The Toyah Phase of Central Texas

NUMBER SIXTEEN
TEXAS A&M UNIVERSITY
ANTHROPOLOGY SERIES

A list of titles in this series appears at the back of the book.

The Toyah Phase of Central Texas

LATE PREHISTORIC ECONOMIC AND SOCIAL PROCESSES

EDITED BY *Nancy A. Kenmotsu*
AND *Douglas K. Boyd*

TEXAS A&M UNIVERSITY PRESS
College Station

First edition
This paper meets the requirements of ANSI/NISO Z39.48-1992
(Permanence of Paper).
Binding materials have been chosen for durability.
♾ ♻
Library of Congress Cataloging-in-Publication Data
The Toyah phase of central Texas : late prehistoric economic and social
processes / edited by Nancy A. Kenmotsu and Douglas K. Boyd.—1st ed.
p. cm.—(Texas A&M University anthropology series ; no. 16)
"This volume contains eight chapters and a peer review. Most were first
presented in a symposium at the 72nd annual meeting of the Society of
American Archaeology in Austin."—ECIP chapter 1.
Includes bibliographical references and index.
ISBN-13: 978-1-60344-690-7 (book/hardcover (printed case) : alk. paper)
ISBN-10: 1-60344-690-7 (book/hardcover (printed case) : alk. paper)
ISBN-13: 978-1-60344-755-3 (ebook)
ISBN-10: 1-60344-755-5 (ebook)
1. Toyah culture—Texas—Congresses. 2. Indians of North America—
Texas—History—Congresses. 3. Indians of North America—Texas—Ethnic
identity—Congresses. 4. Indians of North America—Material culture—
Texas—Congresses. 5. Texas—Antiquities—Congresses. 6. Antiquities,
Prehistoric—Texas—Congresses. I. Kenmotsu, Nancy Adele. II. Boyd,
Douglas K. (Douglas Kevin) III. Society for American Archaeology. Meeting
(72nd : 2007 : Austin, Tex.) IV. Series: Texas A & M University anthropology
series ; no. 16.
E78.T4T69 2012
976.4′01—dc23

2012016413

LeRoy Johnson Jr.

SEPTEMBER 10, 1935–FEBRUARY 4, 2011

We dedicate this volume to LeRoy Johnson Jr., PhD. Dr. Johnson, better known to many of his colleagues in recent years as "Uncle Lee" or just "Lee," spent a lifetime doing archaeology. His contributions to Texas archaeology are many, but his 1995 book—*The Life and Times of Toyah-Culture Folk: The Buckhollow Encampment, Site 41KM16, Kimble County, Texas*—was one of his most important and, some would argue, his best. It is the classic study that best defines the Classic Toyah culture. As is evident in the chapters in this book, he laid a solid foundation for modern archaeologists and ethnohistorians to build upon. We are greatly indebted to Lee for his insights about the peoples we call Toyah and he called "Toyah Folk."

CONTENTS

ACKNOWLEDGMENTS

Understanding the economics and interaction of hunter-gatherers has been and continues to be a focus of archaeological research. The people in these societies often moved in small groups but maintained relationships with "others" across diverse languages and sociocultural barriers.

Texas is particularly suited to the study of hunter-gatherers, for the majority of its lands were home to such groups for thousands of years. This book focuses on the hunter-gatherers who occupied at least 25 percent of the state, particularly its central core, just before and during the early incursion of Spain north of the banks of the Rio Grande, a time frame known as the Toyah phase (AD 1300–1750). The material remains of Toyah phase sites have been of great interest to archaeologists since they were first recorded and investigated over seventy years ago. Although no long-term research projects have been undertaken at any Toyah phase sites, a spate of relatively recent cultural resource management–sponsored excavations and analyses have led to a growing body of data in the past fifteen years. The authors in this volume have mined that body of old and new data to offer their interpretations of the economy and interaction spheres that operated during the Toyah phase, looking at dietary patterns, social networks, and interactions both among Toyah folk and with far-flung friends. It is our hope that these interpretations encourage discussions about this period in Texas and about the broader hunter-gatherer issues that continue to challenge us.

Many people have contributed to this volume and to Toyah studies. J. Charles Kelley was the first to speak of this widespread phenomenon. Dee Ann Story and Ed Jelks investigated Toyah sites in the 1950s and 1960s. Their early insights were used by LeRoy Johnson in his synthesis of what he called the Toyah Folk in the mid-1990s. His contributions to Toyah and to hunter-gatherer studies in Texas were many, and we owe him as well as the other early researchers our gratitude. We also thank many others who have undertaken recent, thoughtful analyses of sites and data related to the Toyah phenomenon. To name only a few besides the authors of this volume: Steve Black, Andy Cloud, Michael Collins, Darrell Creel, Thomas Hester, Betty Inman, Ardi Kalter, James Karbula, Christopher Lintz, John Loshe, Robert Mallouf, Gemma Mehalchick, Timothy Perttula, Michael Quigg,

Robert Ricklis, Robert Rogers, Harry Shafer, Steve Tomka, Abby Treece, and Mariah Wade. We appreciate the ground they broke.

Two anonymous reviewers for the book have earned our appreciation. They offered constructive comments that greatly improved the final chapters. It was clear from their comments that they spent a great deal of time in their reviews, and we are pleased that they considered the final product worth their time.

Other individuals deserve our thanks. Several individuals and institutions were helpful in providing images and maps used in chapter 1, including Virginia Hatfield, Jennifer McWilliams, and Brian Wootan (Prewitt and Associates), Susan Dial (Texas Beyond History), Chase Fountain (Texas Parks and Wildlife Department), Michael Quigg (TRC Companies), Marybeth Tomka (Center for Archaeological Research, University of Texas at San Antonio), and Carolyn Spock (Texas Archaeological Research Laboratory, University of Texas at Austin). Sandra Hannum of Prewitt and Associates was instrumental in preparing and editing many of the figures that appear in several chapters. The staff at Texas A&M University Press, particularly editor-in-chief Mary Lenn Dixon and associate editor Patricia Clabaugh, were generous with their time and helpful advice. John Thomas, our copyeditor, improved the text. We deeply appreciate their efforts to help us and to bring the volume to publication.

It is also fitting that we thank the contributors to this volume. They each expended a great deal of their private time to complete their contributions. They did so in a timely manner, with no complaints about revisions or suggested changes, and always with good humor. Their labor and creative insights are deeply appreciated.

Finally, we received encouragement from many people during the completion of this project. One was Jean Wade, the senior editor's mother, who at niney-one still offers enthusiastic support for anything her children or grandchildren undertake. Our colleagues Myles R. Miller and Jim Abbott also urged us to complete the project and discussed their thoughts about the hunter-gatherers of the Toyah phase. We are grateful to each of them. Their support of this effort has been very important to us.

The Toyah Phase of Central Texas

ONE

The Toyah Phase in Texas

AN INTRODUCTION AND RETROSPECTIVE

Nancy A. Kenmotsu and Douglas K. Boyd

The greater central Texas region was home to hunter-gatherers for thousands of years. As such, the region presents an opportunity to study the economies of small groups, how they interacted with neighbors near and far, how they handled risk, the extent of their mobility, and perhaps how and why their cultures changed through time (Collins 2004). The archaeological record of this large region was first used to study cultural-historical units and their chronometric placements (Kelley et al. 1940; Sayles 1935). Today, there is increasing interest in using the patterns in that record to increase our understanding of social boundaries among hunter-gatherers by focusing on economics, migration, conflict, and interaction. That interest coincides with research in other regions across North America. For example, Stark and colleagues (1998) identified social networks among small-scale groups in the Tonto Basin through analysis of the technological variation in the dominant utilitarian pottery. Vehik (2002) looked at broader-scale patterns in the Southern Plains. She concludes that, as large horticultural village settlements formed after AD 1450, control of access to nonlocal resources became more important and resulted in revisions to trade relationships between groups in that region. Speth (2004) and his colleagues have used the subsistence data from Henderson Pueblo in southeastern New Mexico to investigate both intrasite social boundaries of public versus domestic contexts and boundaries between Henderson and other nearby sites with extraregional groups, especially those in the Southern Plains.

These and other studies hold great promise for explaining social boundaries on the Southern Plains and in adjacent regions. Yet archaeological patterns and their interpretations are not always straightforward. Barth (1969) pointed out that social boundaries, though real, are also quite fluid, and Hitchcock and Bartram (1998:39) in their study of San groups in the Kalahari noted the presence of boundaries within boundaries: "Variability in technology that is seen archaeologically . . . may not reflect differences in the cultures or thought processes of the groups that produced the materials . . . but rather [reflect] the environmental, social, and economic contexts of behavior and problem-solving strategies of individuals within a single group." MacEachern (1998), Stark (1998), and Welsch and Terrell (1998) also recognize that interpreting the causes of patterning in the archaeological record must be approached cautiously. Such caution notwithstanding, we agree with Stark (1998:9) that "the search for social boundaries in material culture patterning is a productive avenue of research."

The chapters of this volume represent an effort to use the Toyah phase to look at social boundaries through migration, hunter-farmer interaction, subsistence, and other issues of anthropological interest. In 1947, J. Charles Kelley (1947a) briefly described the Toyah phenomenon as a focus that rapidly spread across a broad expanse of Texas around AD 1200. Subsequent research, nearly all in the gray literature, has modified Kelley's original descriptions, but the Toyah phase continues to be of keen interest to archaeologists interested in studying small-scale societies. In this introductory chapter, we provide a broad overview of the geographic extent of the Toyah phase and a brief retrospective of the phase from its beginnings to the present day based, in part, on the excellent summaries of Toyah by Johnson (1994) and Ricklis (1994). Figure 1.1 provides a map of selected Toyah and Toyah-related archaeological sites that are discussed in this volume, and table 1.1 provides a key to the site names, numbers, and references for the selected sites.

Toyah in Geographic Perspective

The archaeological pattern known as the Toyah phase is found in the central part of Texas including the Edwards Plateau and the Llano Uplift as well as adjacent portions of the Rolling Plains, Oak Woods and Prairies, Blackland Prairie, Gulf Coast Prairies and Marshes, and South Texas Brush Country (figs. 1.2 and 1.3) This portion of central Texas is within the Great Plains physiographic province as defined by Carr (1967) and thus constitutes the southern end of the Great Plains as identified by most geographers and anthropologists. Within this broad region there exists a collective of shared cultural traits (sensu Kroeber 1939) from approximately AD 1300 to 1700. The region contains enormous biotic, geological, and topographic diversity (fig. 1.4), particularly on the Edwards Plateau (Ellis et al. 1995; see also discussions in Collins 1995, 2004). Comprehensive reviews of the vegetation, soils, climate, and other aspects of these natural regions can be found elsewhere (e.g., Amos and Gehlbach 1988; Arbingast et al. 1973; Diamond et al. 1987; Gould 1962; Hester et al. 1989). Here, we provide only a brief summary that is inadequate to convey the complexity of this large area. Vegetation is generally dominated by oak, juniper, mesquite, hickory, and other hardwoods, but

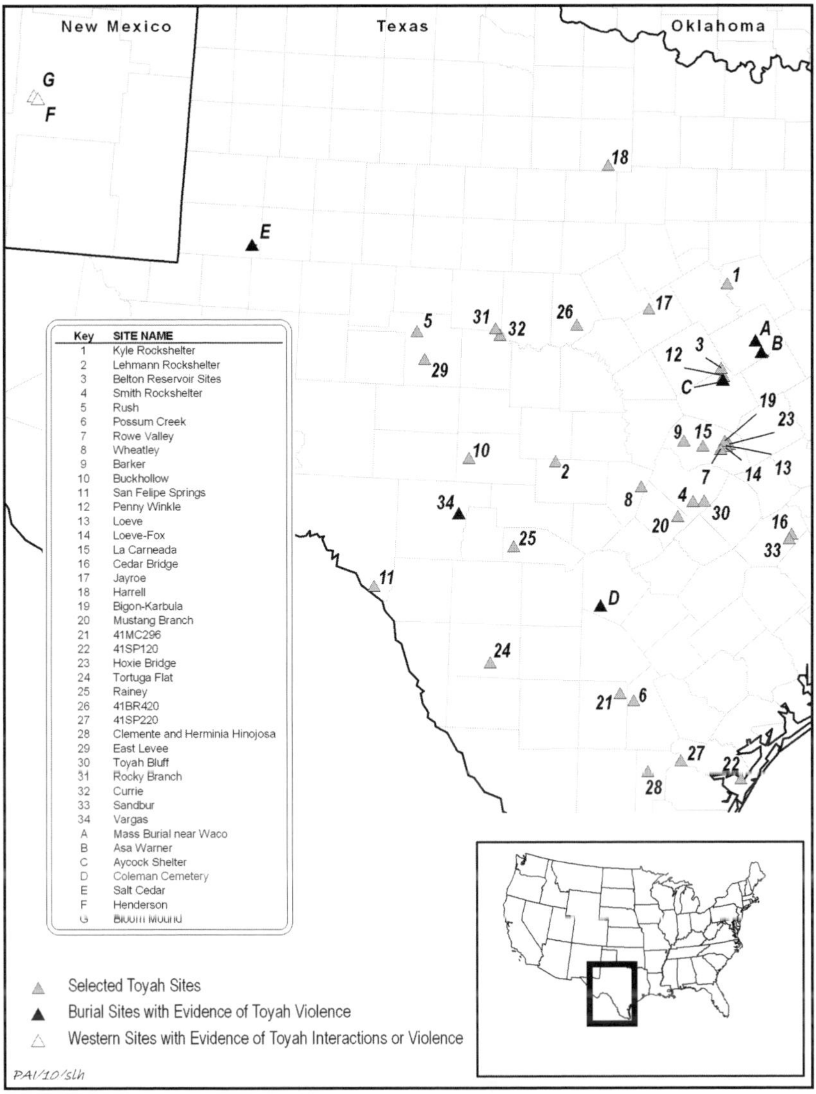

FIGURE 1.1. Map of selected Toyah and Toyah-related archaeological sites mentioned in the text (see table 1.1).

mesquite, thorny scrub, and cacti dominate in the South Texas Brush Country, whereas the prairies to the east and north support grasses with lesser tree cover. A defining geological feature is the Balcones Escarpment, a significant uplift that marks the eastern and southern edges of the Edwards Plateau. East of the uplift are deep, clayey prairie soils; to the south the soils are generally loamy. The plateau itself tends to have thin upland soils amid dissected limestone. On the Edwards Plateau, chert is not only abundant but generally of high quality for stone tool making. In the Blackland Prairie, Gulf Coastal Prairies, and South Texas Brush County, chert is rare except in river drainages. Annual precipitation in the region

TABLE 1.1. Selected Toyah and Toyah-related archaeological sites mentioned in the text

Site Group	*Map Number*	*Site Name*	*Site Number*	*Reference*
Sites in Texas with Significant Excavated Toyah Components	1	Kyle Rockshelter	41HI1	Jelks 1962
	2	Lehmann Rockshelter	41GL1	Kelley 1947b
	3	Belton Reservoir sites	multiple	Miller and Jelks 1952
	4	Smith Rockshelter	41TV42	Suhm 1957
	5	Rush	41TG346	Quigg 1997; Quigg and Peck 1995
	6	Possum Creek	41LK201	Highley 1986
	7	Rowe Valley	41WM437	unpublished; 1982b this volume
	8	Wheatley	41BC114	Greer 1976b
	9	Barker	41WM71	Sorrow 1970
	10	Buckhollow	41KM16	Johnson 1994
	11	San Felipe Springs	41VV444	Mehalchick et al. 1999
	12	Penny Winkle	41BL23	Shafer et al. 1964
	13	Loeve	41WM133	Prewitt 1982a
	14	Loeve-Fox	41WM230	Prewitt 1974, 1982a, 1982c
	15	La Carneada	41WM1012	Rogers and Dixon 2006
	16	Cedar Bridge	41FY74	Skelton 1977
	17	Jayroe	41HM51	unpublished
	18	Harrell	41YN1	Hughes 1942
	19	Bigon-Karbula	41WM258	Prikryl 1982
	20	Mustang Branch	41HY209-T	Ricklis 1994
	21	—	41MC296	Hall et al. 1986
	22	—	41SP120	Ricklis 1990
	23	Hoxie Bridge	41WM130	Bond 1978
	24	Tortuga Flat	41ZV155	Inman et al. 1998
	25	Rainey	41BN33	Henderson 2001
	26	—	41BR420	Mauldin et al. 2003
	27	—	41SP220	Gilmore 2007; this volume
	28	Clemente and Herminia Hinojosa	41JW8	Black 1986
	29	East Levee	41TG91	Creel 1991
	30	Toyah Bluff	41TV441	Karbula 2003
	31	Rocky Branch	41RN169	Treece et al. 1993
	32	Currie	41CC131	Treece et al. 1993
	33	Sandbur	41FY135	Kalter et al. 2005
	34	Varga	41ED28	Quigg et al. 2008
Burial Sites with Evidence of Toyah Violence	A	Mass Burial near Waco	—	Meroney 1936
	B	Asa Warner	41ML46	Watt 1956; Wright 1997
	C	Aycock Shelter	—	Watt 1936
	D	Coleman Cemetery	41BX568	Potter et al. 2005
	E	Salt Cedar	41AD2	Collins 1968
Western Sites with Evidence of Toyah Interactions or Violence	F	Henderson	LA-1549	Speth 2004; Speth, this volume
	G	Bloom Mound	LA-2528	Kelley 1984; Speth, this volume

a

b

c

FIGURE 1.2. Environmental diversity in the central and northern Toyah areas. Photographs show natural regions of Texas as defined by the Texas Parks and Wildlife Department: (a) Edwards Plateau; (b) Llano Uplift; and (c) Rolling Plains. Photographs by (a) Chase A. Fountain, (b) Earl Nottingham, and (c) Virginia Hatfield. Photos used courtesy of the Texas Parks and Wildlife Department (a, b) and Virginia Hatfield (c).

a

b

FIGURE 1.3. Environmental diversity in the eastern and southern Toyah areas: (a) Oak Woods and Prairies; (b) Blackland Prairie; (c) Gulf Coastal Prairies and Marshes; and (d) South Texas Brush Country. Photographs by (a–c) Earl Nottingham and (d) unknown. Photos used courtesy of Texas Parks and Wildlife Department (a–c), and Center for Archaeological Research, University of Texas at San Antonio (d).

c

d

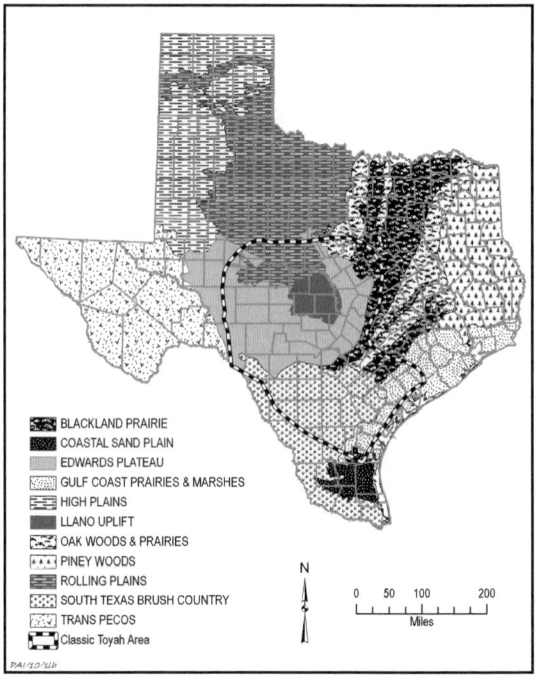

FIGURE 1.4. Map of Classic Toyah culture area (after Johnson 1994:Figure 105) and the natural regions of Texas. After "Natural Regions of Texas" maps by Texas Parks and Wildlife Department, 2001.

gradually decreases from approximately 39 inches in the eastern portions to approximately 22 inches in the west. Natural springs are common throughout the Edwards Plateau, especially along the Balcones Escarpment, but rarer in the adjoining regions (Brune 1981). Numerous streams are present, and the region is bounded on the west by the Pecos River and traversed by several river systems flowing northwest to southeast, particularly the Colorado and Brazos river systems. Much of the Devil's River system is also captured within this area, and to the east and south of the Edward's Plateau the region includes much of the Nueces, San Antonio, Guadalupe, and La Vaca river drainages.

The Toyah phase and its regional extent have been of archaeological interest since the 1930s (e.g., Kelley et al. 1940), but its currently accepted boundaries are based on the synthesis of Toyah by LeRoy Johnson (1994:241–87). That synthesis included a thoughtful review of six well-reported sites (41BN33, 41HI1, 41JW8, 41LK201, 41TG91, and 41TV42) as a final chapter in his analysis and interpretations of the materials from the Buckhollow site (41KM16), a site located along Interstate 10 on the Edwards Plateau (fig. 1.5). As shown on fig. 1.6, the sites cross-cut the region Johnson (1994:243, fig. 105) designated as the homeland for the Classic Toyah culture. Johnson also suggested that there existed around this Classic Toyah culture an area where some but not all Toyah material culture can be found. This he termed the "Shared Toyah area." Since Johnson's (1994) monograph was published, subsequent researchers have frequently borrowed the Classic Toyah culture area (Arnn 2007, 2012; Karbula 2003; Kenmotsu and Wade 2002; Mehalchick et al. 1999), and we employ it here.

a

b

FIGURE 1.5. Views of the Buckhollow site (41KM16). (a) Looking southward down the Copperas Creek valley toward the North Llano River. The Buckhollow site excavations are on the alluvial terrace on the right. (b) Looking south at burned rock features in Excavation Area 6 (see Johnson 1994:Figure 25). Photographs courtesy of Texas Archeological Research Laboratory, University of Texas at Austin. Photo numbers 41KM16 C-277 (a) and 41KM16 C-556 (b).

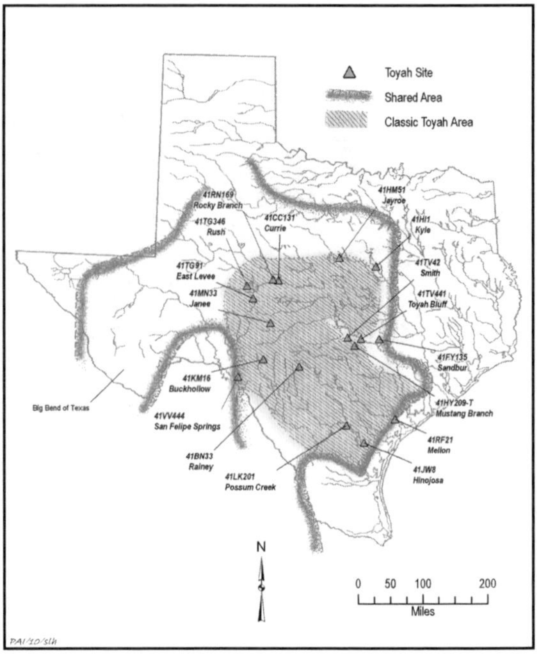

FIGURE 1.6. Classic Toyah culture area, the Shared Toyah area, and selected archeological sites mentioned in the text. After Johnson (1994:243, Figure 105).

The Classic Toyah

Within this greater central Texas region, the period beginning about AD 1300 and ending around 1700 is known variously as the Toyah phase (Johnson 1994: 241; Kelley 1947a, 1947b, 1986), Toyah interval (Collins 2004:122–23), or Toyah technocomplex (Ricklis 1994). This timeframe encompasses the close of the prehistoric period and continues through the time native groups were being buffeted by Spanish colonization and Spain was beginning to establish settlements in Texas. The period is defined by new technologies that appear in the archaeological record of the region, and there is some evidence that dynamics among groups both in central Texas and around its peripheries were changing. The toolkit at Toyah sites is indicative of small groups of hunter-gatherers: small flake arrow points (predominately Perdiz, but also Fresno, Harrell, and Garza), two- and four-beveled knives, Covington knives, simple clay pots (usually with bone temper), flake-blade end scrapers, and flake perforators (Johnson 1994:271–75). Less common, but found in more than rare instances, are double-pointed, unbeveled knives, buffalo-bone spatulas, clay pipes, and shaftstone abraders. This toolkit differs from toolkits in earlier centuries in several ways. Although groups residing on the peripheries of the greater central Texas region had manufactured pottery for many centuries (Miller 1995; Miller and Kenmotsu 2004; Pertulla 2004; Ricklis 2004a, 2004b), it was not made in central Texas until the Toyah phase. Additionally, the lithic assemblages at Toyah sites differ from sites dating prior to AD 1300 in that "most Toyah stone devices (end scrapers, perforators/drills, arrow points)

FIGURE 1.7. View of the Rainey site (41BN33) along Mill Creek in Bandera County (see Henderson 2001:Figure 5). The archaeologist is sitting at the edge of the sinkhole where the site is located. Photograph courtesy of the Center for Archaeological Research, University of Texas at San Antonio.

were made from flakes or blades, and fewer . . . were fashioned by reducing large blades bifacially" (Johnson 1994:259).

Most Toyah sites have activity areas (Creel 1990:223) or living surfaces (Black 1986:225–29). Structures are reported from two (Treece et al. 1993:57–60, 231–35) and have been inferred at two others—Buckhollow (Johnson 1994:33) and Mustang Terrace (Ricklis 1994:284–85). Rib peg alignments found in association with scraping tools have been used to infer hide processing (Ricklis 1994:286; Treece et al. 1993:60–64). Importantly, although Toyah phase sites contain a broad range of economic data, buffalo were an important part of the subsistence base for these people (Collins and Ricklis 1994:14; Johnson 1994:259; Quigg and Peck 1995; Ricklis 1994; cf. Dering 2008), and there are hints that Toyah folk occasionally grew corn or, perhaps more likely, obtained corn through trade with farming peoples (Jelks 1962; Johnson 1994:262). Excavated Toyah sites are variable in their functions, geographic distribution, and type. Several sites are rockshelters (Jelks 1962; Kelley 1947b; Suhm 1955, 1960) and provide some limited data on the perishable items in the Toyah toolkit (basketry, wooden arrow shafts, and notched sticks). The Rainey site (41BN33) (fig. 1.7) was almost wholly contained in a sinkhole that was repeatedly occupied by small Toyah groups beginning around AD 1250 (Henderson 2001:277). This evidence, along with the repeated Toyah occupations at several other sites including East Levee (41TG91) (Creel 1990), Toyah Bluff (41TV441) (Karbula 2003), Sandbur (41FY135) (Kalter et al. 2005:219), and Smith Rockshelter (41TV42) (Suhm 1957), suggest that small family groups repeatedly returned to favored places on the landscape. Two sites (the Rush site in the northern portion of the Toyah regional extent, and the Mustang Branch site in the eastern portion of the region) along with a series of sites at Owen Ivie Reservoir in the western portion of the region (Treece et al. 1993) represent locales of intense processing of large game animals. Others appear, based on butchering patterns, to represent relatively small camps at some distance from kill sites where hunters returned with choice cuts of meat for processing and consumption (Johnson 1994:261).

The lithic and ceramic technologies described from Toyah sites are, of course, among the defining characteristics of Toyah (fig. 1.8).[1] Nearly all researchers have noted that the Toyah lithic assemblage is particularly efficient for the killing and processing of buffalo and other large ungulates, and it is nearly always of locally available raw material. In fact, bison-man interaction has always been an important research issue for Toyah. Some researchers believe bison population changes in the Southern Plains was a key factor in the origin and evolution of Toyah via either migration of people into the region or spread of a technocomplex (cf. Mauldin et al., this volume). Excavations at Mustang Branch (41HY209-T) had abundant evidence that the knapping activities were "primarily for the manufacture of blades and flakes which were either directly suited to the task of butchering or could be quickly made into scrapers and drills for the related activity of hide working" (Ricklis 1994:287). The site had the remains of nineteen adult deer, several antelope, and two bison representing over 1,000 kg of usable meat believed killed in a single event (Ricklis 1994:266). At the Rush site (41TG346), the lithics from Bone Bed 4 (Perdiz points, blades, end scrapers, bifaces, etc.) exhibited extensive tool maintenance, and use-wear studies indicate they were used for hide working on fresh or greased hides (Quigg and Peck 1995:165–68). The partially excavated bone bed at Rush (fig. 1.9) yielded seven bison, and the full bone bed is estimated to have contained at least fifty bison killed and processed in a single event, with perhaps as many as one hundred people aiding in the process (Quigg and Peck 1995:266). In contrast, the Toyah levels in the Rainy sinkhole site (41BN33) have evidence of hunting of both deer and bison with the same lithic toolkit, but the evidence indicates an occupation of no more than a small group of people carrying out domestic activities such as cooking and tool making (Henderson 2001:281–84).

Toyah ceramic vessels are characterized as small, plain, utilitarian. They are represented by just one sherd at the Rainey sinkhole (Henderson 2001), but other sites have yielded several hundred sherds (Treece et al. 1993:205). Ricklis (1994:300) speculates that these vessels were used for fat rendering. Four Toyah vessel types have been identified: a largish, nearly hemispherical bowl; a smaller deep bowl with rounded sides and incurving rims; an olla with somewhat constricted mouth; and a simple tall jar (Johnson 1994:269–70, 274–76). Most have bone temper that is easily seen with the unaided eye or under low magnification, but at times the bone is identifiable only through petrography (Reese-Taylor 1995:F11). Some are painted or have a red wash or slip; often the interiors have a matte finish from the late application of a thin wash. Some interiors and exteri-

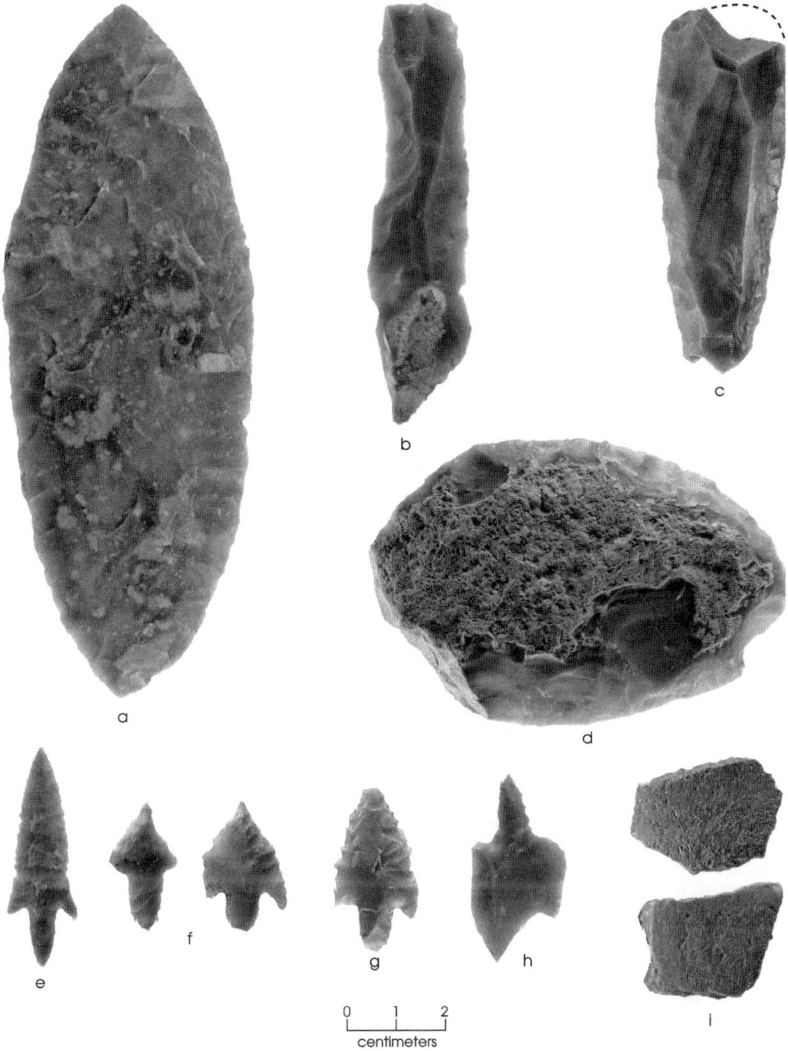

FIGURE 1.8. Typical Toyah artifact assemblage from the Janee site (41MN33): (a) beveled knife; (b) blade; (c) end scraper; (d) side scraper; (e–g) Perdiz arrow points; (h) flake perforator; (i) bone-tempered plainware sherds. Photo by and used courtesy of Jennifer McWilliams.

ors were smoothed with wide sticks or cane. Interior surfaces of vessel rims were thinned or sharply beveled; exteriors were floated and sometimes rubbed to a high luster. Toyah vessels were coiled with thick ropes of clay that were not always well joined during smoothing. Creel (1990:143) notes that in the northwestern part of the greater central Texas region the number of vessels found at any one site is consistently high; Toyah vessels dominate the types found on these sites, but Caddoan wares, Chupadero Black-on-white, Ochoa Indented, and various New Mexican glazewares are present in small numbers. Similar presence of nonlocal wares

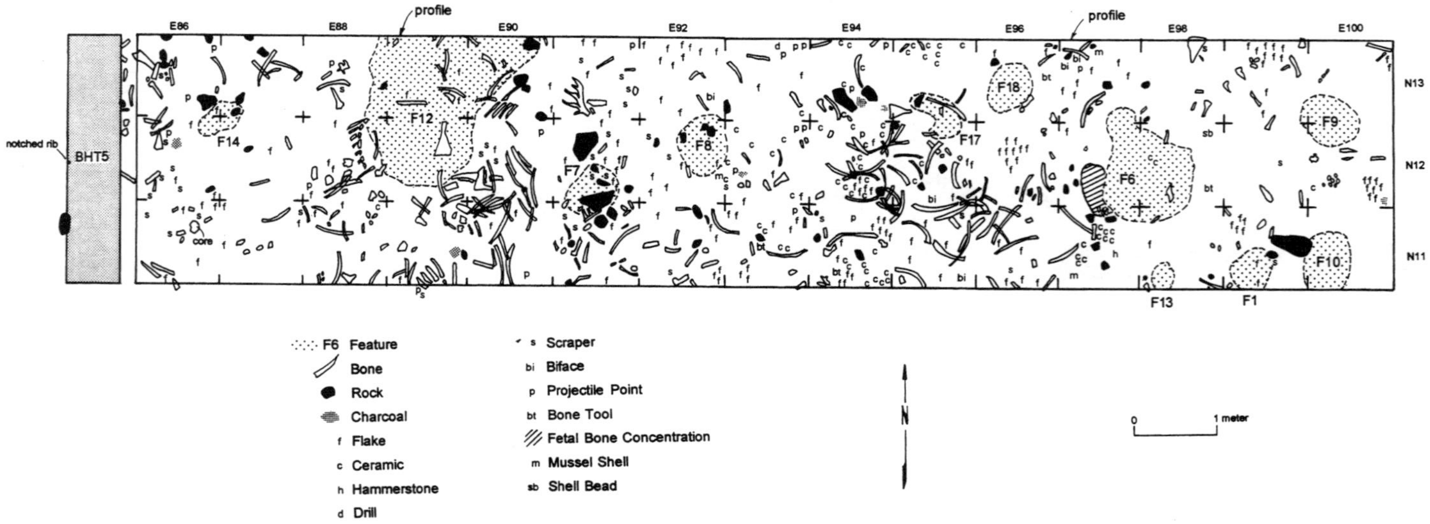

FIGURE 1.9. Map of the Occupation 4 bone bed at the Rush site (41TG346) showing the distribution of animal bones, artifacts, and features in the 3 by 15 m excavation block. Map adapted from Quigg and Peck (1995:Figure 7.1) and used courtesy of the TRC Companies, Austin, Texas.

is found among the pottery recovered from Toyah sites elsewhere, especially along the Balcones Escarpment and in the Gulf Coastal Prairies (Kalter et al. 2005; Karbula 2003; Ricklis 1994:305; see also Kibler, this volume).

Examining Patterns in Toyah Sites

The material culture of the Toyah phase was first described by Sayles (1935:46, 117) for the region around Abilene, Texas, and called the Wichita phase. Later, J. Charles Kelley (1947a:105; see also Kelley 1986:13) renamed the manifestation the Toyah focus[2] after Toyah Creek, a tributary of the Pecos River in Reeves County, Texas, and within the Shared Toyah area shown in fig. 1.6. Kelley (1947a, 1947b; Kelley et al. 1940:145–53) first began to develop his ideas about Late Prehistoric sites while establishing chronostratigraphic sequences with T. N. Campbell in the Texas Big Bend region in the 1930s. As part of this effort, the two men reanalyzed material recovered by A. T. Jackson (1938) from a site in central Texas to correlate their sequences with those from Abilene and the Edwards Plateau; they concluded that Sayles's Wichita phase was equivalent to their findings both in the Big Bend and on the Edwards Plateau and dated to approximately AD 1200–1700 (Kelley et al. 1940).

Several years later Kelley (1947a:103), still working on cultural-historical classifications, became interested in the meaning of the patterns he saw across the greater central Texas region and voiced what has become one of the central themes in Toyah studies: its rapid spread across the region. Referring to it as a horizon, Kelley (1947a:103) stated: "This horizon seems to have appeared first in the extreme western and eastern portions of [Texas], where . . . agricultural econom[ies] and permanent houses are likewise associated, and to have spread in the later prehistoric times to the central and southeastern areas. Several cultural foci have been established for this horizon, including the Toyah Focus of the central and western portions of the state."

Although some of his conclusions have been discounted, the notion that Toyah spread rapidly over the greater central Texas region has been supported by subsequent investigations (e.g., Black 1986:254–57; Dering 2008; Highley 1986; Jelks 1962; Johnson 1994:271; Quigg and Dering 2007). Until recently, researchers believed that Toyah had spread from west to east with a lag of about 100 years (see discussions in Black 1986:255 and Prewitt 1985:225–27). However, radiocarbon dates from several Toyah sites on the Gulf Coastal Plain document its presence in the eastern part of the region as early as AD 1300 (Ricklis 1994:301–304).

Ricklis (1994:299–316), intrigued by this pattern, examined the abrupt appearance of the technological aspects of Toyah sites under two opposing interpretations: immigration of people and diffusion of a technocomplex. Under the immigration proposal, he notes: "If the assemblage represents a major immigration of a single cultural group, then it directly reflects fundamental, nonmaterial aspects of prehistoric life (e.g., society, ethnicity, and their cognitive correlates) . . . [and]

the basic mechanism of change was demographic displacement" (1994:299). Ricklis considers Johnson (1994) the primary advocate for immigration but acknowledges that others (e.g., Prewitt 1985) agree.

Finding little evidence of displaced populations from central Texas moving into southern Texas or the Gulf Coastal Prairies and Marshes, Ricklis (1994:300–301) turns to diffusion of a technocomplex to explain the swift spread of Toyah across such a broad and variable landscape. In part, this derives from his work on sites in the Gulf Coastal Prairies and Marshes dating to the same timeframe but known as the Rockport phase; these people adopted the Toyah lithic assemblage but not its ceramics (Ricklis 1996). At site 41RF21, discrete Toyah and Rockport phase occupations are both present. Other sites along the same drainage where site 41RF21 is located are either Toyah or Rockport, but not both. He argues that Toyah technology was simply a highly efficient toolkit for hunting and processing large game: "If the linguistically and ethnically distinct coastal Karankawans [of the Rockport phase] rapidly responded to the influx of bison onto the coastal prairies and took on bison hunting and an apparently associated lithic tool kit, there is little need to conclude that other indigenous groups of southern and central Texas did not, or could not, do likewise" (1994:304).

Ricklis (1994:311) views cultures as "complex adaptive/informational systems with internally complementary subsystems," and he argues that "not all kinds of cultural information are disseminated for the same reasons or at the same rates or levels of intensity." Under his interpretation, this technocomplex was only a small part of the total behavioral and cognitive systems of any given culture. Therefore, it could easily spread as a technocomplex without the migration of populations. These ideas are interesting and thoughtful. They suggest that social boundaries operating during this period of time were sufficiently fluid to accommodate free exchange of ideas. Despite the exchange of technological information, however, the archaeological assemblages illustrate the presence of a social boundary between Toyah and Rockport that both groups considered important to maintain.

Other models of boundary maintenance need to be tested. For example, Ricklis (1994:305) argues that the lack of decorative attributes on Toyah pottery "renders difficult any inferences of [sociocultural homogeneity] based solely upon ceramics." He further states: "While the stylistic attributes of ceramics cannot necessarily be assumed to represent discrete ethnic or sociocultural groupings (Butzer 1990:100), they do in fact often correlate with social groups as markers of identity (e.g., Graves 1982; Pollock 1983)." Recent studies of technological style challenge this view. Stark (1998:xviii) found that among Dalupa potters the shape of a vessel and key production steps generated regional styles at least as much as decorative elements. In the Tonto Basin, local prehistoric potters produced only utilitarian vessels until the end of the sequence, and only through study of the technology of manufacture were researchers able to begin to detect scales of social boundaries. The paucity of whole or reconstructable vessels in the current Toyah ceramic sample has hampered such efforts to date, but vessel forms could prove to be important regional social identifiers in the future.

Hitchcock and Bartram (1998) advocate a method for studying social boundaries between linguistically and ethnically distinct coresident populations that examines the social uses of space and technology on the basis of individual artifacts, sites, and clusters of sites. Unfortunately, most Toyah studies in the past twenty to thirty years (and there have been a series of excellent ones) have been site-based; each researcher has tried to draw inferences but has often been hampered by lack of time and resources to do much more. Moreover, where studies have been undertaken for highways, pipelines, or other projects with defined construction footprints, excavations are confined to those footprints. If, as is suggested by Kenmotsu and Arnn (this volume), some of those Toyah sites were occupied by groups numbering in the hundreds or thousands, the excavated footprint will give only a tiny view of the occupation and is not likely to reveal much about internal group dynamics. Given that we all agree that the technological style of Toyah is unique and appeared swiftly, it is time to look in detail at social boundaries using artifacts, sites, and use of space at Toyah sites in several subregions of the greater central Texas region. As Stark (1998:5) notes: "Style is not simply decoration, and technical choices are not governed simply by environmental pressures. Rather, these behaviors are socially informed actions that reflect a shared understanding of how things are done. As such, material reflections of technical choices are not neutral."

The Structure of the Toyah Volume

This volume contains eight chapters and a peer review. Most were first presented in a symposium at the 72nd annual meeting of the Society of American Archaeology in Austin. In chapter 2, Nancy Kenmotsu and John Arnn examine the ethnohistorical data for central Texas and suggest that conflict played a greater role in the region in the final century of the Toyah phase. That is followed by two chapters that provide views of Toyah social boundaries by focusing on networks. John Arnn places the available archaeological evidence into a model of social fields. Karl Kibler, working in the Blackland Prairie, explores how small groups can use exotic materials to establish networks with nearby agricultural groups (in this case, Caddo peoples).

Chapters 5 and 6 employ Toyah subsistence data to study group dynamics. Raymond Mauldin, Jennifer Thompson, and Leonard Kemp review the evidence for a florescence of bison around AD 1300 and conclude that it may represent more myth than fact. Instead they argue that the evidence suggests an increase in logistical bison hunting strategies to take advantage of patchy bison availability. Zackary Gilmore, using data from a Toyah site on the Gulf Coastal Prairies, explores economic intensification, in the form of expanded dietary breadth, as a common means of risk avoidance among Toyah groups. The next two chapters view Toyah social boundaries from research conducted outside the Classic Toyah region. Doug Boyd uses his research from the Southern Plains to address boundaries between groups in that region and Toyah groups to their south. John Speth and Khori Newlander look at possible conflicts between Toyah people and people in eastern New Mexico that appear to have surfaced around AD 1300. The final chapter is by Elton Prewitt, who has conducted substantial research on the Toyah phase and here offers his reviews of each of the chapters.

Summary

Archaeological research on the Toyah phase has come a long way in the half century since Kelley (1947a) formalized the concept as a cultural manifestation. With the broad block excavations completed in the past thirty years, the database is rich and detailed and covers a wide swath of Texas. On the basis of work at numerous Toyah sites, archaeologists have learned much about when and how these people lived. The poorly understood parts of Toyah are how social boundaries were defined and whether these boundaries represent a technocomplex. Recent research has begun to focus on these topics, and authors in this volume use several models to investigate social identity and social boundaries within the greater central Texas region and the Southern Plains.

Notes

1. We do not mean to imply that lithics and ceramics made up the entire toolkit found on Toyah sites. In fact, the range of material culture on these sites is much richer and includes bone, shell, and wooden artifacts (Jelks 1962; Johnson 1994).

2. Kelley adhered to the Midwestern Taxonomic Method in his early Texas publications. In this volume we adhere to the Willey and Phillips (1958) classification system, which Kelley eventually adopted and which is used today in Texas.

TWO

The Toyah Phase and the Ethnohistorical Record

A CASE FOR POPULATION AGGREGATION

Nancy A. Kenmotsu and John W. Arnn III

The variability archaeologists observe in material culture (artifacts, features, use of space, etc.) has long been associated with "social groups, whose boundaries are [believed] marked by distinctive patterns in the archaeological record" (Stark 1998:1). Distinguishing social boundaries in order to understand identity and interaction, particularly conflict, on the Southern Plains, including in the southernmost part of the Plains in central Texas, has assumed a prominent role in anthropological and archaeological studies of this region (Buffalohead 2004; Henning and Thiessen 2004; Kelley 1955; Krieger 1946; Perkins et al. 2008; Spielmann 1991a; Vehik 2002; Wykoff and Hofman 1982).

Increasingly, researchers (e.g., Brooks 2002; Vehik 2002; Wade 2003) point to a growing body of evidence from the Southern and Central Plains suggesting that increasing competition over resources shortly after AD 1200 led to population aggregation, with this pattern intensifying after 1450 and continuing through the early nineteenth century. Much of this evidence is supported by historic documents, which are used here and in other regions to inform and refine interpretations of the patterns observed in the archaeological record (e.g., Fowler et al. 1999; Perkins et al. 2008; Rogers and Wilson 1993; Trigger 1989, 2007; Walker 1999). However, as Arnn (2005) points out, many archaeologists in Texas focus their research efforts on subsistence, mobility, technological organization, and other patterns of small-scale groups represented by the Toyah phase (Collins and Ricklis 1994; Jelks 1962; Johnson 1994; Kelley 1947a, 1947b, 1955, 1986; Kelley et al. 1940; Ricklis 1994; Sayles 1935), and it is within this context that the documentary record for central Texas is often brought to bear. In contrast, our study focuses on the documents and what they tell us about the mobility and land tenure of groups in central Texas between 1535 and 1716 by comparing them to the archaeological record (emphasizing archaeological assemblages as an analytical unit) in order to guide future research. Preliminary results indicate that by the seventeenth century the people in central Texas were being inexorably drawn into much broader changes taking place well to the north and south of them.

We begin with a discussion of the pitfalls, but also the value, of using documentary sources and the nature of the documentary record for the greater central Texas region. Then we explore the documentary record for central Texas as it relates to the Toyah phase and what that record may or may not contribute to archaeological interpretations of the assemblages of Toyah groups.

The Documentary Record: Pitfalls and Value Added

The Toyah phase spans the prehistoric and early historic eras (AD 1300–1700). This bridge into the time when the first Euroamericans traveled across the Rio Grande into the southernmost reaches of the Southern Plains and modern Texas offers researchers historical records and maps to enrich their study of the archaeological record. That benefit should not be ignored or understated. However, like the archaeological record, the documentary record is imperfect. Documentary pitfalls consist of broad concerns that would be considered in any documentary interpretation, but also concerns that are specific to documents for a particular region. The problems with the documentary record have been acknowledged by others (e.g., Barnes et al. 1981; Griffen 2000; Hadley et al. 1997; Henige 1993; Loren 2008; Valdez 1995). But because it can be tempting to overinterpret letters and reports written long ago in an era with values and perspectives unique from our own, some problems bear repeating here.

One of the foremost concerns is that most manuscripts related to the time of the Toyah phase were written in Spanish. Only a subset have been translated into English (see discussion in Flint and Flint 2005:5–16). Many archaeologists working north of the Rio Grande are not fluent readers of Spanish, particularly Spanish written prior to modern grammatical and orthographic rules (Haggard 1941:10). These documents also contain abbreviations of hundreds of common words (Arzave 1990; Barnes et al. 1981:19). Although these abbreviations were largely standardized, the same word can have multiple forms, and several abbreviated forms of the same word can appear in the same document. Researchers unfamiliar with these abbreviations can misinterpret whole passages or entire documents.

The Spanish were prodigious documenters, but truly original documents can be elusive. They wanted copies of their manuscripts kept locally, but other copies were sent to viceroys in distant capitals and authorities in Spain or Rome. Thus, nearly all documents were transcribed multiple times, and it was "easy for a scribe to skip words, lines, or paragraphs or change spellings because the script was hard to read" (Wade 2003:xxi). Many Spanish documents on file at North American repositories were transcribed at Mexican and Spanish archives in the early twentieth century, removing the reader still further from the original manuscript. Another problem with documentary research is legibility. The reader must overcome handwriting as bad as our own, water staining, and the effects of time (Barnes et al. 1981:6–9; Kenmotsu 1994:62).

Perhaps of greater concern is that documents contain biases that may or may not be readily apparent. Most researchers recognize that the Spanish were not trained observers and that their statements are incomplete recordings of what they saw or heard (Galloway 1991:455; Griffen 1969, 1979, 2000; Naylor and Poltzer 1986:12; Swagerty 1991:474; Wade 2003). The earliest documents, such as those associated with the Toyah phase, were written at a time when few native people could speak Spanish and fewer Spaniards could speak native languages. Miscommunication must have been common. As Loren (2008:38) notes, "One . . . imagines incoherent babble on both sides of the Native and non-Native language exchange." To illustrate an example, the *requerimiento* was a formal scripted statement read to peoples in the New World telling natives to submit to the rule of a monarch in faraway Spain. The statement was read to people in Southwestern pueblos during the Coronado expedition in the 1540s. As Flint and Flint (2005:2) point out, "The text is replete with concepts and terms that lacked equivalents in the [pueblo] world of that day which rendered it completely unintelligible in its details."

Another bias incorporated into the documents is more subtle: the representation of natives as the "Other." These narratives were written for the elite in Spain, and depictions of natives—who were not considered fully human until the Papal Bull of 1537—as a class of beings different from Spaniards represented a method to assert power over them and even to take possession of them (see Loren 2008:85–88). The enhanced descriptions of the differences between the colonized and the colonizer helped justify colonial institutions such as the *encomienda*. On the other side of the coin, native people could also embellish facts. For example, eighty-six Chizo warriors surprised Spanish authorities when they entered Parral to request military aid against the Tobosos and turn over three boys whom they claimed were not Chizos and had been seized during a battle with the Tobosos (AHP 1655Aa). They asked the authorities to keep the boys. The authorities, who had been unsuccessfully seeking Chizo assistance against the Tobosos for two years, were surprised that the Chizos suddenly appeared before them. They questioned the Chizos about this. The Chizos responded that the first year they had a great sickness among them and could not come; the second year they never got the message (an early example of "it must be lost in the mail"). At first, the Spanish were willing to accept the Chizos' statements. Then they questioned the three boys: all three claimed to be Chizos. The boys said the men wanted to leave them in a "safe" place while they joined the Toboso rebellion against the Spanish. Moreover, their mothers told the three it was good for them to go to Parral because "it is a good land with lots to eat."

Another contributor to bias in documents related to the Toyah phase is that the broad region of central Texas was poorly known because it was not consid-

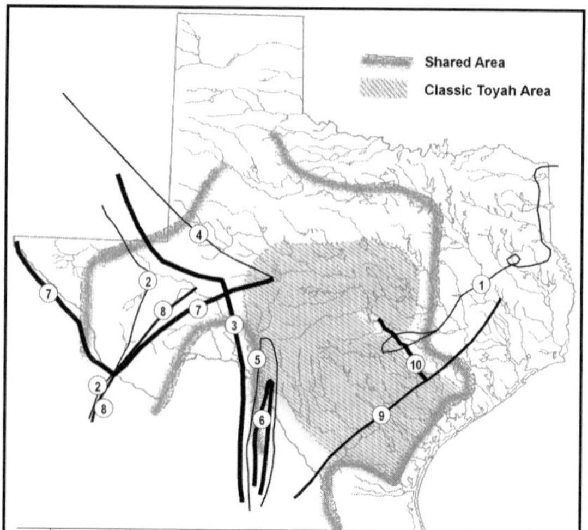

No.	Spanish Visit	References
1	Moscoso, 1543	Biedma 1865, Bruseth and Kenmotsu 1993, Kenmotsu et al. 1993
2	Espejo, 1583	Hammond and Rey 1966, Kenmotsu 2001
3	Castaño de Sosa, 1590	Sosa 1871, Schroeder and Matson 1965
4	Expeditions to the Jumanos, 1629, 1632, 1650, 1654	Ayer 1965, BN 1631, Kenmotsu 2001, Posada 1962
5	Bosque & Larios, 1670	Alessio Robles 1978, SFG 1674, Wade 2003
6	Manuel de la Cruz, 1670s	Alessio Robles 1978, Wade 2003
7	Mendoza, 1683	AGN 1682-1683, AGN 1689-1788, AGN 1683, AGI 1688, Kenmotsu 2001, 2008, Wade 2003
8	Retana, 1689	AGI 1688, Hackett 1926
9	East Texas expeditions 1686, 1689, 1690, 1691, 1693	AGN 1689-1788, 1691, Alessio Robles 1978, Ayer 1691
10	Ramon, 1716	AHP 1716A

FIGURE 2.1. Map of the Southern Plains and central Texas with the areas visited by Spanish expeditions between 1535 and 1716.

ered attractive to Spanish settlement. Located north of what was for the Spanish one of the most inhospitable regions of Mexico—the Bolson de Mapimí (Griffen 1969)—it did not contain lands thought to have exploitable minerals or arable farmlands. When Spanish settlements began to take shape on the eastern margins of central Texas, they were not established until the eighteenth century, when the Toyah phase was ending. These settlements were small and largely confined to San Antonio and mission settlements on the Rio Grande. As late as 1821, Texas (outside of El Paso) had a population of only slightly over three thousand nonnative residents and no settlements west of San Antonio (Chipman 1992:241). Consequently, estimates of distances in early documents are often wild guesses.

Relationships between geographic features were also frequently wrong. Many maps prior to the early nineteenth century show the Pecos River emptying into the Gulf of Mexico, not the Rio Grande, conflating it with the Nueces River, a much smaller river that originates in central Texas. Although up to around 1650 Spanish cartographers were among the finest mapmakers in the world (Wheat 1954), their maps were only as good as the information upon which they were based. They had good maps of Texas's gulf coast as early as 1519 and solid geographic information on Nueva Vizcaya and the corridor to Santa Fe shortly after 1600. For central Texas, however, the information was sparse to nonexistent.

Because central Texas was not targeted for settlement and exploitation, we know of only a very few Spanish expeditions into that region. Figure 2.1 illustrates the general areas visited or traveled by these expeditions during the period 1535–1716 and underscores the very few times the Spanish officially ventured into this large region. Unofficially, the territory was raided for slaves (Alessio Robles 1978:109–16; León 1909). The only expedition to traverse its length, traveling south to north-northwest between the Pecos and Devils rivers, was that of Castaño de Sosa in 1590 (Schroeder and Matson 1965:61; Sosa 1871). Since Sosa had been involved in the slave trade of natives north of Monclova, it is probably no coincidence that the weary travelers did not see any natives until nearing New Mexico. Figure 2.1 also illustrates that the majority of Spanish travel in the region focused on the Concho River drainage in the vicinity of modern San Angelo, the area occupied by the Jumanos.

Beyond the information from these travels into central Texas, there exist a handful of documents that record natives from this region traveling (or being taken) outside of central Texas and being interrogated by authorities (e.g., AGN 1691; SA 1658).[1] Yet even with these interrogations, the total number of documents related to this region of Texas prior to 1716 is small when compared to documents discussing native affairs for groups such as the Tarahumaras, who were situated close to the Spanish silver mines and rich agricultural lands and for which there are hundreds of documentary materials (Cramussel 2000; Deeds 2003; Merrill 1988).

Pitfalls notwithstanding, the documentary record can offer valuable insights into how native peoples organized their societies, carried out their lives, and negotiated their new relationships with colonizers (Cramussel 2000; Loren 2008; Silliman 2005; Wade 2003). Deeds (2003:2), for example, used Spanish documents to study "the persistence of ethnic identity in some cases and not in others under conditions of conquest." She looked at northern Mexico from Durango to Parral between 1560 and 1750. Though acknowledging biases in the documents, she found that the fragmentary record related to native life offered information on "daily economic labors and transactions that went on with or without missionary supervision as well as . . . tantalizing glimpses of beliefs and attitudes, reported sexual liaisons, and shared local knowledge of cures and remedies" (Deeds 2003:10). Álvarez (2000:319–25) reexamined documents of northern Mexico dating from 1600 to 1720 and argues that the Salineros with their nomadic-raiding lifestyle in northern Mexico were actually Tepehuanes (*Tepehuanes del desierto*). The Tepehuanes were semisedentary, small-scale horticulturalists residing near Durango, Mexico. Álvarez concludes that the Salineros were a subset of the Tepehuanes who deliberately chose to change their lifestyle and move east and north of Spanish settlements to avoid the yoke of the *encomienda*. Wade (2003), who conducted research on two groups of documents related to central Texas, notes that documentary research often has to rely on a few sentences, a paragraph, or a few words and piece them together with similar fragments from other documents to build and support ethnohistorical interpretations. Because this is the method required, Wade (2003:xviii) admonishes the reader to recognize "the ephemeral quality of historic interpretation and the absolute need for continued research."

The Documentary Record during the Toyah Phase

We now turn to the documentary record of central Texas from approximately 1535 to 1716. We chose these dates because they bracket, and extend slightly beyond, the portion of the Toyah phase when Spanish manuscripts offer information on mobility and land tenure of the natives of central Texas. The beginning date of 1535 is the year Cabeza de Vaca and three companions fled their captivity under several native groups on the Texas gulf coast, crossed the Rio Grande, and, roughly paralleling that river, walked to La Junta de los Rios (modern Presidio, Texas, and hereafter called La Junta) and ultimately to Mexico City (Krieger 2002; Nuñez 1992).[2] The closing date of 1716 is the year it was reported that a Captain Ramon had traveled into central Texas along the Colorado River (AHP 1716A).[3] Although not all native groups mentioned in this chapter disappear after 1716, after that date native movements both within and outside the region became ever more complex because of the increasing southward Apache movement into central Texas and the Texas Trans-Pecos (e.g., AHP 1716A; Ayer 1714; John 1975; Kenmotsu 2001; Madrid 1992:52). That movement was precipitated by the Comanches and other northern groups who displaced the Apaches from their northern territory (John and Wheat 1989; Kavanagh 1986).

MOBILITY PATTERNS AND THE DOCUMENTARY RECORD

Mobility patterns of hunter-gatherers vary (Barnard 1992; Binford 1980; Kelly 1983; Wiessner 1977; Wilmsen 1989). Hitchcock and Bartram's (1998) ethnoarchaeological research, concentrated in a 28,000 km^2 area of the Kalahari Desert, reflects that variability. Some Kua (Bushmen) people had roughly bounded territories ranging from 1,000 to 2,000 km^2 in size whereas others were much smaller (100–450 km^2). Determinants of the Kua mobility strategies are several and vary by group and through time. Given the aridity of the Kalahari, the location of surface water and water-bearing plants was certainly a significant factor in the size of the area used by a group, but decisions to relocate "become the subjects of exhaustive discussion" within the group considering the move (Hitchcock and Bartram 1998:34). Where to move, when to move, how many should move, whether families should move together or singly, and whether to move to a cattle post were among the issues debated in these discussions. Final decisions were based on weather and knowledge of the land and its resources, but also on debate and personal choice.

The archaeological assemblage of Toyah phase sites has been interpreted to represent the residue of hunter-gatherers. Houses have been inferred at a few (Ricklis 1994; Treece et al. 1993), but most known sites are relatively small (see Henderson 2001 for an example), and it has generally been accepted that they represent small family or kin-based groups residing in a locale for brief periods before moving to another location. In his review of well-excavated Toyah sites, Johnson (1994:263) supports the notion of small groups of hunter-gatherers residing at these sites for a brief period. Some evidence of larger groups has been found. The communal hunting evidence at the Rush site indicates that perhaps as many as one hundred people worked together to kill and butcher a sizable number of buffalo (Quigg and Peck 1995). Treece and colleagues (1993:430) also found evidence of what appears to be cooperative work efforts of perhaps several family-based groups at site 41CC131 on the Concho River. Site 41LK201 may also have evidence of a larger encampment (Highley 1986). The site stretches 800 m along Possum Creek and is some 50 m wide. Unfortunately, excavations focused on only one area of the site, so it is not clear what else is present. The Rowe Valley site may represent a larger encampment (E. Prewitt quoted in Johnson 1994:265) but remains unreported (but see details from it in chapter 9, this volume). Yet most sites appear to be relatively small, and in them Johnson (1994:263) found a pattern of tools and food debris around a heating/cooking hearth that was repeated between sites as well as within the same site, suggesting that each "family was economically independent to the degree that it did its own food preparation and cooking, tool repairing, and the like." At the same time, based on regional distinctions in Toyah pottery and beveled knives, Johnson (1994:267) concluded that group and family mobility among the Toyah was relatively restricted, and the restriction could have resulted in these and other regionally distinct patterns. It should be noted that Johnson (1994:258) considers the Toyah phase to be a prehistoric phenomenon and denies its association with the Jumanos, despite the fact that he dates the end of the Toyah phase at 1600/1650, a time when Spaniards had begun to travel in central Texas and adjacent areas.

When we turn to the documentary record, there is ample evidence that the groups residing in central Texas were hunter-gatherers. The first indication of this is in early reports from central Mexico describing groups residing north of the large towns and villages of central Mexico. Nahuatl speakers of central Mexico told the Spanish that the people in the far north were *chichimecas* based on their similarity to the Chichimecas of Nueva Galícia, who lived without the benefit of clothing "in caves and in the mountains, maintaining themselves with roots" (Motolinía 1971:6). Similar descriptions continued for some time. In the 1595 *carta annua* (annual summary report) sent by the Jesuits to Rome, the people north of Santa Barbara and Saltillo were described thusly: "They wander nude and do not have houses nor specific homes, nor do they sow. They do not have anything to eat other than items that the land voluntarily gives them. They eat [prickly pear] tuna, maguey, mesquite, and other herbs and some fish" (Ayer 1595).

These rather pejorative summaries conform to the account of Cabeza de Vaca. He and his companions lived for six years among native groups near the Texas coast, traveling with them to fields with large stands of prickly pear cacti where they met friends and foes. In those years, they learned nothing to suggest that natives in central Texas west of the coastal prairies had permanent houses or agriculture. Not until they reached the region of La Junta did they encounter such practices (Krieger 2002:222–24).

Despite these sweeping generalizations of the native peoples of the far north of Mexico, including those in Texas, several factors pushed the Spanish to become better acquainted with the many different groups residing in these northern lands. High among these factors were the discovery of silver in Santa Bárbara, Zacatecas, Parral, Indé, and elsewhere in northern Mexico during the second half of the sixteenth century and their continuing interest in colonizing New Mexico. Silver and ranches to grow the food to support the growing population that would mine the silver required a large labor pool to perform the work (Alessio Robles 1978:91–96; Gerhard 1982; Jones 1988). For this, the Spanish harnessed the natives in *encomienda*, an institution claiming to give enslaved natives protection and religious instruction in return for their labor (Himmerich y Valencia 1991). At first, natives close to the mines and ranches were forced into labor, but slaving expeditions quickly ranged at some distance from Spanish settlements. In 1581 natives in La Junta told the Spanish that members of their villages had been forced south to work in the mines (Hammond and Rey 1966:55, 62). During this process of becoming acquainted, documents of soldiers and administrators reveal increasingly greater understanding of the natives residing north of the Rio Grande. Writing in 1649 after considerable experience on the northern frontier of Coahuila, Captain Alonso de León (1909:24) said that the natives of Coahuila and Texas, like those of Nuevo Leon, would stay only a few days in each place, and families would gather together or separate at will. Often their camps had up to fifteen dwellings made of tall grasses or reeds, each with a central hearth. This and other accounts continue to confirm that the natives north of the Rio Grande were hunter-gatherers.

To look at mobility patterns, we examined the documentary record for three of the named groups of central Texas: the Cíbolos, the Hapes, and the Jumanos. These three represent a small subset of the groups listed in the documents. Typically, the Spanish called these groups *naciones*, which literally means "nations" but is also used to indicate that a person is a "native of" one group or another. Griffen (1969:v) says these *naciones* represented bands within larger tribes. Deeds (2003:52) agrees, as does Cramaussel (2000), but both note that they represent quite porous social groups. Because terms like "band" and "tribe" carry certain loaded connotations, we avoid them. We concur that these nations were porous, as were most small-scale societies (Johnson 1989; Spielmann 1991b:3–7). However, we avoid equating "nation" with ethnicity, for we agree with Clark (2004:44) that "ethnicity is situational and varies through time." Thus, we retain the term "nation."

Whereas names of some nations associated with central Texas appear in only one or two documents, others—like the Jumanos—persist for over two hundred years. It is not clear how many of these groups existed in the region, but nineteen nations (see table 2.1) were listed as traveling with Juan Sabeata, a Jumano, as he guided Juan Dominguez de Mendoza and Fray Nicolas Lopez to the region of modern San Angelo (AGN 1684a, 1684b, 1689–1788). Most, if not all, are generally believed to have been residents of this broad region. Fray Lopez wrote there were seventy-six nations between La Junta and the Teyas (the Caddos of east Texas) (AGN 1689–1788). In 1693, Joseph Francisco Marin (Hackett 1926:392–95) listed forty-nine nations occupying the region north of the Rio Grande and between La Junta and the Caddos (table 2.2). Because Marin was a representative of the viceroy and not intimately familiar with these groups, not all he listed were actually from that region, and some of his names may not represent an actual group (Griffen 1969:176–77). Nonetheless, the information gathered by the Spanish in Sabeata's company and lists such as Marin's indicate that the region was populated by a sizable number of nations.

Many nations did not survive colonization (Campbell 1988; Kenmotsu 2001; Salinas 1987), for several reasons. The Masames were slaughtered by their enemies, the Tobosos, around 1652 (AHP 1677C). By the 1650s the Babanes were reduced to only four members from poor conditions suffered in an *encomienda* (SA 1658). The Jumanos, who for nearly a century sought Spanish missions and presidios in their lands, coalesced with the Apaches (Kenmotsu 2001, 2008). Others succumbed to European diseases (Alessio Robles 1978:189–200; Griffen 1969: 83–84).

We now turn to the three nations chosen for closer scrutiny. Table 2.1 lists the Spanish encounters with these three nations, giving the location where the encounter took place, the Spanish estimates of the number of natives present, as well as the names of other nations (if any) that were represented in the group. When the patterns are compared to the archaeological record of the Toyah phase, they show three areas of discordance: the documentary record suggests that there was movement over long distances; that these natives traveled in large groups; and that these three nations traveled in multinational groups.

The Cíbolos (also Civola, Sibola, Sibopora, Sibopolame, Sivolito, Xibulu, Xiabu, Sivoporame, Sipopola, Sipopora, Sipoplame, Sopolame, Sipulame, and Xupulame) are generally believed to have occupied lands south-southwest of the Jumanos (AGI 1693; Griffen 1979:32; Kenmotsu 1994:298). Although this places their homelands in the broad Shared Toyah area (see fig. 1.6), the documents show that the Cíbolos also moved throughout central Texas and beyond. Miguel, a Cíbolo leader in the 1680s, testified in Parral that his land was "from the other part of [e.g., north of] the Rio Grande where there are many . . . Cíbolos" (AGI 1693). In testimony in 1689, another Cíbolo stated that he "lives in a rancheria that typically has war every year with the Caribes Indians on account of their [the Caribes] killing the buffalo herds. They [the Cíbolos] spend part of the year between the Rio Grande and the Nueces River" (AGN 1691).[4]

The Cíbolos are also mentioned in documents related to Spanish encounters with groups south of the Rio Grande (AHP 1651A, 1652A, 1654A, 1677C). Griffen (1969:158) argued that these documents refer to a second, perhaps quite distinct, Cíbolo nation residing south of the Rio Grande. This group is often cited with variants of the name Sibopolame. At present, we find the evidence equivocal. Griffen may be correct. However, many of these documents concern several rebellions, and the documents never say the Cíbolos actually entered the conflict. Rather, they were mentioned as a large nation whose numbers, if they could be persuaded to rebel, would make a significant difference in the outcome of the

TABLE 2.1. Spanish encounters with Cíbolo, Hape, and Jumano groups, 1583–1716

Nation/Date	*Place Encountered*	*Number in Group*	*Other Nations Represented in the Group*	*Reference*
Jumano, 1583	Pecos River near Pecos, Texas	"many" and "tens of Indian men and women"	None	Espejo 1871:123; Espejo in Hammond and Rey 1966:189; Lujan in Hammond and Rey 1929:124–25
Jumano, 1629	"rio de las nueces," or Concho River, near San Angelo	80,000	None mentioned	Ayer 1965
Jumano, 1632	Concho River	Not stated	None mentioned	Posada 1962:466
Jumano, 1650	Concho River	Not stated	None mentioned	Posada 1962:466
Jumano, 1654	Concho River	"a considerable number"	None mentioned	Posada 1962:469, 1982:29
Hape, 1669	East-central Coahuila	29	Ervipiames, Yoricas, Nostli Gueguei, Boboles, Tocoomores, Payoaes, Ocanes, Pamuliem, Dacafoz, Sutoaname, Catuxano, Tercoonome, Xoapoz, Tepogueguei	AHP 1670A
Cíbolo, 1674	South of mouth of the Pecos River	543	Babane, Hueiquechal, Bobole, Xicocoxe, Obaya, Manos Prietas, Penanacam, Baniamaman, Bascoram	BN 1674
Hape, Jumano, 1675	Coahuila, ca. 50 miles south of the Rio Grande	1,331*	Tereodan, Teaname, Teimamar, Queiquezale, Jume, Mavivit, Yorica	Portillo 1886:113–21
Jumano, 1684	Traveled with Mendoza from El Paso to Concho River	515	*Groups traveling with Mendoza and Lopez:* Beitonojame, Chubate, Cujaco, Tareme, Hediondo, Jumano, Oraso, Siacucha, Suajo, Isucho, Cauca, Chinchi, Llame, Cunchuoco, Quitaca, Cuicuchube, Achubale, Hineni, Hanacine *Groups waiting for them in central Texas:* Muele, Flechas Feas, Pescado, Gente que Come, Agua Susia, Tuxaxa, que en unde?, TiJamu, people of the Nueces, Tanaque, Tohajo, Emiti, Caimanes, Toapa, Qui Oborique, Toapari, Geabori, Borobamo, Cocuma, Teanama, Ytaca, Come Cara, Blan, AriLuman, Tumpotoqua, mana, Los Zurdos, Quide, Jumanos	AGN 1683; AGN 1689–1788; Kenmotsu 2001; Wade 2003:103

TABLE 2.1. (continued)

Nation/Date	Place Encountered	Number in Group	Other Nations Represented in the Group	Reference
Hape, Jumano, 1686	Just east of central Texas	"a large number"	Mescale, Yorica, Machomene, Sampanale, Pacuachiam, Tilpayay	Mazanet 1968:8–9
Jumano, Cíbolo, 1688	Pecos River near Pecos, Texas	"a sufficient number of warriors" to help Gen. Retana fight the French	None mentioned	AGI 1688; Hackett 1926:264
Cíbolo, Hape, Jumano, 1689	Just east of central Texas	70	Mescale	Leon 1968:91
Jumano, Hape, 1689	Just east of central Texas	490	Mescale, Ijiaba	Leon 1968:91
Hape, Jumano, 1690		"a large quantity"	Mezcale, Yorica, Sanaque, Sanyau	Leon 1968:136; Mazanet 1968:160
Cíbolo, Jumano, 1691	Just east of central Texas	2,000+ (Mazanet says 3,000)	Cholome, Cantona, Catqueza, Caynaya	Mazanet 1968:240; Teran 1968:178
Jumano, 1693	Just east of central Texas	"a multitude"	None	Salinas Varona 1968:287
Jumano, 1693	Just east of central Texas	"some"	Asinai (Caddo)	Salinas Varona 1968:298
Hape, 1693	Just east of central Texas	No number given	Mezcale, Cacage	Salinas Varona 1968:306
Hape, Jumano, 1700	Missions on the lower Rio Grande	100 families (500+ people)	Mescale, Yorica	AGI 1708
Jumano, 1715	La Junta	180	Conejo	AGI 1715
Cíbolo, 1715	La Junta	550	Pulique, Concho, Polacme	AGI 1715
Cíbolo, 1716	Central Texas	"A large gathering"	Julime, Escomeagamos, Los de Quejolote, Erviapiame, Chizo, Gavilane, Tripas Blancas	AHP 1716A

Table does not include visits of delegations of leaders of these nations to El Paso, Parral, or Saltillo.

* See Wade (2003:40–41) for another translation of this diary entry that documents only 1,172 people in the camp. Regardless of which figure is used, the camp contained a sizable number of people.

TABLE 2.2. Nations listed by Marín living between La Junta and the Caddos in east Texas

Salchomis	Pie de Recacolote	Guacali	Sallas
Cabellos Blancos	Salcocolomes	Bapacores	Cassas Morados
Borrados	Siniples	Dientes Alazanes	Pajaritos
Cavezas	Conejos*	Alzados	Síbolos
Humanas	Come Síbolos	Arcos Tirados	Posalmes*
Apaches	Mesquites	Cacalotes	Topacolmes*
Polacmes*	Oposmes*	Pulicas*	Paiaias Cuchite
Miembros Largos	Comen Todo Manjaar Hecho Pinole	Gaapa	Ymittes
Canaq	Tugues	Cruiamos	Satatu
Rayados	Ysuguaios	Mamuyas	Mapoch
Yaguat	Come Viejos	Cauuares	Otros Borrados
Manos Sordas	Arcos Podridos	Arcos Buenos	
Colas Largas		Sin Orejas	

Source: Hackett 1926:392
* These groups were residents of La Junta (Kenmotsu 1994).

rebellion. The Cíbolos were also contacted well after other native groups had initiated the rebellions, suggesting that their territory was at greater distance from Spanish settlements, and thus less threatened, than those of the other groups. Since we cannot verify from the manuscripts that the Spanish ever saw the Cíbolos in these instances, these documents are not included in table 2.1. Finally, several manuscripts from Saltillo place Cíbolo people in the general region south of the Rio Grande, sometimes in the company of Jumanos (BN 1674; Leon 1968; Mazanet 1968; Terán 1968), a group with whom they enjoyed an alliance, again suggesting that these dispersed encounters and statements all relate to a single group.

In the 1680s the Spanish were struggling to learn more about La Salle's French settlement on the Texas coast. Several documents, written only a few years apart, include statements taken from Cíbolos and others who had seen the French. In November 1688, General Juan de Retana, commander of the San Francisco de los Conchos presidio, questioned three natives from La Junta and two Franciscan friars (AGI 1688). All testified that Don Nicolas, a Cíbolo leader, had sent several of his people to La Junta to tell the people there that he was returning from lands north and east of La Junta, and that he was bringing with him a "Spaniard" who had been among the Caddos. The friars added that in 1687 they first heard of some foreigners whom they said the natives called "Spanish" or "Moors" "because that is what the Indians call the French" (AGI 1688). At that time, Cíbolos and Jumanos in La Junta were about to travel again to the region close to the Caddos. The friars asked the natives to bring them a letter from the Spaniard; in September 1688 they sent word that they were bringing the foreigner instead (Hackett 1926:240–43).

From this series of letters, reports, and testimonies the Cíbolo travel pattern emerges, and it is one of long-distance travel (see table 2.1). Sometime in 1687, some or all of the Cíbolos were in La Junta, where they were engaged in trading. From La Junta they traveled east to trade fairs with the Caddos. It is not clear if the trade fairs were in the Caddoan lands of eastern Texas (a distance of more than 600 straight-line miles from La Junta) or in the prairies slightly west and south of those lands. This trip would have taken the Cíbolos across central Texas, and it appears to have been an annual event because Juan Sabeata, the self-ascribed governor of the Jumanos and Cíbolos, testified that he would have come sooner to Parral, "except that it was time to go to *tierra adentro* [the interior] to fairs with the nations down river from [the] Texas [Caddo] and many other nations" (Hackett 1926:260). This statement coupled with his remark the following day saying he made the decision to go to the fairs and barter sessions "as they [his people] are accustomed to do" (Hackett 1926:262) suggests that the travel east was an annual pattern for the Cíbolos.

In September of the following year, after speaking with the friar who asked that they come back with a letter from the "Spaniard," the Cíbolos first traveled from La Junta down the Rio Grande several days (Hackett 1926:262–66). From there they traveled to fairs held with natives living near La Salle's colony on the gulf coast, and then north to the Caddo villages. Finally, they turned west, meeting General Retana on the Rio Salado (Pecos) in early March 1689. Juan Sabeata told the Spanish that it was approximately twenty-six days from the Caddos to La Junta (Hackett 1926:266). Nicolas, a Cíbolo, contradicts Sabeata, saying the journey took only eight days if the traveler did not make side trips to visit other rancherias (Hackett 1926:272).

Similar long-distance travel is suggested by their presence along the eastern edge of central Texas in 1689 and 1691 (Ayer 1691; Leon 1968; Masanet 1957:362). In both encounters, they again traveled with the Jumanos, and in 1691 they were still under the leadership of Juan Sabeata, suggesting that they were on yet other annual east-west trip to the trade fairs with Caddos and other groups. Few documents include mention of Cíbolos after this date until, in 1715, they are in one of the villages at La Junta (AGI 1715), and the following year among rebel natives on the Colorado River in central Texas (AHP 1716A). In these final two years, then, there are hints of a continuing pattern of long-distance, east-west travel (La Junta to central Texas).

The mobility pattern of Hape people (also Aba, Ara, Gaapa, Hape, Hipe, Iape, Jeapa, Xape, Xiapoz, and Hapoz) differs somewhat from that of the Cíbolos but still exhibits relatively long distances. In the documents that we accessed for this effort, Hapes were first mentioned in 1629 in Benevides's Memorial (Ayer 1965) as residents of the region between the Pecos and Colorado rivers near the southern edge of the Southern Plains. As shown in table 2.1, subsequent Spanish encounters with Hapes in the 1670s place them south of the Rio Grande. Fray Juan de Larios (SFG 1674), who spent considerable time with natives along both sides of the Rio Grande, said that in the 1670s Hapes and several other groups were under the direction of a Don Miguel of the Catujano nation. They briefly settled in Monclova in 1675, but dissension with other native groups caused Hapes and others to leave within two months (Alessio Robles 1978:259; Portillo 1886:159; Wade 2003:19). In the late 1680s they were along the eastern edge of central Texas with the Jumanos and Cíbolos. Then, in 1683, Juan Sabeata listed the Hapes as one of the nations living close to the Jumanos in central Texas (AGN 1683). In 1700 they began to congregate at Mission San Juan Bautista on the lower Rio Grande. Father Espinosa of that mission wrote that, although the Hapes maintained a presence there, they came and went as they pleased: "They were born and reared in *tierra adentro* and often go there" (AGI 1708).

Combined, the documents suggest that this nation moved roughly north-south through central Texas from some point in the northern edge of the geographic extent of the Toyah phase to its fringes on the south in the vicinity of the confluence of the Pecos with the Rio Grande, a distance of approximately 250 miles. The glimpses are few, however, making it difficult to determine if the north-south movement was an annual or occasional choice freely taken, spurred by shifting ecological cycles of drought, caused by internal strife among the nations occupying the region, or some combination of these factors.

The Jumano people (also Chome, Chumano, Humanos, Juman, Xumano, Xume, and Xoman) were first described living in small rancherias along the Pecos River on the western edge of the Toyah macro region (Hammond and Rey 1929:124–25). Documents from the seventeenth century place the Jumano territory between the Pecos and Concho rivers (AGI 1693; AGN 1683, 1684a, 1684b, 1689–1778; Ayer 1965:157–69; Posada 1962, 1982).[5]

Like the Cíbolos, the Jumanos traveled over considerable distances (see table 2.1). When first encountering them on the Pecos River, Espejo and his small band walking south from their trip to New Mexico told the Jumanos they intended to follow that river to return to Spanish settlements in northern Mexico. That would likely have spelled disaster for the ill-equipped expedition, for this was not a direct route to those settlements. The Jumanos said La Junta was a better direction and had no difficulty guiding them there in a trip that took six days (Hammond and Rey 1966). Over the next century, Jumanos were said to be close allies of the Humanas pueblos in New Mexico (Oñate 1871a:266, 1871b:306), indicating that they likely traveled to and from those pueblos. In visits by priests and soldiers to Jumano territory during the seventeenth century, the Spanish learned that by at least 1650 Jumanos had established or were in the process of establishing a relationship with Caddo people residing some 340 miles east of the Concho River (Posada 1962). Friendships require time and effort (Johnson 1989; Rogers and Wilson 1993; Spielmann 1991a; Welsch and Terrell 1998). To make or sustain a friendship with another group residing several hundred miles away implies that Jumanos traveled to Caddo territory beginning at least by 1650, and the continuation of that travel is confirmed in documents from the late 1680s and 1690s (Leon 1968:91; Mazanet 1968:8, 160; Terán 1968:178).

In 1683, Jumano leaders traveled to El Paso to ask that the Spanish put missions and presidios in their territory as protection from Apaches (AGN 1684a 1684b, 1689–1788; Wade 2003:76). The following year, Sabeata led the Spanish to his people who were in the Concho River drainage near modern San Angelo (AGN 1684a, 1689–1788; Kenmotsu 2001; Wade 2003:103). As noted above for the Cíbolos, in the late 1680s the Jumanos, accompanied by the Cíbolos, traveled annually from La Junta through central Texas to the Caddos in eastern Texas, sometimes swinging south along the Rio Grande before reaching Caddo land. In the 1690s they were encountered along the eastern edge of central Texas, again in the company of Cíbolos (AGN 1691).

Jumanos apparently also traveled south to Coahuila as early as the seventeenth century, for some were apprehended there early in that century and placed in *encomienda* near Saltillo (SA 1658). In the 1670s they were reported to be both north and south of the Rio Grande near the mouth of the Pecos (SFG 1674). From 1700 to 1708 they were in missions on the lower Rio Grande but often traveled into central Texas (AGI 1708). In sum, the mobility pattern of the Jumanos was not one of restricted travel in a relatively confined area. Rather, it was an annual movement over considerable distance and was mirrored by the Cíbolos. The travel distance for the Hapes was smaller, but still not restricted to a relatively confined area.

The ethnohistorical evidence also fails to support fully the Toyah archaeological model of mobility taking place in small family groups. Certainly, ethnographic data show that, at times, larger groups of hunter-gatherers travel together. Hitchcock and Bartram (1998:34) point out that the Kan travel part of the year in groups of fourteen to forty-two. Panamint-Timbisha winter camps in Death Valley were typically large gatherings of families (Fowler et al. 1999:55–56), as were winter camps of other Great Basin groups (d'Azevedo 1986; Sucec 2008). For the Cíbolo, Hape, and Jumano peoples, as shown in table 2.1, the evidence indicates that travel in groups well above small kin based group size was not uncommon. Some numbers of natives given in table 2.1 should be viewed with skepticism. They vary from a high of 80,000 souls present at the grand conversion of the Jumanos in 1629 to a low of twenty-nine in 1670 (AHP 1670A; Ayer 1965:132). Although we suspect the 80,000 is greatly exaggerated given the archaeological evidence near San Angelo (Creel 1990; Johnson 1994; Treece et al. 1993), the impression is that the gathering was certainly more than a few small, kin-based families. Similarly, when Sabeata told the Spanish governor in El Paso that he had assembled more than 10,000 souls in that same land in 1683, he was trying to persuade the Spanish that it was worth their time and money to travel some 350 miles east into *tierra adentro*, so we suspect that this figure is too high. We can, perhaps, also assume that the descriptions of the Jumanos in 1629–54 can be discounted or downgraded since these were other occasions where they, as well as the priests, were seeking missions on the Concho River.

In other cases, however, the skepticism should be more guarded. Although not all the remaining encounters with the Spanish were entirely by chance, the natives had not traveled to the locations where they were found for the purpose of meeting the Spanish. Instead, they were usually engaged in buffalo hunting. Moreover, these numbers were provided by experienced frontiersmen, such as Fray Juan de Larios or Alonso de León, who spent considerable time, sometimes years, traveling among or meeting with native groups. Two experienced military men in the late seventeenth century also expressed a healthy respect for the numbers represented by these encounters. Mendoza, who had recently survived the Pueblo revolt, traveled over 300 miles in 1684–85 in the company of a large contingent of Jumanos and their allies with a relatively small party of soldiers and priests (AGN 1684a, 1689–1778; Wade 2003). He typically set up his nightly camps a short distance from the native bed-downs and on a hill if possible. This was a deliberate act of caution. Domingo Terán de los Rios was new to the region, but not new to the military when he made the trip from Saltillo to the Caddos. His party encountered Jumanos, Cíbolos, and Catquezas hunting buffalo along the eastern edge of central Texas during the trek. Although he traveled with a relatively large party, he too refused to join the natives in their camp, setting his up a short distance away, and wrote in his diary: "I observed closely their movements as they outlined their request [for Spanish patents] which I knew to be rather lofty. They [the natives] are numerous and robust, and of considerable haughtiness" (Terán 1968:178). He further said that he believed they had come to this locale to make war on him and his party. Mendoza and Terán would not have had the same concern with small groups of one to several families.

For the 1583 encounter of the Spanish with Jumanos, no numbers are provided, but Lujan and Espejo both describe their rancherias as well populated (Espejo 1871:123; Hammond and Rey 1929:124–25). Adequate food was available to host "a dance between the tens of Indian men and women" at one rancheria, and much merriment with roasted and raw calabashes and prickly pears was available in another (Hammond and Rey 1929:124–25). Fray Larios reported in the 1670s that the Jumanos and Hapes were moving north and south of the Rio Grande among separate groups, some of whom numbered in the several hundreds. When asked why natives moved so often, Larios, who actually traveled among them for several months, explained that because the natives in the group "were very numerous and lived on gathered roots and hunted, in about 15 days they depleted the area where they camped, and were forced to move" (Wade 2003:16).

Travel in large groups was not unique to these three nations. Manuscripts related to Spaniards traveling close to central Texas describe other nations traveling and working in large parties. In the 1670s, Fray Manuel de la Cruz traveled north of the Rio Grande, visiting several nations and taking informal censuses. Population estimates of clergy are sometimes discounted because they augmented counts to justify the continuance of their missions. However, Fray Manuel was one of several priests involved in a series of brief experiments in Coahuila to resolve native unrest (Alessio Robles 1978:231–48; Wade 2003:1–54). At the time of his trip, these priests were trying to settle the natives in missions or new neighborhoods (*barrios*) in Monclova; they needed accurate population estimates to determine the costs for that settlement. Among the groups north of the Rio Grande, he reported 733 Gueiquesales in one group and at least 370 Yoricas in another. Captain Francisco Elizondo (CA 1674), in a separate but related trip north of the Rio Grande, counted 543 adult women and children and 106 warriors in a single camp located in Coahuila a few miles south of the Rio Grande. In another expedition into central and south Texas, Lt. Fernando del Bosque and Fray Larios reported finding several deserted camps with evidence of only a few huts but also encountered occupied camps with groups numbering in the several hundreds (Portillo 1886:111–30). Although these numbers seem high, certainly much higher than expected among hunter-gatherers, they appear to be fairly reliable. Merrill (1994:127) has described a similar large, nomadic group of between three hundred and a thousand people in northern Mexico in the late eighteenth century and argues that these types of groups represent a new cultural form that is a feature "of the interaction that occurred during the colonial period between peoples of the Old and New Worlds."

It must be acknowledged that travel in smaller groups probably also occurred but is simply underreported in the documents. The ethnographic (e.g., Laird 1976; Lee 1979; Spier 1928; Weber and Seaman 1985) and ethnoarchaeological (e.g., Binford 1980; Hitchcock and Bartram 1998; Kelly 1983; Wiessner 1977; Wilmsen 1989) records provide solid evidence that hunter-gatherers often travel in small, kin-based groups, and the documentation is too pervasive to believe that these nations always traveled in large groups. Additionally, León's (1909) summary statement that camps often had no more than fifteen huts certainly indicates that group movement in the region did take place in small groups. When the Jumanos and Cíbolos traveled down the Rio Grande from La Junta in 1688, they stopped after several days at the rancheria of Tomas, a Cíbolo. The impression is that this was a small camp, but no number is given. Similarly, Mendoza (AGN 1684a, 1684b) reported passing Jumano rancherias for several days before arriving at a large camp on the Concho River. Nonetheless, encounters with small groups reported in manuscripts related to central Texas were few.

A final discordance between expectations for mobile hunter-gatherers and the documentary evidence is the evidence that travel was often in multinational groups. Table 2.1 indicates that it was common to encounter multiple nations traveling together. Not surprisingly, the groups a nation traveled with tended to be repeated in subsequent encounters. Table 2.1 shows Jumanos with Cíbolos three times, with Hapes four times, and in the company of Mescales five times. Repeated Spanish encounters with the same or nearly the same cohorts can be found for most other groups. Wade (2003:221) concludes, "It is very likely that the Jumano, in a broad sense, represented a series of groups that included . . . the Jumano proper, the Cíbolo, the Gediondo, the Machome, and Those Who Make Bows." This is one interpretation, but individuals in these mixed groups distinguished themselves from each other. Each nation within the larger group also often had its own leaders, as when Nicolas, the Cíbolo leader, traveled with the Jumanos under Juan Sabeata. Multiple nations residing or traveling together or coming and going from each other's company may have been an artifact of Spanish colonization, but the trait is pervasive. Spanish documents are filled with other examples of multiple nations together in a group (for examples, see AHP 1640c,

1644A, 1653B, 1655B; SFG 1674). In addition, the natives, and eventually the Spanish, consistently recognize who is who, and, as noted above, the self-ascription persists for long expanses of time.

If we look back at the archaeological evidence, this documentary review suggests several things. For one, the model set forth by Johnson (1995) of small groups traveling within restricted territories for short distances may require reconsideration. Additionally, the documentary data suggest that the regional variability seen in the patterning of Toyah archaeological assemblages is unrelated to restricted mobility and needs to be explained by other factors such as personal choice, access to raw materials, or other causes. Alternatively, if the variability is due to restricted mobility, relatively early in the 1600s, for at least the Jumanos, mobility began to be over long distances. By the mid-seventeenth century the Cíbolos and Hapes had followed suit. Interestingly, other than three site (Rush, 41LK201, and possibly Rowe Valley), we have little evidence of sites that might accommodate anything close to three hundred people, much less of groups in excess of a thousand.

Our current inability to identify large encampments may be related to several factors. It may be related to the types of projects where Toyah age sites have been excavated. In the past thirty years, most excavations at Toyah sites have been driven by the limited footprints of highways, pipelines, or development projects (Creel 1990; Quigg and Peck 1995). Even at Buckhollow, the site analyzed and reported by Johnson (1994) and used as the foundation for his "Classic Toyah area" concept, the excavations were limited to the footprint of the highway right-of-way that bisected the site. If one of these sites represented a slice of a larger encampment, that would have been difficult to detect (see acknowledgement of this in Johnson 1994:21, 63). The work of Treece and colleagues (1993) was not restricted by a footprint, but it was restricted by the amount of funding available to spread across several significant sites in a large reservoir.

Another factor is the minimal archaeological investigation undertaken to date in the large central Texas region. It is also possible that our own expectations that Toyah age sites should largely consist of small encampments representing one to several families have contributed to our failure to recognize such sites. Family or kin-based groups within a larger encampment may have set up their camps separately to reduce conflicts, perhaps on opposite sides of a streambank. When we draw boundaries around sites, perhaps they represent edges of kin-based segments within larger camps. Such a profile might not be recognized by current archaeological techniques.

Finally, some of these large camps may have been used for only a night and have limited archaeological expression. Odell's (2008) analysis of excavations at the Lasley Vore site, a large Protohistoric Wichita settlement, found abundant artifactual evidence but no structures. To date "only 11 . . . Wichita lodges [have been excavated] for the entire 600-year period from roughly 1300 to 1900" (Perkins et al. 2008:441). These data suggest that the failure to identify large Jumano/Cíbolo/Hape camps, then, is partially related to the duration of settlement. It should be noted that pottery analysis at Lasley Vore indicates occupation by a multiethnic mix of people (Odell 2008). Regardless of the reasons why large sites are underrepresented in the archaeological record, the documentary evidence strongly argues that they exist.

LAND TENURE

Hitchcock and Bartram (1998:31) note that the twenty-two ethnic groups in the central and eastern Kalahari recognize territorial divisions of the land; for the Kuas, the largest of these groups, those territories "represent far more . . . than simply areas that people use to obtain food and materials for tool manufacture." Kinship and social alliances are the underlying principles of land use and land tenure (Hitchcock and Bartram 1998:21). Land rights are assigned based on group membership but can be acquired through fictive kin, patron-client relationships, or movement to an unutilized area. Territorial boundaries are permeable and overlapping and are generally defended only during periods of resource stress when negotiations are required if a nonlocal group wishes to enter another's territory. These territories have some antiquity. Informants often linked the land they use to ancestors. Hitchcock and Bartram (1998:37) describe territorial behavior as "a complex set of behavior patterns that relate to structural properties of the social and natural environment and to the meanings which people assign to land, resources, and symbolically significant as well as nonsignificant space. Landscapes are not just regions over which people move; they contain places and things that hold tremendous ideological significance to individuals, groups, and societies."

Land tenure can only be inferred from the archaeological record. The Rainey site (41BN33) is a small sinkhole that contains seven superimposed occupations by a small family group dating to the Toyah phase (Henderson 2001). Other Toyah sites have more than one component (Creel 1991; Highley 1986; Treece et al. 1993). Recurring occupation of the same site suggests that people returned to favored locales.

Information on land tenure in the ethnohistorical record is minimal for the Cíbolo and Hape nations but abundant for the Jumanos. The data limitations for the Cíbolos and Hapes are largely related to the few times they testified to the Spanish. In those few cases, however, they reveal a feeling that they did have, in their own words, *their* land. The manuscripts also indicate a widespread and shared understanding of who held what space. Don Santiago, of the Cabeza nation, said he went "to the land of the Cíbolos" (AHP 1673A). Similar statements regarding the "land of" the Cíbolos appear in other documents (e.g., AHP 1651A, 1652A, 1655Ab). Together, they imply that the Cíbolos, like the Kuas, had and held a recognized place on the landscape that was uniquely theirs. Because no Hapes acted as spokesperson for groups when they were among the Spanish, we have less understanding of their tenure on the land. The only hint in the manuscripts is the notion of a repeated north-south movement to and from the same regions.

In contrast to the data limitations for the Hapes and Cíbolos, the Jumanos not only gave testimony, they sometimes sought the Spanish to solicit aid in one form or another, resulting in fairly detailed reports that were sent to civil and clerical authorities. On the basis of those reports, Kenmotsu (2001) argues that the Jumanos, beginning as early as 1583, sought a friendly relationship with the Spanish specifically for the purpose of retaining their homeland. The Jumanos had to know of the Spanish prior to the arrival of the Espejo expedition at their rancherias in 1583. Slaving expeditions had already been to La Junta (Hammond and Rey 1929), and Coronado (1870:260–70; Flint and Flint 2005) traveled to New Mexico and the Southern Plains. Both events must have been topics of considerable gossip and concern. Yet when Espejo and his men arrived on the Pecos, the Jumanos did not treat them as fearful strangers; they received them in a friendly manner and spent six cordial days leading them to La Junta.

In subsequent years their efforts to cultivate Spanish assistance grew more apparent. The Spanish made several visits to the Jumanos between 1629 and 1654 (see fig. 2.1 and table 2.1). In each case they went to the same general vicinity of the Concho River near San Angelo, and in each of these visits the Jumanos spoke of the need for missions and presidios in *their* lands. Over time, these requests show a growing Jumano concern for their homelands. The concern seems to relate to several things. A severe, multiyear drought was in progress in 1629. Waterholes were said to have dried up; the herds of buffalo "on which these nations sustain themselves" moved north, and the people were forced to travel away from their homelands to obtain food (Ayer 1965:161). Disease was also beginning to take its toll on the people living on and close to the Southern Plains by this time (Ayer 1965:162; Kessell 1987:163).

As well, Jumano conflict with Apaches on the Southern Plains was well under way. In 1599 these Apaches requested Spanish aid "against the Xumanos, as they call a tribe of Indians who are painted after the manner of the Chichimecos" (Bolton 1916:225). Only a year later, the Humanas pueblos, allies of the Jumanos, incurred the wrath of Oñate (Zaldiver 1871) and were swiftly punished (Scholes and Mera 1940:279). In the early seventeenth century, perhaps as early as 1618, an unknown number of Jumanos were captured in Coahuila and forced to work on a hacienda there (SA 1658). Conditions were harsh and many died.

It is likely that word of this situation came back to the people on the Concho River. Cleverly, Jumano solicitations were flavored with promises to introduce the Spanish to many nations, with hints that an introduction from the Jumanos would ensure a peaceful reception. The Jumanos were not simply soliciting Spanish visits or treaties. They wanted the Spanish to establish missions and settlements in central Texas "to defend them against their enemies, the Apache" (AGN 1683). We last glimpse the Jumano chief Juan Sabeata in 1691 on the eastern edge of central Texas. He had gone to great lengths in the mid-1680s to persuade the Spanish to settle in his lands, but to no avail. Once again he pleaded with both Terán and Father Masanet that they come to "his" lands. They did not. Given these circumstances, the repeated pleas of the Jumanos for aid indicate that they considered the land on the river of the nuts *theirs*, and they wanted Spanish assistance to hold that land.

Central Texas in Context

The people in central Texas between 1535 and 1716 were not isolated from the broader world; rather, as shown above, they were active participants in that world. As participants, they were affected both directly and indirectly by forces active outside of their own lands. In their case, the broader world included forces that Perkins and colleagues (2008), Vehik (2002), and others have documented to the north, while to the south the forces were the wide-reaching effects of Spanish colonization.

We first turn to the north. Vehik (2002) notes the increasing archaeological evidence, throughout a broad region, of conflict in the form of violent deaths, placement of villages on higher settings where attacks would be more easily defended, and village fortification. That region stretches east-west from the Southern Plains to Arkansas and north-south between the Red and Arkansas rivers. Vehik (2002:43) states: "After AD 1400–1450, conflict increases. By the early historic period, intergroup conflict was a frequently commented upon feature of life in the Southern Plains." She finds that these changes coincide with an increase in the number and distribution of bison on the Plains and argues that much of the competition was over bison (cf. Mauldin et al., this volume). Although her focus is the aggregation of agriculturally based, sedentary villages, Vehik (2002:42) is not unmindful of similar aggregation of more mobile groups. With these larger settlements, there is a concomitant increase in trade of nonlocal goods. Vehik (2002:41) concludes not that the increase in trade was motivated by exchange of food, for both mobile and sedentary groups had adequate food supplies, but rather that trade and aggregation "develop within a context of social disruption and upheaval that resulted from increased conflict."

Perkins and colleagues (2008) agree. As the Wichitas moved into southern Oklahoma and northern Texas in the early eighteenth century, "Wichita life became increasingly intertwined with French trade" for bison and deer hides and eventually dried or salted meat, tallow, and fat (Perkins et al. 2008:435; see also Gregory 1973). Ethnohistorical documents indicate that these Wichita villages were quite large, mirroring the conclusions of Vehik.

Kavanagh (1986), studying Comanche political power and politics in the eighteenth and nineteenth centuries, documents much the same thing. Small family-based groups were present on the landscape, but more often the local headman

> through hunting skill, military bravery, and political charisma, as well as judicious marriages . . . attracted and maintained peripheral families and individuals to the band. The basis of his position was control of the redistribution

> of goods, food, war booty, trade, etc. From this control of access to resources he derived his . . . power. . . . Inasmuch as a series of successful leaders would keep a local band together for several generations, local bands could become corporate bodies with succession to office. However, this was counterposed by the tendency for rivals within a band to split off, taking a portion of the band . . . with them (Kavanagh 1986:49).

Under such leaders, Comanche camps could be as small as 350 or as large as 1,800 (Kavanagh 1986:35).

Looking at interaction as well as the evidence for both conflict and kinship among Comanches, other Plains groups, and Puebloan groups, Brooks (2002) has argued that violence, but also gender, accommodation, and masculine honor, were at stake for all sides in these interactions. He sees "a long and ambivalent relationship between New Mexican villagers and their nomadic . . . neighbors and kin, a relationship both violently competitive and simultaneously mutualistic and cooperative" (2002:4).

The Jumanos, Hapes, and Cíbolos lived along the southern edge of this zone of competition and conflict. There is little doubt that they were aware of these changing conditions (Arnn 2007, 2011; Kenmotsu 2001). Competition and conflict would have spilled toward them as Apaches pressed south from Comanche pressure in the late 1500s and early 1600s. Although Spanish and natives killed large numbers of bison close to the Jumano lands in the mid-1600s, a series of documents from the late 1600s reports Jumanos, Hapes, and Cíbolos hunting bison just east of central Texas and in Coahuila south of the mouth of the Pecos River rather than in their homelands. In 1691, Father Masanet wrote that the Jumanos said they "every year come to the reconocimiento of the Guadalupe River and some of them go all the way to the Caddo. They come to kill bison and carry the skins because in their land there are no bison and when it is cold, they return to their lands" (Mazanet 1968:241). One interpretation of this statement is that bison were by then eradicated in the Rolling Plains and Southern Plains. Alternatively, we interpret it to reflect a situation where those hunting lands were no longer available to these nations. The animals in those lands had been "co-opted" by the Apaches and other northern nations. If this was the case, and we believe it was, the aggregation into large, often multinational groups as shown in table 2.1 represented a show of military strength that was a reasonable response to the aggregation seen in their northern neighbors.

South of central Texas, the Spanish gradually settled the landscape with towns, cities, mining districts, and large haciendas. Although Spanish authorities expressed little interest in settlement of the lands north of the Rio Grande until a French colony was established on the gulf coast, natives of central Texas were not immune to effects from colonization to the south of them. A series of quite large and small rebellions took place there throughout the seventeenth century (Deeds 2003). Diseases had begun to affect indigenous populations south and north of the Rio Grande long before Spanish settlement began there (AHP 1716A; SA 1658; SFG 1674). Territories of other nations to the south were disrupted. Wade (1998, 2003) has argued that these pressures led to conflict over resources (bison as well as fields of prickly pear cacti) within central and south Texas. We agree. Again, as a response to such conflict, travel in large groups would have afforded protection to travelers.

Summary

The documentary record is not perfect. For central Texas it is limited to few documents when compared to the ethnohistorical record of other regions. Still, the documentary record for central Texas from 1535 to 1716 presents a decidedly different perspective of indigenous peoples than prehistoric reconstructions based on archaeological data. For almost twenty years archaeological evidence of Late Prehistoric hunter-gatherers in Texas has been interpreted as the residue of small, kin-based groups of one to a few families, moving within relatively restricted territories. Many, if not most, of these interpretations drew significantly from Johnson's (1994) "Classic Toyah area" model. The fact that his model was used so extensively for so long indicates its utility. It was carefully crafted by the wide body of data that Johnson used, and it offered a big-picture evaluation of hunter-gatherers in central Texas and the surrounding region. It may, however, be time to reevaluate that framework in light of the vast amount of archaeological data gathered since Johnson's seminal work was published. For example, the data point to significant variation throughout both the "Classic" and "Shared" Toyah areas. This makes it increasingly difficult to distinguish between sites in the "Classic" area and the "Shared" area. Are the sites at Owen Ivie Reservoir, with the "Classic" Toyah toolkit, including its ceramic assemblage, just evidence of people who shared traits but were not part of the larger phenomenon? We would not argue that the work of Johnson be left behind. Rather, we suggest that it be considered in light of new and unfolding evidence as research moves forward.

The review of the documentary record presented here also suggests significant variation during the early historic period and supports the idea that the documentary record can be used to inform archaeologists about the prehistoric record. More specifically, there appears to be ample evidence that hunter-gatherers during the Toyah phase were not always small, kin-based groups whose mobility was restricted to a small portion of central Texas. Instead, these people were often described as large social aggregates composed of different groups, some speaking different languages, who traveled long distances. The formation of large, multicultural social aggregates (i.e., Jumanos, Hapes, and Cíbolos) in central Texas may represent responses to social, political, and economic changes occurring outside of the region (both to the north and south) as other groups carried those conflicts into the region during the early to mid-seventeenth century. It may even be possible to demonstrate their formation by documenting differences in site size, spatial patterns, and technological, stylistic, and decorative aspects of site assemblages between Late Prehistoric and early historic indigenous sites.

To date, the archaeological correlates of these large, mobile groups have eluded us, perhaps due to restrictions caused by specific development projects whose footprints restrict the area examined in excavations, but sites generated by such large groups would provide opportunities to explore how communal and individual needs were accommodated in such groups. They would also afford study of how power and decision making were shared in such social aggregates. For example, within the larger group, the Cíbolos had their leaders (AGI 1688; Terán 1968:178), and when the Catquezas were with the Jumanos they also had their named leader, suggesting that a hierarchy of leadership existed within these large, mobile groups. It has also been noted that households represent the basic decision-making unit among hunter-gatherers and other small-scale societies (Clark 2004; Hitchcock and Bartram 1998; Spielmann 1991b). Were sequential hierarchies, consisting of members from different households, negotiating disputes in these large mobile social aggregates, as Johnson (1982, 1989) proposed? Research focused on the identification and documentation of these large social aggregate sites may provide clues to where and with whom decision making continued to reside as well as to broader questions concerning culture change in central Texas.

Notes

1. Slaving expeditions certainly moved in and out of this and other areas of Texas. Although these raids caused considerable disruption of indigenous lives, documentary accounts of them are usually indirect references to explain why a native known to be from a distant area was found elsewhere or to indicate why the native giving testimony might harbor ill will against the Spanish or fear them.

2. Over the years there have been many routes posited by scholars (e.g., Bancroft 1886; Baskett 1907; Casteñeda 1936; Davenport and Wells 1918, 1919; Hallenbeck 1940). We believe the route in Krieger (2002) is the most accurate because it is based on his close personal knowledge of the environment, the indigenous groups of Texas and northern Mexico, and these lands before they were altered by modern development.

3. This document is actually about efforts to control the Acoclame and Cocoyame nations. However, three of the pages of a much longer document represent a summary of an earlier trip by Captain Ramon "to the headwaters of the Colorado River." The headwaters of that river are in the Southern Plains, but elsewhere in the document it is stated that the captain went to the headwaters of the "San Marcos and Colorado rivers," a location that would likely place the area somewhere west of modern Austin.

4. The "río de las nueces" ("River of Nuts") is the Concho River, a tributary of the Colorado in the vicinity of modern San Angelo. It was so named in the early seventeenth century when priests and soldiers from Santa Fe visited the Jumanos in their homelands (Posada 1962). Several centuries later it was renamed the Concho River. Another river, originating in central Texas but well to the southeast of the Concho, is today known as the Nueces River.

5. The Jumanos have been the subject of many studies, which disagree about who these

people were and where they lived (Bolton 1911; Hickerson 1994; Hodge 1910; Kelley 1986; Kenmotsu 2001; Scholes and Mera 1940). In part, the disagreement stems from confusion in the first documents that described them. First encountered in 1583 living in rancherias on the Pecos River near modern Pecos, Texas, during the Espejo expedition (Espejo 1871a, 1871b; Hammond and Rey 1929:124–28), the Jumanos fed the Spaniards and led them to La Junta. Once there, Espejo traveled ahead of the other expeditionaries, anxious to plead his case for having not received permission before going to New Mexico. While he traveled south, he wrote his account of the trip, which has several inconsistencies in names of groups found and where when compared to the travel diary of Diego Perez de Lujan. Espejo conflates the Jumanos with the people living in La Junta in pueblos. Lujan never does, and he makes it clear the two are distinct peoples. Kenmotsu (2001, 2008) discusses this in greater detail. Here, we follow Lujan and consider them a distinct group of hunter-gatherers who lived between the Pecos and Concho rivers in central Texas.

THREE

Defining Hunter-Gatherer Sociocultural Identity and Interaction at a Regional Scale

THE TOYAH/TEJAS SOCIAL FIELD

John W. Arnn III

Toyah represents one of the largest and, arguably, least understood Late Prehistoric archaeological records in North America. Centered in the extreme Southern Plains in what is today central and south Texas, Toyah material culture is distributed across approximately 25 percent of the state (174,000 km²) in a region characterized by wide seasonal fluctuations in precipitation and temperature (Ellis et al. 1995; Hall 1998; Hester 1981, 1995; Stahle and Cleveland 1995). Archaeologists have long recognized Toyah as a distinct archaeological phenomenon dating between AD 1250 and 1700 and ringed by several other distinct prehistoric material cultures as well as early historic Native American groups (fig. 3.1).[1]

In general, Toyah material culture is characterized by the broad distribution of open campsites containing specific lithic and ceramic assemblages in central and south Texas (Black 1986; Creel 1990; Hester 1995; Jelks 1962; Johnson 1994; Lintz et al. 1993; Quigg 1997; Quigg and Peck 1995). The lithic assemblage (fig. 3.2) consists of Perdiz arrow points, beveled knives, scrapers, and perforators based primarily on a flake/blade technology (Johnson 1994:269). The ceramic assemblage (fig. 3.3) consists of primarily undecorated bone tempered bowls, jars, and constricted neck ollas, often with buff- or red-slipped or burnished oxidized exteriors (Ricklis 1995a:196–97). In addition, some researchers (Creel 1990; Johnson 1994) include burned rock features and mussel shell features along with the lithic and ceramics assemblages as representative of the Toyah material culture.

The origins of Toyah are not immediately or obviously visible in the archaeological record; they appear to have emerged suddenly across the region, according to one archaeologist as if "sprung from the brow of Zeus" (Johnson 1994:277). The Late Prehistoric period in Texas is generally divided into the Austin phase, or Late Prehistoric I period (AD 700–1250), and the Toyah phase, or Late Prehis-

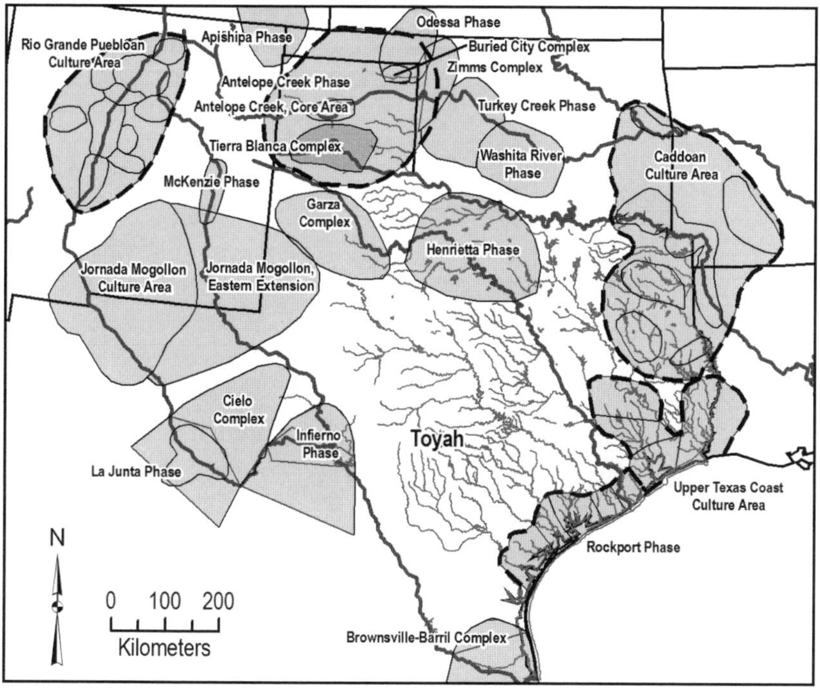

FIGURE 3.1. Toyah and various material cultures and historic groups of the very late prehistoric and early historic periods (ca. AD 1250–1700). Redrawn from Aten (1983), Boyd (1997), Cordell (1980), Drass (1997), Krieger (1946), Lehmer (1948), Mallouf (1999), Perttula (1992), Ricklis (1994, 1995b), Suhm (1957), and Treece et al. (1993)

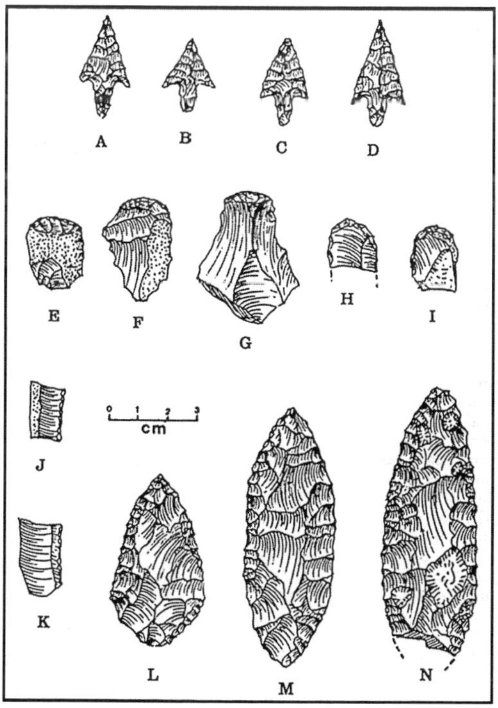

FIGURE 3.2. Toyah lithic assemblage: A–D, Perdiz arrow points; E–I, scrapers; J–K blades; L–N, beveled knives. Redrawn from Ricklis (1994).

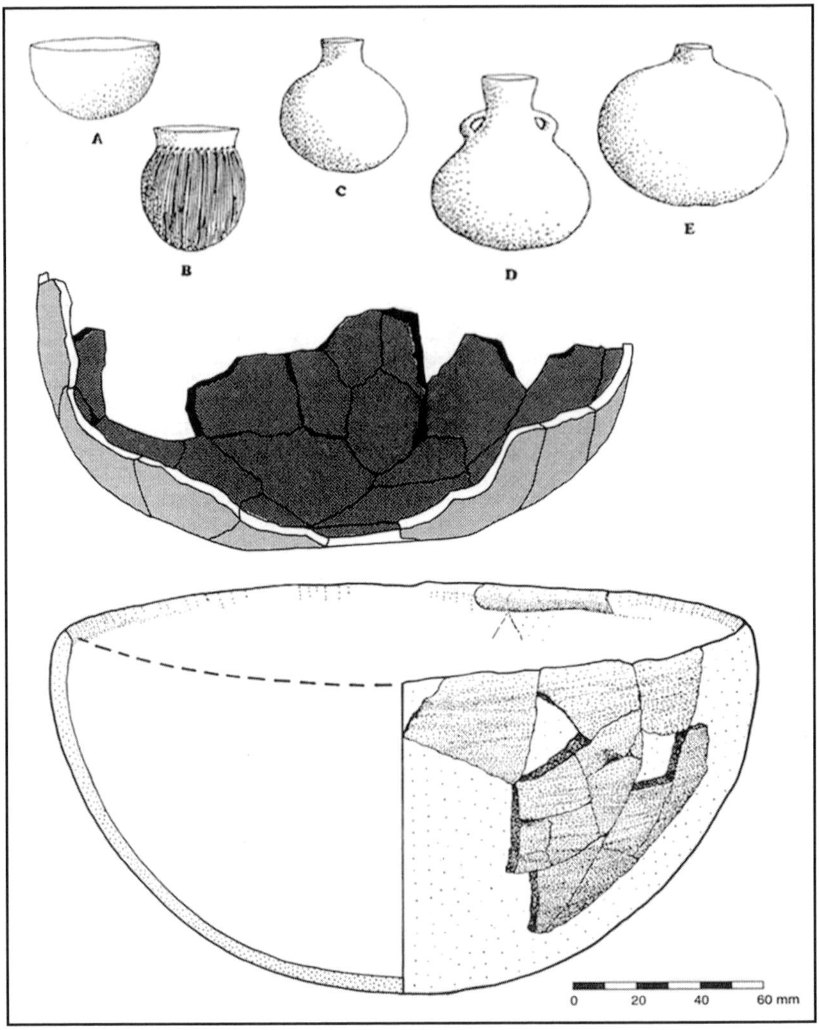

FIGURE 3.3. Toyah ceramics. Above: various bone-tempered pottery forms from select Toyah sites in central and south Texas: A, bowl (41KM16); B, jar with vertical brushing under horizontal rows of punctuations (41HY209); C–E, ollas (d has loop handles) (41LK201, 41RF21); redrawn from Ricklis (1995a). Below: two bowls, the most common ceramic form known for the Edwards Plateau. Top bowl from 41TG346, redrawn from Quigg and Peck (1995); bottom bowl from 41KM16, redrawn from Johnson (1994).

toric II period (AD 1250–1650).[2] The issue of Toyah antecedents is compelling in that Texas is geographically centered between the cultural traditions of Mesoamerica, the American Southwest and Southeast, and the Great Plains and shares much with these regions in terms of biology, geology, and climate. Thus, few regions in North America present a better example of both cultural diversity and a cultural crossroads, suggesting multiple possibilities for Toyah ancestors.

Equally compelling is the ultimate fate of Toyah peoples. Although Toyah is considered a "prehistoric" phenomenon by many archaeologists (Collins 1995; Johnson 1994), radiocarbon assays of Toyah sites across approximately 25 percent of Texas generally fall between approximately AD 1300 and 1700. Direct European contact with Native Americans in Texas began as early as 1528 with the shipwreck of Cabeza de Vaca and his companions on the Texas coast. Thus, more than 170 years (almost half) of the Toyah interval falls within the historic period. Moreover, despite the uniformity in Toyah material culture recognized by archaeologists, historians document significant cultural diversity among Native American groups in this same region during the latter portion of the Toyah interval (referred to by some as the Protohistoric or Early Contact period).

Thus, Toyah presents something of a paradox in which archaeologists have identified one archaeological or material culture in the same region where historians have documented numerous Native American groups and significant cultural diversity. This chapter addresses the dichotomy between prehistoric and historic interpretations and, on the basis of ethnographic, environmental, historical, and archaeological data, presents an alternative interpretation.

Toyah Models

Toyah was first defined by J. Charles Kelley (1947a) as the "Toyah focus" in 1947. Shortly after, others (Hester and Hill 1971; Hester and Shafer 1975; Jelks 1962; Suhm et al. 1954) pointed to significant differences between Toyah and the preceding Austin and Late Archaic periods, emphasizing the initial appearance of ceramics and a flake/blade lithic technology among central and south Texas hunter-gatherers, a broader distribution of the Toyah lithic assemblage, and a specific association with bison (Johnson 1994:241). Combined, these characteristics suggested to many that Toyah was something different than previous prehistoric material cultures and one warranting its own distinct classification (Johnson 1994:241; Karbula 2003:58).

After analyzing most of the available data in the early 1980s, Elton Prewitt (1981, 1985) conceptualized Toyah as a "phase." Prewitt's Toyah phase emphasized a reliance on bison and viewed the lithic assemblage (Perdiz arrow points, beveled knives, various scrapers, and bone tools) as a specific adaptation for procuring and processing bison. In addition, Prewitt (1985) suggested, on the basis of radiocarbon assays from Austin (Late Prehistoric I) and Toyah (Late Prehistoric II) sites, a north-to-south movement or migration of not only bison but also people, beginning sometime in the thirteenth century. Caddoan ceramics were also recovered in several Toyah sites located in the Lampasas Cut Plain and along the western fringes of the Blackland Prairie, suggesting to some Toyah interaction with Caddo peoples to the east.

Prewitt's Toyah phase represented a "remarkably reliable list of traits and a great improvement on anything that had gone before" (Johnson 1994:241), particularly in terms of emphasizing the difference between Toyah and the preceding

Austin phase. Excavations conducted at sites along the northern periphery of the Edwards Plateau (41CC131, 41RN169, 41TG91, and 41TG346) adjacent to the Rolling Plains also contained abundant evidence of bison hunting and processing and were chronologically consistent with other Toyah sites in Prewitt's model (Creel 1990; Quigg and Peck 1995; Treece et al. 1993). Thus, the combined data from sites north and east of the Edwards Plateau tended to support a model in which plains bison hunting populations migrated south following herds into central and south Texas as the bison responded to environmental change (Dillehay 1974; cf. Mauldin et al., this volume).

Although early compilations of radiocarbon assays supported a north-to-south trend in the distribution of Toyah artifacts and assemblages (Prewitt 1985), later compilations indicated an almost simultaneous appearance of Toyah culture throughout the region (Ricklis 1994). With respect to migration, though this particular model addressed the issue of culture change and the perceived uniformity of Toyah material culture, there was generally little or no evidence indicating corresponding abandonment of regions to the north. Conversely, there was little or no discussion of where displaced groups from central and south Texas, likely a sizable population, may have gone once they were inundated with migrants from the north (Kelley 1986; Mallouf 1999; Prewitt 1985). Nor has the subject of migration been addressed in terms of whether these movements were a large, discrete, single event or, for example, a pattern of successive movements by several small groups as is the case with "serial" migration (Bernardini 2005:34). In addition, most supporting data for the migration model were gathered from sites (41BL23, 41HI1, 41ML35, 41SS20, 41TV42, 41WM71, 41WM130, 41WM230) excavated in or adjacent to the Lampasas Cut Plain, Blackland Prairie, and Rolling Plains in environmental settings well suited to large herbivores (i.e., bison) (Prewitt 1981, 1985). Therefore, it is not surprising that these sites presented significant evidence for bison procurement and processing.

During the 1970s and 1980s, other Late Prehistoric sites (41BC114, 41JW8, and 41ZV155) were excavated in central and south Texas, in areas that were not necessarily in or adjacent to prime bison habitat. These sites did not display the same high frequency or prevalence of bison bone as Toyah sites located on the open prairies and plains farther north (Black 1986; Greer 1976a; Hester 1975). In fact, Hester (1975:17) noted twenty-six species represented in the faunal assemblage from site 41ZV155 and stated, "It is possible that the major meat sources were the small mammals—the rabbits and rodents."

Dates from these sites also suggested that the sites were more or less contemporaneous with those located farther north. Prewitt's concept of "phase" was subsequently challenged by Black (1986), who, citing Willey and Phillips (1958:30), argued that the rapid and broad distribution of various aspects of Toyah across several environmentally diverse areas more closely approximated a "horizon" or "tradition" (Karbula 2003:58). Here, Toyah artifacts were viewed as the widespread distribution of technology, or the spread of a "technocomplex" (tools, technology, and ideas), rather than a specific group of people. Although bison may not have been present everywhere in Texas, their presence was assumed to be so pervasive that technology related to bison and bison hunting spread among many different, but local ethnic groups across the region (Black 1986; Collins 1995; Hester 1995; Prewitt 1981; Ricklis 1992).

The latter approach has been described as a cultural ecology–based model (Karbula 2003) in which the regional distribution of Toyah material culture is a result of a specific change in the regional environment (i.e., a general increase in the distribution of bison). At a community level the rapid and widespread distribution of Toyah was transmitted via the "diffusion" of similar ideas and technology among local indigenous groups as bison moved through the region (Ricklis 1994). Nevertheless, this cultural ecology–based model implicitly relies on extensive as well as intensive social interaction in order to spread the bison-related techno-complex. However, beyond "diffusion" it posits no social or cultural mechanisms for the transfer of technology and ideas, and there is the implication that groups in the region were, more or less, spatially fixed entities (within their subsistence ranges) on the landscape.

Although the absence of mechanisms to explain culture change is a common criticism of culture ecology, viewing people as fixtures on the landscape is generally attributed to the culture area concept of the culture history approach, in which some historical groups are viewed as direct ancestors of the original inhabitants of specific areas (Bernardini 2005; Jones 1997). As the distinguished Plains anthropologist Alexander Lesser pointed out more than forty years ago, it is erroneous to assume that human communities exist either in isolation or as fixed points in space (Mintz 1985:76). Models of the "primitive isolate," as Lesser (1961:94) stated, harken back to the days of nineteenth-century evolutionists, and such models are now widely recognized as not only difficult to conceive but generally absent from modern theoretical constructs.

Recent discussions of migration theory indicate that the somewhat vague character of the former Toyah model may be endemic to archaeological concepts of origin and migration in general (Bernardini 2005; Burmeister 2000). As Burmeister (2000) was forced to admit, archaeologists lack even a general definition of migration. Therefore, if migration is to be regarded as a substantive research issue, this line of inquiry requires development. Furthermore, if we accept that no group lives in absolute isolation, it is implicit that whether Toyah peoples moved or developed in situ they did so in interaction with "others." What is argued here is that it was precisely this interaction that created the distribution of material culture recognized by archaeologists as Toyah.

The issue of interaction among distinct sociocultural identities is, however, a point that, with important exceptions (Kelley 1947a, 1955), has been ignored. Thus, in the absence of an explicitly defined mechanism for the transfer of practice and technology, proponents of both models invoke a single regional environmental determinant (essentially climate change resulting in the movement of bison herds) to provide an "either/or" explanation for the archaeological record. Either Toyah people were bison hunters moving with the herds, or bison moved into

Texas and among local groups. Regardless of which model is selected, both rely on bison to explain the widespread and sudden appearance of the Toyah material culture. Thus, interaction and sociocultural identity over a period of four hundred years in an environmentally diverse region encompassing more than 174,000 km^2 is explained in a word: bison.

A fundamental issue emphasized here is that people *are* social/interactive creatures and do not generally live in isolation. Furthermore, there is substantial and significant historical documentation that numerous diverse groups inhabited the same region and interacted for almost half of the Toyah period through a large regional alliance known as Tejas. Thus, there are alternative and compelling reasons and evidence for the transmission of practice and technology besides bison.

Another basic premise emphasized here is that regional interaction and sociocultural identity among indigenous peoples in Texas did not emerge with the arrival of Europeans. Therefore, it is reasonable to infer that there was some persistence of practice, technology, interaction, and sociocultural identity from prehistory into history—and, in fact, the historical record indicates as much. But identity and interaction are precisely the types of things that can be difficult to observe archaeologically, and this is particularly so when archaeologists are either not looking for them or do not think it is possible to observe them in the archaeological record.

Nonetheless, with respect to Toyah, pursuing the issues of sociocultural interaction and identity is in most archaeologists' best interest if only to dispel the various issues identified above with current interpretations. If, for example, archaeologists have indeed identified Toyah material culture as some sort of prehistoric regional phenomenon, it is likely that there is some evidence of continuity into the historic period. This appears particularly likely in the case of a regional phenomenon that spanned 400 years and includes 170 years of the early historic period. Regardless of origin issues, simply establishing some link with a temporally proximal period would only lend credence to Toyah as a valid archaeological concept. Similarly, the ability to distinguish alternative mechanisms for the transfer of practice and technology (something beyond bison and "diffusion") by combining fundamental anthropological theory, ethnographic observations, historical accounts, and archaeological data could only strengthen archaeological interpretations. Toyah studies present several opportunities for reconciling the Late Prehistoric record in Texas with the historic record through multiple lines of evidence. But this requires suspending our belief in monocausal explanations and turning instead to distinguishing multiple sociocultural identities and interaction.

Reconsidering the Toyah Archaeological Record and "The Toyah Problem"

The emphasis on climate change, bison, or migration of peoples or technology has permeated almost every facet of Toyah archaeology, resulting in a generally homogenizing effect with respect to archaeologists' perceptions of sociocultural identity and interaction in the region. That bison were present in Texas during the Late Prehistoric II and early historic periods is not disputed. However, other theoretical approaches may have been sacrificed at the altar of the fatted bison (see Mauldin et al., this volume). Toyah does present an interesting challenge in that there are some remarkable consistencies in terms of artifacts across an enormous, diverse region. Nevertheless, the argument for cultural homogeneity due to external influences (bison, bison technology, and the people who loved them) is assailable on several different points. These issues have been addressed at some length elsewhere (Arnn 2007, 2012); here, a brief summary of key points suffices.

This widespread distribution of Toyah lithics is epitomized by the Perdiz arrow point. Perdiz points are documented in cairn burials in northeast Chihuahua (Mallouf 1987) and the Big Bend (Cloud 2002), rockshelters in southern Coahuila (Taylor 1968), the southern Panhandle Plains (Boyd 1997), Padre Island National Sea Shore (Scurlock et al. 1974), and the Caddo villages of east Texas (Perttula 1998). The high frequency and broad distribution of Perdiz points suggest that they are not indicative of a single prey species or of a single cultural group. In short, many people used the Perdiz point to procure a wide variety of animals. In fact, the frequency and distribution of Perdiz points more closely approximate the frequency and distribution of white-tailed deer rather than bison (Arnn 2007:125–27, 2012). This suggests that Perdiz points and the rest of the Toyah lithic assemblage were well suited for broad-spectrum hunting and foraging, with deer and smaller animals being the common prey in many areas of Texas.

Similarly, the flake/blade technology of the Toyah lithic assemblage is also considered by many to be an innovation associated with the practice of bison procurement and processing with no local antecedent. This does not, however, explain why the assemblage is found in areas where bison were scarce or absent, and there are data to support the existence a flake/blade technology in central Texas immediately prior to Toyah (Arnn 2007:310–14; 2012). Lithic assemblages recovered from Late Prehistoric I or Austin phase sites in central (41BT105, 41UV86) and south Texas (41VT8) do evidence a well-developed lithic technology characterized by the production of flake knives, trimmed flakes, and blades (Creel and Goode 1997:232–33; Johnson 1997:85–87; Shafer 2006a:96–99). In fact, Shafer (2006a:97) states in reference to the Austin phase assemblage at 41VT8, "What was not expected is the prevalence of a prismatic blade technology in the Austin Phase and earlier components." These examples provide local (the Edwards Plateau) antecedents for a flake/blade technology that was once thought to be a very late imported lithic tradition. Furthermore, given the abundance of excellent toolgrade chert and quartzite for hammerstones in and around the Edwards Plateau, there is no reason why the Toyah lithic technology and the innovations associated with it did not evolve in situ.

Johnson (1994:268–69), in one of the most thoughtful discussions of Toyah to date, also addressed variation, or "regionalism," among Toyah sites. According to him the Toyah phenomenon is best represented by both a "Shared Toyah" culture area and a "Classic Toyah" culture area. In essence, Classic Toyah area sites possess all the elements of the Toyah lithic and ceramic assemblages, with little or no exotic artifacts or mixtures of outside cultural traits. In contrast, Shared Toyah area sites reflect Toyah and non-Toyah material culture (ceramics, projectile points, features, etc.).

Sites with mixed Toyah and non-Toyah artifacts in and around the boundaries of the Classic Toyah area have been used to emphasize the variation in material culture within the Toyah region in general (Arnn 2007:340–46). Distinct clusters of sites with similar or shared material culture were also documented on the basis of specific types of ceramics and arrow points found in these sites (fig. 3.4). In some cases these site clusters overlapped with the documented locations of historic linguistic groups (Johnson and Campbell 1992) (fig. 3.5). Examples of sites that display a blend of diagnostic artifacts, characteristic of the mixed assemblages in the Shared Toyah area, include the following:

Blackland Prairie and Lampasas Cut Plain sites (41HI1, 41TV42, 41HM51) with a Toyah lithic assemblage and Caddo or Caddo-like ceramics (Greer 1976a; Jelks 1962; Johnson 1994; Kibler and Broehm 2005; Suhm 1957)

Central Brazos River valley sites (Rodeo Hill and Third Dam) in north-central Texas with Caddo ceramics (Canton and Maybelle incised), mixed arrow points (Alba and Perdiz), side and endscrapers, and bison bones (Smith 1996; see also Kibler, this volume)

Middle Colorado River valley site (41FY135) with complete Toyah lithic assemblage, bison bones, mussel shell features, and Cuney arrow points and sandy paste pottery without bone temper (Kalter et al. 2005)

South Texas site (41MC222) with bison bones (but no endscrapers or beveled knives), bone-tempered plainwares, and Perdiz, Scallorn, Edwards, and unknown stemmed arrow points (Hall et al. 1986)

Rio Grande Plain sites (Mariposa, 41ZV83, and Tortuga Flat, 41ZV155) with mixed arrow point styles (Hester and Hill 1975; Montgomery 1978)

Inland Coastal Plain sites (41JW8, 41LK201, and 41RF21) with distinctive asphaltum-covered, sandy paste Rockport phase ceramics and bone-tempered plainwares (Black 1986; Johnson 1994; Ricklis 1996)

West Texas sites (41PS21 in La Junta district and 41ST87 in northwestern Edwards Plateau) with small quantities of Chupadero Black-on-white and Puebloan polychrome or monochrome wares along with bone-tempered plainwares (Cloud et al. 1994; Kelley 1986; Riemenschneider 1996).

There is also some variation in the vessel forms, decoration, and technological quality of Toyah ceramics. For example, some Toyah pottery is extremely well made, on par with virtually any produced by sedentary farming groups (including Caddo and Pueblo wares), while others are extremely plain and rough. Similarly, Johnson (1994:266) notes considerable variability in Toyah vessel forms and surface treatments throughout the region. Although bowls appear to be more common on the Edwards Plateau, there may be greater variation (ollas and jars) off the Edwards Plateau, particularly in south Texas (see fig. 3.3). Different vessel

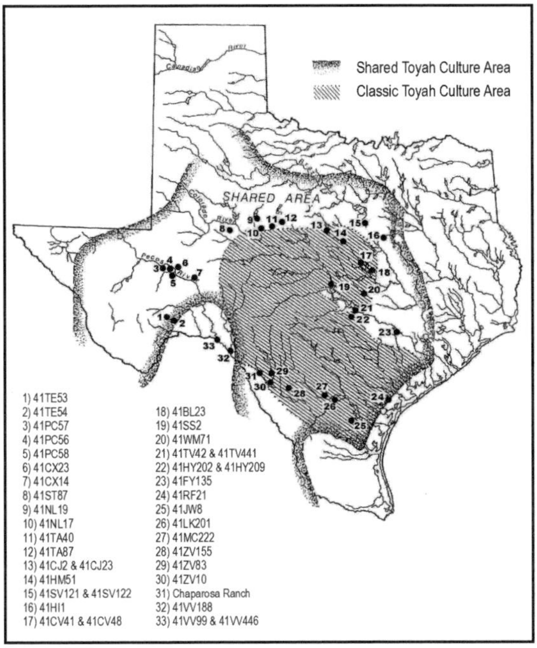

FIGURE 3.4. Map showing sites with mixed assemblages along the boundaries of Johnson's (1994) Classic Toyah culture area.

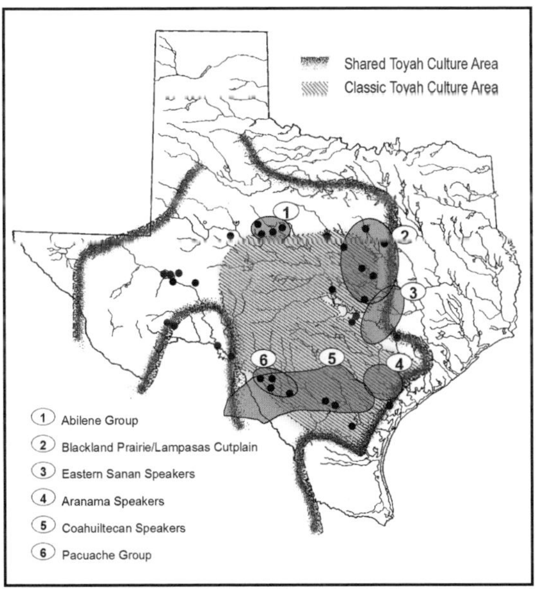

FIGURE 3.5. Map depicting approximate locations of historic linguistic groups and clusters of archaeologically similar sites in relation to the Classic and Shared Toyah areas. Redrawn from Johnson (1994) and Johnson and Campbell (1992).

shapes may someday prove to correspond to different areas in the region, but any consideration of these issues must be tempered by the extremely small samples of Toyah pottery, both in terms of whole or reconstructed vessels and the quantity and sizes of individual sherds.

The reasons for variation in Toyah ceramics are as poorly understood as the origins of Toyah. The fact that this ceramic tradition appeared in all its forms simultaneously suggests that antecedents should be found in adjacent areas. Yet direct linkages to neighboring traditions remain elusive. Indeed, Toyah ceramics seem to embody the mysterious nature of Toyah itself in that they represent variation in material culture while also exhibiting a distinct homogeneity, suggesting significant interaction across the region. It is also true that research into Toyah ceramics is still in its infancy, and many issues concerning the technology and character of these ceramics have yet to be addressed.

For example, particularly well made Toyah ceramics are often found at Toyah campsites throughout the region, albeit in very small numbers. The rare frequency with which this type of fine ceramic appears compared to rougher more utilitarian wares suggests that it had some significance, perhaps similar to the fine ceramics or china found in many homes today. Moreover, its broad distribution is somewhat reminiscent of prestige wares associated with specific religious or political activities (rituals, feasting). The spread of wine in Europe and of fermented corn beverage known as *chicha* in Andean South America has been traced by the distribution of specific ceramic vessels associated with preparing, serving, and consuming these beverages (D'Altroy and Hastorf 2001; Dietler 1990; Dietler and Hayden 2001). At least one such beverage has been identified among many Native American groups in the American Southeast: *asi* ("black drink") from yaupon holly (*Ilex vomitoria*) was nonalcoholic but extremely caffeinated (Hudson 1979). Thus, there are precedents for the widespread adoption of practices and materials among diverse peoples that are not related to a specific utilitarian function (Bray 2003; D'Altroy and Hastorf 2001; Dietler and Hayden 2001; Helwing 2003; Mills 2004).

Many agricultural groups surrounding the Toyah region had ceramics for hundreds of years before ceramics were adopted by Toyah hunter-gatherers. Therefore, it is difficult to understand how and why Toyah peoples suddenly began to manufacture ceramics, even in very limited amounts, unless it involved the adoption of a particular ritual, ceremony, or beverage requiring a specific vessel, as has been documented in many cases around the world (Bray 2003; D'Altroy and Hastorf 2001; Dietler and Hayden 2001; Mills 2004). If this was the case for Toyah, the utilitarian wares of the Toyah assemblage, by far the most common, may have been an ancillary result or by-product of a ceramic tradition that was initiated to produce a particular ware and vessel for a specific ritual, perhaps even one that ended by breaking the vessel into pieces. Such a scenario would explain the widespread and sudden adoption of ceramics by dozens of culturally distinct hunter-gatherer groups and the presence and frequency of similar as well as diverse wares found in the Toyah ceramic tradition.

Archaeologists in Texas have just begun to explore some of the more substantive aspects of prehistoric ceramics, and it should be recognized that these are complex issues and that Texas is not unique. For example, the study of prehistoric ceramics in New England has been dominated until recently by a culture-historical framework developed in the 1940s (Goodby 1998). This typological approach has framed ceramics encompassing most of central and southern New England, dating from 3000 BP to European contact, as the Windsor ceramic tradition and generally corresponding to the historical distribution of Algonquian-speaking peoples (Goodby 1998:166). Robert Goodby (1998:167) suggests this traditional approach has obscured a high degree of variability in size, shape, temper, and decoration during the Late Woodland period (ca. AD 1000–1500). But Goodby (1998:169–70) also acknowledges that within this variation there are similarities (limits on temper size, material used for temper, possible forms of surface treatment, coiling as a method of vessel construction) suggesting "a pattern consistent with a broader cultural unity and shared history, facilitated by centuries of intermarriage, trade and other forms of reciprocal relationships."

Previous archaeological interpretations concentrated primarily on decorative variation as well as social boundaries documented during the seventeenth century to identify tribal affiliations with ceramic traditions (Goodby 1998:171). Goodby, focusing instead on the various technological aspects, noted a remarkable consistency that suggested a single technological style throughout southeastern New England during the seventeenth century and similar to that seen in the Late Woodland period. Moreover, decorative variation was observed virtually everywhere in the region and showed no correspondence with the social boundaries recorded in the seventeenth century (1998:174–175). These data formed the basis for a discussion of the complexities involved in recognizing social boundaries. Goodby's argument was that simply noting a correlation (or in this case the lack of one) between material culture variability and social boundaries does not explain why such a relationship does or does not exist (1998:175). To address this issue, such a correlation "must be supported by an independent archeological argument" (Conkey 1990:11).

The argument or issue that Goodby selected to address the lack of correlation between seventeenth-century social boundaries and ceramic decoration and technological style was, essentially, the character of social identity through time in southeastern New England. Goodby concluded that technological or decorative style did not correspond to documented social boundaries precisely because these boundaries were of recent origin and primarily a product of the pressures of European colonialism. In this particular case, the lack of correlation reflects native people contesting the impositions of European settlers by refusing to demarcate emerging social boundaries (Robinson 1990). Goodby also emphasized the fact that women were responsible for the production and decoration of ceramics, and therefore concepts of gender and faction (Brumfiel 1992) were more useful than ethnicity for interpreting aspects of style (Goodby 1998:178).

The Windsor tradition of New England provides a useful heuristic device for examining the Toyah ceramic tradition. Although we know that this ceramic tradition was distributed across a large swathe of Texas prior to European contact, we do not know how, by whom, or even why it was produced. Archaeologists have recognized that the majority of these ceramics are characterized by bone temper and little decoration. Although there seems to be one particularly well made plain bone-tempered and highly burnished buff-, orange-, or red-colored ware (sometimes referred to as Leon Plain or Doss Redware), most ceramics are simply referred to generically as bone-tempered plainware.

From a technological perspective, some of these ceramic wares appear to have been produced in the same area in which they were found—in short, they appear to be locally manufactured. For example, ceramic collections from the Harrell, Fall Creek, and Buckhollow sites all appear, to the naked eye as well as under magnification, to share some of the characteristics of what LeRoy Johnson (1994) referred to as Classic Toyah ceramic ware consisting of plain, buff-colored, and burnished pottery. On the other hand, and with the important exception of the Buckhollow ceramic assemblage, the Harrell and Fall Creek sites also possess abundant examples of plainware that were technologically different from Classic Toyah ware as well as from each other. However, these differences were primarily in the type of aplastic or temper. For example, Fall Creek plainware exhibits numerous mineral inclusions resembling nothing so much as quartzite and granite, both commonly associated with the Central Mineral Region of Texas in which this ware is found. Plainware ceramics from the Harrell site often exhibit mussel shell temper and paste that appears somewhat sandy, again consistent with the area in which it was deposited.

The preliminary results of the Central Texas Ceramic Study, a geochemical ceramic sourcing project using neutron activation analysis, seem to support the idea that there are many local variants of bone-tempered Toyah wares made in central Texas, but interpretations are complicated by the high degree of mobility and transport of vessels across the Toyah region (Taff 2006). Nevertheless, these findings are consistent with cursory observations of uniformity in Toyah ceramics. Although some Toyah ceramics exhibit different types of tempers, most are plain, and there does appear to be a remarkable consistency across a large region in technological patterning (i.e., surface treatment, vessel construction, and temper, but particularly size and the materials used). This is precisely what Goodby (1998:169–70) was referring to when discussing the development of the Windsor ceramic tradition and the ramifications of "shared history, facilitated by centuries of intermarriage, trade and . . . reciprocal relationships." Still, the fact that at least some Toyah ceramics were produced locally suggests that various groups had established social boundaries within a much wider field of social contact.

How diverse and wide this field of interaction became and what its material correlates are can be addressed to some extent by projectile points. Although Perdiz is by far *the* dominant arrow point type from the Red River into southern Coahuila, Mexico, and from western Louisiana to the Davis Mountains of west Texas, it is notable that other points frequently represent 5–10 percent of the total arrow points recovered from Classic Toyah sites. But precisely what these other point types mean in terms of functionality or sociocultural identity remains a mystery. Several sites within Johnson's (1994) Shared Toyah area and along the margins of the Classic Toyah Culture area exhibit some mixing of arrow points and ceramic assemblages from other areas. Along the Pecos River, Chupadero Black-on-white and Caddoan wares and Perdiz, Fresno, Toyah, and Harrell arrow points are documented in several sites (41PC56, 41PC57, 41PC58, 41CX19) (Rogers 1972). Sites farther south along the canyons of the Rio Grande (41TE53, 41TE54) yielded no ceramics but mixed arrow points (Perdiz, Cliffton, Toyah, Fresno, and Harrell) (Bandy 1980). Henrietta focus sites contain most of the Toyah lithic assemblage along with a diversity of point styles (Perdiz, Cliffton, Toyah, Fresno, and Washita) (Fox 1939; Hughes 1942; Krieger 1946; Prewitt 1964). Many sites in the Abilene area produced all or most of the Toyah lithic assemblage, along with a diversity of points (Perdiz, Fresno, Washita, and Harrell), Rio Grande glazewares, and plainware ceramics made with a wide variety of tempers (mussel shell, grog, bone, and limestone) (Griffin 1935; Ray 1935:84).

Many archaeologists have distinguished several Late Prehistoric material cultures corresponding to early historic cultural groups. Some of these groups were sedentary or semisedentary, did not practice broad-spectrum foraging, and were located some distance from the Classic Toyah area (Rockport Phase/Karankawa, Frankston Focus/Hasinai, La Junta/Abriaches, and dozens of Puebloan groups), yet many possessed elements of Toyah assemblages (Perdiz points, bone-tempered plainwares, etc.). Thus these groups do not necessarily characterize the mobile foragers who once inhabited the Classic Toyah area. In contrast, it is likely that the many groups who occupied Johnson's Shared Toyah area relied upon a variety of different subsistence strategies reflecting a greater diversity of environmental settings and attendant resources.

Toyah as a regional material culture presents something of an enigma. Although some sites reflect a wide variety of artifact classes and types (especially arrow points and ceramic wares), others may demonstrate little or no variation. The problem for archaeologists is to both explain the large-scale homogeneity and address the growing body of evidence for diversity. Previous archaeological constructs of Toyah scarcely mention this diversity and what it may mean. But it is clear that previous perceptions of Toyah as a homogenous bison-hunting cultural entity blanketing most of Texas are no longer tenable. Mixed assemblages hint at the diversity that was once present and suggest a pluralistic cultural setting. At the same time, the broad distribution of Toyah material culture cannot be ignored and instead should be recognized as evidence for individual and group participation in social, economic, and political networks within a regional social field.

Fundamental Forager Identities and Interactions and Archaeological Visibility

The terms *cultural group* and *cultural identity* are used here to denote a specific type of social aggregate composed of several endogamous forager bands or communities. I argue here that hunter-gatherer cultural groups in the Toyah region, particularly the Classic Toyah Culture area, can be conceptualized as marriage/linguistic groups. Anthropologists have long recognized that forager bands, as a basic human organizational unit of between twenty-five and seventy-five people, are simply too small to be endogamous (Birdsell 1953; MacDonald and Hewlett 1999; McBrinn 2005; Wobst 1974). People require a larger social network or marriage group to acquire suitable marriage partners. Most anthropologists now acknowledge that social aggregates of approximately five hundred persons, perhaps slightly smaller, constitute a minimum size for a population breeding unit (Kelly 1995:210). In short, to remain reproductively viable forager bands must participate in a broader scale of social interaction beyond the immediate community or band.

But marriage partners are not the only things exchanged in an endogamous group. Language, cosmology, and technology are also shared among the various bands that form a marriage group, sometimes referred to as a linguistic group. Therefore, it is reasonable to infer that several contemporaneous and archaeologically identical residential base sites (occupied by several small bands or communities) located in the same general area may represent a larger social aggregate related through kinship and language. I view this social aggregate as approximately equivalent to a marriage group (McBrinn 2005) or maximal band (Wobst 1974) of perhaps two hundred to six hundred individuals who exhibit a fundamental level of sociocultural cohesion beyond the band or local community. It should be noted that at this scale (the site to area scale) similarities are apt to be easier to discern than differences. This is due primarily to the proximity of all groups to similar environmental resources as well as to each other.

At a broader scale, encompassing several thousand square kilometers, it may be possible to recognize specific culture groups (marriage/linguistic groups), each composed of several endogamous hunter-gatherer communities/bands. Although residential bases may display similar material culture, the style, material, and design of artifacts and features may differ or some parts of the material culture may be absent altogether from one group to another across the region.

Returning to central Texas, soils in much of the region are generally shallow, and limestone was commonly used in construction and as heating elements in prehistoric cooking and warming hearths. But farther north in a different physiographic zone there is a significant drop in the frequency of rock used in hearth features (fig. 3.6). North of the Concho and Colorado rivers on the Rolling Plains, the frequency of unlined hearth features increases significantly. This area also shows a significant increase in non-Perdiz arrow points (Garza, Harrell, and Washita points) and non-Toyah ceramics (Caddoan brushed wares, Nocona Plain, and a sandy paste plainware) that are typically associated with areas farther north in the grassland environment of the Great Plains and to a lesser extent east Texas. In fact, the overlying Quaternary alluvium and wind-blown sand that constitute the soils of the Great Plains can be as much as 150 feet thick, and stone may not be easily or readily available in many areas. Not surprisingly, hearth features on the Plains are often unlined, reflecting, perhaps, a practice related to specific environmental conditions. To be sure, rock-lined hearths are found on the Plains, albeit where rock is available; at the same time, unlined hearths can be found in sites on the Edwards Plateau, albeit where there is sufficient soil. But practices, like habits,

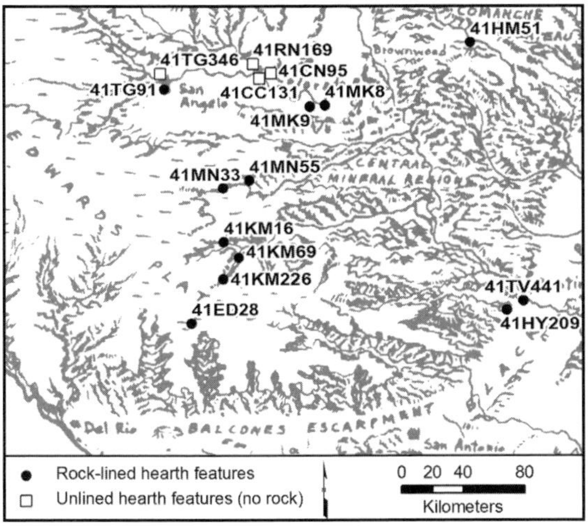

FIGURE 3.6. Map depicting the approximate margins of Late Prehistoric II sites with and without rock-lined hearths.

can be difficult to break and are often retained even when new materials and practices are readily available and apparent.

In addition, Late Prehistoric II sites on both banks of the Colorado and Concho rivers also generally reflect a mixture of all point styles, ceramic assemblages, and to a lesser extent features from areas to the north and south. Thus, when considered together the artifacts, assemblages, and features from sites located along these rivers suggest that these campsites were locations where multiple cultural identities/groups met and interacted. The mixing of artifacts also indicates a permeable rather than solid boundary where people, objects, and ideas were exchanged. Nevertheless, such sites may be considered to approximate social or cultural boundaries, albeit permeable ones, between different groups (Stark et al. 1998). The mixed artifacts, assemblages, features, and materials found in these sites may also be considered somewhat atypical of residential campsites or bases located closer to the interior or core of a marriage/linguistic group area. For example, residential base camps located closer to the core of the group area would be expected to contain a more locally homogenous archaeological record with fewer foreign or exotic artifacts and materials than sites located on the periphery.

Alternatively, different culture groups may have little or no contact with each other, and this may be reflected in abrupt truncations in the distribution of material culture. As the case above suggests (absence vs. presence of rocks in hearths), the distribution of specific artifact classes, feature types, or materials could be linked to distinct environmental boundaries. Changes in artifact styles or decoration in the same environmental setting can, however, also indicate social rather than ecological factors at work. Steve Black (1997:169) makes such an observation in an article devoted specifically to burned rock features on the northern Edwards Plateau: "The Colorado River may have served as a cultural boundary or buffer zone at some times and as a travel route at others."

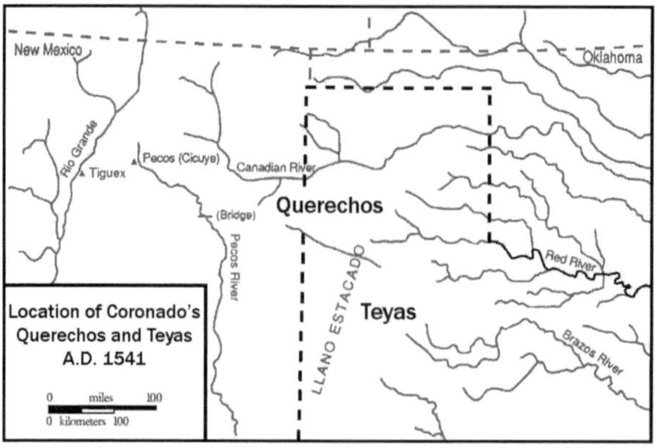

FIGURE 3.7. Approximate location of Coronado's Querechos and Teyas, AD 1541. Redrawn from Habicht-Mauche (1992:250).

Similarly, in the earliest historical accounts from the Panhandle (ca. 1540), Coronado's expedition documented two groups with virtually identical subsistence and settlement patterns, the Querechos and the Teyas, who were openly hostile. Both groups were highly mobile, subsisted almost entirely off of bison, and lived in tents on the high plains. Nevertheless, they were distinguishable from each other by differences in language, body adornment, and geographic range (the Querechos lived generally north of the Teyas) (fig. 3.7). This situation presents a classic archaeological problem in terms of recognizing sociocultural identity in that the distinguishing characteristics of these groups do not lend themselves to archaeological visibility. Language and tattoos, for example, are the types of things that ethnographers may note but are not generally present in the archaeological record, and shared similarities in Teyas and Querecho subsistence and settlement patterns blur distinctions between the two. In addition, Coronado's expedition was lost for a good portion of its time on the Plains and, thus, the precise location of these groups must also be called into question.

Doug Boyd's (2001:8, see also Boyd, this volume) work provides archaeological evidence that during the Late Prehistoric II period there were two distinct archaeological complexes in the Texas Panhandle Plains (fig. 3.8), each possessing a ubiquitous and functionally diagnostic suite of artifacts consisting of arrow points, beveled knives, and end scrapers. Although the artifact classes represented in the two suites are the same, the stylistic attributes of at least one artifact type—arrow points—are not. Boyd (2001:10) points to the abrupt dropoff in Garza points north of the Colorado and Brazos river drainages and the absence of these points north of the Red River drainage as evidence of a distinct ethnic boundary. The Red River also marks the northernmost distribution of Perdiz points—the most common point type found throughout Texas during the Late Prehistoric II period. Johnson (1994:241–27) described the southern Llano Estacado as a "Shared Toyah area" where both Toyah and Garza occupations are found alongside each other

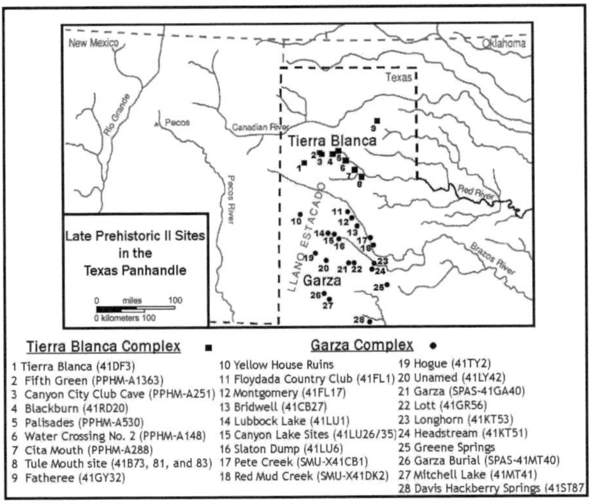

FIGURE 3.8. Tierra Blanca/Querechos and Garza/Teyas sites. Redrawn from Habicht-Mauche (1992:252) and Boyd (1997:370, 382).

and Perdiz and Garza points are found together at many sites. Yet Garza and Perdiz are rarely, if ever, found north of the Red River drainage on the Llano Estacado.

Boyd (1997, 2001) conceptualizes both Querechos and Teyas as ethnic groups and links them to the Late Prehistoric II/Protohistoric Tierra Blanca and Garza complexes, respectively, on the basis of corresponding geographic, ethnohistorical, and archaeological evidence. Such a conclusion might at first appear to be an essentialization of arrow points and people (i.e., different arrow points equal different groups). But in this particular context the combination of archaeological and historical data provides evidence that distinctive arrow points may, in part, represent cultural identities and the absence of social interaction mark a general sociocultural boundary.

Thus, at a regional scale differences in the material record from one area to the next may appear significantly more pronounced than at smaller scales of analysis. For example, sites excavated in the same general area may very well show striking similarities reflecting intermarriage, shared practices, and similar environmental conditions. Discerning multiple cultural identities in the archaeological record can also be obscured by restricting synthesis to specific areas—whether central Texas (Collins 1995, 2004), south Texas (Hester 1995, 2004), east Texas (Perttula 1992, 1998, 2004), or Panhandle Plains (Boyd 1995, 2004). This certainly appears to be the case for Toyah, where a spatial (regional) and temporal (Late Prehistoric and early historic) synthesis has only recently been presented (Arnn 2007).

In addition to its cultural diversity, Texas was and still is geographically diverse, exhibiting marked differences in topography, geology, rainfall, flora, and fauna. These differences are generally most evident in the variation and relative abundance of food and water resources from one area to the next. Thus, the subsistence resources of all plants, animals, and humans are influenced in some way by conditioning factors specific to the area. Most archaeologists who have studied Toyah agree there is a strong correlation between the relative abundance of various resources (plants, animals, water, fuel, etc.) within the community range and the size, distribution, duration of stay, and function of Toyah sites. Johnson's (1994:263) interpretation of Toyah material culture suggests that Classic Toyah communities consisted of several small nuclear families inhabiting a specific territory or range that consisted of residential campsites and special-purpose sites occupied on a seasonal basis.

Residential base camps represent a specific location on the landscape within the community range where several families gathered to take advantage of a particularly abundant resource or resources found only at that location at a specific time of the year. There may have been several large residential bases corresponding to specific resources, locations, and seasons within a single community range or perhaps just one, depending on the environmental conditions. Alternatively, during other times of the year bands may have dispersed in smaller groups or perhaps even as single families across the band/community territory.

As Hester (1981) pointed out, resource density and abundance vary in south Texas throughout the year and across the landscape depending on the vagaries of climate and seasonal cycles. Ellis et al. (1995) argued that in central Texas relatively minor climatic fluctuations across this environmentally diverse landscape could result in dramatically different combinations of concentrated or dispersed resources in the area. Perhaps the most significant factor for virtually all living things in this region is the seasonal fluctuation in precipitation and the corresponding availability of water. During the dry season and times of drought, the productivity of plant forage can decrease dramatically along with the output of springs and running streams. Such a situation can drastically reduce the range of animals, including humans, in terms of foraging area, further concentrating resources around the most dependable water sources (Taylor 1964).

Therefore, it should come as little surprise that residential bases are often found along major river drainages in precisely the locations where people as well as plants, animals, and water are often most concentrated. River bottoms and terraces in many parts of central and south Texas offer the additional bonus of large stands of nut-bearing native pecan trees (Hall 1998, 2000). Given the strong case made for carbohydrate- and fat-rich foods (particularly linoleic fatty acid) in hunter-gatherer diets (Kelly 1995; Speth and Spielmann 1983) and the high carbohydrate and fat (particularly linoleic fatty acid) content in pecans (Hall 2000:110), groves of pecan trees were an exceptional fixed resource. Nonetheless, despite the ethnographic emphasis on similar fatty plant resources such as mongongo nuts (Kelly 1995) and direct comparisons between the fat content of bison and pecans (Hall 2000; Speth and Spielmann 1983), most archaeologists, with notable exceptions (Hall 1998, 2000), have generally ignored both the nutritional aspect of pecans and their strategic location on the landscape.

Although the weather and temperature of this region are generally associated

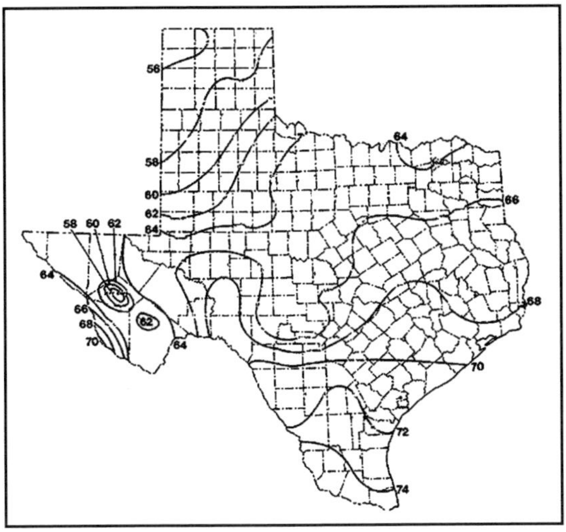

FIGURE 3.9. Mean annual temperature in degrees Fahrenheit depicting north-to-south trends in Texas temperatures. Adapted from Griffiths and Orton (1968).

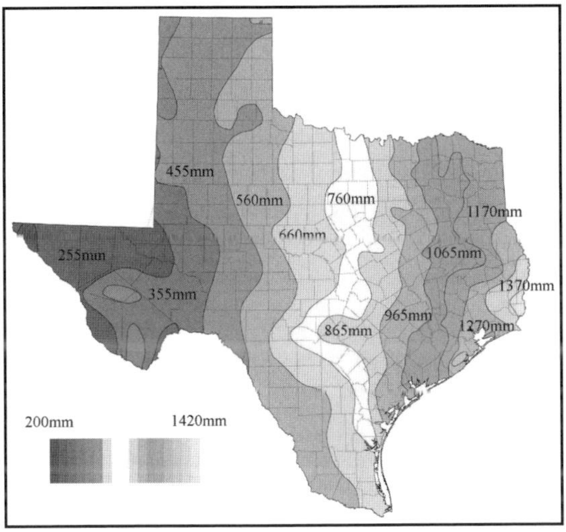

FIGURE 3.10. Annual precipitation depicting east-to-west trends in Texas rainfall patterns. Redrawn from Texas Parks and Wildlife Department precipitation map.

with seasonal changes, dramatic fluctuations in temperature are not uncommon. Canadian cold fronts move south across the Southern Plains virtually unimpeded and can drop temperatures as much as 50° F in just a few hours. In the summer, high pressure systems may remain stationary over the region for weeks at a time, resulting in month-long heat waves with afternoon temperatures exceeding 100° F. In general, though, mean annual temperature throughout the region is oriented north to south and, to a lesser extent, along elevation clines (fig. 3.9). Precipitation too can be extremely erratic. For example, despite annual precipitation averages (fig. 3.10), widespread droughts lasting more than five years are rather frequent—on the order of three to four every seventy-five years. In short, an individual can expect at least one if not two significant droughts to occur in his or her lifetime.

Modern agriculture is limited to some extent by these same erratic weather conditions, and much of this area today is devoted to raising hardy mobile browsers such as sheep, goats, and white-tailed deer. These conditions would have presented a challenge to anyone subsisting directly off wild plant and animal resources. At the same time, because of the north-south orientation of isohyet lines a group caught in such a drought could move east approximately 50 km (a two- to three-day walk) and encounter significantly better environmental conditions—if they had access to such areas. One way to ensure access to other territories is through social networks. Certainly, ethnographic data indicate that foraging societies around the world often develop and participate in extensive long-distance social relationships and exchange networks (Hardesty 1977; Hitchcock and Bartram 1998:23; Kelly 1995:187; Lee 2003; Welsch and Terrell 1998:51; Wiessner 1983; Yellen 1977). Individuals, families, and groups have all been documented participating to varying degrees in long-distance social, political, and economic relationships with "others" (culturally different individuals, families, and groups). Some anthropologists (Hardesty 1977; Lightfoot 1983; Taylor 1964; Yellen 1977) argue that hunter-gatherers living in variable environmental regions established and maintained some of these networks, at least initially, to offset variations in resource abundance.

This does not mean that one environmental determinant (bison) is being substituted for another (variable environment) to explain the Toyah phenomenon. Forager social behavior, even at the band level, is almost inherently geared toward external social interaction. Individuals must look beyond their own community/band for a suitable mate and often have relatives or offspring who live in distant bands or even other culture groups (Kelly 1995; Lee 2003; Yellen 1977). In one region of the Kalahari (roughly the same size as central and south Texas combined) ethnographers documented numerous bands of foragers who spoke four mutually unintelligible languages. Ethnographers also noted that hunter-gatherer groups in that region shared 90 percent of the same material culture (Lee 2003; Wiessner 1983).

The point argued here is that twentieth-century foragers are frequently documented spending significant time involved in social interaction, and there is no reason to believe that this did not occur in the past. It is likely that many prehistoric hunter-gatherer individuals, families, bands, and distinct cultural groups within large regions, particularly environmentally variable regions, interacted frequently through numerous social relationships based on kinship, exchange, and alliance. In other words, they participated in a social field and, despite vast distances, the level of integration in these fields, in terms of the cultural interaction of the general population, was significant.

The very things that sedentary social groups use to signal difference and define group membership or cultural identity (e.g., stylistically and functionally distinct artifacts, features, and architecture) might be passed or shared among several distinct forager groups over many generations. Thus, the Toyah lithic and ceramic assemblages, rather than symbolizing a specific ethnic group, may simply reflect some degree of participation in a broad social field composed of numerous different groups. The permeable and flexible character of social boundaries and relationships in foraging societies combined with a relatively light complement of durable and visible material culture may mask the material signature of distinct groups (Lourandos 1997; McElreath et al. 2003; Wiessner 1983). Beyond the scale of communities, marriage/linguistic groups and long-distance social networks might appear or present another level or aspect of social identity encompassing whole regions—for example, Toyah. In this respect the distribution of the Perdiz arrow point may more closely approximate the range of this social field.

When combined, these data point to significant cultural diversity throughout most of Texas during the final two hundred years of prehistory. These data also suggest that the Toyah region is more accurately conceptualized as a large "playing field" filled with numerous environmental settings, peoples, languages, and customs connected through various networks, resulting in the widespread distribution of specific types of material culture as people interact. Thus, the apparent homogeneity in the material record that archaeologists recognize as either a "Toyah" ethnic group or "technocomplex" can be explained by various social, economic, and political relationships that together formed a large, regional social field.

Historical Data

The archaeological, ethnographic, and environmental data beg the question: if Toyah was composed of several distinct very late prehistoric cultural groups linked together by numerous individual, family, band, and group social, economic, and political relationships, then where is the historical evidence for such a broad social field? More simply, why is there no continuity with the historic period? Surely there must be some inkling of such a large social field in the documentary record.

In fact, there are numerous accounts from the early historic period of Texas that document scores of distinct groups speaking approximately a dozen different languages.[3] Table 3.1 documents just some of the names recorded by various early expeditions and parties in Texas. Despite some repetition, the shear number of indigenous groups recorded is impressive (see Kenmotsu and Arnn, this volume). Some names were mispronounced and rendered in various spellings.

The first list in Table 3.1 represents thirty groups identified in Spanish ecclesiastical and civil records between approximately 1675 and 1700 who occupied or used the lands adjacent to and north of the Amistad National Recreation Area (Amistad), which abuts the Edwards Plateau on the southwest (Kenmotsu and Wade 2002:33–39). Amistad includes the area where the Rio Grande is joined by the Pecos and Devils rivers but also a broader area of the Stockton Plateau and the region to the north of the confluence of the Pecos (Kenmotsu and Wade 2002:8). The second list is based primarily on documents from the Bosque-Larios expedition of 1675 and the Mendoza-Lopez expedition of 1683–85 compiled by Wade

TABLE 3.1. Documented Native American groups, ca. 1670–1700

Amistad Reservoir, south Texas 1700 (Kenmotsu and Wade 2002)	*Edwards Plateau 1673–1684 (Wade 2003)*	*South Texas 1689–1693 (Foster 1995)*		*South and east of the Edwards Plateau 1684–1687 (Foster 1998)*	
Apache	Apache	Agualohe	Pacuasin	Ahehouen	Nasoni
Ape	Ape	Aguapalam	Pamaya	Ahouergomahe	Ointemarhen
Bagname	Arame	Alachome	Papanac	Arhau	Omenaosse
Bibit (Mabibit)	Arcos Tuertos	Ape (Hape)	Parchaque	Ayenny	Onapiem
Bobole	Bagname	Apaysi	Pastaloca	Bracamo	Orcan
Cacaxtle	Bobole	Cacase	Pataguo	Cascosi (Clamcoeh)	Palaquechare
Cibolo	Ervipiame	Cacaxtle	Patchal (Pachal)	Cenis	Panequo
Ervipiame	Gediondo (Hutaca or Parugan)	Caisquetebana	Patsua	Chancre	Pechir
Gediondo	Geniocane	Cantona	Payaya	Chaumene	Peinhoum
Gueiquesale	Gueiquesale	Catqueza	Pitahay	Choumay (Jumano)	Peissaquo
Julime	Jumano	Cava	Quem	Coyabegux	Petao
Jumee	Jumee	Caynaaya	Sacuache	Ebahamo	Petsare
Machome	Mabibit (Bibit)	Chaguan	Samampac	Exepiahohe	Piechar
Manos Prietas	Manos Prietas	Chalome	Sampanal	Kannehouan	Quouan
Mescal	Ocane	Cibola	Sana (Sanac, Xanac)	Keremen	Serecoutcha
Mesquite	Pataguache	Coco	Saquita	Kemahopihein	Spichehat
Muruame	Pinanaca	Emet	Simaoma	Kiabaha	Teao
Ocane	Siano (Sana)	Hasinai	Tepacuache	Kiabahe	Tehauremet
Pacuache	Teaname	Jumano (Chomene, Chome, Comane)	Toboso	Koienkahe	Teheaman
Pacuachiam	Tereoodan (Terecodam)	Mescal	Tohaha (Toaa)	Komkome	Telamene
Papanac	Xaeser	Momon	Toho (Too)	Kouyam	Temerlouan
Pinanaca	Xoma	Muruam	Vanca	Kuasse	Tohau (Toho)
Saesse	Yorica	Naaman	Xiabu (Ijiaba)	Meghey (Mayaye)	Tohaha
Siano (Sana)		Ocana (Ocane)		Meraquaman	Tsepcoen
Teaname		Odoesmade		Naodiche	Tserabocherete
Teimamar		Paac			
Teneimamar		Pacpul			
Terocodame		Pacuache			
Tilijae					
Tilpayay					

(2003), who identified twenty-three Native American groups on the Edwards Plateau. Combining the first and second lists results in about thirty-six different groups recorded between 1673 and 1700. Sixteen or so names from both lists match; most of those that do not match come from the later and longer list. It is also significant that by 1700 the Apaches had moved farther south and begun raiding well into central and south Texas as well as Mexico (Wade 2003; see Kenmotsu and Arnn, this volume). Therefore, the later and larger list of groups produced in 1700 may represent displaced or remnant social groups who once inhabited areas farther north.

The third list of names, compiled from Foster (1995), presents fifty-one Native American groups recorded by various Spanish expeditions (primarily León, Terán, and Salinas) between 1689 and 1693. Documents from these expeditions clearly state that the Spanish followed Native American trails, some marked by stone cairns, across south Texas. In short, the documentary record from these expeditions indicates widely recognized primary routes linking various groups from what is today Amistad with groups living in east Texas along the Trinity River. Although this list dates to roughly the same period as the previous lists, it represents a far larger and somewhat more eastern reporting area. Therefore, it is understandable that many names in this table do not match the first two lists. Nevertheless, there are some matches, with a total of eleven group names shared by the first, second, and third lists.

The fourth list, compiled from the journal of a Frenchman, Henri Joutel (Foster 1998), documents fifty Native American groups observed between the Nueces and Sabine rivers of south and east Texas from 1684 to 1687. Joutel's journal provides an interesting contrast from various Spanish accounts. Although the number of groups recorded is almost identical to that in Spanish accounts recorded just a few years later, many names appear to be different. There is, however, poor correlation between Spanish and French renderings of Native American group names, and it is not clear if other group names could be correlated. This suggests that resolving linguistic inconsistencies between various French and Spanish versions of indigenous group names would be a significant contribution to ethnohistorical research.

Even allowing for duplication from one list to the next, the number of groups documented in these lists shows several distinct social groups living in central and south Texas during the early colonial or historic periods. Although it is unclear precisely what sort of social organization these names represent, there is little question as to their existence. Furthermore, this type of documentary evidence makes it difficult to ignore the deep division between Texas prehistory and history and the almost complete absence of continuity between the two. Where archaeologists have observed or imposed homogeneity, historians and ethnohistorians (Campbell 1988, 1989; Foster 1995, 1998; Hickerson 1994; Johnson and Campbell 1992; Kenmotsu and Wade 2002; Wade 2003) researching the early Spanish and French colonial records (ca. 1528–1700) in Texas have documented heterogeneity, identifying dozens of Native American cultural groups in the Toyah region that spoke several different languages. A recent tabulation by Collins (1999) documented no less than 160 names for Native American groups recorded during the sixteenth and seventeenth centuries in central and south Texas.

Early European accounts note that despite vast distances and different languages indigenous peoples frequently traded, formed alliances, visited, and intermarried.[4] The fact that Native Americans invariably identified themselves and others as members of specific groups and participated in long-distance social interaction during the early historic period indicates that identity and interaction figured prominently in local as well as regional social, economic, and political arenas. Yet, despite significant temporal overlap (approximately two hundred years, from 1500 to 1700) and a relatively robust data set, archaeologists and historians maintain diametrically opposing interpretations concerning the cultural identity of people in this region. Where archaeologists observe cultural homogeneity in the regional archaeological record, historians present data that indicate heterogeneity. Perhaps the most revealing account concerning historical networks and relationships among distinct cultural groups was written by Fray Francisco Casañas de Jesús María in 1691 in east Texas. During the late seventeenth century, Casañas worked among the Hasinais, one of several Caddo groups in the province of Tejas. In fact the word *Teja* has been widely interpreted as a Caddoan word for friend or ally. In August 1691, Casañas (translated by Hatcher 1927:2) had this to say concerning the term *Tejas:*

> I notice that this name Tejas includes all the friendly tribes. The name is common to all of them, even though their language may be different. And, since this name is a general term, it must be used for no other reason than to indicate the long-standing friendship which they entertain towards each other. And, therefore, among all these tribes "Tejas" means friends.

Casañas goes on to name "the friendly tribes called the Tejias," giving the general direction and distance these tribes lived from the Hasinais:

> The Guaza, Yaduza, Bata, Cojo, Datana, Chuman, Cagaya, and the Assenay—different from the Asinai—live toward the south and west about eighty leagues from this province. To say that the latter have become separated from the rest of the Asinai is a mistake. The Caquiza, Quintanuaha, Coai, Canu, Tiniba, Vidix, Sico, Toaha, Cautouhaona, and Nepayaya are located toward the southwest; the Canonidiba, Casiba, Dico, Xanna, Vinta, Tobo, Caquixadoquix, Canonizachitous, and Zanomi toward the southeast. All these I have named up to this point are allies. The enemies of the Province of the Asenay are the following: Anao, Tanico, Quibaya, Cauzeaux, Hauydix, Naviti, Nondacau, Quitxix, Zauanito, Tancaquaay, Canabatinu, Quiguayua, Diu-Juan, Sadammo. This is a very large nation. Others are called Apaches, Ca-au-cozi, and Mani. These are all enemies. Only three or four of these tribes are located toward the southeast; the others live toward the west. They communicate with the province of the Asinai, and they know that some are friends and some enemies.

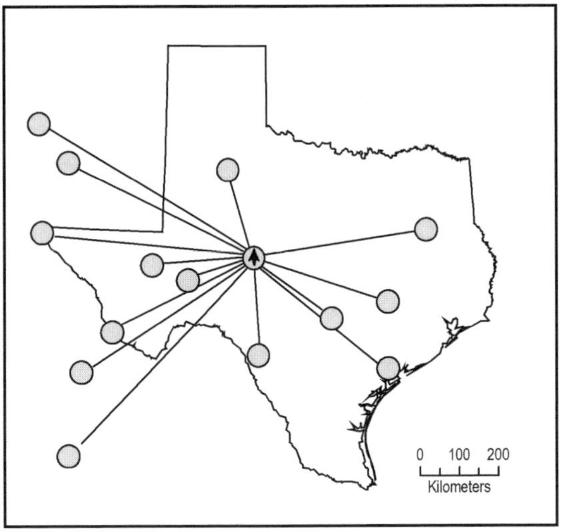

FIGURE 3.11. Jumano homeland and various trade destinations and sightings, AD 1542–1592. Redrawn from Kenmotsu (2001).

What is so remarkable about Casañas's account is that he states so clearly and emphatically what the term *Tejas* means and to whom it applies. According to Casañas it refers to almost fifty distinct groups who are allied with one another, "even though their language may be different." Toward the end of the list he reaffirms that they are "allies." Thus, there is little doubt that the region of Tejas included central and south Texas and was a broad social field consisting of numerous distinct groups who were all allies.

In addition, many of these groups visited, traveled, and traded extensively with each other. Several documents (including Casañas's) list the almost omnipresent Jumanos (see other renderings of the name in Kenmotsu and Arnn, this volume), a group of Native Americans who were reported throughout this region. The most generally accepted description of the Jumanos locates them in west Texas and the western Edwards Plateau (fig. 3.11), where they lived as hunter-gatherers in small rancherias (Hammond and Rey 1966; Kelley 1986; Kenmotsu 2001; Wade 2003). They are also known to have traded and cohabitated with Puebloan agriculturalists living in the Salinas district of central New Mexico in the late sixteenth and early seventeenth centuries, and during the late seventeenth century with the small agricultural pueblos of the La Junta region in the Texas Trans-Pecos and Chihuahua, Mexico (Bolton 1911; Hammond and Rey 1966; Kenmotsu 2001). The Jumanos were also observed on numerous occasions by both the Spanish and the French in south and east Texas in the company of various Native American groups and noted as allies of the Caddo group in Joutel's journal (Foster 1998:247). In fact, Jumano individuals and groups were reported by almost every European expedition into Texas from 1581 until the early eighteenth century. Jumanos frequently served as heralds, delivering important news to various groups throughout the region (Kelley 1955). Thus, as a historic forager group the Jumanos are significant because they give some measure of the extensive contacts and influence that some prehistoric foraging groups in the region may have possessed.

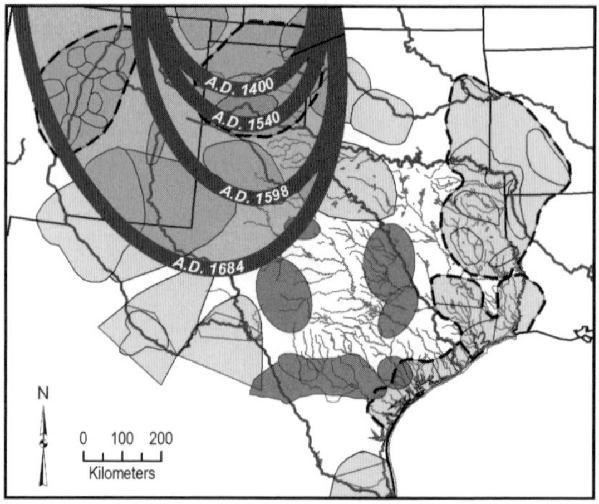

FIGURE 3.12. Map depicting external forces affecting the Tejas alliance during the late seventeenth century. From Arnn (2007).

A combination of events including increasing pressure from Athapaskans to the north, European pressure from the south, east, and west, as well as European-introduced diseases led to the apparent collapse of the Tejas social field and forced many Native Americans into Spanish missions in northern Coahuila and south and east Texas during the late seventeenth and early eighteenth centuries (fig. 3.12). During this period, most stylistic variation in arrow points began to fade and by approximately AD 1700 had disappeared altogether (including Cliffton, Cuney, Garza, Harrell, Perdiz, Toyah,[5] and Washita). These events may correspond with the increased access and use of firearms among Native American groups, a point rarely acknowledged, at least in print, among archaeologists. At about this same time (ca. 1700), the Guerrero or "Mission" point began to appear in the San Juan Bautista and San Bernardo missions near Guerrero, Coahuila, in what is today the Texas/Mexico border close to the cities of Eagle Pass and Piedras Negras (Inman 1997:129–28; Ricklis 1999:142). Native Americans living in the Spanish mission system had no access to contraband firearms, and the Guerrero point along with a plain, often bone- or sand-tempered ceramic ware, sometimes referred to as "Mission" ware, would soon spread throughout most of the southern and eastern portions of the former Tejas social field.

The Perdiz arrow point is known for its ubiquitous presence throughout Texas, and this distribution also corresponds to the later Tejas social field. Perdiz points have not, however, been observed in good archaeological contexts with historic artifacts, prompting some (Johnson 1994) to suggest that, despite their ubiquity in the prehistoric record, they were discontinued just prior to the dawn of the historic period. Nevertheless, the prehistoric distribution also corresponds with the historic boundaries of specific cultural groups such as the Jumanos, the Caddos, and various other groups documented as members of the Tejas alliance. What I argue here is that the widespread distribution of the Perdiz point may have marked the boundaries of the Tejas alliance in prehistory, recognized archaeologically as Toyah, but that by the time of the Tejas collapse many of the surviving Native

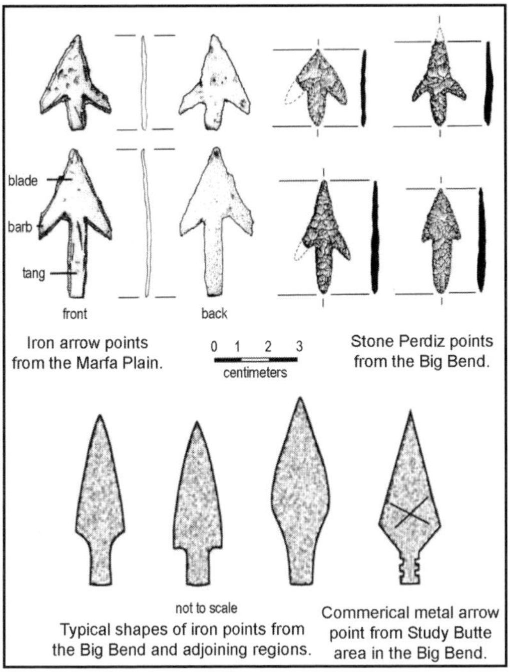

FIGURE 3.13.Perdiz and metal arrow points from the Trans-Pecos. From Mallouf (2004:6–7).

Americans had already started using firearms or had entered missions. As a result, overall numbers of Perdiz points deposited in historic contexts were extremely low. But even if this was the case, should archaeologists not expect still to see some continuation of the Perdiz point style into the historic period?

Mallouf (2004) and Walters and Rogers (1975) have documented metal arrow points in the Trans-Pecos area, and although metal points are typical for this period these particular points were wrought into shapes resembling Perdiz arrow points (fig. 3.13). The metal points documented by Mallouf (2004) on the Marfa Plain and those noted by Walters and Rogers (1975) recovered along the Pecos River were all within the former distributional range of the prehistoric Perdiz point. Interestingly, the shape of the Perdiz-like metal points is quite distinct from several different examples of commercially available or trade points, suggesting a significant intent or certainly considerable effort to achieve a specific shape. Farther east, along the southeastern margins of the Balcones Escarpment, a Perdiz arrow point made of vitreous glass was recovered from the San Antonio de Valero Mission in San Antonio (Lohse 1999:268). Glass Perdiz points of unknown context are also present in collections at the Witte Museum in San Antonio, Texas (Hindes 2005, personal communication).

These arrow points, made of foreign materials but wrought by Native American hands into familiar regional forms, may represent an attempt by indigenous peoples in missions to maintain continuity with their past by incorporating a ubiquitous symbol of an indigenous alliance into European materials. Furthermore, the almost simultaneous emergence of another distinct point type (Guerrero) among a specific population (if not group) of Native Americans within the Spanish mission system suggests the persistence of prehistoric practice into the historic period. In short, a specific point style may have been adopted by various cultural groups living in the missions to reflect their participation in a broader social arena and, thus, their shared identity within the same social field.

Conclusion

This chapter presents evidence for the existence of multiple sociocultural identities in Texas linked through a broad social field (Toyah/Tejas) that operated for approximately four hundred years spanning both the prehistoric and historic periods, between AD 1275 and 1700. The data presented suggest several reasons (location, environment, ethnographic analogy, specific resources, etc.) why this particular location and these particular people (broad-spectrum foragers) lend themselves to the development of extensive social networks. These concepts also do not conflict with the basic premise that Toyah presents a widespread archaeological phenomenon; they simply strengthen this position by proposing its continuity into the historic period as the Tejas alliance. There is little doubt that people, ideas, and technology passed through central and south Texas. There is also significant evidence that groups of broad-spectrum foragers in the Toyah region significantly influenced the people, ideas, and technology of the Southern Plains (Arnn 2007). In short, the Tejas social field may have been the most significant social, economic, and political organization in this region for some four hundred years (fig. 3.14).

These concepts constitute a decidedly different approach to archaeology in Texas. For more than fifty years archaeologists have sought to explain culture change in Texas through migration or external contacts from the north, east, south, and west rather than focusing within the region. The blame for at least some of this can be laid squarely at the feet of three prominent anthropologists who declared Texas a “cultural sink” (Swanton 1924), “cultural sump” (Kroeber 1939), and “ethnographic sink” (Sjoberg 1953:280). It is now clear that Texas was home to numerous distinct sociocultural groups who spoke a dozen or so languages. In addition, this region presents a remarkable and enduring foraging tradition, perhaps on par with that of the Great Basin. However, the Tejas social field (including Toyah) presents something altogether different in that it points to the potential for complex but nonhierarchical or bottom-up social, economic, and political organization among numerous and diverse peoples—particularly foragers. Therefore, Toyah, Tejas, and Texas appear to be unique in North America, and a second and, one would hope, more enlightened look is warranted. The fact that this was not immediately apparent to three anthropologists more than a half-century ago is certainly no reason to continue to dismiss it now.

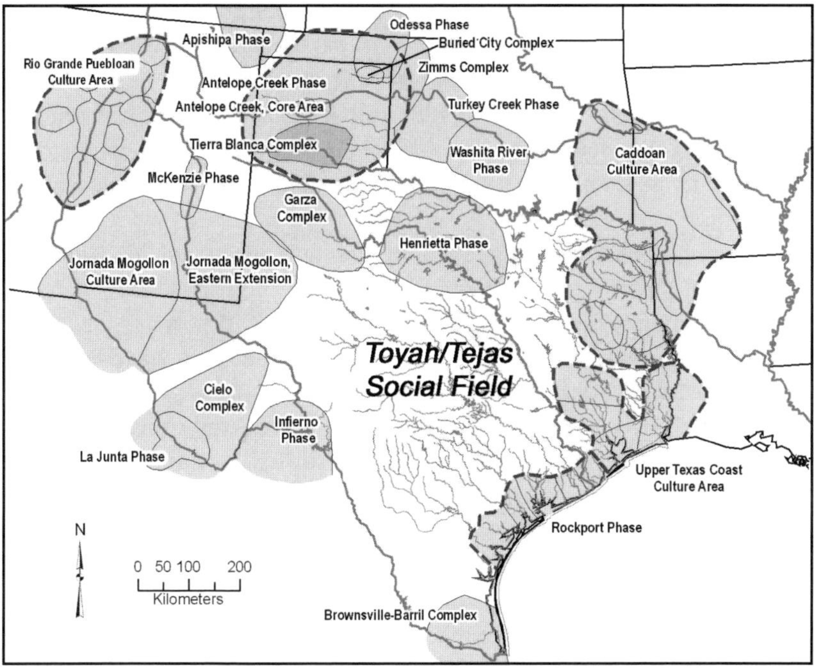

FIGURE 3.14. Map depicting the extent of the Toyah/Tejas social field and reflecting various archaeological, historical, and linguistic groups as well as hypothetical community/band ranges.

Most of the archaeology in this region to date can be characterized by a consistent focus on chronology, technology, and subsistence (Arnn 2005). That focus has contributed significantly to our understanding of several issues. But it has not been able to address the dichotomy between historic and archaeological interpretations of Toyah identity or the underlying social mechanisms responsible for the Toyah phenomenon. On the other hand, many of the methods employed by cultural ecology studies can and in many cases have already provided the raw data necessary for addressing precisely these types of issues among broad-spectrum foragers. This as well as the historical, environmental, linguistic, and ethnographic data strongly suggest that it is only through the combination of various disciplines, theories, and methods that prehistoric identities and interactions can be observed and, ultimately, understood.

A similar issue of significant import is the continuity of prehistoric identities and social interaction into the historic period. The fact that that prehistory and history have traditionally been researched by different academic fields (history vs. anthropology) and treated as two completely different subjects (archaeology vs. history) has almost certainly contributed to divisive interpretations and an artificial truncation of Native American social organization, as it has elsewhere (Lightfoot et al. 1998). Although archaeologists investigating the Late Prehistoric period recognized something unique in the Toyah phenomenon and historians researching the early colonial period no doubt recognized the significance of indigenous alliances, combining the two provides a far more complete picture of past peoples and their interaction. Furthermore, the artificial division imposed between prehistory and history does not appear to serve a useful purpose and, in this case, has obscured the identity, interaction, and continuity of an indigenous regional population.

The concepts presented here are admittedly simple. Prehistoric Toyah is ancestral to the historic Tejas social field or, alternatively, the Tejas social field represents the continuity of Toyah traditions. Three scales of identity and interaction (community/band, marriage/linguistic group, and long-distance social networks) are presented as the constituent elements of a vast regional social field. Far more identities and interactions were undoubtedly at work, but these three may represent the base from which almost infinite complexity sprang. Ethnographers have demonstrated that these particular scales of identity and interaction existed in similar contexts, and it is also possible to discern their correlates in the archaeological record. Therefore, they represent fundamental sociocultural tenets that were likely operative in the region between AD 1300 and 1700, and Texas retains its name as an alliance of sorts to this day.

Notes

1. For example, Rockport Phase/Karankawa, Frankston and Allen phases/Hasinai (Caddo), La Junta Phase/Abriaches, and dozens of Puebloan groups in New Mexico (Aten 1983; Boyd 1997; Collins 1971; Drass 1997; Hester 1995; Jelks 1962; Kelley 1947a; Krieger 1946; Lehmer 1948; Mallouf 1990; Miller and Kenmotsu 2004; Perttula 1992; Ricklis 1996; Speth 2004; Speth and Spielmann 1983; Suhm 1960; Turpin 1995).

2. The term "phase" that appears elsewhere in other chapters of this book has been eliminated here due to its specific spatial, temporal, and cultural implications when applied in an archaeological context. Instead, I use Late Prehistoric I (AD 700–1250) and Late Prehistoric II (AD 1250–1650) to denote these broad chronological periods. I retain the terms "Austin" and "Toyah" and use them interchangeably and in conjunction with Late Prehistoric I and Late Prehistoric II to provide some overlap with previous studies. However, unless otherwise noted in the text, Late Prehistoric I/Austin and Late Prehistoric II/Toyah are indicative only of temporal periods and should not be viewed as culturally or spatially descriptive terms. In fact, some archaeologists (Boyd 1997; Hall 1998; Mauldin et al. 2003; Ricklis 1995b) have begun to substitute absolute dates in place of archaeological chronologies altogether. This approach emphasizes the evolution of cultural material in well-stratified intrasite components as well as intersite comparisons of components across large geographic areas combined with settlement and subsistence patterns and paleoenvironmental studies. In the interest of brevity, I employ Late Prehistoric I/Austin and Late Prehistoric II/Toyah here merely as broad chronological designators for cultural identities and interactions discussed at length in this chapter.

3. For example, Álvar Núñez Cabeza de Vaca, Benavides, Bosque and Larios, Casañas, Castañeda de Nájera, Coronado, De Soto, Douay, Espejo, Jaramillo, Joutel, Luxán, Mendoza and Lopez, Morlete, Oñate, Pichardo, Rodríguez and Chamuscado, and Zaldívar (see Kenmotsu and Arnn, this volume).

4. Early European accounts are associated with these travels: Alonso de León expedition in 1689, Álvar Núñez Cabeza de Vaca in 1528–36, Bosque-Larios expedition in 1675, Castillo-Martin expedition in 1650, Guadalajara expedition in 1654, Mendoza-Lopez expedition in 1683–84, Joutel in 1687, Salas in 1629, and Terán expedition in 1691–92.

5. This particular Toyah is named after a town in far west Texas and generally is not associated with Toyah components.

FOUR

The Role of Exotic Materials in Toyah Assemblages in a Late Prehistoric Economic and Social System

Karl W. Kibler

Exotic materials in Toyah assemblages, although relatively uncommon, are reminders that Toyah peoples had alliances and contacts with neighboring peoples. Artifacts and other cultural materials, such as Caddoan pottery, obsidian, and marine shells, offer us unique opportunities to examine this economic and social network. Using exotic artifacts, I examine the interactions between Toyah peoples and neighboring non-Toyah groups on a broad interregional scale. These interactions may signal the maintenance of an economic and social system established to reduce risk in a world of fluctuating and unpredictable resources.

The presence of exotic materials in Toyah phase sites broaches the subject of interregional exchange, its function and nature among Toyah groups of central Texas and adjacent areas of the Gulf Coastal Plain to the south and southeast.[1] The subject of exchange in archaeology, particularly the exchange of exotic materials, provides insights into the social and economic relationships between groups (e.g., Baugh 1982). Social and economic relationships between groups and the social boundaries associated with them have been the subject of recent archaeological studies in other regions of North America (e.g., Stark et al. 1998; Vehik 2002). Studies of the Toyah archaeological record, particularly those focused on the exchange of exotic materials, can provide similar insights into the nature of the Toyah social field and the Toyah people's relationships with non-Toyah groups.

Exotic materials within Toyah phase site assemblages in the greater central Texas region examined in this chapter are Caddoan pottery (particularly in the eastern portion of the region); obsidian, primarily from Valles Caldera (Jemez Mountain) sources in New Mexico; and marine shells and shell artifacts from the Gulf of Mexico and possibly Pacific coast (table 4.1 and fig. 4.1). Overall, however, the most obvious aspect of exotic materials on Toyah sites is how few

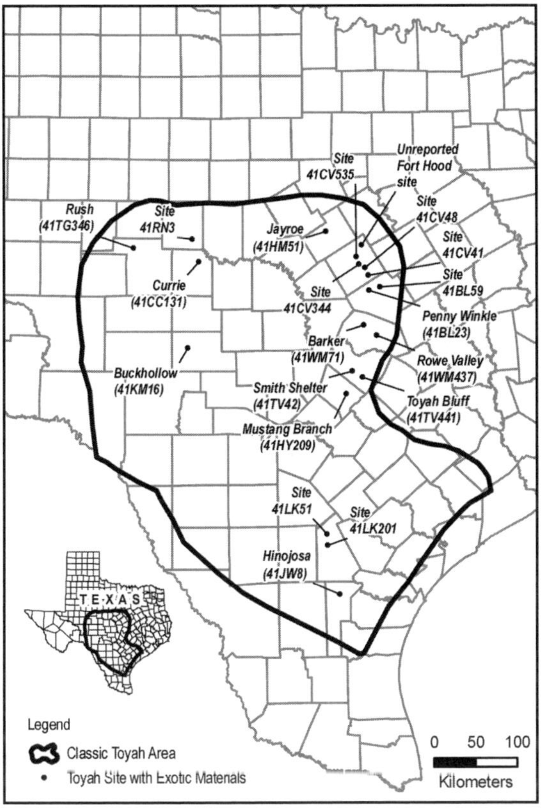

FIGURE 4.1. Toyah sites in central and south Texas with exotic materials.

of these sites actually contain exotic materials, particularly compared to earlier Late Archaic sites in the region. The decline in exotic artifacts from the Late Archaic to the Toyah phase is not unexpected, for "exchange does not uniformly increase through time" (Earle 1994:420). In fact, the archaeological record of North America shows that the expansion and collapse of exchange systems were both common and cyclical in nature (Earle 1994:432). Given the rarity of exotic materials in Toyah assemblages, I argue that it is unrealistic to view the Toyah as a link in an economic interaction sphere that tied together the adjacent Caddoan people, Plains Villagers, and Puebloan peoples of the Southwest.

I also argue that some of the exotic items, such as nonutilitarian marine shell artifacts and even some items that are utilitarian, were not really necessities for the groups who occupied the Toyah phase sites. For example, Toyah folk did not need Caddoan pottery, since they made their own serviceable bone-tempered pottery. The same can be said of obsidian, since much of the classic Toyah region contains a plentiful and ubiquitous supply of high-quality knappable stone (i.e., Edwards chert). Nor can it be said that exotic materials from Toyah phase sites, even the pottery, were associated with the exchange of food, at least at a level where exchange was a major source of food for the group. This too is not unexpected. As Earle (1994:422) points out, moving an amount of food that would

TABLE 4.1. Exotic materials from Toyah sites in central and south Texas

Site	*Exotic Material*	*Place of Origin*
1. Barker (41WM71)	29 incised bone- and grog-tempered sherds (Vessel 1)	east Texas, north and south of Sabine River *
2. Buckhollow (41KM16)	2 rim sherds (Vessels 12 and 13)	Southern High Plains or easternmost pueblos?
3. Currie (41CC131)	1 obsidian flake	unknown
	3 *Olivella* shell beads	Texas gulf or Pacific coasts
	1 marine shell pendant	Texas gulf or Pacific coasts
4. Hinojosa (41JW8)	19 marine shell fragments	Texas gulf coast
	1 piece of asphaltum	Texas gulf coast
5. Jayroe (41HM51)	3 obsidian flakes	Valles Caldera (Cerro Toledo), New Mexico *
	1 obsidian flake	Valles Caldera (Cerro del Medio), New Mexico *
	1 obsidian arrow point fragment (Perdiz)	Valles Caldera, New Mexico
	44 brushed sherds (Bullard Brushed)	east Texas?
6. Mustang Branch (41HY209)	5 Poynor Engraved sherds	east Texas *
7. Penny Winkle (41BL23)	1 incised rim sherd	east Texas, north and south of Sabine River *
	1 parallel brushed sherd	east Texas, north of Sabine River *
8. Rowe Valley (41WM437)	1 brushed sherd (Boothe Brushed, Vessel 1)	east Texas, probably north and south of Sabine River *
	1 Patton Engraved sherd (Vessel 2)	east Texas, Neches-Angelina River basin *
	1 plain bone-tempered sherd (Vessel 5)	east Texas, north and south of Sabine River *
9. Rush (41TG346)	3 brushed sherds	east Texas?
10. Toyah Bluff (41TV441)	15 fine sandy paste sherds (Rockport Plain)	central Texas coast?
11. Smith Shelter (41TV42)	27 sandy paste sherds (Goose Creek Plain)	Galveston Bay, Texas?
12. Site 41BL59	1 obsidian biface fragment	Valles Caldera (Obsidian Ridge), New Mexico *
13. Site 41CV41	7 bottle sherds (Taylor Engraved)	east Texas, north of Sabine River *
14. Site 41CV48	8 grog-tempered brushed sherds (Boothe Brushed)	east Texas, south of Sabine River *

TABLE 4.1. (*Continued*)

Site	*Exotic Material*	*Place of Origin*
15. Site 41CV344	5 grog-tempered sandy paste sherds (Vessel 1)	east Texas, south of Sabine River *
	4 plain grog-tempered rim sherds (Vessel 3)	east Texas, north and south of Sabine River *
	4 engraved grog-tempered bottle sherds (Vessel 4)	east Texas, south of Sabine River *
16. Site 41CV535	1 obsidian triangular arrow point	Mule Creek, New Mexico *
17. Site 41LK51	1 obsidian core or biface fragment	Malad, Idaho *
18. Site 41LK201	1 marine shell bead	Texas gulf coast
	4 marine shells or shell fragments	Texas gulf coast
	1 piece of asphaltum	Texas gulf coast
19. Site 41RN3	1 obsidian flake	Valles Caldera (Obsidian Ridge), New Mexico *
20. Unreported Fort Hood site	4 engraved grog-tempered rim sherds	east Texas, south of Sabine River *

Sources: (1) Perttula et al. (2003), Sorrow (1970); (2) Johnson (1994); (3) Lintz et al. (1993), Treece et al. (1993); (4) Black (1986); (5) Prewitt and Associates; (6) Ricklis and Collins (1994); (7) Perttula et al. (2003); (8) Perttula et al. (2003); (9) Quigg and Peck (1995); (10) Karbula (2003); (11) Suhm (1957); (12) Hughes (1989); (13) Perttula et al. (2003); (14) Perttula et al. (2003); Trierweiler (1996); (15) Perttula et al. (2003); (16) Hughes (1989); (17) Hall et al. (1986); (18) Highley (1986); (19) Lintz et al. (1993); (20) Perttula et al. (2003), Thomas (1978).

* Confirmed through various trace element or petrographic analyses.

play a significant subsistence role any distance is cost prohibitive and not feasible without markets. He suggests that the exchange of food as part of the subsistence strategy was of little significance in prehistoric North America. I agree that it was of little significance for the people occupying the Toyah phase sites in the greater central Texas region. What role, then, do the exchange and acquisition of relatively few exotic materials play in the Toyah cultural system if they do not represent utilitarian items or meet functional and economic needs that are otherwise met by local materials and resources?

For the Toyah peoples, and most other hunting and gathering societies, exotic materials are better understood within a context of subsistence insecurity, where fluctuating and unpredictable resources must be dealt with through various strategies. All hunter-gatherers are exposed to some level of risk (i.e., resource deficits or production shortfalls) in their environments, as evidenced by the various risk reduction strategies they employ (Kelly 1995). Toyah peoples were no different; their environment was one of risk. In this chapter I explore the environment of risk where the Toyah phase sites are situated and offer comments on how these people reduced that risk through interregional economic and social networks.

The Toyah Homeland: An Environment of Risk

The Toyah homeland, central Texas and adjacent areas of the Gulf Coastal Plain (fig. 4.2), has often been described in bountiful terms by researchers who provide extensive lists of available food resources (e.g., Collins 1995:383; Hall 1998; Thoms 2004:21–28, 2005). I would counter these Garden of Eden–like views by noting that these researchers fail to consider two basic factors: the dynamic seasonal and annual climatic patterns of the region, which can be quite variable, particularly in terms of rainfall; and the cost of acquiring these resources in terms of search, acquisition, and processing times. The former I believe shapes the latter by affecting the resource density and predictability (sensu Dyson-Hudson and Smith 1978) of the environment. I argue that the Toyah homeland was a risk-laden environment, best characterized by low resource predictability and fluctuating resource densities.

In many environments there is a high correspondence between seasonal fluctuation and resource predictability. Regular or expected seasonal temperature fluctuations impose a sense of predictability for resource availability and scheduling (Jochim 1981:53). In central and south Texas, however, the links between seasonal change and resource predictability are weak or nonexistent for at least two reasons. One is the lack of a lengthy cold or winter season in most years. Although seasonal temperature variations for these regions are high, with daily average differences between January and July ranging from approximately 17 to 22° C (30 to 39° F) (Brooks 1978; Hyde et al. 1992; Minzenmayer 1979; Wiedenfeld 1986), an average year endures as few as 11 days (Jim Wells County in the south) to as many as 45–57 days (Hill and Irion counties in the north and west, respec-

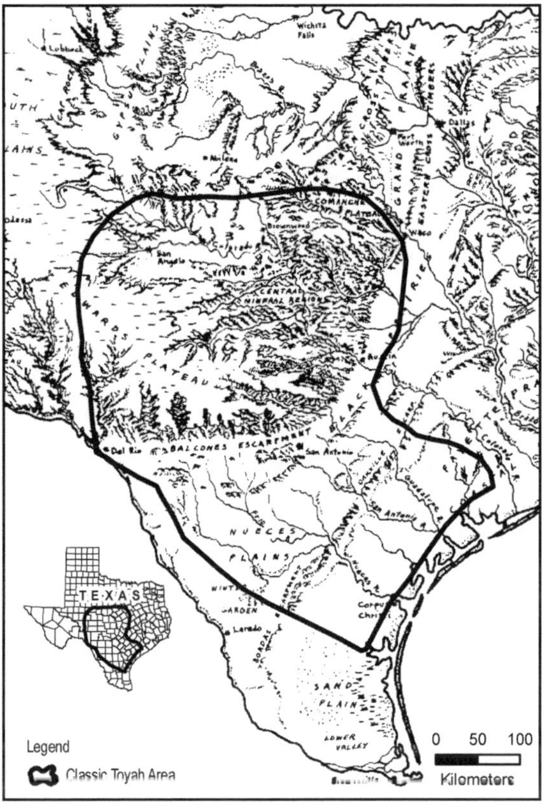

FIGURE 4.2. Eco-regions of the Classic Toyah area.

tively) with below-freezing temperatures and a growing season of 232–289 days (Natural Fibers Information Center 1987:239, 257, 271, 307). Periods of freezing temperatures are usually short-lived, and overnight freezing temperatures often give way to sunny and warm daytime conditions during the winter months. Lack of snow cover and frozen ground makes certain roots, tubers, and bulbs available year round (though their nutritional value may vary seasonally) rather then being limited to warmer spring and summer months, as they are in more northern temperate climates. The same lack of snow cover and relatively warm temperatures also provide access to adequate forage for animals and eliminate the need for migration or hibernation for most warm-blooded species. Even cold-blooded reptilian species such as turtles can be observed out and about on warm, sunny days during winter months.

Another reason for the low resource predictability is the lack of large topographic features that would host different environments with distinct sets of resources due to differences in elevation—sets of resources that would be available at different times of the year.

Clearly, then, in central Texas the availability of many resources is not predicated on seasonal changes or distinct ecological zones found in different elevations. Many resources are readily available throughout the year, and therefore sub-

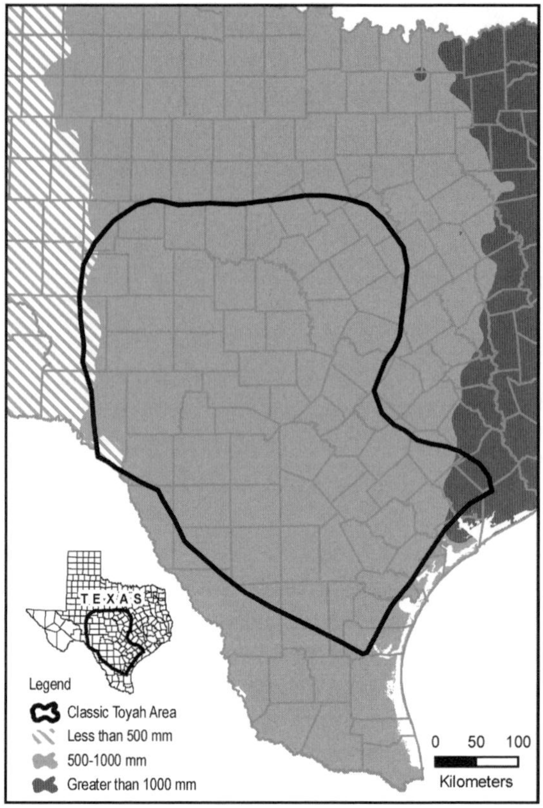

FIGURE 4.3. Annual rainfall across Texas.

sistence activities would not vary much throughout the year. That is not to say the region lacks seasonally available resources, but even they can vary in density in unpredictable ways (see below). In fact, the densities of most resources in the region can vary randomly throughout the year and from year to year.

The region's proximity to the semiarid plains to the north, arid deserts to the west, and more humid woodlands and forests to the east makes it particularly vulnerable to oscillating yet relatively unpredictable periods of rainfall deficit and surplus (fig. 4.3). The annual rainfall pattern, though bimodal with late spring and early fall peaks, is often interrupted by prolonged droughts or short periods of torrential rains that can occur at any time of the year. Across the region, annual rainfall amounts range from 965 mm (38 inches) in the east (Lavaca County) to 457 mm (18 inches) in the west (Irion County) (Natural Fibers Information Center 1987:257, 307). Annual rainfall amounts can vary from about 40 to 200 percent of the annual average across the region (Natural Fibers Information Center 1987:6–15). The region itself also contains one of the most flash flood–prone areas in the United States—the Balcones Escarpment of the eastern Edwards Plateau (Caran and Baker 1986; Patton and Baker 1977). Overall, the chaotic rainfall patterns in the region can deliver paralyzing blows or setbacks to many resources, dramatically affecting their density and availability to local populations. As rainfall patterns become less regular, uncertainty regarding resources and how foragers can deal with them increases (Jochim 1981:55).

Even resources in this region such as nut crops (pecans, walnuts, and acorns), prickly pear fruits, and mesquite beans, which are typically thought of as seasonally available and generally predictable, can nonetheless vary in production from year to year with rainfall amounts and distribution. For example, on the Gulf Coastal Plain south of the Edwards Plateau, prickly pear tuna and mesquite bean production have been found to vary considerably from year to year depending on rainfall amounts during the preflowering and flowering periods (Windberg 1997). Moreover, acorn production is highly variable from year to year, even among trees of the same species (Tarr 2004). Oaks produce low to moderate acorn crops in most years, with abundant yields once every two to five years. Abundant crop yields may be 80 percent higher than yields in a low-production year, varying by hundreds of pounds of acorns per acre. This natural cycle of production can be confounded by other factors such as erratic rainfall. Poor acorn production can result from extended periods of rain or high humidity during the flowering period, which reduces the tree's ability to pollinate. Poor acorn production would directly impact hunter-gatherer food supplies as well as devastate deer populations that also depend on acorns. Annual pecan production is similarly cyclical. Pecan groves do not naturally produce abundant crops every year but rather do so every two to four years (Hall 1998:6). Thus, even those resources that are truly seasonal can be unpredictable in terms of yield because of natural cycles of production and climatic factors. In short, the Toyah homeland is a risky environment of low resource predictability and fluctuating resource densities.

Risk Management and Exotic Materials

Dyson-Hudson and Smith (1978) suggest that hunter-gatherer groups in regions of irregular resource density and unpredictability would practice a high degree of residential mobility and be receptive to information sharing within ill-defined or fluid territories that for the most part were not defended. Residential mobility is a risk reduction strategy commonly attributed to the Toyah peoples, often in terms that convey a very high level of mobility (e.g., Collins 1995:388). A high level of mobility is reflected in the Toyah toolkit, which comprises many tool forms with durable edges that can be repeatedly resharpened to extend their use life. Toyah knives, end scrapers, and arrow points are often heavily curated.

Given a strategy of mobility to mitigate resource uncertainties, it becomes important to "remain as informed as possible about conditions in adjacent or even distant areas" (Johnson 1989:372). The exchange of information becomes a vital risk reduction strategy under such circumstances. Exchange and acquisition of information of this type requires broad social networks, and hunter-gatherers establish these networks to secure themselves against fluctuating and unpredictable food resources (Braun and Plog 1982; Wiessner 1982a). The exchange of information is often coupled with the exchange of material goods, sometimes using goods that are exotic or extralocal in origin. In this context, then, nonperishable exotic materials in the archaeological record are simply the physical representation of groups monitoring each other under conditions of considerable uncertainty and maintaining social relationships over large areas—relationships that can be called on in times of need (Johnson 1989:384–85; Wiessner 1982b).

Social Relationships and Exotic Materials

In examining social networks of the Toyah peoples, we have a certain advantage over those who study earlier archaeological cultures of central and south Texas. This advantage is that the Toyah phase (AD 1250–1700) chronologically overlaps the initial period of interaction between Native American groups and Europeans (Kenmotsu 2001; Wade 2001, 2003; and see Kenmotsu and Arnn, this volume). The ethnohistorical literature provides us a glimpse of how Toyah social networks might have functioned and a better understanding of the significance of exotic materials in the Toyah cultural system. Although much of the ethnohistorical literature is presented in a context of European relationships with Native Americans, Wade (2003:228, 231) suggests that these social networks and mechanisms did not rise in response to the presence of Europeans and also argues that their complexity indicates that they existed in prehistory.

During the seventeenth century at least twenty-one different Native American groups inhabited the Edwards Plateau (Wade 2003:222), an area over which a single coeval archaeological material culture, the Toyah phase, is found. This fact alone suggests a high level of interaction, communication, and information sharing between these groups, since they shared largely the same material culture or toolkit. The rancheria of the Gediondos encountered on the Pecos River by the Mendoza-Lopez expedition in 1684 housed various Jumano groups and other groups as well, but it is likely that the material culture of all these groups would appear archaeologically as Toyah phase sites. Wade (2003:226–29) notes that these groups composed an enormous socioeconomic network that was maintained through alliances, dual ethnicity, ladinos (individual translators, intermediaries, or facilitators between groups), and information sharing (see also Arnn, this volume). Various groups within these twenty-one members formed coalitions and alliances based on common socioeconomic interests, the lifespan of which likely reflected the duration or resolution of each current dilemma (e.g., resource inequities, threats from other groups) that spawned the alliance (Wade 2003:226). These alliances were often cultivated and sustained through the exchange of goods (no doubt some exotic) and information (Kenmotsu 1994; Wade 2003:227).

Exotic materials in Toyah sites, then, primarily represented alliances and social relationships with groups outside the Toyah homeland. Hence, their presence in sites along the margins of the Classic Toyah area and their near absence in the center are not surprising, a pattern that mimics Johnson's (1994) Classic Toyah area and surrounding Shared Toyah area model. In the core area, which is nearly devoid of exotic materials, it is difficult to examine social relationships using the archaeological record. Even though intraregional variability in tool forms, styles, and raw material use probably exist, these attributes are currently not easily recognized or well understood. Surely those living in the core area established and participated in social networks, as evidenced by the multiple distinct groups occupying the Edwards Plateau, even though they are expressed archaeologically as a single material culture. Their social networks simply did not include groups outside the Classic Toyah area, and therefore their access to exotic materials was very limited.

Marginal to the core area, Toyah sites yielding exotic materials are for the most part found close or adjacent to the source area of those materials. Although Caddoan pottery is present across central Texas, its quantity, distribution, and cultural associations are not well known or understood. Across the region Caddoan pottery is often found in undated contexts lacking other diagnostic materials, or, when the age of a site yielding Caddoan pottery is known, it often predates the Toyah. The latter tends to occur throughout the middle Brazos River basin, a phenomena that Shafer (2006b) attributes to Caddo peoples inhabiting that river valley between AD 1000 and 1300 and serving as the sustaining population for a Caddoan ceremonial center at the George C. Davis site, located some 180 miles east of the middle Brazos River valley and in the southern heart of the Caddoan culture region. It is also possible that some ceramic vessels that are Caddoan in style and appearance were not manufactured in east Texas, as chemical analysis of sherds from site 41BQ285, a Toyah site in Bosque County, seems to demonstrate (Griffith et al. 2010).

Eliminating from consideration Caddoan pottery that predates Toyah or is found in poorly defined temporal or cultural contexts, true Toyah sites yielding Caddoan pottery are most common along the eastern and northeastern margins of the Classic Toyah area (fig. 4.4). The ethnohistorical literature indicates interaction between various groups in this marginal area. We know that Caddo people were present on the Blackland Prairie east of the Edwards Plateau for bison hunts (Ricklis and Collins 1994:19). We also know that this part of the Toyah homeland periodically hosted large encampments of ethnically diverse groups, including Caddos and other groups not from the immediate area (Campbell 1988; Ricklis and Collins 1994).

Near the northwestern margin of the Toyah homeland, the Buckhollow site and site 41RN3 yielded pottery sherds of possible Plains or Puebloan manufacture and Valles Caldera obsidian, respectively (fig. 4.5). The Currie site, which is also located in this part of the Classic Toyah area, yielded obsidian from an unknown source, *Olivella* shell beads, and a marine shell pendant. Given the site's location, these items were probably obtained by Toyah people from neighboring Plains groups who participated in the more extensive Plains-Pueblo exchange system to the north and northwest (Vehik and Baugh 1994). Archaeologically, we find sites in this marginal area with mixed Toyah, Plains, and Southwestern archaeological

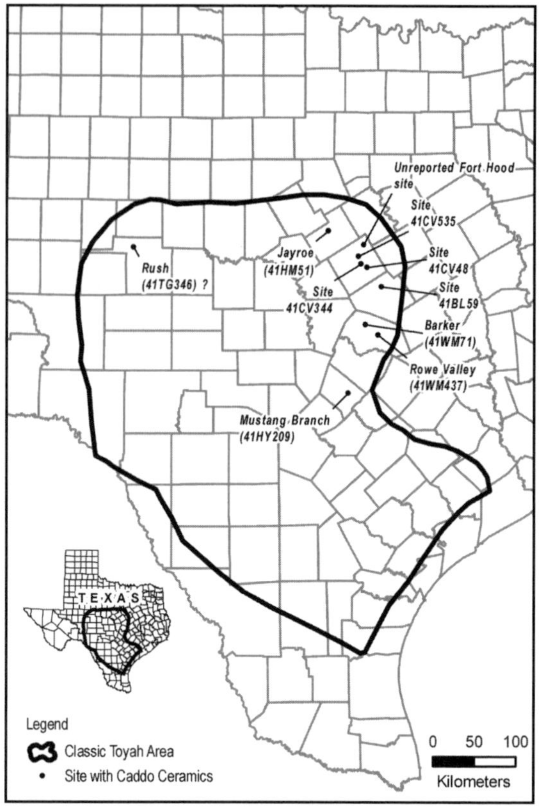

FIGURE 4.4. Toyah sites yielding Caddo pottery.

assemblages, suggesting that Toyah peoples in this part of the Toyah homeland were engaged in relations with their Plains and Puebloan neighbors. These include such sites as the Davis Hackberry Springs site (Riemenschneider 1996) in Sterling County, the Bridwell site (Parker 1990) in Crosby County, and several sites (Rogers 1972) along the Pecos River in Pecos and Crockett counties. It should be noted that this social network probably broke down when Apachean groups moved into the area in the sixteenth century. The ethnohistorical literature is replete with reports of native groups, particularly Jumanos, making requests for Spanish protection from Apaches (Kenmotsu 1994, 2001; Wade 2003).

Near the southeastern margin of the Classic Toyah area, the Hinojosa site and site 41LK201 yielded marine shell artifacts and fragments and asphaltum, which were probably obtained from the neighboring coastal Karankawas. Both Toyah and Karankawa (or Rockport Phase as it is known archaeologically) groups used similar lithic toolkits that included Perdiz points, end scrapers, bifacial knives, sometimes with alternately beveled edges, and flake drills, but they made different types of pottery (Ricklis 1992).

This pattern of social relationships marked by exotic materials from a single source area with a neighboring outside group or groups along the margins of the Toyah homeland holds true for almost all Toyah sites examined here, except for

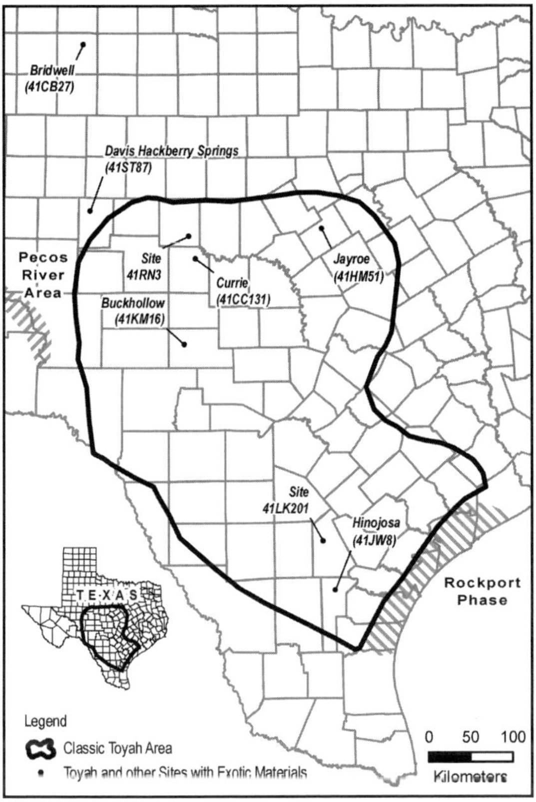

FIGURE 4.5. Peripheral Toyah and other sites, and adjacent culture areas.

the Jayroe site in Hamilton County. Very few Toyah sites contain multiple types of exotic artifacts, and even fewer contain exotic materials from different, widely dispersed source areas. The Jayroe site, which dates to AD 1400–1640, yielded multiple types of exotic materials from different areas: obsidian from two Valles Caldera sources (Cerro del Medio and Cerro Toledo) and Caddoan pottery (Bullard Brushed) (Kibler and Broehm 2005). Obsidian artifacts are rare in Toyah sites and, when present, usually consist of a few small flakes or small tool fragments. Those obsidian artifacts that have been identified to source locations through various trace element analyses are primarily from Valles Caldera sources, sources that became largely available to Southern Plains groups through trade with northern Puebloan groups after AD 1450 (Baugh and Nelson 1987). Bullard Brushed is a Late Caddo utilitarian pottery type commonly associated with the Frankston phase (AD 1400–1600) of the Neches and Angelina river basins and Titus phase (AD 1400–1680) sites located between the Sabine and Sulphur rivers in east Texas (Pertulla 1992:107, 1995; Story and Creel 1982). It is also known from central Texas as a trade ware (Suhm and Jelks 1962:21).

The Jayroe site, located near the northern margin of the Classic Toyah area in the Western Cross Timbers region, is nearly equally distant from contemporaneous Frankston and Titus phase sites to the east and Plains Village sites to

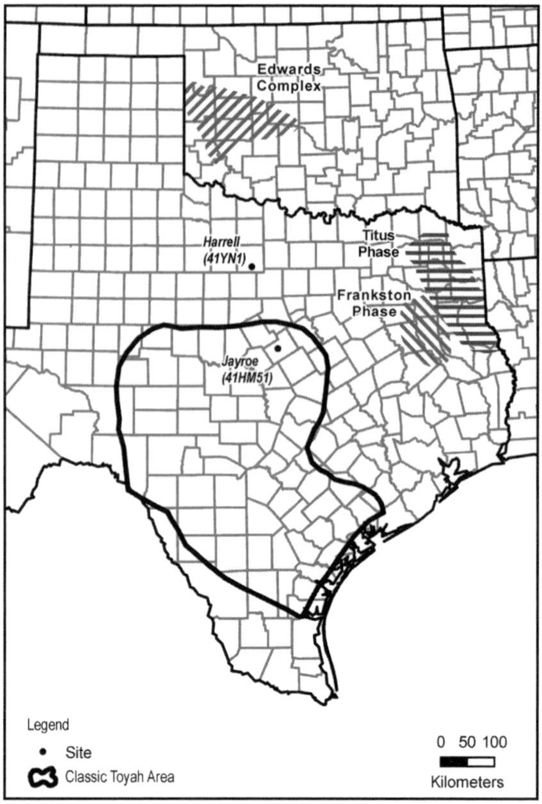

FIGURE 4.6. Possible social field for the Toyah occupants of the Jayroe site.

the north (fig. 4.6). In southwestern Oklahoma, sites of the Edwards complex (AD 1500–1650) have yielded Caddoan and Puebloan pottery as well as obsidian from Valles Caldera sources (T. Baugh 1982, 1986; Hofman 1984). Even closer to the Jayroe site, near the confluence of the Brazos and Clear Fork of the Brazos rivers in Young County, is the Harrell site (Krieger 1946:87–120). Although not well dated or understood, the Harrell site represents the southernmost manifestation of the southern Plains Village tradition. The site assemblage includes such exotic materials as Poynor Engraved sherds, a Late Caddo pottery type associated with the Frankston phase, a small obsidian biface (source unknown), and an *Olivella* shell bead. As documented by several researchers (e.g., T. Baugh 1982, 1986; Hofman 1984; Vehik 2002), these materials clearly indicate that Plains Village groups, around the time the Jayroe site was occupied, were engaged in a large social and economic network with Puebloan and Caddoan peoples. On the basis of the exotic materials recovered from Jayroe, it appears that Toyah peoples had social relationships with their Plains Village and Caddo neighbors, neighbors who participated in a much larger social and economic network with access to resources from east Texas across the Southern Plains and into the northern Pueblo areas of New Mexico.

The Jayroe site is unique with its multiple types of exotic artifacts from distinct areas, but at the same time the pattern we see at Jayroe parallels some of the patterns we see at other Toyah sites with exotic materials. For example, the Jayroe site is situated along the margins of the Classic Toyah area, and its site assemblage indicates that its occupants had social relationships with adjacent non-Toyah groups. Unlike many other Toyah sites, the Jayroe site is situated a relatively short distance between two sedentary groups of horticulturalists (Caddo and Plains Village), who were participating in an extensive social and economic network. Being "neighborly," the Toyah folk took advantage of their proximity to these groups and their exchange network to reduce risk in their own world. In return, the Toyah people certainly must have provided the Caddos and Plains Villagers with materials or information to cement these social relationships, though it is not clear what material things they might have offered (Edwards chert, bison hides?). Foraging groups interacting with neighboring horticulturalists and more sedentary groups in mutually beneficial ways or to reduce risk is quite common worldwide, and the archaeological, ethnographic, and ethnohistorical literature is replete with examples (e.g., Bahuchet and Guillaume 1982; Hart and Hart 1986; Kenmotsu 1994; Spielmann 1982, 1983). It appears that the Toyah occupants of the Jayroe site represent another example of a social network to reduce risk during uncertain times.

Conclusion

In this chapter I examine and interpret exotic materials found in Toyah sites as archaeological markers of the social relationships of Toyah peoples on a broad interregional scale. Though rare, exotic materials in Toyah sites represent the establishment and maintenance of social networks with groups outside the Toyah homeland. The Toyah central and south Texas home was a risk-laden environment of unpredictable and fluctuating resources, risks that were mitigated through a high degree of residential mobility and various social relationships, which included non-Toyah peoples. To examine these relationships more closely, in future studies we should conduct more rigorous and systemic sourcing or provenance of artifacts. These studies can expand upon the interpretations of Toyah social relationships and networks presented here, including small-scale intraregional relationships between Toyah groups as well as the broader interregional relationships between Toyah and non-Toyah peoples.

Note

1. In this chapter, "Toyah" refers to Johnson's (1994) Classic Toyah culture, and central Texas comprises the Edwards Plateau, Balcones Canyonlands, Llano Uplift, and Lampasas Cut Plain.

FIVE

Reconsidering the Role of Bison in the Terminal Late Prehistoric (Toyah) Period in Texas

Raymond Mauldin, Jennifer Thompson, and Leonard Kemp

Since 1974, Dillehay's influential article detailing bison on archaeological sites on the Southern Plains has shaped views of subsistence in south and central Texas. This has especially been the case in the Toyah phase. The supposed return of large numbers of bison around AD 1300 (650 BP), combined with the appearance of a host of traits including beveled knives and hide scrapers, led most researchers to envision Toyah subsistence as geared primarily to bison exploitation. Our examination of 141 components from seventy-seven Late Archaic and Late Prehistoric sites within a 150,000 km² area of central and south Texas does not support the previously defined Initial Late Prehistoric (Austin) period of bison absence. Although bison remains are nearly ubiquitous on Toyah occupations, they are also present on Austin occupations. Our review of paleoclimate data suggests that conditions for bison probably deteriorated throughout the Late Prehistoric, resulting in a patchy distribution. Rather than being a response to the return of bison to Texas after 650 BP, Toyah subsistence may in part reflect an increase in logistical bison-hunting strategies in the context of declining, fluctuating bison availability.

Throughout the thirteenth and into the fourteenth century across central and south Texas, a suite of new material cultural items appeared (see fig. 1.8). Characterized by beveled knives, formal end scrapers, long-shafted flake drills, blade technology, ceramics, and contracting-stem arrow points termed Perdiz, the distinctive suite of items was formally named the "Toyah focus" by Kelley (1947b:121–24; Stephenson 1950:154; Suhm et al. 1954:113). Consistent with the theoretical position of the period, researchers interpreted Toyah material as reflecting ethnic groups and made tentative links between the material remains and historically identified entities, such as the Jumanos (Kelley 1947b:121; Stephenson 1950:154) or Coahuiltecan-speaking groups (Johnson 1994:278–81). These historic links appeared to account for the ultimate disposition of Toyah populations, but researchers looked to the north for the origins of the complex. Shafer (1971a, 1977) was among the first to note explicitly the "Plains-like" nature of much of the Toyah material and link the appearance of that material to a focus on bison hunting. Shortly after Shafer's observations, Dillehay (1974) published his extensive review of bison on the Southern Plains. He proposed a series of bison "presence" and "absence" periods for the region. Researchers were quick to link the return of bison in Dillehay's Presence period III (750–650 to 400 BP) to the sudden appearance of Toyah material culture in Texas (e.g., Greer 1976a:141–48; Hester 1975:122; Huebner 1991:350–51; Prewitt 1981:74, 84, 1985:228). Subsequently, some researchers argued that Toyah material culture reflected the movement of Plains populations south, following bison back to Texas (e.g., Johnson 1994; Prewitt 1981). Others (e.g., Black 1986; Ricklis 1994) argued that Toyah technology, a toolkit that seems well suited for hunting and processing (Brown et al. 1982; Sollberger 1971), diffused among a variety of indigenous groups focused on the returning bison. Aspects of this debate are ongoing (Collins 2004:122–23; Wade 2003:217–23).

We review the presence of the Plains bison (*Bison bison*) on 141 components in a large area of central and south Texas. Though focused on the Late Prehistoric (1250–400 BP), we include Late Archaic material for comparative purposes. Our review does not support Dillehay's (1974; see also Huebner 1991) suggested Bison Absence period II (1450 to 750–650 BP). Although our interpretations are hampered by the use, in many cases, of presence/absence data on bison, underreporting and underanalysis of older excavations, and a dearth of direct dates linking bison with particular periods, it appears that bison were present on about 40 percent of archaeological sites dating between 1250 and 700 BP in central and south Texas. Since bison never left Texas, Toyah material is unlikely to be a simple response to their return.[1] In fact, our reviews of several different paleoenvironmental data sets suggest that conditions for bison were probably deteriorating throughout the Late Prehistoric period (1250–400 BP). This deterioration potentially resulted in a decline in the number of bison and an increase in year-to-year variability in bison availability in central and south Texas. Rather than being a response to the return of bison to Texas after 650 BP, we suggest that Toyah material culture reflects, in part, an increase in the importance of logistical bison-hunting strategies.

Late Holocene Bison Availability in Central and South Texas

Although there were earlier observations (e.g., Baerreis and Bryson 1965; Collins 1968; Dibble and Lorraine 1968), Dillehay's (1974) study represents the first significant attempt to model shifts in bison on the Southern Plains. Using published and unpublished data from about 150 archaeological and paleontological sites from throughout the Southern Plains, he mapped bison presence/absence over nearly 12,000 years. Time periods were assigned either by reference to associated radiocarbon dates or, more commonly, through association with artifacts argued to be temporally diagnostic. Dillehay (1974:181) proposed a series of intervals for which he argued that bison were either present or absent across much of the region. Of specific concern here are patterns of bison in Texas suggested for the Late Archaic and, more importantly, for the Initial (Austin) and Terminal (Toyah) Late Prehistoric portions of Dillehay's sequence. Dillehay argued that after a roughly 3,000-year presence (Presence period II; 4450–1450 BP), bison were "absent" from Texas from 1450 to 750–650 BP (Absence period II; roughly equivalent to the Austin phase). Bison returned at around 750–650 BP (Presence period III), a time coeval with the development of Toyah material culture. Dillehay suggested that both the 700-year absence of bison as well as their return in the latter half of the Late Prehistoric period were related to unspecified climate changes (1974:184–87).

After the publication of Dillehay's model, several researchers evaluated the suggested patterns of bison availability in the Late Prehistoric in detail. Results were mixed. Focusing on north-central Texas, Lynott (1979) argued that, although bison probably were never present in large numbers in the area, they were clearly present in the Toyah period. Lynott (1979:98) also found evidence of bison in the Initial Late Prehistoric, Dillehay's Absence period II. Working in central and western Oklahoma, Susan Baugh (1986) demonstrated that bison were common throughout the Late Prehistoric. She found that bison were present on 11 of 14 sites (78 percent) that were dated to between 1650 and 850 BP (S. Baugh 1986:84–91), a time that encompassed much of the Dillehay's Absence period II. Huebner (1991) undertook an extensive study of Dillehay's model focusing on central and south Texas, as well as along the South Texas Coastal Plain, and on the Late Prehistoric period (AD 700–1550). He reviewed the presence/absence of bison, as well as the temporal placement of faunal remains, using data from 77 sites (1991:346–51). Consistent with Dillehay's results, Huebner found that bison were common on Late Prehistoric sites dating after AD 1250. No "definitive" evidence of bison on sites dating between AD 700 and 1250 was reported (1991:347).

These studies and others (e.g., Creel 1990:223–29) support Dillehay's earlier observation that bison were present in sites throughout the region after AD 1300. Clearly, during the Terminal Late Prehistoric, bison were a component of subsistence across the Southern Plains and in central and south Texas. Results regarding the absence of bison in the Initial Late Prehistoric are less obvious. Whereas Huebner's (1991) work supports an absence period, the results of both Lynott's (1979) and S. Baugh's studies (1986; see also Greer 1976b:238) demonstrate that bison were present during this time in north-central Texas and Oklahoma. Though Toyah material within Texas is coeval with evidence of bison, whether the Toyah material culture reflects a response to an influx of bison into central and south Texas remains uncertain because the pattern of bison presence/absence prior to the Terminal Late Prehistoric is unclear.

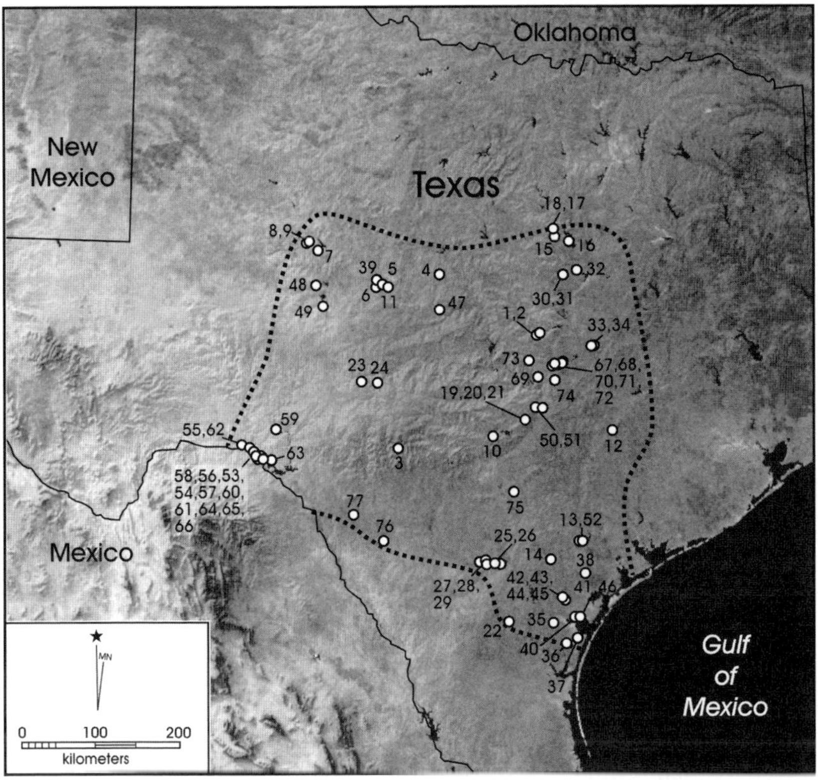

FIGURE 5.1. Central and south-central Texas sites used in the analysis. See table 5.2.

Central and South Texas Bison Reconsidered

To clarify the pattern of bison presence in the Late Prehistoric, we focused on a roughly 150,000 km² area, shown in figure 5.1. The area overlaps significantly the earlier study by Huebner (1991). Those sites listed in Huebner (1991) and those listed by Dillehay (1974) that were within our arbitrary figure 5.1 boundary formed our initial dataset of 86 sites. An additional 28 sites within the region, most of which have been excavated within the past fifteen years, were also reviewed. In all, we reviewed publications from 114 sites reflecting 181 Late Archaic and Late Prehistoric components, gleaning information on bison presence, temporal placement, and the strength of association between bison and the assigned temporal component if bison were present. We relied only on published data in primary sources.

We sought radiocarbon dates as primary temporal indicators, but most assignments were based on the presence of temporally diagnostic artifacts. Table 5.1 presents the temporal ranges and diagnostic artifacts used to assign material to components. We arbitrarily split the relatively long Late Archaic into three blocks

TABLE 5.1. Temporal periods and associated diagnostic artifacts for central and south Texas

Time Period	*Diagnostic Projectile Point Types and Other Artifacts*
Initial Late Archaic 4450–2500 BP (2500–550 BC)	Pedernales, Bulverde, Kinney, Langtry, Val Verde
Middle Late Archaic 2500–1600 BP (550 BC–AD 350)	Marcos, Montell, Castroville, Lange, Marshall, Williams, Shumla
Terminal Late Archaic 1600–1250 BP (AD 350–700)	Darl, Ensor, Frio, Fairland, Godley, Figueroa, Ellis, Edgewood
Initial Late Prehistoric 1250–700 BP (AD 700–1250)	Scallorn, Edwards, Alba
Terminal Late Prehistoric 700–400 BP (AD 1250–1550)	Perdiz, Clifton, Livermore; ceramics (including Rockport)

(Initial, Middle, Terminal), hoping to clarify temporal trends, and we divided the Late Prehistoric along traditional lines, with our Initial Late Prehistoric equivalent to the Austin phase and the Terminal Late Prehistoric equivalent to Toyah. Only components in which a researcher had clearly identified bison were considered as having bison "present." Specimens identified as "bison size," "bovid," or "very large mammal" were not counted as bison.[2] In cases where bison were identified, we further assessed the association between bison and either radiocarbon dates or temporally diagnostic artifacts. When bison were present, we eliminated cases if the deposits appeared to be mixed. In cases where bison were absent from a component, we were primarily concerned with identifying what temporal periods were represented. Mixing of deposits was not an issue in these "bison absent" cases.

After our elimination of problematic components, we had 141 components from 77 archaeological sites that fell within the figure 5.1 boundary and had sufficiently detailed temporal and faunal information. Site locations are shown in figure 5.1, with the assigned numbers in the figure linked to table 5.2, which provides data for each component by site (see Mauldin et al. 2010:Figs. 8–2 through 8–6, for bison presence/absence by time period). When a component is absent from a site, the cell in table 5.2 is blank. When a component is present but bison are absent, a "0" appears. When bison are present but the number of specimens identified as bison (NISP) are not known, an "X" appears in the cell. Finally, when we could ascertain NISP for bison from a component, we list that number in the cell. Overall, 18 Initial Late Archaic components, 20 Middle Late Archaic, and 30 Terminal Late Archaic components are listed. For the Late Prehistoric, 73 components are listed, with 53 of these assigned to the Terminal Late Prehistoric.[3]

Table 5.3 provides summaries of the table 5.2 data. Included in table 5.3 is the relative frequency of components with bison present for each of the five intervals. The frequency of components with bison present seems to decline slightly throughout the Late Archaic, dropping from 38.9 percent in the Initial period to 20.0 percent in the Terminal Late Archaic. Perhaps the most interesting aspect of the table 5.3 summaries is that our review does not support the Initial Late Prehistoric (Austin phase) absence period proposed by Dillehay (1974) and supported by Huebner's (1991) work. Bison are not merely present during this period but

TABLE 5.2. Component-level bison presence data (NISP)

Figure 5.1 Reference	Site Trinomial	Initial Late Archaic	Middle Late Archaic	Terminal Late Archaic	Initial Late Prehistoric	Terminal Late Prehistoric	Primary Reference
1	41BL104	21	15	17		1	Sorrow et al. 1967
2	41BL85	X					Sorrow et al. 1967
3	41BN33				9	23	Henderson 2001
4	41BR420			0	3		Mauldin et al. 2003
5	41CC131					3,421	Treece et al. 1993
6	41CC222	X				X	Lintz et al. 1993
7	41CK30					X	Shafer 1969
8	41CK76					4	Shafer 1971b
9	41CK79					1	Shafer 1971b
10	41CM1		2	X	0		Johnson et al. 1962
11	41CN95			0		938	Treece et al. 1993
12	41FY74					28	Lord 1977
13	41GD21	1				3	Fox 1979
14	41GD4					X	Hester and Parker 1970
15	41HI1				0	4	Jelks 1962
16	41HI117	1	1			3	Lynott 1978
17	41HI54				0	0	Stephenson 1970
18	41HI55		0	0	0	0	Stephenson 1970
19	41HY202A					32	Ricklis and Collins 1994
20	41HY202B		46				Ricklis and Collins 1994
21	41HY209T			0	1	121	Ricklis and Collins 1994
22	41JW8					15	Black 1986
23	41KM16					5	Johnson 1994
24	41KM69			0	0	1	Thompson et al. 2007
25	41LK201	1				15	Highley 1986
26	41LK67	0		0		0	Brown et al. 1982
27	41MC222					33	Hall et al. 1986
28	41MC296		1		5	4	Hall et al. 1986
29	41MC55					X	Hall et al. 1986
30	41ML35			0	0	0	Story and Shafer 1965
31	41ML37			0			Story and Shafer 1965
32	41ML39					0	Watt 1965
33	41MM340	0	1	0			Mahoney et al. 2003
34	41MM341				0/0*		Gadus et al. 2006
35	41NU221					19	Ricklis 1987
36	41NU37					6	Patterson and Ford 1974
37	41NU4					0	Campbell 1956
38	41RF21					289	Ricklis 1990
39	41RN169					10,666	Treece et al. 1993
40	41SP103					3	Ricklis 1987
41	41SP120				2	8	Ricklis 1990
42	41SP160					2	Ricklis 1990
43	41SP167					23	Ricklis 1990
44	41SP168					6	Ricklis 1990

TABLE 5.2. Continued

Figure 5.1 Reference	Site Trinomial	Initial Late Archaic	Middle Late Archaic	Terminal Late Archaic	Initial Late Prehistoric	Terminal Late Prehistoric	Primary Reference
45	41SP170					31	Ricklis 1990
46	41SP43				0	0	Ricklis 1990
47	41SS20					X	Green and Hester 1973
48	41TG346**					1,111	Quigg and Peck 1995
49	41TG91		0			143	Creel 1990
50	41TV42			X	0	X	Suhm 1957
51	41TV441					3	Karbula et al. 2001
52	41VT66					60	Huebner 1987a
53	41VV161		0	0			Collins 1969
54	41VV162	0	0	0			Alexander 1974
55	41VV167	0		0			Ross 1965
56	41VV186	0					Collins 1969
57	41VV187	0		0			Alexander 1970
58	41VV189	0		0			Epstein 1963
59	41VV213	0	0	0			Word and Douglas 1970
60	41VV215	0	0	0			Nunley et al. 1965
61	41VV216		0	0			Nunley et al. 1965
62	41VV218		2,152				Dibble and Lorraine 1968
63	41VV260		0	0		0	Greer 1968
64	41VV74	0		0			Parsons 1965
65	41VV82	0	0	0			Nunley et al. 1965
66	41VV87			0		X	Collins 1969
67	41WM118			1		1	Eddy 1973
68	41WM130			4	1	1	Bond 1978
69	41WM2	X		X			Campbell 1947
70	41WM230		0	0	1	0	Prewitt 1974, 1982c
71	41WM267		0	0			Peter et al. 1982
72	41WM437					X	Prewitt 1982b; this volume
73	41WM56		0	0	0		Peter et al. 1982
74	41WM815		0				Brownlow 2003
75	41WN88					1	Nickels 2000
76	41ZV155				1	2	Inman et al. 1998
77	41ZV202				0		Mauldin et al. 2010

*Two separate Initial Late Prehistoric components present at this site.
**Only Occupation 4 considered here (see Quigg and Peck 1995).

present with a frequency (40 percent) comparable to Late Archaic components. In terms of frequency of presence, the presence of bison on components shows little change during the Archaic and Initial Late Prehistoric time frame. But bison are nearly ubiquitous on Terminal Late Prehistoric period components, being present on 83 percent of the 53 components considered.

The radical shift in bison presence seen in the component frequency between the Late Archaic/Austin phase pattern and Toyah is visible in the NISP portion of

TABLE 5.3. Component summary statistics for bison presence data in table 2

Time Period	Components	Bison Present	Percentage with Bison	NISP Data Present	Total Bison NISP	Average Component NISP
Initial Late Archaic	18	7	38.9	4	24	6
Middle Late Archaic	20	7	35.0	7	2,218	316.9
Terminal Late Archaic	30	6	20.0	3	22	7.3
Initial Late Prehistoric	20	8	40.0	8	23	2.9
Terminal Late Prehistoric	53	44	83.0	36	17,057	473.8

table 5.3. For the 36 Toyah phase components with NISP values, just over 17,000 bison specimens were recorded. The average of about 475 items per Toyah component is a dramatic jump over all earlier time periods, and especially over the average of about three bison specimens per Initial Late Prehistoric (Austin) component. The high Toyah average, however, is somewhat misleading. Table 5.2 shows that 7 of the 36 Toyah components with NISP data account for 98 percent of the 17,057 specimens, and 50 percent of the 36 cases have an NISP below 10. Thus, as a group, Toyah components differ from earlier periods primarily in that there are a handful of cases with extremely high bison NISP counts. However, the most frequently occurring value during all periods, including Toyah, is a bison NISP of 1. MNI counts would have almost certainly generated different patterns in the data, but the quality of the faunal data available in Texas did not lend itself to such analysis. MNI data were reported in only a few of the more recent studies.

The data presented in tables 5.2 and 5.3 suggest that bison were present in much of central and south Texas from the Initial Late Archaic through the Terminal Late Prehistoric. It is tempting to use the relative frequency of presence of bison on components within a period, perhaps in combination with the NISP values, as a measure of bison availability in the environment. It would, however, be wise to avoid that temptation. Ignoring issues related to sampling, analytical vigor, and preservation, for the archaeological data presented in table 5.3 to directly reflect bison availability in the environment several statements must be true. Hunter-gatherers must pursue bison when encountered; they must encounter bison at a rate consistent with their true environmental density; and they must have a consistent success rate in their pursuit of these animals. They must have organized mobility and subsistence in similar ways. Once they acquire bison, they must use roughly similar butchering, transport, processing, and discard tactics (Dickens and Wiederhold 2003), and occupation lengths for components must be roughly equivalent between periods. Because these elements did not remain constant over the 3,500 years represented by the Late Archaic and Late Prehistoric, it is unlikely that the table 5.3 data provide an adequate measure of bison abundance.

For example, hunting weaponry and associated hunting tactics changed at around 1250 BP with the introduction of the bow and arrow (Collins 2004). Toyah technology itself represents a toolkit that seems to hint at shifts in game-processing methods at around 700 BP (Brown et al. 1982:59–63; Sollberger 1971; and see Kenmotsu and Boyd, this volume). It is likely, in fact, that the magnitude of the NISP shifts associated with Toyah (table 5.3) and the appearance of a small number of components with extremely high NISP bison counts signal a change in hunting organization, and possibly in processing and transport strategies (Quigg 1997). Unfortunately, because faunal assemblages during some periods in Texas are extensively fragmented, perhaps in association with grease and marrow extraction, detailed skeletal element frequencies that might provide clues to organizational or transport strategies (e.g., Emerson 1993; Speth and Rautman 2004) are seldom available. In short, developing reliable, independent measures of the relative frequency of bison in the natural environment from the archaeofaunal data currently available in Texas will be difficult. Below, we consider several paleoenvironmental datasets to create an independent, though admittedly indirect, measure of bison availability.

Estimating Bison Availability by Proxy

Plains bison (*Bison bison*) first appeared in the Northern Plains sometime around 6000 BP and spread rapidly south as grasslands replaced woodlands and forests during the latter portion of the Middle Holocene. They appear to have arrived in latitudes comparable to Texas sometime around 4500 BP (McDonald 1981; cf. Lewis et al. 2007). Though certainly present at times in woodland settings, the primary range of bison extended from central Texas in the south to Alberta, Canada, in the north, approximating the limits of the Great Plains grasslands (McDonald 1981:104). Because studies show that grasses and sedges consistently constitute over 90 percent of their diet across all seasons (Coppedge et al. 1998; Peden 1976; Peden et al. 1974), the association of bison with grasslands is expected. Here, we use two long-term data sets—changes in stable carbon isotopes in sediments, and shifts in grass pollen from bogs—and a short-term data set—tree ring–based drought indices—to monitor shifts in grassland productivity during the Late Archaic and Late Prehistoric periods. We use these measures of grassland productivity as an indirect measure of bison availability.

Clearly, there are several assumptions in this indirect approach, including the assumption that at the southern extent of their primary range bison densities are conditioned solely by the quantity of available forage. In reality, other factors interact with forage quantity to produce shifts in bison density. Minimally, these factors include forage quality, water availability, weather patterns, landforms, grazing pressure, and predation levels (Emerson 1990; Frank and McNaughton 1992; Kemp 2008; Knapp et al. 1999; Steuter et al. 1995; Van Vuren and Bray 1986). The principal advantage of our approach, however, is that it provides a measure of bison density shifts that is independent of the archaeological record.

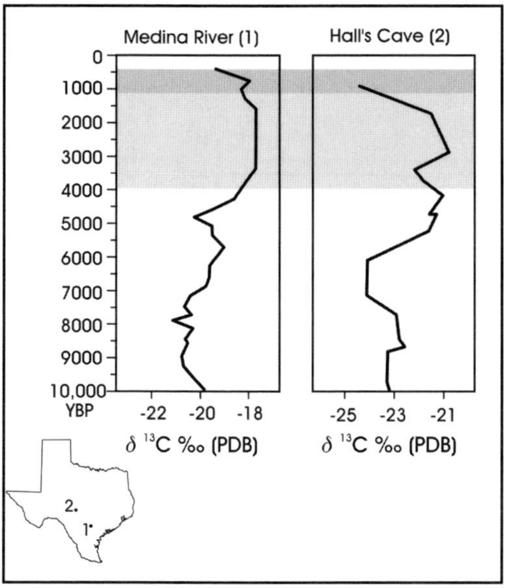

FIGURE 5.2. Carbon isotope data on soils from central and south-central Texas. Data from Nordt et al. (2002) and Cooke (2005).

LARGE-SCALE, LONG-TERM PATTERNS OF PALEOVEGETATION

The first type of data used here consists of stable carbon isotopic values on buried soils. Given the latitude and temperature regimes in Texas, plants that use a C_4 photosynthetic pathway are primarily grasses (Epstein et al. 1997; Paruelo and Lauenroth 1996; Teeri and Stowe 1976). Shifts in the relative contribution of C_4 plants in paleosols are, in effect, monitoring shifts in the contribution of grass to the isotopic signature. Figure 5.2 presents two carbon isotope sequences from within the study area. The Medina River data, presented and discussed by Nordt et al. (2002), reflect carbon isotopic values derived from a series of buried, dated soils. The Hall's Cave carbon isotope data are derived from buried sediments from an extremely well-dated deposit (Cooke 2005). Both of these data sets show responses to shifts in the relative contribution of C_3 and C_4 plants. Although we are primarily concerned with the past 4,000 years of the sequence, we present the past 10,000 years for comparative purposes.

Figure 5.2 illustrates that the two carbon isotope data sets differ slightly over the past 4,000 years. Unfortunately, the Medina River sequence has only two data points within the Late Archaic. Nevertheless, this sequence shows an increase in C_4 grass at the start of the Late Archaic and a decline in C_4 grass at the close of the Late Archaic. That decline accelerates near the end of the better-sampled Late Prehistoric period. The well-dated Hall's Cave sequence shows a slight decrease in C_4 in the early portion of the Late Archaic, with an increase of C_4 at around 3000 BP. A sharp decline is then present into the Late Prehistoric period. Interestingly, both sequences show a decline in C_4 late in time, with the decline initiated

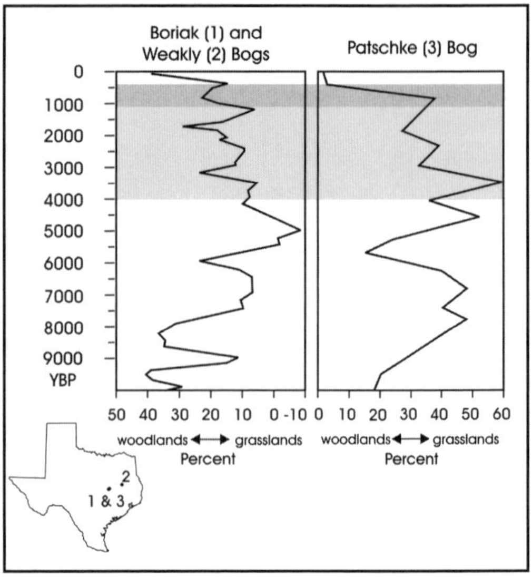

FIGURE 5.3. Bog pollen data from central and east-central Texas. Data from Bousman (1998) and Nickels and Mauldin (2001).

at about 1200 BP in the Medina River area and at about 2000 BP in the Hall's Cave sequence.

Figure 5.3 presents two paleovegetation shifts based on two long bog pollen sequences from near the eastern edge of the study area. The Boriack/Weakly bog series is from Bousman (1998). Bousman (1998) used selected pollen counts from Boriack and Weakly bogs to estimate large-scale shifts in canopy cover over the past 18,000 years. Critically, Bousman's analysis eliminated local marsh pollen from consideration, producing a record that relied primarily on regional pollen data. Nickels and Mauldin (2001), using data developed by Camper (1991), took a similar approach with pollen from the slightly better dated Patschke Bog deposit.[4] They eliminated local "contaminants," focusing on shifts in grass pollen frequencies during the Holocene. Comparison of the two sequences in figure 5.3 suggests some regional variability encompassed by similar overall trends. The Boriak/Weakly sequence shows a decline in grassland after about 5000 BP. The Patschke pollen data suggest an increase in grass pollen, and by extension grasslands, which reached a peak at around 3,400 years ago. Grass pollen percentages then begin a slow, though variable, decline. That decline accelerates in the Terminal Late Prehistoric, especially in the Patschke Bog sequence.

The illustratated data sets reflect long-term shifts in vegetation communities at variable spatial scales. Overall, they suggest that C_4 grasslands were increasing during the Initial Late Archaic in much of central and south Texas. Grasslands seem to be at their peak in most sequences in the Middle or early Late Archaic and then began a slow, gradual, variable decline until the close of the Late Archaic. All data sets seem to show a pattern of declining grasslands through the Late Prehistoric.[5] To the degree that these large-scale patterns in grasslands implicate bison density, these data suggest a declining bison density throughout much of the Late Prehistoric, including the Toyah period.

MONITORING VARIABILITY IN PALEOVEGETATION AT SHORT TEMPORAL SCALES

The data sets discussed above reflect shifts in grasslands that occur on a temporal scale of hundreds of years, reflecting long-term climate change. Although documenting these scales is critical if we are to understand long-term changes in bison populations, bison, as well as human hunter-gatherers, respond not to temporal scales of hundreds of years but to daily, seasonal, and yearly shifts in resource structure. For example, several authors have documented that shifts in location and amount of rainfall on a short-term basis can dramatically change production in grasslands (Bamforth 1988:58–64; Cable 1975; Knapp et al. 2001; Lauenroth et al. 1999; Pieper and Herbel 1982; Sala and Lauenroth 1982). Variable forage production, in turn, can influence short-term responses in ungulate mobility and group size (e.g., Epp 1988; Frank and McNaughton 1992). Though difficult to monitor, short-term variability in forage production, and bison responses, should dramatically affect bison availability.

To examine this shorter scale, we turn to recently compiled tree ring–based drought indices (Cook and Krusic 2004). These data provide a high-resolution view of climate variability in the Late Prehistoric in central and south Texas. Grouping data at 25-year intervals and focusing on absolute differences in the summer Palmer Drought Severity Index (PDSI), our results suggest that during the later portion of the Initial Late Prehistoric (950–700 BP) year-to-year fluctuations in PDSI values were low. After 700 BP, however, high variability in PDSI values are present for a given 25-year segment. That high variability in moisture should produce high year-to-year fluctuations in bison availability within central and south Texas.

The PDSI, developed in the early 1960s as a way to quantify drought (Palmer 1965), is a relative measure of soil moisture. Several factors, including temperature, rainfall, potential evaporation, transpiration, soil type, and runoff, are used in calculating the index (Alley 1984; Karl 1986). Although higher and lower values are possible, the index generally ranges from a value of 4 (extreme wet spell) to −4 (extreme drought), with a normal period designated as zero. Cook and Krusic (2004; see also Cook et al. 1999) developed the reconstructed summer PDSI database used here from tree rings using a point-by-point regression method and 835 tree ring chronologies from across North America. They established a 2.5° latitude by 2.5° longitude grid, consisting of 286 locations, that provides yearly drought data for the United States, Canada, and Mexico. We focused our investigation of summer PDSI values on four of these 286 grid points, designated as points 180, 181, 165, and 166. Figure 5.4 provides the location of these points within central and south Texas. These grid points provide PDSI values for the region that stretch from the modern period back, in all cases, to at least 950 BP. The four reconstructions are, however, somewhat dependent on each other; they are built on a small number of original tree ring chronologies, especially early in the respective sequences. In addition, the same chronology influences more than one data point.

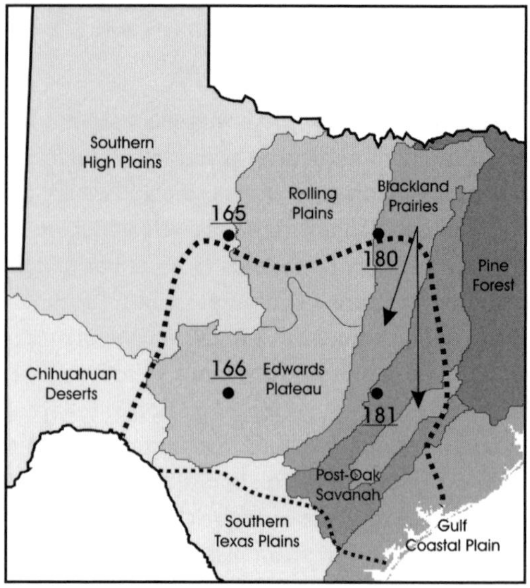

FIGURE 5.4. PDSI data locations with study area boundary and major ecological zones identified. PDSI from Cook and Krusic (2004).

For all 286 grid points, Cook and Krusic (2004) calibrate and verify their tree ring–based reconstructed summer PDSI values against actual summer PDSI values derived from modern weather stations. Figure 5.5 (top) provides an example of the relationship between actual PDSI values and reconstructed PDSI values between 1950 and 1999 for grid point 181. Pearson's correlation coefficient (R) for these 50 points is .918 (R^2 = .8419), and there are no significant outliers. Figure 5.5 (bottom) provides the reconstructed PDSI values for these same data sets by year for the 1950–1999 time frame. Note that the "1950s drought" (e.g., Bomar 1995) is evident in the reconstructed PDSI values.

Figure 5.5 shows that the PDSI reconstruction is a strong reflection of the actual PDSI values, and that the reconstruction can identify multiyear events, such as the 1950s drought. Still, relating the PDSI values to grassland production within the study area is not clear-cut. PDSI is a relative measure of soil moisture. At least for the past century, there is a significant, positive relationship between precipitation and PDSI values within central and south Texas (Mauldin 2003; Thompson et al. 2007). It is probable that for much of the semiarid study area there is a positive relationship between PDSI values and grass production; that is, high PDSI values should correlate with grassland expansion and increased forage, whereas low (negative) values should correlate with the contraction of grasslands and reduced forage production. For other areas (e.g., woodlands, parklands, savannahs), negative PDSI values may actually result in the expansion of grass, which is frequently present in the understory, and increased bison forage.

Rather than focus on differences that are difficult to interpret directly in terms of forage, figure 5.6 uses the PDSI data for each of the four grid points to measure variability in available moisture and, by extension, variability in grass production. We computed the absolute difference between PDSI scores for consecutive years

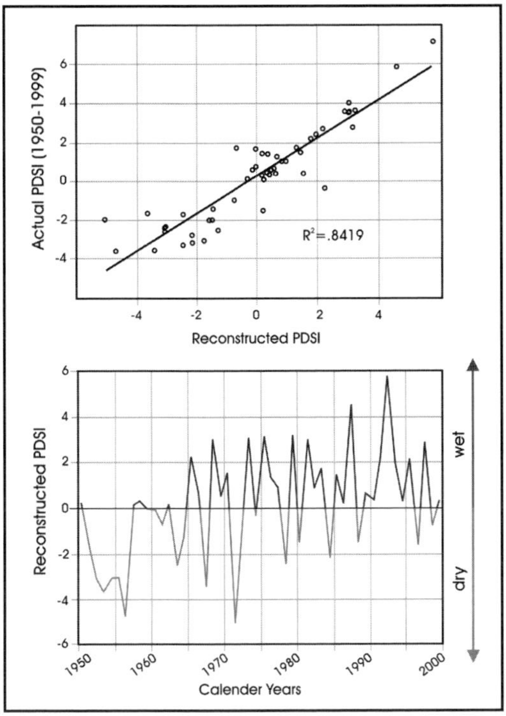

FIGURE 5.5. Above: PDSI actual vs. tree ring–reconstructed PDSI for grid point 181, 1950–1999 data. Below: Reconstructed PDSI between 1950 and 1999, grid point 181. Note 1950s drought at extreme left. Data from Cook et al. (1999).

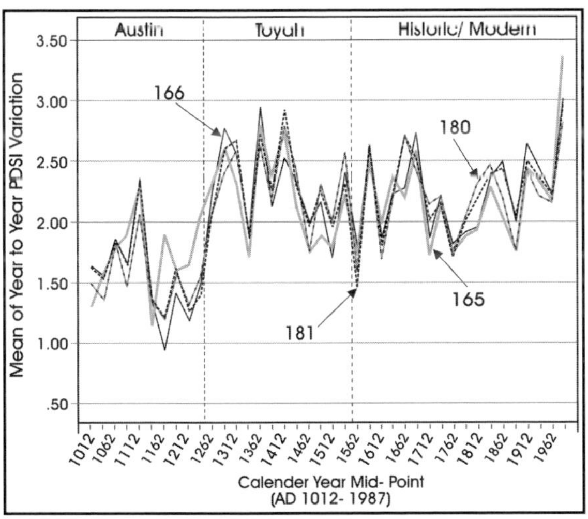

FIGURE 5.6. PDSI variability from 1012 through 1987 for locations in figure 5.4. Grouped at 25-year increments. Data from Cook and Krusic (2004).

during a given 25-year period. For example, in AD 1000 a reconstructed PDSI of −2.283 was present at grid point 181. The following year the PDSI value was 1.542, producing an absolute difference of 3.825 between these two years. We performed similar calculations for all years for each sequence and summarized mean absolute differences at 25-year intervals. Figure 5.6 plots these 25-year segment averages for the 1,000-year period. Higher mean values are associated with periods of high

TABLE 5.4. Summary information on PDSI variability at 25-year segments and the average number of tree ring chronologies used in estimates.

PDSI Grid Point	Initial Late Prehistoric		Terminal Late Prehistoric		Historic/Modern Era	
	Absolute Difference	Average No. of Chronologies	Absolute Difference	Average No. of Chronologies	Absolute Difference	Average No. of Chronologies
180	1.52	3.00	2.30	3.95	2.19	24.20
181	1.59	3.00	2.33	3.08	2.24	20.31
165	1.72	2.86	2.21	3.37	2.17	22.60
166	1.55	3.00	2.30	3.09	2.25	17.96

variability in PDSI values and, by extension, high variability in both soil moisture and forage production. Table 5.4 provides summaries of the absolute differences as well as the number of tree ring chronologies used in the calculation for each temporal block.

All four sequences in figure 5.6 show roughly similar patterns. During the latter portion of the Initial Late Prehistoric (AD 1000–1250), variability in PDSI is low in all four sequences. For this 250-year period, the average between-year difference is between 1.52 (grid point 180) and 1.72 (grid point 165), below the mean value of 2.08 for all four sequences. In the subsequent 300 years that correspond to the Terminal Late Prehistoric, between-year differences in PDSI values increase substantially, with all sequences in excess of 2.21. The higher-than-average year-to-year fluctuations continue throughout the subsequent 450 years of the historic and modern period.

The number of tree ring chronologies available for use in the PDSI reconstruction increases through time. It is possible that the pattern of increasing variability seen in figure 5.6 is simply a function of more chronologies rather than more climate variation. To consider this possibility, table 5.4 also includes the average number of tree ring chronologies used for each of the three periods. For the Initial Late Prehistoric, an average of 2.96 tree ring chronologies were used in the reconstruction over the 250 years between AD 1000 and 1249. Although this figure did increase slightly to 3.37 chronologies during Toyah, the substantial increase in year-to-year variability between the Initial and Terminal Late Prehistoric is probably not a function of this small addition. In contrast, more than twenty-one tree ring chronologies are available for the post-1550 reconstructions. Thus, the high variability during the historic/modern portion of figure 5.6 may be attributed to the larger number of chronologies in use. The figure 5.6 data suggest a substantially different pattern of variation in yearly PDSI values in the Terminal Late Prehistoric relative to the Initial Late Prehistoric. That variability probably signals a different climate regime. Critically, the high year-to-year variation should have resulted in dramatic fluctuations in forage production, possibly producing higher levels of bison mobility and variable herd sizes during some years and clusters of bison with reduced mobility during others.

SUMMARY

On the basis of analyses of several long-term data sets from different regions of central and south Texas, we suggest that an accelerated decline in grasslands occurred throughout much of the Late Archaic and Late Prehistoric periods. This decline should have resulted in restricted areas of forage for bison. Tree ring–based PDSI values provide a short-term perspective on variability in forage production. These data suggest that short-term fluctuations in production were at their highest during the Terminal Late Prehistoric. This climate variability would have produced dramatic differences in forage quantity and quality over a given 25-year period. Those differences should have resulted in significant fluctuations in levels of bison mobility and herd size. These climate variables suggest declining overall bison numbers accompanied by high year-to-year variability in bison availability during the Toyah period.

Toyah Reconsidered

The picture provided by the climate-based reconstruction of bison during the Terminal Late Prehistoric is contrary to other recent interpretations of the role bison may have played in Toyah adaptations (e.g., Ahr 1998; Collins 2004; Dickens and Wiederhold 2003; Tomka 2001). It is certainly different from the traditional concept that Toyah was a response to the return of large numbers of bison to the region (e.g., Dillehay 1974; Huebner 1991; Johnson 1994; Prewitt 1981; Shafer 1977). During a time when more than 80 percent of Toyah components in the study area have bison present and when the average NISP of bison on these components was higher than at any other time considered, climate data suggest that bison population levels in the environment were declining and that there were high year-to-year fluctuations in bison numbers. The archaeological patterns appear to be at odds with the reconstructions based on paleovegetation.

There are several ways to resolve this apparent conflict. First among these is to discount the paleoclimate data. Several of the long-term data sets (e.g., Boriack/Weakley Bog) are poorly dated, and others (e.g., soil carbon isotopes in Hall's Cave) are probably monitoring local, rather than regional, conditions. Additional sequences may dramatically change this picture, but at present all four data sets seem to reflect the same general pattern of vegetation shifts throughout the study area, especially at the close of the Late Archaic and into the Late Prehistoric (see figs. 5.2 and 5.3). Discounting all four sequences may be premature.[6] It is also possible to question the link between grasslands and bison abundance. Bison have occupied a variety of ecological settings, many of which we would not characterize as grasslands. Yet bison diets are primarily composed of grass, and the core area of the distribution of bison is within the Great Plains grasslands (McDonald 1981:104). A third path toward resolution, and the one that we find most interesting, is to consider the possibility that the paleoclimate data sets, the links between increased grasslands and greater numbers of bison, and the archaeological patterns of bison presence are all correct. Rather than revealing a weakness in methods or application, the apparent conflict between the data sets is telling us something about Toyah subsistence organization.

If the vegetation reconstructions are close to accurate, grasslands were shrinking in size during the Late Prehistoric period. One outcome of the shrinking grasslands would have been an increasingly patchier spatial distribution of forage across the landscape. Reduced forage over the long term would reduce the number of bison, thereby concentrating a smaller number of animals in fewer patches. The PDSI data suggest increased temporal fluctuations in climate at this same time (see fig. 5.6 and table 5.4). These fluctuations should have affected short-term grass production and, by extension, bison distribution on the landscape. During some years, some locations would have received high rainfall throughout the year, producing consistent forage. During other years, rainfall would have been spotty at these locations, and forage would have been quickly exhausted. Thus, the presence of bison in any one area was increasingly unpredictable in time. Overall, the distribution of bison would have become more predictable in space but less predictable in time (see also Kemp 2008).

If hunter-gatherers chose to pursue bison under these conditions, and the data in tables 5.2 and 5.3 clearly show that these animals were hunted during the Toyah period, success would be highly variable. Pick the wrong location, arrive too early or too late, and returns from bison would be nonexistent. Arrive at the right time and place, and returns could be substantial. Under these conditions, a viable strategy might be to use a logistical strategy increasingly to pursue bison. Logistical strategies are likely to be used when critical resources (e.g., water, wood, staple foods) exhibit increased spatial incongruence (Binford 1980, 2001:269). Regardless of whether bison are a "critical" resource, a patchier bison distribution would increase spatial incongruence between bison and other resources. The use of small task groups geared specifically to acquire, process, and transport selected portions of bison, if required, would provide opportunities for substantial returns while minimizing requirements associated with the presence of larger residential groups should bison be absent. Such a scenario is consistent with the presence of specialized, expensive tools that appear to be designed for bison processing (e.g., Creel 1990, 1991; Sollberger 1971; Tomka 2001) and with the high variability in bison NISP values for Toyah components shown in table 5.2. There are hints that some historic groups used such a strategy in the late sixteenth, seventeenth, and early eighteenth centuries (e.g., Folmer 1940; Wade 1998:app. E, 2003:152–57).[7]

The development of the Toyah toolkit, which includes specialized tools such as beveled knives, end scrapers, and Perdiz projectile points, possibly emerges with increasing pressure on hunters to find and procure bison when overall bison availability is falling but where bison are increasingly localized by shrinking grasslands (Kemp 2008; Mauldin et al. 2010). In the face of such pressure, hunting strategies and tools that increase successful hunting trips and increase processing efficiency are worth the time invested in manufacturing such items (Bleed

1986; Torrence 1983, 1989). Alternatively, in times when bison are a more reliable resource and the opportunity for hunting is high, there is less need to invest time making specialized tools; such conditions are exemplified in the tool assemblage of the Austin phase, which is notable for the use of arrow points for the first time in Texas but otherwise contains general-purpose tools. The technological developments from relatively unspecialized tools of the Austin period to the highly specialized tools of the Toyah are striking and consistent with a change to a logistical hunting strategy. The development of specialized Toyah tools that may have been designed for bison procurement and processing could be a response to intensification of bison procurement in a time of waning overall bison populations but increased spatial clustering of these very large mammals (Kemp 2008; Mauldin et al. 2010). Under these conditions, logistical hunting strategies using specialized tools would make the most of dwindling bison hunting opportunities.

If logistically organized strategies were increasingly used after 700 BP to hunt bison, and if that increase was associated with falling, variable, bison populations, we would expect additional patterns to be present in the Toyah record. Minimally, two primary site types, residential sites and hunting-focused special-purpose locations, should be recognized through differences in artifact and faunal diversity (Binford 1978:488–97; Dering 2008; Thomas 1983). We would expect some residential locations to have a high frequency of specialized tools characterized by manufacturing breaks, as populations "geared up" for logistical hunts, whereas at some special-purpose hunting locations tool breakage patterns would be dominated by use rather than manufacturing breaks (Binford 1977, 1979; Bleed 1986; Tomka 2001). As bison populations fell, intensification on resources, perhaps evidenced by new processing tools (e.g., ceramics) and increased use of extant processing technologies (e.g., oven features made of fire-cracked rocks [FCR]) that would allow access to increasingly marginal elements of resources, would occur. Finally, we would expect an expansion of the diet through the addition of low-ranked (low return/high handling cost) resources (e.g., snails, reptiles, amphibians, geophytes, and a variety of small seeds).

Several recent studies are consistent with many of these expectations. For example, Dering's (2008) examination of Late Prehistoric subsistence on the Edwards Plateau concludes that Toyah subsistence does not reflect a narrowing of diet breadth relative to the earlier period, as would be expected if bison returned to the state in large numbers. He concludes that Toyah subsistence was "not dominated by hunting, the environment of the Edwards Plateau was not conducive to supporting large populations of bison," and Terminal Late Prehistoric subsistence was "based on a broad suite of plant and animal resources" (Dering 2008:59). Consistent with an intensification on low-return plant resources, Thoms' (2009, 2008:127–32; see also Black and Creel 1997) data on the presence of FCR features from the Edwards Plateau and Cross-Timbers area of Texas show a dramatic increase late in the prehistoric sequence. Thompson and Mauldin (2008) and Mauldin et al. (2008, 2009) have demonstrated a similar increase in FCR feature density, as well as in the intensity of feature use, in the Terminal Late Prehistoric for sites in central and south Texas (see also Karbula 2003). Speth and Newlander's work (this volume) clearly suggests, at least on the periphery of the Toyah distribution, that there was intense competition for access to bison, a situation that would not necessarily be expected if bison were ubiquitous (see also Wade 2003). In addition, emerging patterns in human isotope and bioarchaeological research (Hard and Katzenberg 2008; Munoz 2004; Potter et al. 2005) are consistent with intensification and subsistence stress during the Terminal Late Prehistoric.

Conclusions

In central and south-central Texas, Toyah adaptations reflect a broad diet breadth. Populations are increasingly investing labor in relatively expensive processing technologies (e.g., ceramics, FCR features) that are designed to acquire increasingly marginal returns from resources, expanding diet to include lower-ranked resources, and pursuing high-ranked resources, such as bison, with shifts in mobility strategies (Mauldin et al. 2010; Thompson et al. 2007). We suggest that densities of bison are generally declining throughout the Terminal Late Prehistoric, not completely absent, but that these densities are highly variable from season to season and across space. The long-term decline in bison is a result of regional climate shifts that are reducing C_4 grasslands, and the increased local variability in bison density is related to high year-to-year variability in rainfall as demonstrated by PDSI values in the Late Prehistoric. Additional research, such as that of Gilmore (this volume) will ultimately clarify the utility of our particular view of Toyah adaptations, but there is mounting evidence that views of Toyah as focused primarily on the acquisition of abundant bison are no longer viable.

Acknowledgments

Much of the research presented here has developed over several years in association with a series of ongoing projects conducted by the Center for Archaeological Research (CAR) under contracts with the Texas Department of Transportation (TXDOT). Thanks go to G. Lain Ellis and Owen Lindauer, former directors of the archaeology division at TXDOT, as well as James Abbott and Scott Pletka, currently with TXDOT, for providing insightful comments on the overall research strategy. Discussions with Phil Dering, Jacob Freeman, John Speth, and Steve Tomka were also helpful. We gratefully acknowledge comments by Steve Black, Tom Dillehay, Robert Hard, and Nancy Kenmotsu. In addition, comments by Antonia Figueroa, Cynthia Munoz, David Nickels, and Lynn Wack greatly improved an early draft of the paper. Thanks also for the continued support of the staff at CAR, including Bruce Moses for help with the graphics. Finally, thanks to Doug Boyd and Nancy Kenmotsu for undertaking the substantial task of putting together both the 2007 SAA symposium and this volume.

Notes

1. The question here, as well as at several other points in this analysis, is one of both temporal and spatial scale. The spatial scale of bison migration has been widely debated (e.g., Barsness 1985; Epp 1988; Morgan 1980:157). Cahalane (1954:77) notes that herds may remain in a region for several weeks if forage is adequate, then move rapidly to new grazing areas. Bison certainly may have been absent from much of Texas on a seasonal or yearly basis for brief periods during the long period considered here. Such absences would, however, be invisible at an archaeological time scale. In his original characterization of the "presence/absence" argument, Dillehay (1974) appears to have used those terms in a similar sense. He subsequently has suggested that "frequent" and "infrequent" may be terms that are closer to his original meaning, given the immense size of the region considered and the temporal resolution available (Dillehay, personal communication, 2008).

2. The context of the majority of "bovid," "bison size," and "very large mammal" recoveries, and the lack of alternative mammals in this size range in the region, suggests that these remains represent bison that simply lacked diagnostic elements. We chose, however, to select parameters in which we had strong confidence. The inclusion of these excluded elements would probably change the details of the patterns presented here by increasing both the numbers of components with bison and the NISP counts on those components. This increase may differentially occur on earlier components (e.g., Initial Late Archaic) that are more likely to have degraded faunal assemblages and thereby lack diagnostic elements. We do not think that the relative patterns produced by the inclusion of "bovid" and "bison size" elements would be dramatically different from those shown here. However, researchers are certainly encouraged to take this alternative view in any future data compilations.

3. There are certainly going to be additional sites and components that we missed within the figure 5.1 boundary, as well as cases where the temporal assignment and association of bison that we propose are open to question. However, given the overall strengths of the patterns, it is unlikely that these missed components would alter our conclusions. In addition, note that questions focused on the association of bison with a given temporal period can easily be overcome by directly radiocarbon-dating bison bone. We hope that future researchers will consider this direct dating option.

4. Data used by Camper (1991) are archived at the World Data Center System, www.ncdc.noaa.gov/paleo/datalist.html. The data set used is the North American Pollen Database, made available by the NOAA Paleoclimatology Program, National Climatic Data Center, Boulder.

5. We are primarily concerned with the shape of the overall curves in figures 5.2 and 5.3 rather than the absolute values of the stable carbon isotopes or the pollen percentages. The absolute values, especially in the case of the stable carbon isotope data sets, are certainly reflecting local conditions. However, the general shapes of all four curves are potentially reflecting regional changes in climate variables. At this general level, the shapes are similar over much of the 10,000-year sequence.

6. With the exception of the Hall's Cave data (Cooke 2005), the temporal resolutions of the data sets are less than ideal, with some relatively long periods in some sequences (e.g., Late Archaic in Medina River, fig. 5.2) being primarily defined by only two data points. In addition, we are, in effect, comparing geological and archaeological chronologies, both of which are imprecise. Nevertheless, these four data sets spatially bracket the figure 5.1 study area, reflect a significant time depth, and are the best data sets of which we are aware for the region. Given the rough similarity in shapes of the four curves, it is likely that there are some larger-scale climate variables underlying the patterns shown in all four sequences.

One anonymous reviewer suggests that our climate model is not relevant because Native Americans may have increased grasslands through intentional fires, and that bison may have actually enhanced the growth of grass through fertilizing and mixing topsoil. The reviewer suggested that these processes would have enhanced grasslands, even if our view that climatic conditions for grasslands were deteriorating is correct. Note, however, that our paleoenvironmental interpretations are based primarily on data sets that directly reflect C_4 plants, which in this part of Texas are primarily grasses. Consequently, no matter what the proximate cause of the shifts in C_4 grasslands, the soil isotopic signatures and pollen frequencies both show that grasslands are declining. Any attempts by Native Americans to enhance grasslands, if in fact they did occur, were apparently unsuccessful, given that C_4 proxies all decline late in the sequence.

7. There are several accounts of bison availability at specific points in Texas during the early historic period (Parkman 1883:216–33; Weniger 1984:178), but Wade (1998, 2003) summarizes bison sightings from a variety of early Spanish expeditions in much of central and south Texas. Her appendix E provides detailed route and camp information, along with game observed, on ten different years when expeditions visited the region between 1675 and 1767, along with information on 246 camps used by these expeditions. Overall, these early expeditions noted bison on 39 of the 246 camps; that is, roughly 84 percent of all camps lacked any mention of bison. Those data also show extreme year-to-year and seasonal variability in bison observations. In two of the ten years with data (1683, 1691), bison were observed at roughly 40 percent of camps. Four of the remaining eight years also note bison as present in the area, though the frequency is always less than 11 percent. In the remaining four years, members of these expeditions did not note bison as present. Seasonal observations of bison were lowest in the winter months of December and January (8.3 percent of camps) and highest in the summer months of May, June, July, and August (21 percent).

SIX

Bone Processing and Subsistence Stress in Late Prehistoric South Texas

Zackary I. Gilmore

On the basis of diet breadth theory, archaeologists often use the intensity of marginal food exploitation to measure the level of subsistence stress experienced by prehistoric peoples. The frequent occurrence of subsistence stress among Toyah phase groups inhabiting the south Texas plains can be investigated using ecological, ethnohistorical, and bioarchaeological evidence. This chapter examines the potential of marginal bone fat exploitation as an archaeological indicator of Toyah phase subsistence stress using evidence from site 41SP220, a late Toyah site in south Texas. I argue that although economic intensification, in the form of expanded dietary breadth, may have been a common means of risk avoidance among Toyah groups, more attention should be paid to the social environments and historical circumstances in which the Toyah people made subsistence decisions.

Substantial seasonal variation in available sources of nutrition is widespread among hunter-gatherer economies (Jenike 2001:9). This variation is often a product of extreme or unpredictable environmental conditions and often results in periodic increases in subsistence-related stress (Low 1990). As a result, virtually all ethnographically recorded hunter-gatherer groups have developed effective strategies to both avoid and cope with instances of food shortage. It is unlikely that Toyah groups inhabiting the highly variable Late Prehistoric environment of the Gulf Coast Coastal Prairies and Marshes would have been an exception.

Multiple lines of evidence seem to confirm that dietary stress was a common concern for Toyah hunter-gatherers. In this chapter, I review evidence for subsistence stress among Late Prehistoric groups on the southern margin of the Classic Toyah area, which extends across most of the central and south Texas portions of the Southern Plains. I then examine the role of marginal bone fat exploitation in stress avoidance using zooarchaeological data from site 41SP220, a Toyah phase campsite in San Patricio County. The results of this study suggest that the site's animal bone fragmentation patterns, which could easily be interpreted as evidence of intensive human processing activities, are actually largely the result of postdepositional taphonomic processes. Studies of bone-processing activities have the potential to contribute a great deal to knowledge of the state of Toyah subsistence economies as long as relevant social and historical factors are also taken into account.

South Texas Coastal Prairies and Marshes: A Stressful Environment?

The Gulf Coast Prairies and Marshes ecosystem is located within Blair's (1950) Tamaulipan biotic province, a region that includes essentially all of south Texas below the Guadalupe River along with a significant tract of extreme northeastern Mexico (see figs. 1.3c and 1.4). The climate in this region is characterized as semi-arid and generally entails long, hot summers and relatively short, mild winters. For example, the modern average high temperature in the summer in the south Texas county of San Patricio is 96° F, and the average low temperature in the winter is 46° F (Guckian and Garcia 1979:82). Average annual rainfall in San Patricio County is 74.4 cm and varies considerably between seasons. More than 60 percent of total precipitation usually falls between the months of March and September, meaning that on average the region sees only 21.6 cm (8.5 inches) of rain during the five-month period between November and March (Guckian and Garcia 1979:Table 1). Total rainfall is also exceedingly unpredictable from year to year. For neighboring Jim Wells County, Black (1986:22) reports that major droughts lasting for more than one year occur on average once every twenty years, and shorter droughts lasting up to a year occur once every ten years. In addition, there are periods of months with little or no rain almost every year.

Because of moisture deficiencies and modern cattle grazing, much of the Tamaulipan province is now largely dominated by thornbrush chaparral. Primary species include mesquite (*Prosopis juliflora*), various species of acacia and mimosa, granjeno (*Celtis pallida*), lignum vitae (*Porliera angustifolia*), cenizo (*Leucophyllum texanum*), white brush (*Aloysia texana*), and prickly pear (*Opuntia leptocaulis*) (Blair 1950:103). Prior to the mid-1800s, however, the distribution of thornbrush species was much more restricted (Johnston 1963), and much of the region in question was likely relatively productive grassland. Maintenance of prehistoric grassland in south Texas was probably aided by the native tradition of prairie burning, thought to have been used by Native American groups to rejuvenate plant growth and thereby increase bison and deer numbers (Albert 1999; Drolet 2005).

Today, as in the past, the south Texas open savanna is broken into multiple parcels by thin bands of hardwood forest that line the basins of southeastward-flowing rivers and streams. These bands, known as gallery forests, contain a variety of larger, economically significant tree species uncommon elsewhere in the region. Within the Lower Nueces River valley common trees include various live oaks, elm (*Ulmus crassifolia*), hackberry (*Celtis laevigata*), anacua (*Ehretia anacua*), mulberry (*Morus microphylla*), pecan (*Carya illinoensis*), and willow (*Salix* spp.), the branches of which are commonly intertwined with the vines of mustang grape (*Vitis mustangensis*) (Drolet 2005:10). Gallery forests would have provided prehistoric inhabitants of the river valley with several important resources including fruit and nuts, firewood, construction materials, and a variety of economically significant animal species (Drolet 2005:10).

According to Blair, the vertebrate fauna of the Tamaulipan province include, or have until recently included, at least sixty-one mammalian species, including three large ungulates: bison (*Bison bison*), deer (*Odocoileus virginianus*), and pronghorn (*Antilocapra americana*) (Blair 1950:103). Other mammals in the area include collared peccary (*Pecari tajacu*), coyote (*Canis latrans*), bobcat (*Lynx rufus*), raccoon (*Procyon lotor*), opossum (*Didelphis virginiana*), skunk (*Mephitis mephitis*), jackrabbit (*Lepus californicus*), cottontail (*Sylvilagus* spp.), and badger (*Taxidea taxus*), along with various squirrels, rats, and mice (Hall et al. 1982:7). This region is also home to a large variety of birds, snakes, lizards, turtles, and fish, as well as freshwater mussels and land snails that were often important prehistoric nutritional resources (Hall et al. 1982:7).

Hall (1998:7) suggests that the relatively large Holocene floodplain produced by the Lower Nueces River would have provided the Late Prehistoric inhabitants of this portion of the Gulf Coastal Prairies and Marshes with concentrated "resource patches," including prickly pear groves, live oak, and mesquite concentrations along with oxbow lakes, which together would have formed a relatively rich subsistence base. Despite these concentrations, however, it is likely that the region's extreme temperatures and unpredictable rainfall patterns would have produced conditions that resulted in frequent periods of heightened dietary stress. Throughout south Texas, the leanest period of most years would have occurred during winter and early spring as rainfall subsided. During this time of year, the availability of carbohydrate-rich plant foods including prickly pear, mesquite beans, acorns, pecans, and other seeds and fruit would have declined significantly (Ricklis 1996:21–22). At the same time, the condition of high-ranking animal prey including bison and deer would also have declined as forage quality grew worse and body fat reserves of these animals diminished (Speth 1983). In short, south Texas Toyah groups inhabited a natural environment that was both unpredictable and highly variable seasonally. This likely resulted in subsistence conditions in which food shortage was a common concern.

Toyah Phase Subsistence and Stress in South Texas

Most of the archaeological evidence for Toyah phase (AD 1300–1750) subsistence in south Texas consists of animal remains and the lithic tools used in food processing. Plant remains are rarely preserved in south Texas archaeological sites. Fortunately, several sites have fairly well preserved faunal assemblages, although

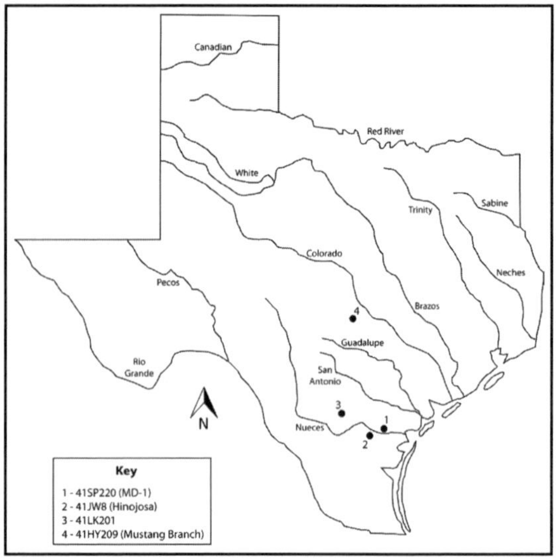

FIGURE 6.1. Map showing the approximate locations of sites mentioned in the text.

only a few have undergone a level of analysis thorough enough for the extraction of detailed subsistence data. Nevertheless, zooarchaeological studies have consistently yielded data that suggest the exploitation of a wide array of animal taxa from multiple south Texas habitat types. These include large and small mammals, birds, reptiles, and a variety of freshwater fishes. That stated, bison and deer remains generally dominate most Late Prehistoric assemblages, resulting in interpretations of a Toyah horizon economy based largely on the hunting and processing of large mammals (Black 1989).

Archaeological evidence from sites in south Texas confirms the importance of these large mammals to the region's Late Prehistoric economy. For example, at site 41LK201, a stratified prehistoric site in Live Oak County (fig. 6.1) (Highley 1986), zooarchaeological analysis shows a marked increase in the dietary importance of large mammals relative to small fauna between the Late Archaic and Late Prehistoric periods (Steele 1986a:208, Fig. 47). This direct association of large mammal remains with implements of the classic Toyah lithic toolkit at the site supports the view of these tools as specialized implements designed for the efficient hunting and processing of large mammals (Highley 1986:141).

Another example is the Hinojosa site, a large Toyah horizon base camp in Jim Wells County just to the southwest of site 41SP220 (see fig. 6.1). The entire suite of Toyah stone tools discussed above was found in association with clusters of large mammal remains at the Hinojosa site (Black 1986:240). Analysis of use-wear and breakage patterns of the tools confirms their use in large mammal exploitation. Perdiz arrow points from the site show the type of wear expected from hunting large mammals, end scrapers have patterned wear consistent with hide scraping, and the beveled knives show wear from meat or hide cutting (Black 1986:241). The faunal remains from the Hinojosa site also indicate an economic focus on large mammal exploitation. According to Steele (1986b), mammals were by far the most abundant class recovered during excavation. Of these, artiodactyls (i.e., bison, deer, and antelope) and lagomorphs (rabbits and hares) were the most numerous, with large artiodactyls contributing the vast majority of estimated meat weight (1986b:124).

Because pollen is rarely preserved in this region, the role of plants in subsistence strategies often must be inferred primarily from early historic descriptions of native plant consumption. One important plant food that was widely distributed in prehistoric south Texas is prickly pear cactus (*Opuntia* spp.) (Hall 1998). Nineteenth-century travelers describe large impenetrable thickets of prickly pear within the Lower Nueces Valley through which neither people nor animals dared to pass (Helm 1884:181). Spanish explorer Cabeza de Vaca, during his stay with the Mariames of south Texas between 1533 and 1534, described the harvesting of large quantities of prickly pear fruit during the ripening season as well as the drinking of prickly pear juice as a water substitute (Campbell and Campbell 1981:18). Scholars often place Cabeza de Vaca's prickly pear collecting ground within the Lower Nueces Valley (Campbell and Campbell 1981:6–7).

Another group, the Avavares, resided year-round near the prickly pear collecting grounds somewhere in the area of San Patricio County (Campbell and Campbell 1981:24). According to Cabeza de Vaca, prickly pear and the seeds of a plant tentatively identified as Texas ebony (*Pithecellobium flexicaule*) were staples during the warm weather, and roots were an important food during the winter months (Campbell and Campbell 1981:26). This same basic pattern is also indicated by Cabeza de Vaca for several other south Texas native groups, suggesting that it may have been widespread in the region during the Late Prehistoric period.

The earliest explorer accounts of south Texas also describe an environment in which food shortages were common throughout much of the year and a particular problem during the winter months. Cabeza de Vaca wrote that during six of the eight months spent with the Avavares, the Spaniards and natives struggled to find enough to eat (Campbell and Campbell 1981:25). During the winter, the Mariames sometimes went up to three or four days without food. Cabeza de Vaca also commented that these people were adept at surviving long periods of hunger (Campbell and Campbell 1981:15), although he unfortunately does not elaborate on how subsistence strategies were altered during food shortages. Campbell and Campbell (1981:35) speculate that dietary deficiencies may explain the purported historic consumption of marginal foods such as pulverized bone and deer droppings by indigenous peoples of south Texas.

Powell's (1987) study of the adaptive success of hunter-gatherer groups in central and coastal Texas also provides some information related to subsistence security. He utilizes bioarchaeological evidence of various pathologies to estimate the relative amount of biological stress endured by the inhabitants of three different geographic regions: the Texas coast, the coastal plain, and the Edwards Plateau in central Texas. Two of the pathologies considered, porotic hyperostosis and enamel hypoplasias, have been linked directly to serious nutritional deficiencies, although they may also be a result of infection or other stressors (Larsen 1999). Powell's investigations indicate that both of these pathologies occurred slightly more frequently among inhabitants of the coastal plain than among populations living near the coast but much less frequently than people who resided in the Edwards Plateau region (Powell 1987:Table 2).

Thus, although the evidence is limited in each case, both ethnohistorical and bioarchaeological data seem to suggest that subsistence stress was a significant concern for Toyah hunter-gatherers in south Texas.

The Role of Skeletal Fat in Stress Avoidance

During times of stress, hunter-gatherers frequently expand their dietary breadth to include more marginal resources, often referred to by biological anthropologists as "fall-back" foods (Marshall and Wrangham 2007). Fall-back foods are, by necessity, extremely reliable nutritional resources under a range of environmental conditions. Generally they do not form a significant portion of the normal nonstressed diet because they require labor-intensive processing techniques for extraction that yield relatively small amounts of edible substance. Because fall-back foods often require greater processing time and effort than other normally abundant resources, they may not be commonly utilized under normal conditions, although their reliability in times of stress means that they may be vital for group survival.

One common form of marginal food exploitation among hunter-gatherers is the processing of large mammal bones for the extraction of small fat deposits (e.g., Binford 1978; Outram 2001; Speth 1983). Animal fat, in general, serves several essential nutritional functions, and bone fat makes for a particularly effective fall-back food because of its reliability even within the harshest environmental conditions. In fact, even when an animal has died from starvation its bones still contain significant amounts of highly nutritious fats (Outram 2001). In archaeological studies, bone fat exploitation can be an especially useful signature of marginal food use and dietary stress because the relatively frequent preservation of bone and the patterned nature of bone-processing activities make them highly visible within the archaeological record.

The preference shown by many hunter-gatherers for fatty foods has been observed by anthropologists working within a variety of natural environments (see discussion in Jochim 1981:81). Only in the past twenty-five years, however, has it been recognized that this widespread taste for fat makes great nutritional sense (e.g., Jochim 1981; Speth 1983, 1987; Speth and Spielmann 1983). Thus, it is now recognized that in addition to adding desirable flavor animal fat also performs essential biological functions, especially in environments where extreme temperatures or low rainfall limit available plant foods and force hunter-gatherers to rely periodically upon animal foods for the majority of their sustenance (Speth and Spielmann 1983, and references therein). In these types of marginal environments, ones that are usually marked by periodic instances of extreme cold or drought, hunter-gatherer caloric intake often declines significantly as carbohydrate sources become less available and the condition of hunted animals correspondingly worsens. During these periods of heightened subsistence stress, hunter-gatherers often avoid high-protein lean meat and instead turn to economic activities associated with the acquisition of animal fat (Speth 1987:14).

A diet consisting primarily of lean meat from fat-depleted animals can, over a period of weeks, lead to severe nutritional deficiencies, even when relatively large quantities of meat are being consumed (Speth and Spielmann 1983:5). This phenomenon, sometimes referred to as "protein poisoning," is largely a result of two aspects of human metabolization of protein. One involves the relatively high "specific dynamic action" (SDA) of a high-protein diet compared to a diet based on fat or carbohydrates. SDA refers to the variations in the body's metabolism that result from ingesting different foods (Chaney and Ross 1971:45). According to Speth and Spielmann (1983:6), the SDA of a diet composed mostly of fat is about 6–14 percent, whereas a largely protein diet may have an SDA as high as 30 percent. This means that up to 30 percent of the calories consumed in a high-protein diet are needed simply to compensate for the jump in metabolism that arises from consuming protein. This phenomenon is what allows modern adherents of the Atkins diet to eat large amounts of red meat and actually lose weight. For prehistoric hunter-gatherers, however, a diet based largely on lean meat during the winter and early spring would increase energy requirements at a time of year when other sources of calories were at a low point (Speth and Spielmann 1983:6).

A second important aspect of protein metabolism involves a process known as protein sparing. When subsistence stress is high and caloric intake is reduced, consumed protein may be converted directly into energy instead of performing its normal body functions such as maintaining cellular integrity and boosting immune responses. Fat and carbohydrates, on the other hand, have a protein-sparing effect, meaning that they reduce the amount of protein utilized for energy needs (Speth and Spielmann 1983:14).

In addition to staving off the negative biological effects of a lean meat diet, fat serves other positive functions. Fat is the most concentrated source of energy in the body, providing more than twice the number of calories as an equal amount of either carbohydrate or protein (Jochim 1981; Mead et al. 1986). Fat contains essential fatty acids and is important in ensuring that the body has adequate amounts of the fat-soluble vitamins A, D, E, and K (Mead et al. 1986:459). For all of these reasons, fat would likely have been important in the normal diet of most hunter-gatherers and would have taken on even greater importance during times of heightened nutritional stress.

Like other major sources of nutrition, however, animal fat also becomes scarce during periods of extreme cold or drought. Among large ungulates (including bison and deer), as forage quality diminishes and malnutrition becomes a problem, fat reserves are catabolized as an energy source (Brink 1997:270). In many ungulate species, fat mobilization seems to occur in a consistent sequence. The large deposits of body fat covering the back and abdomen are the first to go, followed by the fat within the bone marrow (see discussion in Speth 1983). The small amounts of fat contained within the structure of the bone itself (i.e., bone grease) are the last to be catabolized and are thus the most reliable of all animal fats (Brink 1997:271). This sequence is important because during particularly stressful periods the bones of large mammals would likely have provided hunter-gatherer groups with the only consistently available source of fat. Because of this, archaeologists have increasingly recognized the role of within-bone fat deposits in the subsistence strategies of prehistoric hunter-gatherers (e.g., Brink 1997; Marshall and Pilgram 1991; Outram 2001).

The dependability of bone fat makes it an extremely effective fall-back food during times of stress. As with many other marginal food resources, however, exploitation of certain types of bone fat requires labor-intensive extraction techniques, which makes these resources unattractive when subsistence security is relatively high. Bone fat exists in two basic forms: marrow fat within the shafts of long bones and a few other elements, and bone grease within the structure of long-bone ends and the axial skeleton. Marrow acquisition requires only the cracking open of marrow cavities and thus entails relatively little effort unless smaller, denser bones such as mandibles and phalanges are involved. Bone grease production, on the other hand, is a much more elaborate and labor-intensive process. Vehik (1977) describes the process of grease rendering as it would have taken place in prehistoric times before the introduction of metal pots. First, bones were crushed into small, fine fragments on a ground cover made of skin or some other material and then placed in a pot over a fire or in an earthen hearth, where they were heated using hot stones. The bones were boiled until the grease rose to the surface, where it was skimmed off and stored as cakes or in liquid form.

The exploitation of marginal bone fat resources, as with other fall-back foods, can best be understood in terms of diet breadth theory, which holds that the more difficult high-ranked food items are to procure, the more low-ranked items are consumed. Although this logic is most often applied when researching the number of different animal or plant species utilized, it can also be applied to prehistoric decisions regarding which bone fat resources to exploit. If conditions are good and alternative fat resources are relatively abundant, only the highest-ranking marrow deposits may be utilized. In contrast, if food is scarce and stress levels are high, virtually every bit of skeletal fat may be exploited, including the smallest, least-accessible grease deposits (Outram 2004:79). As a result, the decisions of ancient hunters about which bones to process and how intensely to process them can be used to infer the state of their subsistence economy and whether or not they are suffering from subsistence stress (Outram 2004).

Case Study: Site 41SP220

Given the high potential for stress in south Texas, as well as the importance of bison and deer within Toyah subsistence regimes, the study of bone fat exploitation has a great deal of potential for evaluating subsistence security among Toyah groups. Despite this fact, the degree of bone processing is rarely discussed in zooarchaeological reports of the region except to say that high fragmentation levels may be a result of processing activities (e.g., Steele 1986a, 1986b). Outram (2001) has outlined a method for quickly and accurately evaluating the intensity of bone-processing activities based on bone fragmentation patterns and an easily applied tool for evaluating the impact of noncultural fragmentation called the fracture freshness index (FFI). I recently utilized Outram's method to examine bone fat exploitation at site 41SP220, a single-component Toyah campsite located in the south Texas coastal plain (Gilmore 2007).

Site 41SP220 was identified in 2002 during systematic survey of the Lower Nueces River valley by participants of the Summer Anthropology Field School directed by Robert Drolet. The site is situated on a high flat terrace fronting the eastern bank of the Nueces River in San Patricio County (see fig. 6.1). It consists of a long, narrow strip of cultural remains lining the river's edge (fig. 6.2), a pattern typical of Late Prehistoric inland sites across much of south Texas (Hester 1995). A series of twelve radiocarbon dates suggest the site was inhabited between AD 1470 and 1770 (Drolet 2006), and the growth annuli of four fish drum otoliths from different areas of the site suggest spring as the major season of occupation (Gilmore 2007).

Between 2003 and 2006, excavations focused primarily on Midden 6, the southernmost habitation area identified at the site. By the end of the 2006 field season, 42 m² of Midden 6 had been uncovered, yielding relatively dense deposits of Toyah phase cultural materials including all major implements of the Classic Toyah lithic assemblage (Kelley 1947b), several hundred bone-tempered ceramic sherds, and more than 4,200 animal remains (Drolet 2007). Zooarchaeological analysis revealed that at least twenty-two distinct animal taxa are represented in the assemblage, with bison (*Bison bison*) and white-tailed deer (*Odocoileus virginianus*) making up the majority in terms of both NISP and bone weight (Gilmore 2007).

Site 41SP220 was thought to be a likely location of subsistence stress because of its occupation during the spring when food resources were presumably at low point. Furthermore, the relatively large number of highly fragmented large mammal bones uncovered during excavation seemed consistent with intensive bone-processing activities usually associated with stressful conditions. To assess the level of subsistence security experienced by Toyah phase inhabitants of the site, a detailed study of bone fragmentation patterns was conducted, designed to determine whether bison and deer carcasses were exploited for marrow, were processed for bone grease, or both. Specific processing activities were evaluated using Outram's (2001) method of bone fragmentation analysis.

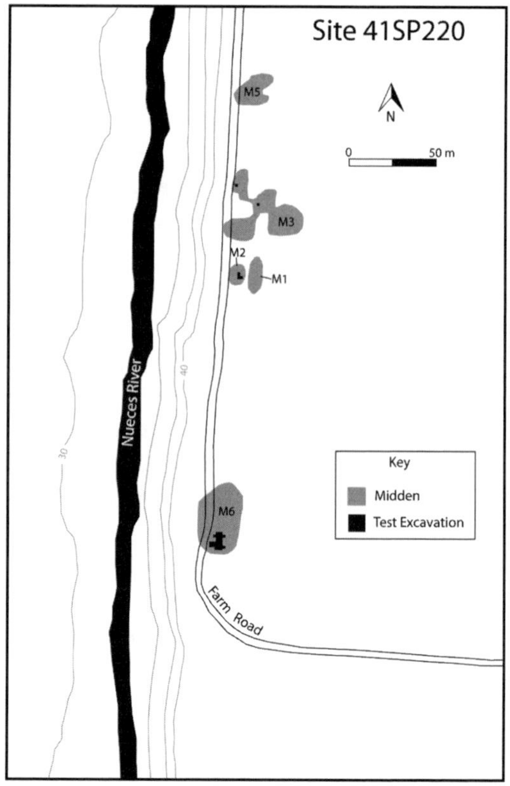

FIGURE 6.2. Map showing midden locations and excavated areas of site 41SP220. From Drolet (2007).

As suggested by Outram (2001:405), all bone fragments were first separated into a series of size classes (<1.5 cm, 1.5–3 cm, 3–6 cm, 6–9 cm, >9 cm) to gauge the overall fragmentation level of the bison and deer samples. Figure 6.3 shows the proportion of bison bone fragments in the different size classes. The smaller size classes clearly dominate, with more than 50 percent of all bison bones measuring 3 cm or less in diameter. Only four complete bison long-bone epiphyses survive in the assemblage and only two complete elements. The smaller size classes also dominate when deer bones are examined, with more than 60 percent of all bone fragments measuring 3 cm or less (fig. 6.4). Seven complete deer long-bone epiphyses and 12 complete elements survive in the assemblage. Almost all of the complete elements for both bison and deer are small, compact foot bones such as carpals, tarsals, and phalanges. In general, these data closely resemble those expected for an assemblage having undergone intensive processing for bone fat resources.

The second part of Outram's (2001) method involves calculating the relative proportions of different bone types that make up each of the size classes in order to infer the specific types of processing activities that are likely to have been conducted. Because marrow exploitation requires only the cracking open of long-bone shafts, it is expected to result in significant proportions of shaft splinters in all size classes. As noted above, bone grease production requires that cancellous

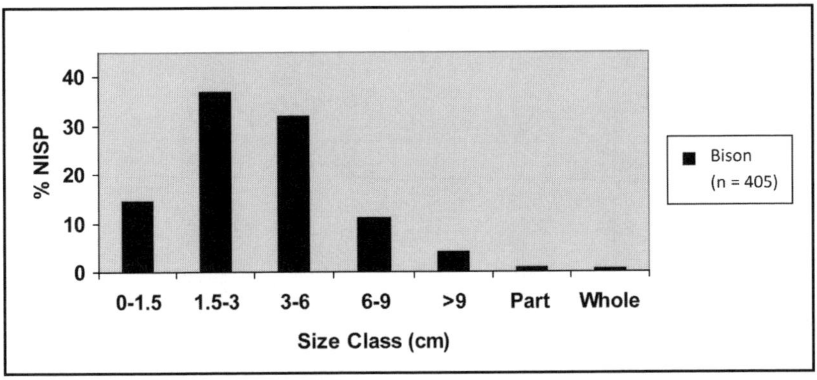

FIGURE 6.3. Proportion of bison bone fragments in various size classes from site 41SP220.

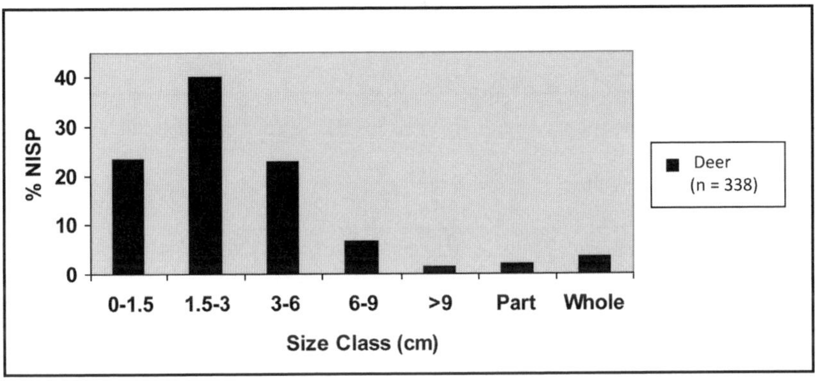

FIGURE 6.4. Proportion of deer bone fragments in various size classes from site 41SP220.

bones be crushed into small, fine fragments before being boiled and are therefore expected to yield large proportions of long-bone epiphysis and axial fragments only within the small size classes. Few cancellous elements or fragments would be expected to survive complete or within the larger size classes.

Within the 41SP220 bison sample, long-bone shaft fragments largely dominate, making up 41–64 percent of the NISP in all size classes (fig. 6.5). As noted above, this is typical of the pattern expected from an assemblage processed for marrow extraction. Ribs also make up a significant proportion of all size classes, accounting for 24–50 percent of fragments in each case. Because virtually no bison axial elements were recovered from the site (probably because of transport decisions), few cancellous fragments exist in any of the size classes. The general lack of cancellous fragments suggests that grease was not produced at the site using bison bone.

A somewhat different fragmentation pattern exists for the deer bone from the site (fig. 6.6). The fragmentation of deer long bones, like those of bison, conforms well to what one would expect for an assemblage processed for marrow. Shaft fragments represent 39–55 percent of the total number of bone fragments

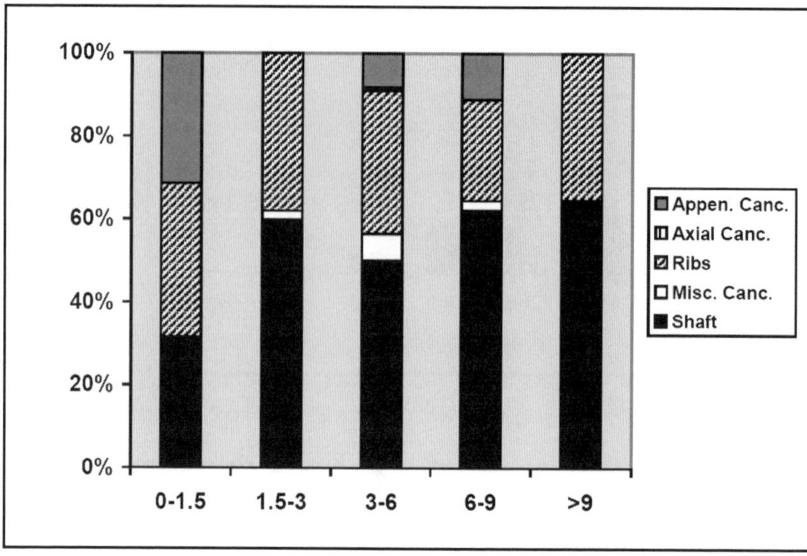

FIGURE 6.5. Proportion of bison bone types within various size classes from site 41SP220.

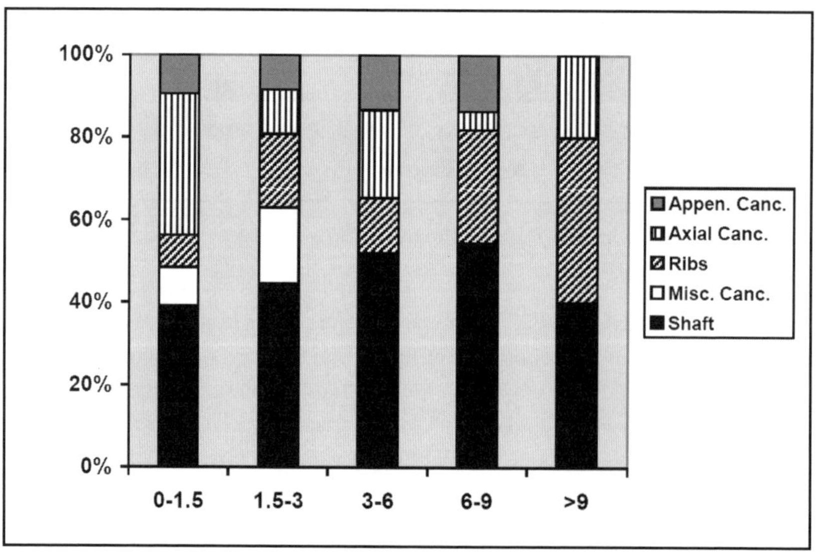

FIGURE 6.6. Proportion of deer bone types within various size classes from site 41SP220.

in each size category. Ribs make up less than 8 percent of the smallest size class and gradually increase in relative abundance as size increases. Deer cancellous bone, on the other hand, is much more abundant than that of bison. Cancellous fragments in this case account for the highest proportion of fragments within the smallest size classes and generally decrease in abundance as size increases. This pattern of cancellous bone fragmentation is similar to that expected from an assemblage that has undergone grease production.

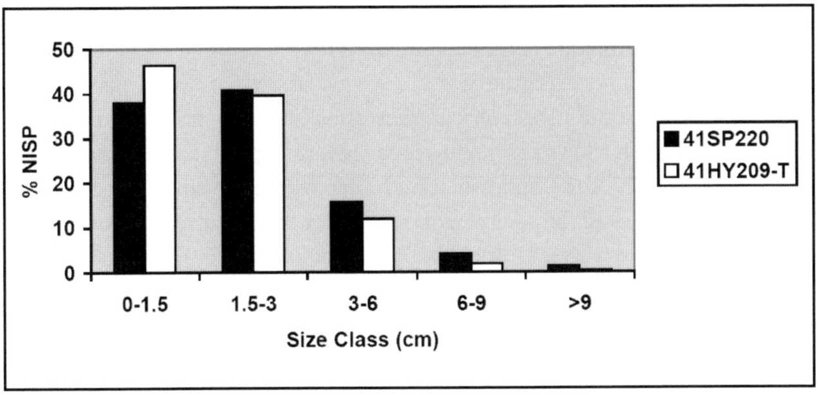

FIGURE 6.7. Percent NISP of all large mammal bone fragments in various size classes from 41SP220 and 41HY209-T (Mustang Branch).

To add perspective to this fragmentation pattern, I compared fragmentation data from site 41SP220 to that from the Toyah component of the Mustang Branch site (41HY209-T) in Hays County (Ricklis and Collins 1994). The Mustang Branch site has become almost synonymous with intensive processing and has produced by far the strongest evidence of bone grease production of any site within the Toyah sphere. Like site 41SP220, the Mustang Branch site was occupied during the spring when high levels of subsistence stress may have increased the value of even the smallest fat deposits (Masson and Holderby 1994). In terms of the level of fragmentation, the site 41SP220 assemblage is comparable to that from Mustang Branch. Figure 6.7 shows the proportion of fragments in the various size classes for both sites. In both cases, the smallest two size classes dominate, containing approximately 75 percent of the 41SP220 bone fragments and approximately 85 percent of those from Mustang Branch. The small fragment sizes resulted in a high proportion of unidentifiable fragments from both sites. Just over 90 percent of large mammal bones from site 41SP220 and approximately 74 percent from the Mustang Branch site were unidentifiable to element (Masson and Holderby 1994:278).

On the basis of fragmentation levels alone, therefore, the data would seem to suggest that the site 41SP220 large mammal assemblage was subjected to an array of intensive processing activities. The final step of Outram's (2001) method, however, offers a means of evaluating the extent to which the observed fragmentation patterns are a result of cultural practices rather than nonhuman taphonomic processes. Outram's FFI utilizes three primary criteria—fracture angle (the angle of the fracture surface to the bone's cortical surface), fracture outline (the fracture's basic shape, e.g., spiral, transverse, longitudinal), and fracture edge texture—to assess whether or not a bone was fractured while fresh. Each large mammal shaft fragment is scored between zero and 2 on each of these criteria. The three separate scores are then summed to arrive at the overall FFI score for the specimen. Overall scores range between zero and 6, with zero indicating a fragment exhibiting only fresh fracture characteristics and 6 indicating a fragment with almost no attributes of fresh fracture (Outram 2001, 2002).

The average FFI score for the 41SP220 large mammal assemblage is 3.6, indicating a mixture of both fresh and nonfresh fractures. This mixture can be seen in figure 6.8, which shows the frequency of the different FFI scores. These scores indicate that much of the fragmentation visible within the site 41SP220 assemblage is likely the result of natural taphonomic processes rather than prehistoric bone-processing activities. Although a significant number of fragments scored at either zero or 1, suggesting marrow cracking, the large proportion of higher FFI scores within the assemblage indicates that the high degree of cancellous bone fragmentation is likely to be a result not of bone grease production but rather of other taphonomic processes. One contributing factor is likely the highly acidic soils at the site, the effects of which can be seen in figure 6.9. The higher fragmentation levels noted for cancellous bone are probably a result of the lower relative density of these bones, which might make them more vulnerable to natural fragmentation.

Discussion

The lack of intensive bone processing at site 41SP220 obviously does not mean that the site's inhabitants occupied a stress-free environment, but it does mean that subsistence conditions were such that when processing decisions were being made the labor-intensive procedure of grease production was not found to be a worthwhile pursuit. These results are somewhat unexpected given the highly fragmented condition of large mammal bones from the site and the fact that it was occupied during the spring, presumably the most stressful time of year. Nevertheless, there are several possible reasons that bone-processing activities were geared toward only the highest-ranking bone fat resources.

One possible explanation is that the site was occupied during a particularly prosperous period of time when the threat of subsistence stress was minimal throughout the year. As discussed earlier, the south Texas climate is unpredictable, and short-term fluctuations in rainfall probably led to substantial variability in the availability of plant and animal resources from year to year. The apparent lack of stress suggested by the processing strategies at site 41SP220 therefore may not necessarily be indicative of normal subsistence conditions in the area during the Late Prehistoric period but rather of one exceptionally abundant interval.

Another potential explanation is that the relatively small number of bison and deer available to the site's inhabitants rendered grease production an inefficient option even during periods of heightened stress. Because individual bones produce very small quantities of usable grease, grease production generally involves the accumulation of large numbers of grease-producing bones before processing takes place. The relatively warm climate of south Texas may therefore have posed serious challenges to grease production due to the difficulty of storing up large

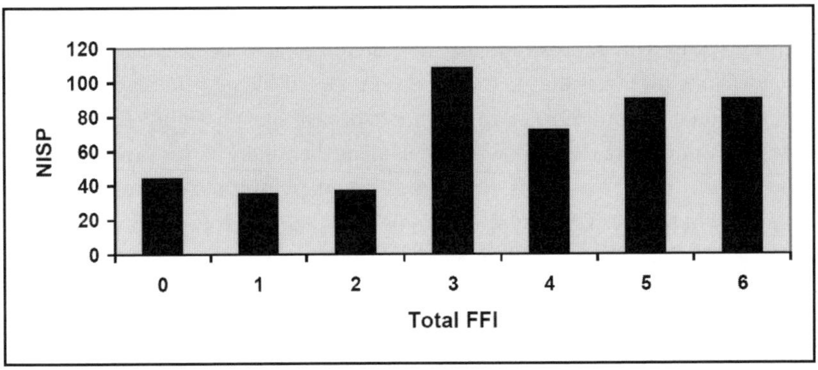

FIGURE 6.8. Frequency of large mammal fracture freshness index (FFI) scores from site 41SP220.

FIGURES 6.9. Examples of bison long-bone fragments showing signs of extreme chemical weathering.

quantities of cancellous bones before they spoiled (Outram 2001:402). This problem may have been overcome in some cases, including at site 41HY209-T (Mustang Branch), by killing a large number of animals at once (Masson and Holderby 1994). However, the small number of bison and deer represented at site 41SP220 may have yielded an amount of grease so small that it was not worth the amount of labor required to access it.

An alternative strategy that may have been employed is the expansion of diet breadth to include a larger number of lower-ranked species. This may at least partially explain the abundance of small rodents and snakes in the faunal assemblage. Although these animals are usually considered to be commensal species, there are examples of them being consumed under certain conditions. This strategy would not, however, have added significant amounts of either fat or carbohydrates to diets of the site's inhabitants and may not, therefore, have been particularly effective at staving off stress during the harshest times of the year. The same strategy, though, could be applied to marginal plant species. One possibility is that Toyah groups in south Texas were able to supplement their diets with a variety of plant roots in order to attain enough nutrients during the winter and early spring. Ricklis (1996:22) suggests that coastal groups consumed a large amount of cattail roots during this time of year, and Spanish explorers document a similar practice by hunter-gatherers farther inland (Campbell and Campbell 1981). The paucity of botanical data from site 41SP220 makes any firm conclusions regarding specific subsistence strategies tentative at best.

A final possibility, and one that deserves more attention in Toyah studies, is that south Texas hunter-gatherers engaged in a variety of social rather than ecological activities to avoid and alleviate subsistence stress. Although the behavioral ecological approaches within which hunter-gatherers are often considered tend to treat each foraging group as an isolated, environmentally determined unit of analysis, ethnographic research consistently shows a powerful social influence on foraging economies (e.g., Cashdan 1985; Wiessner 1982a). Eighteenth-century records of south Texas indigenous groups describe an incredibly complex social environment involving literally hundreds of linguistically independent hunter-gatherer groups who communicated with each other using a fully developed sign language (Goddard 1979:356). In fact, Troike (1987:301) describes south Texas as "one of the most linguistically complex areas of the world." The sheer complexity and historical fluidity of Toyah social systems may forever prevent their complete archaeological understanding, but the importance of prehistoric social networks should be given greater consideration in archaeological interpretations. At this point, the only evidence of economic interaction from site 41SP220 is the presence of asphaltum-decorated pot sherds (Griffiths 2006) and a single marine shell bead, both of which suggest trade with native coastal groups. Although no clearly nonlocal food remains have been identified, social mechanisms for avoiding stress almost certainly existed.

Conclusions

The often harsh natural environment of the south Texas plains would have posed constant and significant challenges for Toyah hunter-gatherers. Because of this, research centered on subsistence-related stress has the potential to contribute a great deal to our archaeological understanding of the nature of virtually all aspects of Toyah societies. Because of the relatively frequent preservation of bone at Toyah sites and the importance of large mammals to Toyah subsistence efforts, studies of bone fat exploitation may often represent an efficient means of examining the state of Toyah economies, especially given the relative quickness with which bone-processing strategies can be assessed using the methods developed by Outram and others. Additional attention, however, should also be directed toward the role of social strategies such as trade and aggregation in avoiding and alleviating subsistence stress. Ultimately, a more holistic approach is necessary for us to achieve a complete understanding of the impact of stress on the lives of Toyah hunter-gatherers.

SEVEN

What Is Northern Toyah Phase? The Toyah Phenomenon on the Texas Southern Plains

Douglas K. Boyd

Bone-tempered pottery, Perdiz arrow points, and bison-processing tools are hallmarks of the Toyah phase in central and south Texas between AD 1300 and 1700. What, then, do the northernmost Toyah-like remains found on the southern Llano Estacado represent? An expansion of Toyah culture tradition northward from their central Texas homeland? Or adoption of Toyah material culture by Southern Plains groups? Did Toyah peoples and other social groups maintain friendly relations and cooperate on communal bison-hunting ventures on the Southern Plains? In this chapter I summarize current archaeological evidence for northern Toyah and offer some thoughts on future archaeological research needs.

I begin by saying that I cannot answer the broad research questions proposed in the paragraph above. Questions of population migration versus trait diffusion and intercultural interaction have long been debated for the Toyah phenomenon in Texas. These are important questions, but they have not yet been adequately addressed for the Toyah culture itself, much less for the northern Toyah area, using currently available archaeological data. Thus, I examine the archaeological remains in the northern Toyah study area (fig. 7.1) using a perspective slightly different from previous research, and I describe how the use of social identity and social fields concepts form the appropriate context for framing future archaeological research on Toyah in this region.

Archaeological Background for Toyah Culture Regionalism

It has long been recognized that Toyah phase components are most concentrated in central and south Texas, but Toyah-like materials are found over a much

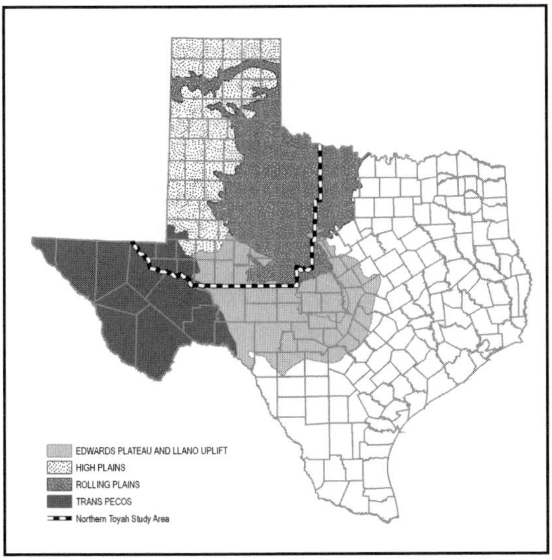

FIGURE 7.1. Northern Toyah study area in the Texas Southern Plains. This area includes portions of four natural regions: the southern end of the High Plains (including the Llano Estacado); the southwestern portion of the Rolling Plains; the northwestern edge of the Edwards Plateau; and the western edge of the Trans-Pecos. Base map is from "Natural Regions of Texas" map by the Texas Parks and Wildlife Department, 2001.

broader area. Johnson (1994:241–87) introduced the concept of a core region that he called the Classic Toyah culture area within a Greater Toyah area (see fig. 1.4). The Classic Toyah area encompasses some 51,958 mi² (134,570 km²), 19 percent of the state of Texas (at 268,601 mi², or 695,676 km²). The Greater Toyah area encompasses 121,622 mi² (315,000 km²), 45 percent of Texas, and it includes what Johnson calls the "Shared Toyah area" (see fig. 1.4). The Shared Toyah area alone is nearly one-quarter the size of Texas, and the largest portion of it is located to the north and west of the Classic Toyah area. Johnson (1994:Figure 105) notes that the boundary of the Shared Toyah area is "tentative," but he extends it northward into the Texas Panhandle Plains. It is notable that he intentionally left a gap in the northernmost boundary to imply the degree of uncertainty in our understanding of Toyah cultural interactions. This is precisely why a consideration of the northern Toyah area is needed.

Classic Toyah is assigned to the period from about AD 1300 to 1700. Its material culture includes a range of stone tools that are typical of Plains Village occupations, such as beveled knives, end scrapers, perforators, and grinding stones. When found in the northern Shared Toyah area, only two kinds of material culture—Perdiz arrow points and bone-tempered pottery—are distinctive to Toyah and not generally associated with any other cultures in the Texas Panhandle.

As is discussed later in this chapter, pottery is key to understanding the Toyah phenomenon and social identity in the Shared Toyah area. Toyah plainware pottery is tempered with variable amounts of bone fragments and ranges from very well made and highly burnished pots to crudely made pots. The pottery has been called Leon Plain or Doss Redware in the archaeological literature (Kelley 1947b:123; Suhm and Jelks 1962:95–96). Johnson (1994:210) notes that these names are virtually meaningless now because of the generic nature and wide distribution of bone-tempered plainware. Trace element analyses, such as instrumental neutron activation analysis, may prove to be the best way to differentiate source areas for these bone-tempered wares (Creel 2002), but currently available data have not yet produced meaningful insights into the Toyah phenomenon. All of the pottery appears to be utilitarian in nature, and vessel forms are generally limited to simple bowls, jars, and ollas (Johnson 1994:206). The ollas sometimes have simple loop handles (i.e., tenoned or riveted) on their necks (Johnson 1994:275; Perttula et al. 2003:Figure 6), and this trait may prove to have significant implications for social identity and Toyah origins.

Johnson (1994:261, 262, 268) notes that occasional finds of maize at Toyah sites suggests that Toyah peoples grew some corn or obtained some in trade from neighboring farming groups (e.g., Caddo groups). Current evidence is debatable, and there is no strong evidence that Classic Toyah peoples practiced any farming. Crop raising by Classic Toyah peoples, if it occurred at all, was probably very limited, otherwise more evidence would have already been found. But even if Classic Toyah peoples did no farming, that does not mean that Toyah peoples in the northern and western Shared Toyah area did no farming. In fact, it is notable that the Kyle Rockshelter is one of the few sites where corn may be in a Toyah context (Jelks 1962:92–93, 113–15; Johnson 1994:261–62). Kyle is not within the Classic Toyah area but is located in the northeastern Shared Toyah area (see figs. 1.1 and 1.4).

Most researchers have characterized Toyah peoples as relatively mobile hunter-gatherers whose primary pursuit was bison. This view seems applicable for some parts of Texas—such as the Buckhollow site in Kimble County and the Rush site in Tom Green County (Johnson 1994; Quigg 1997; Quigg and Peck 1995). But it has been challenged in other parts of Texas where deer and antelope remains are more common than bison—such as 41HY109-T in Hays County (Ricklis 1994; see also Mauldin et al., this volume). There is certainly a great deal of diversity in habitats across the Greater Toyah area, and it is reasonable to assume that people hunted more deer in savanna or mixed forest-grasslands and hunted more bison or antelope in open grasslands (Johnson 1994:259–60; also see Shay 1978 for a discussion of bison and deer hunting in forest-grassland transition zones). The importance of bison hunting is certainly an issue that has relevance to our understanding of the northern Toyah phenomenon in the Panhandle Plains.

Most open Toyah sites are interpreted as short-term hunting and processing camps or longer-term residential base camps (Johnson 1994:242–56). Intensive archaeological work at the Rowe Valley site (41WM437) just north of Austin resulted in the discovery of spatial patterning that probably reflects ephemeral huts laid out around a central plaza (Elton Prewitt, personal communication, 2003; Prewitt 1984). In all likelihood, this represents a residential site of a single community of Toyah peoples. In his summary of prehistoric houses in central Texas, Johnson (1997:56–62) notes that possible Toyah structures have been found at two sites near San Angelo—41CN131 and 41RN169 (Treece et al. 1993)—and Ricklis (1994:283–84) notes a probable Toyah structure in Hays County. Toyah occupations also are present in rockshelters in central Texas, such as at the Kyle Shelter in Hill County (Jelks 1962; Johnson 1994:246–48), Smith Rockshelter in Travis County (Suhm 1957), and numerous unnamed shelters on Fort Hood in Bell and Coryell counties (Mehalchick et al. 2003:190). On the basis of faunal and macrobotanical data, Dering (2008) proposed that most Toyah peoples had a diverse diet that included a wide variety of resources other than bison and deer. A fair amount of specialized plant processing must now be acknowledged, since plant remains from well-dated contexts show that much plant processing was done in earth ovens and burned rock middens by Toyah peoples in central and west-central Texas (Black et al. 1997:282–84; Karbula 2003:77–78). It is notable that, although there is limited evidence for structures and subsistence activities in the Classic Toyah area, it is not clear how this evidence may relate to the northern Shared Toyah area where there is little or no archaeological evidence of structures and subsistence.

Ethnicity and Social Identity

It has been suggested that the Toyah phase represents the prehistoric manifestation of the native peoples the Spanish called Jumanos during the period AD 1580–1750 (Kenmotsu 2001:34–37; Wade 2003:230–31), although not all researchers agree and some have linked the Jumanos with other archaeological groups (e.g., Hickerson 1994:220–30). The Toyah-Jumano connection is certainly an idea worthy of careful consideration, and it may certainly be used to formulate testable hypotheses and archaeological research problems. However, both the Toyah and Jumano concepts are so confusing and broad, in terms of the geographic areas and sociopolitical phenomenon they represent, that they are not well suited as the beginning point for archaeological research on the Toyah phenomenon (see Kenmotsu and Arnn, this volume). Any attempt to interpret Toyah archaeology in the context of a Toyah-Jumano connection must be supported by large amounts of high-quality archaeological data from many well-excavated sites across a vast region, combined with continued study and reanalysis of the limited Jumano ethnographic records. Unfortunately, even if better archaeological and ethnographic data sets were available, there would still be considerable disagreement regarding the ethnic identity of Toyah.

As advocated in recent works by John Arnn (2005, 2007, 2012), including his chapter in this volume, archaeological research should focus on the concept of self-ascribed social identity, defined by distinct communities of people interacting within broader social fields. Perhaps a better approach to conducting archaeological research on the Toyah phenomenon is to start at the smaller scale and examine evidence for local social identity, then work outward to the regional scale and look for evidence of larger social fields. The logic behind this approach may be summarized in the following five arguments (see Arnn 2007, 2012; Arnn, this volume).

1. The Toyah phenomenon, as exemplified in large part by the distribution of

Perdiz arrow points, is too geographically widespread to reflect a single culture. Anthropological theory and ethnographic evidence tell us that many distinct social groups, or communities, probably inhabited this vast area (Arnn 2007, 2012). In addition, we may predict the existence of many social groups, and interactions among those groups, based on the extreme environmental variability across this vast area (Binford 1980:13–17).

2. The primary goal of archaeological research for Toyah should be the recognition, description, and understanding of social identity in the form of communities and social fields. To begin the process of recognizing social identity, we need to focus on detailed comparative archaeological studies that look for similarities and differences in Toyah sites and material culture across the entire geographic range. In his article "Interregional Interaction in Prehistory: The Need for a New Perspective," Edward Schortman (1989:52) argues that for prehistoric archaeological research "our most basic task at present is to develop a theoretical framework that will facilitate the study of intersocietal contact." The organizing principle for this theoretical framework, Schortman says, should be *social identity*.

Humans are social creatures, and we must belong to a group in order to survive. Groups use "highly visible" and "redundant" symbolic expressions—what archaeologists call diagnostic "material culture"—that define group membership and differentiate "us" from "them." Schortman (1989:54) defines social identities as "culturally defined and accepted categories that guide interpersonal behaviors and are symbolized by distinct cues." He goes on to say that each individual has a salient identity that is a combination of that person's ethnic identity and social class, both of which are self-ascribed conceptual categories. "Salient identities then serve as the basis for unified groups who act in concert to obtain resources and maintain control of them by limiting access to their members" (Schortman 1989:55).

When the social-identity concept is employed for archaeological research, the result is that "a focus on 'culture' is replaced by one on networks of interaction maintained by significant social categories." This shift in perspectives allows archaeologists to adopt a new conceptual approach: "Rather than trying to identify cultures, we must turn our attention to recovering evidence for the existence of social affiliations, ethnic or class based, from the patterns of recovered material remains. We must seek to define the conditions that call these identities into existence, the mutual concerns around which they cluster, and how shifts in the total environment of a group lead to changes in the existence and importance of affiliations" (Schortman 1989:56).

3. If we accept the premise stated above, archaeologists must acknowledge that Willey and Phillips's (1958:22) "phase" concept does not apply very well to Toyah. Rather than consider it as the Toyah phase as described by Elton Prewitt (1981, 1985), we should think of it as the Toyah phenomenon, which is more akin to what Willey and Phillips (1958:33, 37) called a "horizon" or "tradition." This is precisely the point made by Steve Black (1986:262) when he called Toyah a horizon and by LeRoy Johnson (1994:241–42) when he defined the Classic Toyah culture

area. By calling Toyah a culture area, Johnson was trying to get away from considering it as an archaeological phase.

4. To understand Toyah at the broadest scale, archaeologists must first start to examine the Toyah phenomenon at the smallest scale—and this involves social identity at the community level. Social identity is self-ascribed and is recognizable in the archaeological record because people use various social identifiers as a means of demonstrating group identity. Social identifiers may be a specific physical appearance (e.g., hair styles, tattoos, body piercing, clothing, jewelry), distinctive material remains (e.g., various styles of tools, weapons, houses), or unique technologies (ways of doing things). Archaeologically, material remains generated through daily practice include many things that served as social identifiers, which is equivalent to what Schortman (1989:55) called "cultural diacritics" or "salient affiliation diacritics." I prefer the simpler term, "social identifier," which is defined here following Schortman (1989:55): material signifiers that served as symbolic expressions of group identity and facilitated the unambiguous recognition of group affiliation. As such, social identifiers were "highly visible and redundant" to "ensure the rapid recognition of proclaimed identities and decrease the possibility of misidentifications."

The community level is the smallest identifiable social grouping, and this is what we seek initially when we examine social identity. Communities interacted at the regional level, and this is expressed as social fields across vast areas. Using the definition proposed by Murdock (1949:79, as cited in Willey and Phillips 1958:49), a community is "the maximal group of persons who normally reside together in a face-to-face association."

5. The archaeological search for social identity and social fields in prehistory should be done independent of considerations of ethnicity or linguistics, at least initially. Social identity at the community level crosscuts broad ethnic and linguistic groupings, and focusing on these concepts has generally been a distraction for prehistoric archaeological research. This is especially true given the limitation of ethnohistorical records and the nature of the current archaeological evidence. Even if the seventeenth- and eighteenth-century Jumanos may serve as a prototype for constructing behavioral models applicable for examining Toyah archaeology (Kenmotsu 2001:35–37), we should not simply assume that all Toyah manifestations will fit a Jumano hunter-gatherer-trader model. It is likely that archaeologists may never reach a consensus on identifying the ethnicity or language groups of many communities of people who lived 300–700 years ago across much of Texas. Furthermore, it appears that the whole concept of Jumano, as recognized by sixteenth- to eighteenth-century Spaniards, is really not a distinct ethnic group as much as it is a vast social field.

Johnson's "Shared Toyah Area" Concept and Toyah Social Identity

When Johnson (1994) defined the Classic Toyah region of central and south Texas, he also mapped and discussed the Shared Toyah area to the north of the Classic Toyah (see fig. 7.1). This concept was based in large part on the fact that Perdiz arrow points and bone-tempered plainware pottery were commonly found in these northern sites along with other types of contemporaneous arrow points and pottery and decidedly non-Toyah lithic assemblages. He recognized that there was subtle regional differentiation between Toyah sites within the Classic Toyah region, but he also recognized the widespread distribution of "Pan-Toyah" material culture that "helps link together widely spread communities into a single cultural tradition." Clearly, the Greater Toyah Culture Area reflects a large social field where many communities lived and interacted.

Given this view of the Greater Toyah Culture Area, Schortman (1989) would argue that our primary task as archaeologists is to begin the process of identifying communities (i.e., social identity) and the complex interaction networks (i.e., social fields) they participated in. In the northeastern periphery of the Toyah region, Shafer (2006b) has identified sites with mixed Toyah-like and Caddo-like assemblages as the Prairie Caddo, a group that may represent Caddoan people who interacted frequently with the Toyah. In the southern end of the Greater Toyah region, Ricklis (1992, 1995a, 1995b, 1996) has recognized a similar interaction with a distinct (but perhaps fluid) social boundary between the coastal Rockport culture and the south Texas Toyah culture. Given these situations, it is not surprising that Johnson's northern Shared Toyah area may also be characterized as a complex social boundary where the northernmost Classic Toyah groups came in contact with other groups living in the Southern Plains (defined here as the southern end of the Panhandle Plains region, including the southern Llano Estacado and Rolling Plains).

ARCHAEOLOGICAL DIVERSITY IN THE NORTHERN TOYAH AREA

In his 1995 summary of projectile point distributions in Texas, Prewitt (1995:Figure 41) shows that Perdiz points are found across almost all of the state of Texas, except in the uppermost counties in the Texas Panhandle. This evidence also shows that Perdiz points are found far to the north of the Classic Toyah area. Prewitt's 1995 study can now be updated, and a more comprehensive literature review shows that many archaeological sites have produced Perdiz points in the northern portion of Texas (table 7.1). Figure 7.2 shows that Perdiz-producing sites are scattered over a vast portion of the Southern Plains, in what I am calling the northern Toyah region. The question is, what does this northern Toyah phenomenon represent?

The northern Toyah area is characterized by the presence of multiple styles of arrow points and many distinctive pottery types during the period AD 1300–1700

TABLE 7.1. Summary of archaeological sites in the Panhandle-Plains region yielding Perdiz arrow points

County	*Site Name (Number), Component**	*Reference*
Andrews	Salt Cedar (41AD2)	Collins 1968
Callahan	Bear Branch (41CA13)	Katz and Katz 2002
Coleman	Elm Creek (41CN95), Cultural Unit 1	Treece et al. 1993:307–86
Concho	Currie (41CC131), Cultural Unit 2	Treece et al. 1993:307–86
Crosby	Bridwell (41CB27)	Parker 1982, 1990
	Unspecified site	Runkles 1962
Dickens	Dockum Springs (SMU- X41DK1)	Parsons 1967
Floyd	Floydada Country Club (41FL1)	Skinner 1975; Word 1963, 1991
	Montgomery (41FL17)	Word 1965; Northern 1979
Gaines	Unspecified site	Runkles 1962
Garza	Lott (41GR56)	Runkles and Dorchester 1987
	Unspecified site	Runkles 1962
Lamb	Unspecified site	Randall 1970
Lubbock	SPAS-LU29	Brown 1985
Lynn	SPAS-LY4 (near Tahoka Lake)	Riggs 1965
	SPAS-LY42	Hart 1976
	Unspecified site	Runkles 1962
Martin	SPAS-MT40	Gates and Hart 1977
Midland	Bull Hill (41MD2)	Shawn 1975
Randall	Canyon City Club Cave (PPHM-A251)	Hughes 1969
Runnels	Rocky Branch (41RN169), Cultural Unit 1	Treece et al. 1993:31–118
Scurry	Greene Springs	Portis et al. 1968
Sterling	Davis Hackberry Spring (41ST87)	Riemenschneider 1996
Terry	Hogue (41TY2)	Pope 1991
Tom Green	Rush (41TG346), Occupation 4	Quigg and Peck 1995:83–88; Quigg 1997
Winkler	Blue Mountain Rockshelter (no #)	Holden 1938
Yoakum	White	Suhm 1962

Source: Much of the information in this table is derived from site discussions and tabulated data in Boyd (1997:337–430).
* Abbreviations other than trinomial site numbers: PPHM, Panhandle Plains Historical Museum; SMU, Southern Methodist University; SPAS, South Plains Archeological Society.

(Boyd 1997). If we use Prewitt's (1995) data to compare the distributions of various arrow point types, it is clear that Perdiz points appear in the northern Toyah area along with at least five other contemporaneous point styles (fig. 7.3), and these types are found together in many sites. What is most intriguing, as discussed below, is that Perdiz points are often found in archaeological contexts that demonstrate they were used in conjunction with many of these other points.

The diversity of point styles might suggest that people from many different cultural groups were occupying the Texas Southern Plains after 1200 or 1300. If we look at the pottery types found across this same area, we see a similar pattern. The first attempt to look at the diversity of pottery on the Llano Estacado was by Watts (1963). The tabulated ceramic identification data show a large number of Puebloan

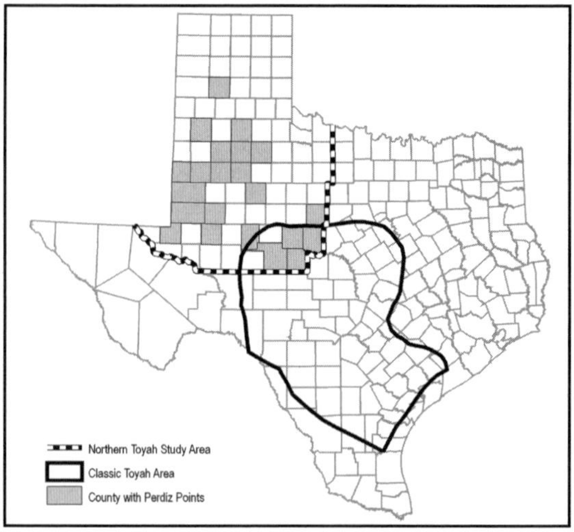

FIGURE 7.2. Distribution of archaeological sites yielding Perdiz arrow points in the Texas Panhandle-Plains region. See table 7.1.

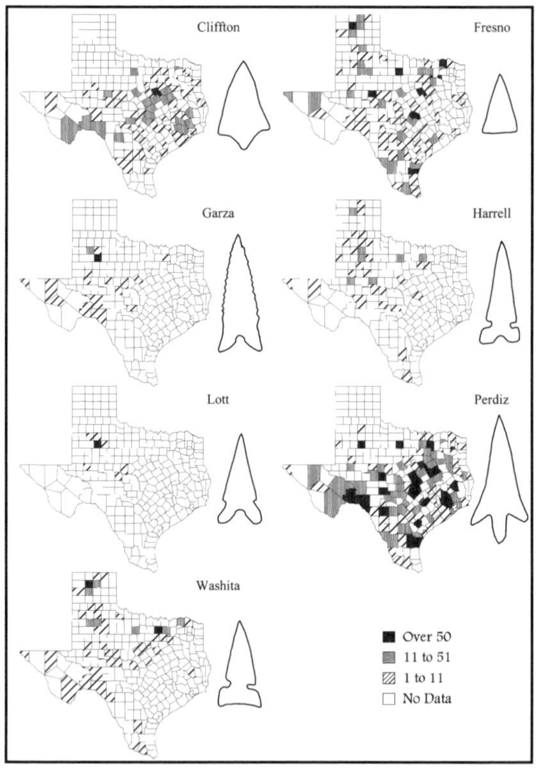

FIGURE 7.3. Geographic distribution of Perdiz and contemporaneous arrow points by county. Map based on Prewitt (1995: Figures 11, 20, 21, 23, 29, 40, and 48). Note that all of these contemporaneous styles are found in the northern Toyah area.

pottery types across his study area on the southern Llano Estacado (table 7.2). Other ceramic styles or types mentioned in the article by Watts are rare in the region but include cord-marked, engraved, and shell-tempered (possible Caddoan), corrugated wares (Reserve Plain Corrugated, Tularosa Indented Corrugated, Seco Corrugated), and Ochoa Brown Smudged Indented.

TABLE 7.2. Age and relative frequency of Puebloan pottery types found on the southern Llano Estacado in Texas

	Relative Frequency				*Age Estimate**			
Ceramic Type	*Very Common*	*Common*	*Rare*	*Very Rare*	*Early Ceramic*	*Middle Ceramic*	*Late Ceramic*	*Unspecified*
Undifferentiated brownware	X				X	X	X	
Jornada Brown		X			X	X	X	
Three Rivers Red-on-terracotta			X			X	X	
El Paso Polychrome		X				X	X	
Chupadero Black-on-white	X					X	X	
Rio Grande Glaze I/A		X				X	X	
Rio GranDe Glaze II/B			X				X	
Rio Grande Glaze III/C			X				X	
Rio Grande Glaze IV/D			X				X	
Rio Grande Glaze V/E		X					X	
Rio Grande Glaze VI/F		X					X	
Tewa Polychrome/Tewa Red		X					X	
Los Lunas Smudged				X				X
Mimbres Black-on-white (undifferentiated)				X	X	X		
Kowina Black-on-white				X				X

Sources: From Boyd (1997:Table 83), based on data from Watts (1963). Age estimates are based on ceramic manufacturing dates presented by Runyan and Hedrick (1987), Snow (1982), and Whalen (1981).

* Approximate dates for periods are Early Ceramic, AD 1100; Middle Ceramic, AD 1100–1300, Late Ceramic, post–AD 1300.

More recently, Wiseman et al. (1999) conducted the Llano Estacado Pottery Project (LEPP) specifically to update the previous ceramic study by Watts (1963). For the LEPP study, ceramic analysts examined pottery found in local collections, primarily from the southern Llano Estacado. There is some overlap with collections studied by Watts, but the LEPP study had a much larger sample. Wiseman et al. (1999) examined 955 sherds from eighty-one sites in twenty-two counties and identified them to ceramic types. The ceramic identifications and temporal assignments for these types are summarized in table 7.3. Of the ceramic types they identified, at least thirteen different types fall into the late ceramic period, being manufactured after about AD 1300 (acknowledging that there are some differences of opinion in the dating of these types and that some of these types were also manufactured before 1300). For the LEPP study, Wiseman (1999; Wiseman et al. 1999) plotted the distributions of the ceramic types by counties, and figure 7.4 is a map summarizing the LEPP study area that I compiled from these data. It shows the diversity of pottery types across this region. Not surprisingly, the counties with the largest site and sherd samples have the greatest number of different types represented. For example, the sample for Lubbock County is 344 sherds from fourteen sites, and it includes ten different types that date between 1300 and 1700, including Toyah bone-tempered plainware. Similarly, the Pecos County sample (95 sherds from sixteen sites) contains Toyah plainware and seven other

TABLE 7.3. Ceramic types identified in the Llano Estacado Pottery Project

Group	Type	Estimated Dates of Manufacture (AD)*	Period of Manufacture and Use**		
			Early Ceramic	Middle Ceramic	Late Ceramic
Painted and Other Service Wares	Chupadero Black-on-white	1050–1500	X	X	X
	Three Rivers (4 types)	1000–1350	X	X	X
	El Paso Polychrome and Brown	1100–1400		X	X
	Red Mesa Black-on-white	850–1125	X		
	White Mountain Red Ware	1000s–1100s	X		
	Rio Grande glazes	1275–1700		X	X
	Tewa Red Ware	1700s–1800s			X
Utility Pottery	Corona Corrugated and Plain	1225–1672		X	X
	Jornada Brown	100–1400	X	X	X
	South Pecos Brown	900–1300	X	X	
	Middle Pecos Micaceous Brown	900–1300	X	X	
	McKenzie Brown	1100–1300		X	
	Ochoa Plain Brown, Corrugated Brown, and Indented	1350–1500			X
Texas Types	Leon Plain or Doss Red Ware	1300s–1700s			X
	Bullard Brushed (Caddoan)	1200–1500		X	X
	Borger Cordmarked	1100–1450		X	X
Other Types	Pueblo/Apache Micaceous	1600s–1700s			X
	Cuahuatitlan Burnished	1600s			X

Sources: For the Llano Estacado Pottery Project, Wiseman et al. (1999) and Wiseman (1999). The finds of Cuahuatitlan Burnished, a Mexican ceramic type, are discussed by Wiseman (1999).

* Most dating is from Wiseman et al. (1999), but dates for some types are from other sources: Bullard Brushed from Suhm and Jelks (1962:21, 95); Leon Plain from Pertulla et al. (1995:195–97); and Pueblo/Apache Micaceous from Perttula et al. (1995:208).

** Approximate dates for periods: Early Ceramic, AD 1100; Middle Ceramic, AD 1100–1300; Late Ceramic, post–AD 1300.

types that date between 1300 and 1700. What is striking about this map is the wide geographic area covered by so many different pottery types that represent diverse cultural traditions.

What does all this arrow point and ceramic data mean? It is acknowledged that there are sample size issues, and the sampling was by no means systematic or random. Taken together, however, both the arrow point and pottery distribution data suggest that many cultural groups ventured onto the southern Llano Estacado or were interacting with groups who lived there. Archaeological evidence suggests that such interactions were common in the Late Prehistoric I period and became even more common after 1200 in the Late Prehistoric II period that correlates with the Toyah phenomenon (Boyd 1997, 2004; Boyd et al. 1993). Ethnohistoric evidence indicates that this area was dynamic in terms of sociocultural interactions during the Protohistoric and historic periods (Boyd 1997:481–86). Numerous studies that have looked at Late Prehistoric, Protohistoric, and historic cultures and exchange on the Southern Plains attest to the complexity of the social interactions (e.g., T. Baugh 1986, 1991; Boyd 2001; Creel 1991; Habicht-Mauche 1992; Hofman 1989; Kessell 1987; Spielmann 1983, 1989; Vehik 1990, 2002). The key

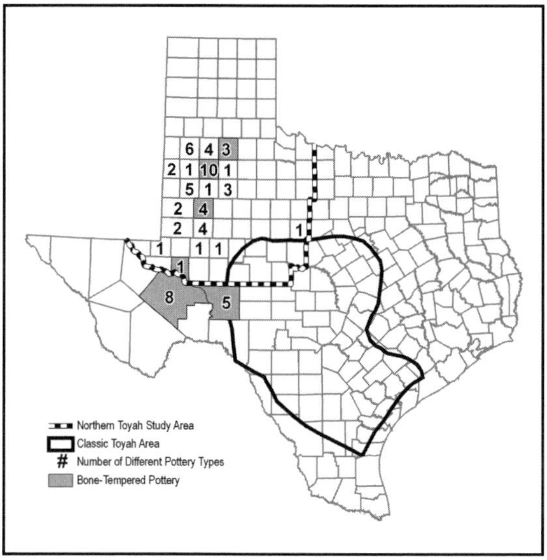

FIGURE 7.4. Distribution of ceramic types, by county, for the Llano Estacado Pottery Project. Data derived from numerous distribution maps in Wiseman et al. (1999) and one map in Wiseman (1999).

point here is that the Toyah groups who lived at the northern edge of the Classic Toyah area were probably among the many groups who ventured onto the Southern Plains, most likely to hunt bison, and some Toyah groups may have settled there. When they did venture onto or settle in the Southern Plains, these northern Toyah peoples were not alone.

There are several sites where the material culture evidence, found in good archaeological contexts, seems to indicate interactions between northern Toyah and Southern Plains groups, as well as the possibility of group cooperation in communal bison hunting ventures. This evidence includes Toyah and Plains tradition pottery types found at the Buckhollow site and Perdiz and other arrow points found together at the Elm Creek, Currie, Rush, and Lott sites. Such evidence gets to the heart of the problem—recognizing social identity in the archaeological record. The evidence from these sites warrants a brief look.

Although the Buckhollow site in Kimble County is not located in the northern Toyah study area (see fig. 1.1), it is one of the northernmost of the Classic Toyah sites. The pottery from Buckhollow is particularly revealing in terms of social identity. Johnson (1994:210) notes that most of the pottery was made by Classic Toyah potters but that at least two vessels "were made by potters who assuredly were not Toyah-culture people, and their affinities are maybe with the Llano Estacado or Rolling Plains of Texas." A third vessel may have been made by a Classic Toyah potter, but it came from "far south of the Edwards Plateau." Regardless of how these nonlocal vessels got to the site, Buckhollow represents a Classic Toyah community that was well connected to outside communities in a larger social field.

Excavations at the Elm Creek site in Coleman County revealed a campsite where bison butchering and hide processing were primary activities (Treece et al. 1993:307–86). The arrow points associated with this site include Fresno (3), Lott (4), and Perdiz (1), and it appears that these points were used contemporaneously.

Excavations at the Currie site in Concho County revealed another bison-processing campsite not far from the Elm Creek site (Treece et al. 1993:119–306). Cultural Unit 2 within the site was interpreted as a Toyah phase occupation, but the point types included Perdiz (44), Fresno (2), Harrell (2), Garza (1), and Cliffton (1). The ceramic assemblage consists of 700 sherds, all of which are bone-tempered, and a small number of these have engraved or incised lines and red paint. An arc-shaped soil anomaly and burned daub concentrations were interpreted as evidence of wattle-and-daub structures (Treece et al. 1993:231–35).

On the basis of his synthesis of Classic Toyah culture, Johnson (1994:260, 286) suggested that Toyah people did not engage in "dedicated large-scale communal hunting" of bison as was done in many parts of the Great Plains. However, about the same time Johnson was writing this, a bison-butchering campsite in Tom Green County called the Rush site was being excavated by Mike Quigg (Quigg 1997; Quigg and Peck 1995). Quigg found evidence of repeated occupations and a dense bison bone bed, called the Occupation 4 level. The excavation was restricted to a 15 m long segment within a 3 m wide pipeline right-of-way. For the Occupation 4 level, Quigg (1997:153) concluded that "it is evident from the excellent context that Perdiz, Harrell, Garza, and Cliffton projectile points co-occur and are contemporaneous in this one brief occupation at the Rush site." Quigg and Peck (1995:i) further interpreted the situation: "Direct association of three different types of projectile points coupled with the postulated frequency of 50 killed bison implies this location may have resulted from a combined effort by several culturally distinct hunting groups gathered together to perform a communal bison kill operation in the fall (November)."

Thus, this site provides the first evidence that northern Toyah groups were participants in a Southern Plains social field that may have involved cooperative communal hunt. Logically, there is no reason to doubt that there are many other sites in the northern Toyah area where communal hunting was done, but finding such superb contextual evidence as at the Rush site is rare indeed.

The Garza site is apparently a short-term campsite where Garza complex peoples were involved in bison processing (Runkles 1964). No Perdiz points were found there, but 13 Garza, 15 Harrell, and several Fresno points were recovered. In contrast, the Lott site, a campsite located 1.7 km away with a large inventory of bison bone, yielded a diverse assemblage of points and pottery (Runkles and Dorchester 1987): 56 Lott, 49 Garza, 58 Perdiz, and 6 Harrell. The pottery recovered consists of one sherd probably from Oklahoma (Edwards complex), 75 sherds of probable Caddoan pottery with fingernail punctate decorations, 60 sherds of probable Caddoan incised pottery, 1 sherd of Rio Grande Glaze I, and 500 sherds of bone-tempered plainware. Of particular importance, the original investigators noted that each of the three main point types—Lott, Garza, and Perdiz—came from separate areas within the site, hinting that multiple groups were occupying the site simultaneously (Boyd 1997:400–402). Burned daub with impressions suggested the presence of wattle-and-daub structures at the Lott site. Unfortunately, the published archaeological data are not sufficient to allow researchers to evaluate the interpretation of spatially separated groups, but a similar situation has been documented along the Texas coast. Ricklis (1996:97–99) considers the Melon site (41RF21) to be an "encampment shared by coastal [Rockport-Karankawa] and inland [Toyah] peoples for the purpose of hunting and processing bison and deer." As at the Lott site, this interpretation is based on a distinct horizontal pattern of pottery distributions, with the northern half of the site dominated by bone-tempered wares and the southern half dominated by Rockport wares.

COMMUNITIES AND SOCIAL FIELDS IN THE NORTHERN TOYAH AREA

In light of the evidence presented above, I conclude that the Southern Plains was home to many different social groups who interacted in complex ways that are not well understood. In terms of the social identity concept suggested by Arnn, the Southern Plains was occupied by an unknown number of distinct communities of people from very different sociocultural backgrounds throughout the period 1300–1700. During this time, the northern Toyah area seems to represent a major boundary between two or more large social fields that include, at a minimum: the Classic Toyah and a Southern Plains social field. Viewed more broadly, the northern Toyah area could also represent the eastern edge of a frontier Pueblo social field and the western edge of an extended Caddoan social field.

These social fields represent the exchange of ideas, technologies, and materials between communities, and they indicate that the Late Prehistoric social interactions and exchange systems in the Southern Plains were quite complex indeed. If a social field can be defined by the material culture that was shared by communities who interacted regularly through various alliance networks, and if the northern Toyah area is a zone where multiple social fields merge, then this region is ideal for the study of social fields and territorial boundaries. I agree with Schortman (1989) when he argues that exchange systems and territorial boundaries should be a major focus of archaeological research.

In reality, there is no single line that defines the cultural boundary of one social field from another. Because of the cultural dynamics during the Late Prehistoric and Protohistoric periods, we must view the northern Toyah area as a rather broad zone in which two or more social fields overlapped. It was a zone where Toyah-influenced communities interacted with Southern Plains communities for more than 400 years, and this zone was undoubtedly an area of fluid social movement and constantly changing social alliances. In such areas, we may expect not only complex exchange networks between allies (e.g., Baugh and Ericson 1994) but also conflicts and violence between social groups. There are, in fact, several burials that have Perdiz points as cause of death in the Toyah region (Prewitt 1981:83, 1982c:50–51; Rogers 2000). Shafer (2006:40) describes the central Texas Balcones Escarpment zone as "a seriously contested region" from AD 1000 to 1300, just preceding the advent of the Toyah phenomenon. Evidence of Late Prehistoric violence is fairly common across the Southern Plains (Boyd 1997:329–31,

364, 2004:324–29; Brooks 1994; Prewitt 1982c:42–43, Figure 13, Table 4; Seacat 1997:92–123; Vehik 1990, 2002; and see Speth and Newlander, this volume). As suggested by Keeley (1996) in *War before Civilization: The Myth of the Peaceful Savage*, it is not likely that so many different groups could have converged to hunt bison in the Southern Plains during the past millennium without some amount of conflict and warfare arising. The fact that alliances, exchange systems, and territorial boundaries were extremely dynamic is what makes the Late Prehistoric archaeology of the Southern Plains, and the study of the northern Toyah phenomenon, so challenging but also so exciting.

There is evidence for considerable regional cultural diversity within the vast Classic Toyah area (see Johnson's 1994: 265–68 discussion "Evidence for Toyah Regionalism"). Most notably, sites in the northern part of the Classic Toyah area appear to be different from those in the southern part. Bison remains and bison-hunting technology (points, beveled knives, and end scrapers) are best represented in the northern sites nearest the Great Plains. The northernmost Classic Toyah sites exhibit more Plains-like traits, such as four-beveled knives (instead of two-beveled) and sandstone shaft abraders. Regional diversity also is evident in Classic Toyah pottery. Some variability in composition is due to differences in local geology, but variations in vessel form and decorative style are due to geographic location and proximity to outside influences. Caddoan-like decorative techniques, for example, are more common on Toyah pottery in the eastern portion of the Edwards Plateau.

There is little evidence that Classic Toyah peoples traded directly with southwestern Puebloan cultures, although a few sherds of sandy paste pottery found in northern sites may have come from Puebloan or Plains sources. Micaceous pottery, generally attributed to Apachean peoples (Eiselt 2006), is notably absent from Toyah sites. Classic Toyah peoples living along the eastern margin of their homeland left Caddoan potsherds behind in the sites they abandoned. It was, however, apparently traded with Caddoan peoples on a more or less regular basis, with some Caddoan pottery even making its way as far west as Abilene and San Angelo (Creel 1991; Kibler, this volume). It is presumed that the Toyah-Caddo trade (or Toyah-Prairie Caddo trade, as recently defined by Shafer 2006b) involved bison meat and hides exchanged for crops, but there is no hard evidence for this type of mutualistic exchange. What is clear is that Classic Toyah peoples, unlike some of their Southern Plains contemporaries (i.e., Garza, Edwards, and Wheeler complex peoples), were not middlemen in any extensive Puebloan-Caddoan interaction sphere, nor does it appear that they participated directly in the Southern Plains-Pueblo exchange (Spielmann 1983, 1991a). In contrast, it appears that the northern Toyah communities may have interacted with many Southern Plains groups, especially the Garza complex peoples. The Garza complex is rather restricted geographically, and these people were well connected with the southwestern Puebloan peoples to the west, and to a lesser extent with Caddoan-influenced groups to the east.

In a regional ceramic study, Leonard (2006) examined Puebloan glazeware pottery (dating to ca. 1450–1700) found in Garza and Tierra Blanca sites on and adjacent to the Llano Estacado. She mapped the distributions of temporally distinctive glazeware styles (Glazes A through F based on bowl rim forms) manufactured in different Puebloan source areas (Pecos, Salinas, Galisteo, and other) relative to the various sites attributed to the Garza and Tierra Blanca archaeological complexes. In the northern part of the Texas Panhandle, Tierra Blanca sites contain Glaze C and D wares made almost exclusively at pueblos in the Galisteo Basin. In contrast, the more southerly Garza complex sites contain Glaze C, D, E, and F wares that were made in all three of the main Puebloan source areas—Pecos, Salinas, and Galisteo. Furthermore, different Garza sites have varying proportions of glazewares from these different sources, but the ceramic assemblage at each individual site is usually dominated by one source. At one Garza site, more than 90 percent of the glazewares are from Galisteo, and two other sites have more than 50 percent Galisteo pottery. Two sites are dominated by glazewares from the Salinas district, and two sites have between 70 and 100 percent glaze pottery made at Pecos Pueblo. Finally, two Garza sites have substantial amounts of glaze pottery from both Pecos Pueblo and the Salinas district (more than 30 percent of both types). Acknowledging some limitations due to sample size, this evidence led Leonard (2006:251–52) to conclude that there were "relatively formal ties of exchange between individual Plains and Pueblo communities" and that "the long-term persistence of these ties may, in turn, have been maintained through such social institutions as marriage . . . or the inherited trade partnership." In simple terms, this means that the Garza complex most likely encompasses many distinct communities. The interactions between these Garza communities and distinct communities of northern Toyah peoples are of considerable interest.

The very nature of Toyah regionalism suggests that there were many distinct communities of people dispersed across much of Texas. These groups shared many generic aspects of Toyah material culture, but this simply reflects the fact that these communities were connected to one another through a vast social field. In conclusion, current archaeological evidence indicates that the northern Toyah area is a boundary zone between communities from two or more distinct social fields that evolved from significantly different cultural backgrounds. As I view it, the northern Toyah region of AD 1300–1700 is quite analogous to the Prairie Caddo region (Shafer 2006). Although Shafer's work refers to an earlier period (AD 1000–1300), he concludes that the archaeological evidence indicates the presence of a complex boundary zone between the central Texas and Caddoan social fields.

Thoughts on Future Archaeological Research in the Northern Toyah Area

This final section examines several interrelated aspects of the Toyah phenomenon, focusing somewhat on the role of communal bison hunting in the northern Toyah region. Archaeological evidence for communal hunting is of considerable importance because it relates to human social organization, group identities, and territorial boundaries between groups. This evidence from the northern Toyah area may well shed light on the ultimate origins of the peoples we call Toyah, especially if we apply more rigorous archaeological field and analysis methods to address the broader regional research issues.

COMMUNAL HUNTING, SOCIAL ORGANIZATION, AND TERRITORIAL BOUNDARIES

For Plains archaeologists, the concepts of communal hunting, social organization, and territorial boundaries are intimately related. Many prehistoric and historic Plains peoples were large-scale bison collectors who used a logistical resource procurement strategy (Binford 1980:10–12). For many groups, this involved seasonal communal hunts where relatively large numbers of people worked together to trap and kill large numbers of animals. Bamforth (1988) describes the complex relationships among climate (particularly rainfall and temperature), grassland habitats, and ungulate ecology (particularly bison migration and aggregation patterns) on the Great Plains. He goes on to explain how humans adapted to increasing bison populations by adopting communal hunting methods. The shift to more sophisticated hunting methods required people to have a more complex social structure than was needed for a simpler hunter-gatherer lifestyle. Frison (1978:243–48) notes that people could not begin to consider communal hunting until bison populations had reached a minimum critical level. When animals were too few in number, communal hunting was simply too much effort for too little return.

Schortman (1989:59–61) suggests that archaeologists should focus on recognizing social identity by defining the cultural interactions between social groups that are most evident along their territorial boundaries. The exchange systems that archaeologists are fond of studying are only the physical manifestation of social alliances. It is notable that the northern Toyah area is buffalo country, extending from the northern edge of the Edwards Plateau onto the southern Rolling Plains and Llano Estacado. For any groups living or traveling through this area between 1300 and 1700, buffalo hunting would have been an important subsistence activity, and it is likely that many social alliances were formed so that the participants could maintain access to buffalo hunting grounds. All archaeological evidence suggests that the bison population in the Southern Plains was quite high after about 1100 (e.g., Dillehey 1974), and many groups of people became bison hunters (e.g., Boyd 1997; Boyd et al. 1993 [Tierra Blanca and Garza complexes]; Johnson 1994; Quigg and Peck 1995 [northern Toyah area]). As mentioned above, one response to substantial bison populations in the Southern Plains grasslands was for people to adopt communal hunting methods (Bamforth 1988:128, Forbis 1978; Frison 1978:243–48). This required changes in their social organization and may have frequently involved cooperative hunting by multiple groups. Hence, one important research avenue for the northern Toyah area relates to identifying archaeological evidence for communal hunting and the existence of cooperative hunting by different groups. This involves identifying communities of people and defining their territorial boundaries.

The environments people lived in, including the relative population density and behaviors of large game animals within their area, were key factors dictating how people made a living. Bison, antelope, and deer are the primary large game animals found in the Greater Toyah area, and they are well represented in Toyah archaeological assemblages. However, these animals were not of equal importance all across this vast and diverse region. The extreme environmental diversity of the Greater Toyah area, along with different habitat preferences and behavioral characteristics of these animals, meant that the population densities of bison, antelope, and deer varied from region to region. People could hunt large game animals using a variety of different techniques, but the choice of techniques was not random. The population density and behavioral characteristics of each animal dictated the selection of hunting methods.

Archaeologically, it appears that Toyah peoples probably hunted more deer than bison over most of central Texas, whereas bison was hunted more intensively in the northern Toyah area. This presumably reflects the relative population densities of the animals, with deer having been more plentiful across most of the Edwards Plateau and bison having been more abundant in the grasslands of the Southern Plains. When bison populations were sufficiently large, as they tended to be in Plains grassland environments, communal hunting was often selected as the principal hunting technique. Opportunistic hunting and communal hunting are very different ways of procuring large grazing animals, and they denote very different types of social organization (Bamforth 1988:125–28). The choice selected by each group affected how people organized their society and is a key factor that must be considered if one hopes to recognize social identity and communities in the archaeological record.

DEVELOPING MODELS OF SOCIAL IDENTITY, INTERREGIONAL INTERACTION, AND COMMUNAL BISON HUNTING

In the future, archaeologists must begin to develop explanatory models for cultural interactions in the Southern Plains using social identity as the organizing theme. A wide variety of hunter-gatherer theoretical orientations—such as behavioral ecology, optimal foraging strategy, diet breadth, and collector-forager models—have been proposed and remain valid research tools (e.g., Bettinger 1991; Binford 1980, 1983; Kelly 1980, 1983, 1995; Winterhalder and Smith 1981). Any of these, and many others yet to be developed, may be employed for hunter-gatherer research that is focused on social identity. Although I do not propose any specific models or formulate testable hypotheses herein, I believe that we need to construct explanatory models at different scales in order to begin to understand the sociopolitical complexities of the northern Toyah area. Some models may require examination of material remains to recognize social identity at the local scale. Other explanatory models need to be regional or pan-regional in scale and require intersite comparisons across a larger area in order to define social fields and community interactions.

In his article, Schortman (1989) defines five research issues that provide an excellent framework for examining the northern Toyah phenomenon. These research issues were formulated specifically for looking at societies that were more complex and had a higher degree of social stratification than most hunter-gatherer groups, but the concepts can be applied to societies at various levels of social complexity. I see no reason why these five research issues cannot be applied directly to the study of social fields using the northern Toyah phenomenon as well as to all types of egalitarian hunter-gatherer communities (1989:59–61):

Causal relations: "To what extent is there a causal relation between the development of sociopolitical complexity and the appearance of salient-identity [exchange] networks transcending local social boundaries?"

Interaction increases social stratification: "As intersocietal interaction increases, there is a greater dependence among societies, especially the elites, for needed goods."

Warfare and intraidentity competition: "The sharing of identity may even facilitate intraidentity competition by providing a common set of criteria against which to measure the relative accomplishments of the participants." In addition, "people who share an affiliation . . . may compete with each other even to the point of warfare."

Trade as communication: "It is important to realize . . . that trade is embedded within a broader context of communication and that the goods themselves may well be as important for their symbolic meaning as for their quotidian uses."

Nonelite interaction: "It is at least possible for nonelite, under certain circumstances, to engage in intense contacts which transcend local social boundaries and, hence, form interregional salient identities."

I believe that these five research issues form a rather appealing contextual framework for building models applicable to the study of social identity and interregional interactions in the northern Toyah area. The theme of warfare is, for example, of considerable importance but has not been examined closely in the context of northern Toyah. Similarly, the concept of trade as communication is one that has not been stressed for hunter-gatherer groups, with rare exceptions (e.g., Hegmon and Fisher 1991). Studies of Late Prehistoric and Protohistoric exchange provide an important baseline for understanding Southern Plains groups and regional interactions (e.g., Creel 1991; Habicht-Mauche 1987; Spielmann 1983, 1989; Vehik 2002), but the pivotal role of information exchange has not been adequately addressed. In a review of the Jumano trader Juan Sabeata and evidence for Protohistoric interregional trade, J. Charles Kelley (1955:981) observed that the traffic in news was, "perhaps, more important culturally than the bison products, the salt, the bows and arrows, the turquoise and cotton, the feathers, and shells, that made up the tangible currency of trade." Because hunter-gatherer peoples have long used exchange systems as means of maintaining critical social ties to minimize risk in variable environments, trade as information is an especially appealing theme for organizing archaeological research. So much of what was traded were perishable remains that are lost in the archaeological record, but indirect evidence of exchange survives in the form of ideas and technologies spread by diffusion.

In conclusion, it may be surmised that during the period from 1300 to 1700, the Southern Plains was home to many dozens of separate communities of people who were organized into complex social fields. These communities interacted in many different ways that ranged from cooperative communal hunting ventures to elaborate exchange networks to raiding and open warfare. During this dynamic period of prehistory, the communities involved came and went, and the interactions between communities were constantly changing. In the midst of all this change, and for a brief period of no more than a few hundred years, northern Toyah communities were among those who lived on the Southern Plains.

POSSIBLE NORTHERN ORIGINS FOR TOYAH

One research question that warrants consideration is related to the search for Toyah social identity. What are the origins of the Classic Toyah material culture? Except for Perdiz points and bone-tempered pottery, Classic Toyah material culture is similar to that of the many Southern Plains Village cultures. When, how, and from where the Plains-adapted toolkit made its way into Toyah culture is not known, but a northern origin is suspected. It has been suggested that the Perdiz arrow point and distinctive bone-tempered pottery probably originated from slightly different sources. Using data from the Buckhollow and other Toyah sites, Johnson (1994) examined these questions: Who were the Classic Toyah people? From where did they originate? He did not accept the idea of indigenous development for Classic Toyah culture. Rather, he stated, "My preference is for the notion that Classic Toyah material culture, with its unique pottery, was first brought into its homeland by outsiders who may have been members of one or a small number of related social groups." He does not propose any prototypes for the Perdiz arrow point style, but he thinks it denotes use of a compound cane arrow shaft that might be "more a Southwestern or northeast Mexican (or even Southeastern) implement than a Plains device." Considering the pottery, he sees no real conclusive evidence of genesis in the use of bone temper, but he acknowledges that this technology may have come from "Caddoan-speaking areas of the prairie-plains and Woodlands." Stylistically, however, he believes Toyah pottery has many traits that were derived from the Jornada Mogollon tradition (Johnson 1994:268, 271–81).

When all the evidence was considered, Johnson suggested that Toyah culture may have come from multiple sources and offered the following conclusions (1994:277):

- "The ultimate homeland of most Toyah buffalo-hunting and bison-processing tools of stone is the Plains Village area."
- Perdiz arrow points "cannot be traced to that or any other homeland unless it be far western Texas or eastern Chihuahua," where the Perdiz points may predate the Perdiz points in the Edwards Plateau.
- "Compound cane arrows may not derive from the Plains but from the Southwest or northeastern Mexico."
- Bone tempering may have come "from the northern plains or prairie-plains or even the Caddo-speaking area of the Woodlands, although perhaps by a very circuitous route," or "Toyah immigrants may have developed it themselves."
- "Classic Toyah vessel forms . . . as well as several quite specific manufacturing and firing methods point to the U.S. Southwest and northeastern Mexico in a general way, and more specifically to the large region where the various Mogollon/Mogollonized pottery traditions developed. Of course, Southwestern pottery occurs on the Southern Plains, and the route of this Mogollon-like pottery into the Toyah regions may have been via the Llano Estacado or the plains southeast of there.
- "Late-period Toyah tenoned olla handles . . . may have a protohistoric northern prairie-plains origin.

Johnson ultimately concluded that "it is too soon to answer the question about where the first Toyah people originally came from. . . . Yet the Southern Plains cannot be eliminated as the original homeland, since that area was strongly influenced by Mogollonized people in pre-Toyah times" (1994:287). Following up on this idea, I suggested that the Palo Duro complex is a likely candidate as an ancestor for many traits of the Classic Toyah culture (Boyd 1997:333–34, 2004:329). It seems logical to look toward the Southern Plains for a culture that immediately predates the Toyah phase and had roots in, or was extensively influenced by, the Jornada Mogollon of southeastern New Mexico. The Palo Duro complex, and perhaps the related Blow Out Mountain phase in the Callahan Divide region defined by Creel (1990:15–16), may fit this bill. Archaeological evidence suggests that northern Toyah communities were rather familiar with the Southern Plains—an area where bison hunting became a dominant subsistence activity after 1100 or 1200. At the time of its disappearance from the Caprock Canyonlands between 1100 and 1300, the Palo Duro culture possessed a possible prototype arrow point style (i.e., stemmed arrow points typed as Deadman's or Alba- and Bonham-like), a connection with Mogollon pottery-making technology and styles, and the initial contact with Plains bison-hunting tools and technology. This is precisely the time when the Toyah culture suddenly appeared in central and south Texas.

A few research questions related to social fields immediately come to mind:

- Was the Palo Duro complex the source for one or more of the traits of the Classic Toyah culture?
- Was the disappearance of the Palo Duro complex in the Southern Plains and the sudden appearance of Classic Toyah culture in central and south Texas related to climatic events that caused a population increase and southward spread of Southern Plains bison?
- Did northern Toyah peoples adopt communal bison-hunting techniques as a result of these changes?
- Did Palo Duro peoples migrate southward to become the earliest manifestations of the Toyah phase?
- What is the relationship between the Palo Duro complex and the more southerly Blow Out Mountain phase, and what bearing does this have on Toyah origins?

All of these questions relate directly to social identity. Defining these relationships hinges on our ability to recognize the differences between social groups and trace social identifiers through time and across space (admittedly a task much easier stated than accomplished).

ARCHAEOLOGICAL METHODOLOGY FOR NORTHERN TOYAH RESEARCH

My final thoughts on archaeological research for northern Toyah relate to method. Current archaeological data on Toyah sites in the Southern Plains are insufficient to begin even a cursory examination of social identity, and we have only the vaguest concepts of the extent and complexity of group interactions. For example, of all the sites where Perdiz points have been found (see table 7.1), most are known only through surface collections or minimal testing, and extensive excavations have been done at only a few of them. Thus, the sample of data useful for detailed comparative studies is extremely small for such a large area. Although it would be wonderful to initiate some type of systematic regional archaeological site sampling as advocated by Binford (1964), this is not likely to happen. Most archaeological research will likely be done in CRM contexts, and sites will be chosen for investigation on the basis of threats by development rather than regional research concerns. To maximize the data potential for future investigations involving northern Toyah sites, bear in mind the following considerations:

Regardless of the level of investigation undertaken, more (and more accurate) chronological data are essential. Certainly the resolution of current dating techniques, like radiocarbon analysis and optically stimulated luminescence, is less than desired. But many dates are needed to establish, with a fair degree of confidence, the age and duration of occupations at each Toyah site.

Sampling is critical. Archaeological sites are a sample of human activity across a landscape, and features and artifacts are samples of activity areas and residue left behind at a site. To investigate social identity issues, we must have large samples of excavated sites in a local area and multiple clusters of excavated local sites within a region. As noted by Binford (1964) more than forty years ago, for a single site investigation to be useful for such purposes it must be investigated using horizontally extensive excavations that produce large samples of artifacts and features that enable inferences of site function, spatial patterning of activities, and the like.

We need better definition of site types, and we need to be able to recognize which social groups created them. We expect social identity to be most clearly expressed at residential base camps, but we must work toward identifying the full range of special-activity sites associated with northern Toyah communities.

We need to search systematically for evidence of structures and site layout at residential bases (see Johnson 1997:56–62, for a discussion of prehistoric dwellings across greater central Texas). Hunter-gatherer houses, such as those found at Toyah occupations mentioned above, will be ephemeral and difficult to identify. In some cases, such as at site 41HY209-T, the only surviving evidence of structures may well be the spatial patterning of artifacts and faunal remains discarded around a dwelling (Ricklis 1994:283–84).

The foods that people ate and the technologies used to gather, process, and store them are important social identifiers. We need more thorough studies of all types of subsistence data to understand fully geographic and temporal differences in the subsistence technologies and diets of northern Toyah communities (Dering 2008). This includes all types of botanical and faunal evidence in conjunction with studies of artifacts and features representing subsistence technology. An emphasis on the social aspects (e.g., communal feasting) of subsistence is needed to tie remains to social identity.

Extensive sampling and detailed analyses of ceramic assemblages are critical to understanding Toyah regionalism and social identity. This must include analyzing vessels forms, manufacturing traits and decorative styles, and geochemical composition through time for the Greater Toyah area.

More intensive sampling and analysis of archaeobotanical remains from all types of sites are critical. This should include a great deal more flotation to recover charred plant remains and all types of specialized studies (pollen, phytolith, starch grains, isotope data, etc.). Special attention should be paid to looking for evidence of cultigens and incipient agriculture.

Whether animal bones are found at residential bases or at specialized hunting camps or butchering/processing sites, we need more complete and thorough analyses of faunal data following the lead of researchers like Frison (1978), Quigg and Peck (1995), and Speth (1983). There is considerable disparity in the quality of published faunal data for previously excavated sites. For example, the faunal data published for the Rush site (Quigg and Peck 1995) are very good, whereas the faunal data for the Garza and Lott sites are not adequate to allow reanalysis or reinterpretation.

Finding, investigating, and analyzing human burials constitute an important avenue of research for the northern Toyah region. Comparative interregional mortuary studies, like those described by Beck (1995) and Perttula (2001), are critical to understanding social identity and cultural interactions in the northern Toyah region; for discussions of important Late Prehistoric II burials in the northern Toyah area, see (Boyd 1997:350–77, 418), Collins (1971:90), and Seacat (1997:92–123). In his study of social interactions in the central Texas Prairie Caddo region, which represents a good sociopolitical analogy for the northern Toyah area, Shafer (2006b) concluded that "evidence for violence should be an integral part of bioarchaeological studies." The study of prehistoric mortuary remains in central and south Texas by Perttula (2001) shows clearly the value of the evidence for interregional exchange and violence associated with burials. Evidence for prehistoric social identity, social fields, and group interactions will be expressed more clearly in human burials than in any other class of archaeological remains.

EIGHT

Plains-Pueblo Interaction

A VIEW FROM THE "MIDDLE"

John D. Speth and Khori Newlander

Bloom Mound, gutted by vocational archaeologists and pothunters more than sixty years ago, is a tantalizing enigma on the prehistoric landscape of southeastern New Mexico. Despite its apparent diminutive size (only ten rooms were known to local amateurs) and its remote location far out in the grasslands of southeastern New Mexico, Bloom was tightly enmeshed in developments in the broader Pueblo world, producing the easternmost record of copper bells as well as quantities of turquoise, obsidian, marine shells, and ceramics from as far afield as northern Chihuahua, western and southwestern New Mexico, and southeastern Arizona. The University of Michigan's excavations at this intriguing little trading entrepot have shown not only that Bloom is larger than all of us had once thought but that its florescence in the 1300s and 1400s provides us with a priceless record of the early stages of intensive interaction between peoples of the Southern Plains and the Pueblos to the west. Bloom is also revealing the heavy price the villagers may have paid for engaging in this interaction, as they came into intense, sometimes deadly competition over access to bison herds, and perhaps access to trading partners, with other Southern Plains groups, some from as far away as central Texas and the Texas Panhandle.

To most, whether tourist or long-term Southwest resident, the Roswell area epitomizes the "middle of nowhere." Most archaeologists, it would appear, share much the same view. And in New Mexico, when archaeologists talk about "the Southwest," you can be pretty sure they are thinking about "the Pueblos," spelled with a capital "P." Were you to ask them where they would place the eastern edge of the Pueblo world prior to contact with Euroamericans, most would agree that it stopped at the last major range of mountains fronting the Plains—the Sangre de Cristos in the north, followed to the south by the Sandias and Manzanos, and finally by the Sacramentos (the Guadalupes, which lie still farther to the south, are generally excluded). Whatever might be found to the east of the mountains is something else, but almost certainly not Pueblo.

Even the culture historical framework used by Southwestern archaeologists reflects eastern New Mexico's perceived marginality in the prehistoric scheme of things. Thus, we have the Mogollon culture area, a fully respectable division within the cultural geography of the ancient Southwest, and one that has been with us for decades. Occupying much of southwestern New Mexico, the Mogollon stands front and center with its equals, the Anasazi and Hohokam, and features prominently in any serious discussion of Southwestern prehistory (e.g., Cordell 1997).

Moving eastward across southern New Mexico, we come to the Jornada branch of the Mogollon (or Jornada Mogollon for short), an entity centered on the El Paso area, and one that is not so mainstream even though it too has been with us for a long time (Lehmer 1948; Miller and Kenmotsu 2004). The Jornada Mogollon does get discussed by archaeologists who work outside the Jornada area, but most often as a kind of backwater occupied by "less-developed" cultures that somehow missed the boat while important things were happening elsewhere. Cordell's (1997) most recent edition of the *Archaeology of the Southwest* clearly shows just how little impact Jornada archaeology has had on mainstream thinking in the profession; using the index as a guide, in the book's 522 pages only two paragraphs are devoted to the Jornada Mogollon.

Moving still farther to the east, we come to the eastern extension of the Jornada branch of the Mogollon. This mouthful, which encompasses most of southeastern New Mexico and a bit of adjacent Texas, is largely the creation of local amateurs who for years unsuccessfully sought help from mainstream Southwesternists but were pretty much ignored (Corley 1965; Leslie 1979; Miller and Kenmotsu 2004). Then, from the early 1980s onward, the area was given over to contract archaeologists who have been buried up to their proverbial ears pounding out an endless stream of "boilerplate" surveys of well pads, pipeline right-of-ways, power lines, and potash mining leases. Although thousands of "sites" (read "picked-over, deflated, surface manifestations") have been recorded in State files, to the consternation of both State and federal officials, there still is no real "prehistory" for this vast area, no archaeological record that provides palpable grist for the mills of mainstream theorizing about cultural developments in the Southwest or elsewhere in North America. The area gets occasional lip service in broader treatments of the Southwest, but it remains very poorly known and, for the most part, ignored. Not surprisingly, the post-Paleoindian archaeology of southeastern New Mexico is not even mentioned in Cordell's (1997) text.

From the perspective of the Southern Plains archaeologist looking the other way, the picture is not all that different, though when viewed from the east what constitutes "interesting" now lies squarely in the Texas Panhandle and Edwards Plateau, and in the adjacent Rolling Plains of Oklahoma, with the cultural record attracting less and less attention as one's focus drifts progressively westward off the Llano Estacado (e.g., T. Baugh 1986; Hofman et al. 1989; Hughes 1989).

In sum, Roswell and the stretches of the Pecos Valley that lie to the north and south, a strip of land some 250 km wide, really does lie in a kind of scholarly "no-man's land," not just in reference to the area's intermediate geographic setting but in terms of its perceived importance to archaeologists in their discussions of what was going on in the "core" of their respective culture areas. What then, if anything, makes this "middle ground" interesting and worth considering? The answer is simple—Plains-Pueblo interaction—a topic that has garnered a respectable share of scholarly attention over the years by historians and archaeologists alike (Spielmann 1983, 1991b). The Spanish chronicles provide tantalizing, though frustratingly terse, descriptions of nomads coming off the plains, leading veritable "trains" of heavily laden dogs, some dragging travois, en route to the Pueblos to overwinter and trade. Other accounts tell of raids on the Pueblos, when these same nomads (or their close cousins) stole food, livestock, and women from the farmers, took hapless captives as slaves, and sometimes sacked the homes and villages of their erstwhile trading partners. But regardless of whether one is a Plains archaeologist or a Southwestern archaeologist, both stand (metaphorically speaking) in the heart of their respective culture areas and gaze into the hazy distance toward the heart of the other's culture area, envisioning the homelands of these ancient partners-in-trade (and conflict) to have been separated from each other by a vast "hinterland" that was essentially uninhabited, at least on any sort of permanent or significant basis. Thus, for Southern Plains bison hunters to trade with the Pueblos, and vice versa, the determined travelers had only to trudge across the vacant lands that separated them. Even today, we suspect a lot of the automobile traffic moving east or west between New Mexico and Texas is guided by motivations that are not all that different.

The apparent emptiness of the terrain between the western edge of the Caprock or Llano Estacado and the eastern fringes of the Pueblo world may be more illusion than reality, an artifact of the lack of sustained, problem-oriented archaeological research throughout much of the area. Other factors have contributed to this illusion as well. One is the a priori assumption that what does exist in this vast "no-man's land" is ephemeral, insubstantial, and hence basically uninteresting. Another stems from a methodological uncertainty—the current difficulty in determining a terminal date for the manufacture of Rio Grande Glaze A. For years, work in southeastern New Mexico has been guided by the assumption that the absence of glazewares later than Glaze A (the earliest type in the traditional Rio Grande sequence) meant that much of the region had been abandoned by around AD 1400. There is a growing suspicion among Southwestern ceramic specialists, however, that Glaze A continued in use well after 1400, perhaps to as late as 1500 or even later (Eckert 2006; Snow 1997, 2007). If this revised dating should turn out to be correct, the absence of the so-called later glaze types in southeastern New Mexico may tell us little or nothing about whether the area was occupied or abandoned by village horticulturalists during the fifteenth and sixteenth centuries.

Regardless, there are no Chaco Canyons or Mesa Verdes in the Pecos Valley; but the archaeological record is sufficient to show us that during the Late Prehistoric period there was a fairly substantial presence of peoples there, and in the area that is the focus of this particular endeavor—Roswell—the local inhabitants lived in multiroom communities of abutting pitrooms or above-ground adobe structures and practiced a semisedentary mixed economy based on farming, gathering, and hunting (Speth 2004). Of particular interest in the Roswell case is the abundant evidence for bison hunting, many of the animals apparently being taken at considerable distances from the villages; as well as quantities of Southern Plains cherts, particularly Edwards Plateau and Tecovas or Tecovas look-alikes; nonlocal ceramics from as far afield as southwestern New Mexico, southeastern Arizona, and northern Chihuahua; marine shell from the Gulf of Cortez; Jemez-area obsidian and turquoise; and even a macaw, northern cardinal (another bird with red plumage of nonlocal origin), and several copper bells (Kelley 1984; Vargas 1995). These "exotics" provide ample testimony to the fact that the folks in Roswell were not isolated hillbillies who knew not of the goings-on in other parts of the Southwest or Southern Plains. They were bona fide participants in Plains-Pueblo interaction, and their communities sat squarely between the High Plains and the Pueblo world (however defined), offering both opportunities and potential obstacles to others who wanted to engage in interregional trade. We need to explore the role of these "middleman" communities within the broader social, political, and economic matrix in which such interaction was embedded in order to better understand how Plains-Pueblo interaction came about and how it may have influenced what was going on within the culture areas—Plains and Pueblo—that bounded southeastern New Mexico on its eastern and western flanks.

Late Prehistoric Roswell

Most of us know Roswell because of its dubious link to little green men from outer space. Beyond that, tourists on summer vacation who find themselves heading through southeastern New Mexico on their way to Carlsbad Caverns, or possibly Big Bend, are made painfully aware of four things: the area is big, it is flat, it is hot, and it is dry. With the curious exception of some deep, water-filled sinkholes at Bottomless Lakes State Park east of Roswell, little oases that most passers-by are unaware of, there seems to be nary a drop of surface water anywhere that is not pumped from deep underground wells. For much of the year even the Pecos River is more mud flat than river. So why would there be anything archaeological there, save a smattering of ephemeral campsites left by small bands of foragers passing through on their seasonal peregrinations across this desolate inland sea of parched grama grass and snakeweed?

The answer is that Roswell was once one of the best-watered oases in the Southwest, boasting seven permanent rivers that all converged on this one locale: the Pecos, Hondo, North and South Spring, and North, Middle, and South Berrendo. Before 1900 these rivers teemed with fish and provided what to the early Roswell settlers seemed like an inexhaustible water supply. F. H. Newell (1891:285), in the annual report of the U.S. Geological Survey, described Roswell as having "the finest and most easily controlled supply of water in the [New Mexico] territory, and an equally good body of land to be irrigated." Unfortunately, through rampant abuse and mismanagement, by the 1930s almost all had been destroyed and, along with it, much of Roswell's archaeological record. The southward-bound tourist passing through Roswell today, amid the usual strip of shopping malls, fast-food establishments, and gas stations, unknowingly crosses the remnants of five of the original seven rivers, their channels now little more than barren, trash-filled gullies where water once flowed in almost unimaginable abundance.

The character of these rivers, and the remarkable fish resources they once possessed, are eloquently described in a letter written in 1876 by one of Roswell's early settlers, Marshall Ashley Upson. His description is so vivid that it is worth quoting at length:

> [The North Spring] river is as transparent as crystal and about forty feet wide. . . . The Pecos is fully as large as the Rio Grande, although the Rio Grande is several hundred miles longer. . . . Besides North Spring River there is South Spring River which has its rise just four miles south of this house, and makes its junction with the Hondo at its mouth, where they both, or rather all three [including North Spring] empty into the Pecos. . . .
>
> Besides these four rivers, there are two smaller ones, their rise being from springs not more than two and one-half and three and one-half miles from this house, and emptying into the Pecos two and three and one-half miles below the mouth of the Hondo. Six rivers within four miles of our door—two within pistol shot—literally alive, all of them with fish. Catfish, sunfish, bull pouts, suckers, eels, and in the two Spring Rivers and the two Berrendo (Antelope) splendid bass. These four rivers are so pellucid that you can discern the smallest object at their greatest depth. The Hondo is opaque and the Pecos is so red with mud that any object is obscured as soon as it strikes the water. Here is where the immense catfish are caught. I pulled one out four and one-half years ago that weighed fifty seven pounds. Eels five and six feet long are common. Bass in the clear streams from two to four pounds is an average. (Shinkle 1966:16; see also Wiseman 1985)

Later in the same letter, Upson goes on to provide additional fascinating details about fishing in Roswell:

> Fishing will be my amusement, as well as profit. We have two dams in the acequia, about twenty yards apart. We have eight catfish there now, which will average sixteen pounds each. We set out lines in Spring River at night, visit them in the morning, carry our fish 200 or 300 yards, and drop them between the dams. When we want them to ship, we open the gate of the lower dam, running off the water, pick up the fish, take out the entrails, and ship them to Fort Stanton and Las Vegas [New Mexico] where they are worth twenty cents per pound. We could by labor ship 500 pounds per week. We will send off 100

pounds tonight all caught by two visits per day to only three lines. (Shinkle 1966:18)

Destruction of the valley's rich nonrenewable natural resources, along with much of its archaeological record, occurred on an unprecedented scale. Toward the close of the nineteenth century and in the opening decade of the next, J. J. Hagerman, a New Mexico entrepreneur (who happens to have graduated from the University of Michigan in 1861), spearheaded construction of a massive earthen dam—the Hondo Reservoir—in an unsuccessful attempt to irrigate thousands of acres of farmland around Roswell. In addition, to prevent flooding of the growing downtown area, the major river courses were artificially moved and channelized, and, over the years, thousands of acres of potentially arable land along the Hondo were leveled, some by stripping, others by burying, in order to increase the amount of land that could be irrigated. It is not altogether surprising, therefore, that by the late 1930s all but four Late Prehistoric villages—Fox Place, Rocky Arroyo, Bloom Mound, and Henderson—had been either obliterated or sealed beneath many feet of overburden, and the three most conspicuous of the survivors became repeated targets of vandalism as well as more systematic digging by well-intentioned but untrained amateurs.

Fortunately, despite decades of illicit digging, not all was destroyed. Recent work at all four villages has begun to reveal the broad outlines of Roswell's fascinating thirteenth- through fifteenth-century prehistory and in the process is yielding insights into the dynamic role that Roswell played in the development of Plains-Pueblo interaction (Emslie et al. 1992; Speth 2004; Wiseman 2002).

The Henderson Site

When we began to work in the Roswell area in the late 1970s, local lore held that the only worthwhile Late Prehistoric village had been Bloom Mound, but everyone assured us that the digging that had gone on there in the late 1930s had essentially emptied it out. According to local collectors, the same amateurs who systematically stripped Bloom of its archaeological deposits also occasionally dug at another site on a nearby ridge, but that one—known today as the Henderson site (Speth 2004)—had the reputation of not being worth the effort. In fact, Henderson had been reported by R. A. Prentice to the Museum of New Mexico in 1934 as nothing more than "a serpentine pile of small rocks about 50′ long and varying in width from 2′ to 3′."[1] This "serpentine pile of rocks" turned out to be a village of seventy-five to one hundred or so rooms. That the site survived at all is a miracle, given that it is prominently labeled "Indian Ruins" on the 1949 edition of the 7.5 minute topographic map for the area. Fortunately, today both Henderson and Bloom are well protected by their owner, the Archaeological Conservancy, and by the ranchers whose land surrounds the sites.

The Henderson site sits atop a limestone ridge overlooking the right bank of

FIGURE 8.1. Map of U.S. Southwest showing approximate location of Henderson site and Bloom Mound (asterisk). Henderson is on the south side of the Hondo Valley and Bloom Mound is on the north side less than one mile downstream.

the Hondo River, about 17 km southwest of downtown Roswell (fig. 8.1). The site, like the few others that are known in the area, had suffered from extensive pothunting in the past, evidenced nearly everywhere by shallow depressions and low mounds of grassed-over backdirt. A gaping and very fresh pothunter's pit near the center of the site clearly had destroyed an important part of the settlement. Despite the obvious vandalism, our work at Henderson quickly revealed that a surprising amount of the site still remained more or less intact.

This good fortune is due in large part to the peculiar architecture of the village. Many of the room floors had been sunk well below the original ground surface, and the walls were constructed by setting a series of upright limestone slabs (including several deliberately broken metates) at ground level and then raising the adobe (or occasionally jacal) superstructure above these. Apparently, the pothunters usually stopped digging when they reached the base of the uprights, assuming, not unreasonably, that they had reached or passed the level where the floor should have been. After considerable testing, we realized that the actual floors lay anywhere from 35 cm to as much as a meter below the bases of the upright slabs, and most of these floors, aside from extensive rodent burrowing and occasional deep pothunting, were reasonably intact. Such rooms are referred to in local parlance as "bathtub" rooms. In essence, they are like pitrooms, except that they share all four walls with adjacent structures so that together they form genuine room blocks rather than isolated pithouses.

In five seasons of excavation, two of which lasted for three full months, we sampled slightly under 20 percent of the site. Our work showed that the village was an adobe "pueblo" with more than seventy (perhaps as many as one hun-

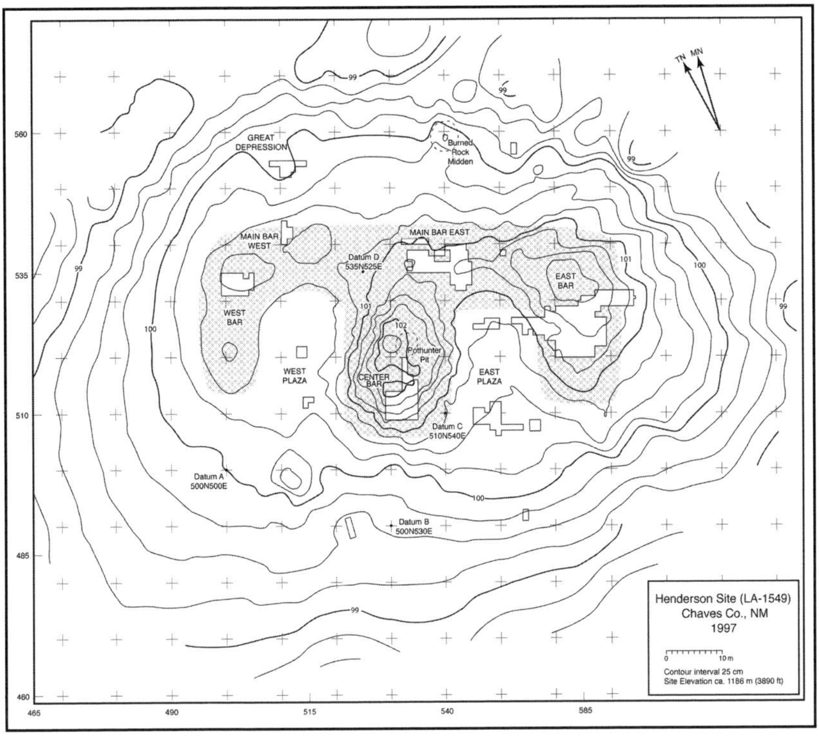

FIGURE 8.2. Map of Henderson site (LA-1549) at close of 1997 field season, showing "E"-shaped layout of room blocks and University of Michigan excavation units.

dred or more) contiguous, single-story, square to rectangular rooms. Ceramics (mostly El Paso Polychrome, Chupadero Black-on-white, Lincoln Black-on-red, and Corona Corrugated; see Wiseman 2004), projectile points (mostly Fresnos and side-notched Washitas; see Adler and Speth 2004) and a suite of conventional and AMS radiocarbon dates all converged to show that Henderson was occupied during the latter part of the 1200s and first quarter to half of the 1300s (these dates must be regarded as fairly crude approximations since current radiocarbon calibration schemes leave a lot of room for guesswork [see Speth 2004]).

The room blocks are laid out like a capital "E," open to the south, with small plaza-like areas between the arms of the "E" (fig. 8.2). Entry into the rooms was by ladders through hatches in the roof. None of the rooms we sampled had doorways or windows. Internal features consisted mostly of centrally located hearths, some with an adobe lip or collar, as well as small subfloor cylindrical "storage" pits (almost invariably empty), subfloor burial pits close to the walls, and four upright support posts near the corners of the rooms. The rooms were arranged in tiers, with four or five parallel tiers constituting the long or main bar of the "E," at least at its eastern end, and four or perhaps five tiers making up the center and east bar. The west bar, which is shorter than the others and more poorly preserved, may have had only two, or possibly three, tiers.

Unfortunately, most of the deposits at Henderson were quite shallow, not surprising given its exposed location on the crest of a limestone ridge. The lack of stratified fill was frustrating, because we were particularly interested in looking at economic change over the lifetime of the community. Then in 1981, following the advice of the late Robert H. (Bus) Leslie, a knowledgeable and dedicated vocational archaeologist from Hobbs, New Mexico, we shifted our focus from rooms to plazas. We soon encountered a huge roasting feature in a natural karstic depression in the limestone bedrock of the east plaza. This depression was filled with tons of fire-cracked rocks (some of which were recycled manos, metates, grooved mauls, and flaked limestone choppers that would feel right at home in the Oldowan) and literally thousands of bones of bison, pronghorn antelope, deer (probably mule deer), butchered domestic dogs, cottontails and jackrabbits, prairie dogs, small numbers of gophers and muskrats, birds (mostly coots but other waterfowl as well, plus a few turkeys and many passerines and raptors, including hawks, owls, and at least one eagle), freshwater molluscs (mostly a locally extinct species of bivalve known as *Cyrtonaias tampicoensis*), and fish (mostly channel catfish, but including at least three other catfish species).

We also found other sizable roasting features, one we affectionately dubbed the "Great Depression," both because of its depth and "uncooperative" fill and because of the record high temperatures the crew had to endure during the 1994 summer field season when we excavated it (several days hit 110° in the shade and one reached 114°, and our only "shade" at the site was a single, forlorn-looking mesquite bush). Thanks to the many roasting complexes, we soon had a wealth of economic data (Speth 2004), though still no real stratigraphy. The big roasting features all had been emptied out when they were no longer needed, a closure offering—typically a bird of some sort, but in one case an infant—put at the bottom of the pit, and then backfilled. In other words, what little stratigraphy there was in these deep deposits meant nothing chronologically.

Then we had another stroke of luck. Despite the relatively brief occupation span of the community (almost certainly less than a century), the rim profiles of one of the site's principal ceramic types—El Paso Polychrome jars—seriated, allowing us to distinguish two arbitrary occupation phases—early phase and late phase (Speth 2004; Speth and LeDuc 2007; Zimmerman 1996). The seriation also allowed us to place the area's four major surviving Late Prehistoric villages, all of which appeared to be roughly contemporary on the basis of their nearly identical ceramic assemblages, in chronological order. From early to late, the sequence revealed by the El Paso Polychrome seriation is Fox Place, Rocky Arroyo, Henderson, and Bloom Mound. The seriation does not preclude the possibility that the occupations at these villages overlapped in time, perhaps substantially, but they clearly form an ordered sequence, with Bloom Mound marking the latest Roswell area village occupation for which we presently have evidence.

With two phases identified at Henderson, we were able to look at economic change, albeit spatially rather than stratigraphically, and the patterning that emerged was striking (Powell 2001; Speth 2004). In the early phase, which we guestimate to date between about AD 1275 and 1300 or slightly later, the villagers made their living by a mix of farming (corn kernels and cobs were rare, but cupules were nearly ubiquitous in flotation samples), wild plant gathering (especially grass seeds of various sorts but also yucca, mesquite, and many other species), hunting of a wide spectrum of taxa from pocket gophers to bison, and fishing (mostly channel catfish). Bison were important in the early phase, but only moderately so. Despite the large number of rooms and the investment in permanent architecture, the village was probably semisedentary—with most of the able-bodied inhabitants leaving after the harvest was in, presumably to hunt bison, and returning in late winter or early the next spring. The principal reason we suspect the village was never totally abandoned is that we could not find any evidence of clandestine storage—that is, storage in below-ground pits well away from rooms that would have concealed the contents from unwanted visitors to the vacant community (DeBoer 1988). In the early phase, Henderson appears to have been quite insular; we found very little ceramic or other evidence of long-distance exchange (Speth 2004).

We should digress briefly here to comment on how we decided which ceramics were local wares and which had come to Henderson through long-distance exchange, since this distinction is important in our subsequent discussion. The truth of the matter is that we do not really know where any of the "local" ceramics were made. Until such knowledge becomes available, we simply assume that if a ceramic type is abundant in the assemblage it was locally made, and if it is rare it was nonlocally made. Fortunately, at least the distinction between "abundant" and "rare" is pretty obvious at Henderson. Out of some 35,000 sherds that have been analyzed thus far (the first two seasons' worth; see Wiseman 2004), just four types make up 95 percent of the total—El Paso Polychrome (53 percent), Chupadero Black-on-white (17 percent), Lincoln Black-on-red (15 percent), and Corona Corrugated (10 percent). These are the types we assume are local. Another 3 percent of the analyzed assemblage, just under a thousand sherds, are unidentifiable. The remainder (about 2 percent of the total), an eclectic hodgepodge of sherds representing more than twenty different types, is the category that we consider nonlocal. Prominent among these are Salado wares (Pinto, Tonto, and especially Gila), Chihuahua polychromes (especially Babicora but also a few Carretas and Ramos), White Mountain redwares (St. Johns, Springerville, Cedar Creek, and especially Heshotauthla), and Rio Grande glazes (mostly Agua Fria but also Los Padillas and Arenal).

While acknowledging that all four of the local ceramic types could have been made many kilometers from Roswell (e.g., Chupadero Black-on-white may have been brought in from the Sierra Blanca region, 100 km or more west of Roswell; Clark 2006; Creel et al. 2002), the most problematic among them is El Paso Polychrome. Consisting mostly of jars, this distinctive though not particularly elegant ceramic type was in common use over a huge area of the Southwest, from Roswell in the northeast all the way to Casas Grandes in the southwest, a distance of over 480 km as the crow flies. In fact, they were so common at Casas Grandes that Di

Peso et al. (1974:141) referred to them as "tin cans," an appellation that might just as easily be applied to these vessels at Henderson, where they (or at least their sherds) are more abundant than all of the other ceramic types combined. If these jars, many of which were large, fragile, and probably quite heavy (Burgett 2007; Speth and LeDuc 2007), were hauled to Roswell from as far away as El Paso or beyond, we would have to conclude that Henderson and Bloom Mound were engaged in trade on a much grander scale than we have envisioned. Clearly, the source areas for these cumbersome "tin cans" need to be identified with some degree of certainty if we are to gain a better understanding of the nature and spatial extent of the exchange system in which the Roswell communities participated.

Let us now return to the discussion of the economic changes at Henderson. During the late phase, probably beginning in the first few decades of the 1300s, the quantity of nonlocal ceramics, turquoise, marine shell, and other "exotic" items from distant parts of the Southwest increased significantly. The five seasons of excavation at Henderson yielded a total of 1,560 sherds of types that came from at least as far west as the Rio Grande (the glazes) and many from considerably farther afield.[2] Virtually all of Henderson's extraregional ceramics (nearly 95 percent) were found in late phase contexts. Turquoise, marine shells (especially *Olivella* but also some *Glycymeris*), and obsidian, though never abundant at Henderson, also became noticeably more common in the late phase, both as items placed in burials and in general room fill (Speth 2004). In essence, what Henderson's late phase shows us is a comparatively early stage in the development of the classic pattern of Plains-Pueblo interaction so vividly described by the Spanish a few centuries later (Speth 2004; Spielmann 1991b).

In time with the increase in exotic trade goods, the quantity of bison brought to Henderson also increased, both in absolute numbers of bones and in density of bones per cubic meter of excavated deposit. Not surprisingly, the number and density of projectile points rose substantially as well, more or less tracking the quantity of bison that was coming into the village. And the bison bones that were brought back were strongly biased in favor of moderate- to high-utility upper limb parts (utility measured using Binford's 1978 MGUI and Marrow Index), implying greater average transport distance between kills and village, larger numbers of animals taken per kill event, or some combination of the two (Speth 2004). The communal importance of bison also increased. Whereas in the early phase we found roughly half of the bison bones in domestic contexts (i.e., room trash), in the late phase over 80 percent were recovered in and around public roasting features. In addition, trade involving dried meat appears to have risen sharply in the late phase, as evidenced by a significant drop in the quantity of bison ribs, the most easily dried portion of the animal (Speth and Rautman 2004). That this decline is not a taphonomic artifact of the bone-crunching proclivities of hungry village dogs is indicated by the fact that the abundance of much more delicate antelope and deer ribs, which should have been the first to be destroyed by village dogs, remained more or less unchanged.

The bison remains suggest that the Henderson villagers in the late phase had become increasingly engaged in long-distance treks to hunt these animals, but the bones by themselves do not tell us where. By analogy with ethnohistorical information, we can speculate that the most likely direction would have been eastward or northeastward toward or onto the High Plains of the Texas Panhandle, or southeastward toward or onto the Edwards Plateau in central Texas. Though we lack a direct way to demonstrate this at the moment, strontium isotope and trace element chemistry of the bison bones may one day help us identify likely hunting areas, at least on a relatively coarse scale (e.g., Ezzo et al. 1997; Price et al. 1985). These areas have very different bedrock geologies, which we can expect to be reflected in the chemistry of the plants the bison ate and hence in the chemistry of their bones. Of course, if the Southern Plains herds regularly migrated between areas with different bedrock geologies, the picture is likely to become more complicated, though bone chemistry offers a promising approach.

In the meantime, the cherts may help us identify probable hunting areas. It goes without saying that visual identification of chert sources is fraught with uncertainty, because so many materials, regardless of source, can look very much alike. For example, the most abundant Roswell area cherts are smallish nodules that range in color from light gray to bluish-gray to beige or tan, some vaguely banded, some mottled, and some fairly homogeneous, waxy, and eminently knappable. These "bluish-gray" cherts can be found eroding out on the surface of many of the limestone outcrops between Roswell and the Sacramento-Sierra Blanca mountains to the west. No one has studied these potential sources systematically, so we have no idea just how variable the cherts may be in color, texture, nodule size, amount of cortex, and knappability. Visually, many of these local variants broadly resemble the grays from the Edwards Plateau. However, Edwards is notorious for its panoply of colors, patterns, and textures (e.g., gray, tan, brown, white, even a black variety known as "Owl Creek chert"; Frederick and Ringstaff 1994; Frederick et al. 1994). The justly famous waxy gray "Georgetown" variety of Edwards is by no means the only one found in central Texas. Thus, we should be forthright in pointing out that in our earlier publications on the Henderson projectile points and lithics (Adler and Speth 2004; Brown 2004) we assumed that almost any gray or bluish-gray chert was local, a call that in many cases may have been wrong.

There are two other major sources of chert, both from the Texas Panhandle, that were widely used in the region during the Late Prehistoric period—Alibates (along the Canadian drainage north of Amarillo) and Tecovas (sometimes called Quitaque, south of Amarillo). Again, these materials are quite variable (Holliday and Welty 1981; Mallouf 1989; Shaeffer 1958). Alibates provides a case in point. To most archaeologists who work in New Mexico, Alibates' appearance is almost always likened to raw bacon, with the pale grayish to bluish portion (resembling the fatty part of uncooked bacon) confined to small mottles and thin stringers sandwiched between the more prominent rust- or bacon-colored zones. However, fist-sized and larger chunks of the gray to bluish-gray variety (i.e., just the fatty portion of the bacon) are commonplace in some of the quarry areas at Alibates and were widely used prehistorically for making projectile points, end scrapers, and beveled knives. Again, these Alibates variants can be hard to distinguish by eye alone from some of the Edwards varieties and from some of the Roswell area materials.

Although ultraviolet (black light) fluorescence (UVF) is clearly no substitute for the precision and replicability of trace element studies carried out using instrumental neutron activation analysis (INAA) or other high-tech methods, it has proved quite useful as a preliminary means for distinguishing some of the major Southern Plains sources, particularly Alibates, Tecovas, and Edwards Plateau. Work by Hofman et al. (1991), Hillsman (1992), Frederick and Ringstaff (1994), Frederick et al. (1994), and Wiseman (2002), as well as analyses conducted by one of us (K.N.) using chert type collections at the Museum of New Mexico (Santa Fe) and Eastern New Mexico University (Portales), has shown that both Alibates and Tecovas commonly produce a light to dark green response under shortwave UV light (Hofman et al. 1991). In contrast, Edwards Plateau cherts, regardless of their color in ordinary light, almost invariably yield a yellow or orange response under both short- and longwave UV light (Frederick et al. 1994).

Thus, we decided to examine the points from Henderson and Bloom Mound using UV light. Our first step was to get an idea of the characteristic fluorescence responses of cherts that we can be reasonably confident are local in origin. Given the "expedient" nature of the lithic assemblages from Henderson and Bloom (e.g., Parry and Kelly 1987), with almost no formal tools other than projectile points and preforms/ovate bifaces, much of the raw material used in these villages could well have come from sources close to home. However, in light of the evidence that the Roswell villagers were heavily involved in interregional trade and also made extended hunting forays into the Southern Plains, we cannot rule out the possibility that some significant portion of the debitage had been flaked from nonlocal raw materials. To circumvent this problem, we turned instead to surface collections consisting of debitage and a few formal tools from five ephemeral campsite/quarrying localities situated directly on the chert-bearing limestone outcrops west of Roswell. These sites were investigated by Charles Hannaford (1981) as part of a highway right-of-way survey, and the materials he collected are now curated at the Museum of New Mexico in Santa Fe: "Beginning approximately at the Chaves County line and extending to the western limit of the survey, a number of lithic scatters were encountered. In each case the sites were located on a hill, the result of geologic folding of the limestone bedrock. Of importance to prehistoric populations utilizing a stone based technology was the resultant exposure and concentration of a reducible lithic material embedded in the limestone" (Hannaford 1981:94).

We examined the UVF responses of 788 pieces, which is slightly under 20 percent of the total museum Hannaford collection (N = 4,339). Although light green (19.3 percent), dark green (1.1 percent), and yellow-orange (7.4 percent) responses were all observed in the Hannaford sample, for the most part the responses were readily distinguishable from those we observed on comparative materials obtained directly from chert sources in the Texas Panhandle and Edwards Plateau. The latter produced relatively uniform, continuous UV responses over the entirety or major portions of the specimens; most of the Hannaford material yielded only small, discontinuous spots or blotches of color, some or much of which could easily be an artifact of weathering on these surface-collected materials. In contrast, most of the projectile points and bifaces from Henderson and Bloom that responded to UV light did so with a relatively uniform response much like what we observed on the Texas materials. Thus, in the discussion that follows we proceed on the assumption that the Henderson and Bloom Mound points and bifaces that responded with relatively uniform green (light or dark) or yellow-orange emissions were made on materials derived from Southern Plains sources, not from local outcrops. Ultimately, of course, this assumption needs to be checked by more precise and reliable methods.

Many of the projectile points from Henderson and Bloom were undoubtedly made on local materials. However, if the Roswell villagers were making extended treks out into the plains to hunt bison, it is likely that they had to manufacture replacement points while they were away, some of which would have found their way back to Roswell upon completion of the hunt (some as still-hafted broken bases in need of replacement, others as complete spares). And if we are right that the villagers did a fair amount of their bison hunting in the Texas Panhandle or on the Edwards Plateau, then we might expect some projectile points to yield either a uniform light/dark green or a yellow-orange UV response comparable to what we observed on our sample of Texas comparative materials. Thus, the UVF response of the points may help us identify the area(s) within the Southern Plains where the majority of their hunting took place (i.e., Panhandle vs. Edwards Plateau), and whether the geographic focus of their hunting activities changed in any significant way over time.

The total sample upon which the UVF analysis is based consists of 993 projectile points (mostly Washitas, Fresnos, and unidentifiable tips), of which 250 are from Henderson's early phase, 603 from the late phase, and 140 from Bloom Mound. There are also 92 ovate bifaces—33 from Henderson's early phase, 58 from the late phase, and, interestingly, only one from Bloom, despite the fact that we excavated there for two full seasons.

Figure 8.3 shows the UVF responses for the projectile points. Three interesting patterns are evident in the figure: (1) green responses (Panhandle) are consistently more frequent among the points than yellow-orange ones (Edwards Plateau); (2) both green and yellow-orange responses fall off sharply by the time of Bloom's occupation; and (3) the frequency of points displaying a yellow-orange response falls off sooner, and declines farther, than points with a green response. Taken together, these results suggest that the Roswell villagers during the late thirteenth and fourteenth centuries were interacting with, and probably hunting in, both the Panhandle and central Texas, though seemingly more frequently, or for more extended periods, in the Panhandle. In addition, access by the villagers to both the Panhandle and the Edwards Plateau region appears to have declined

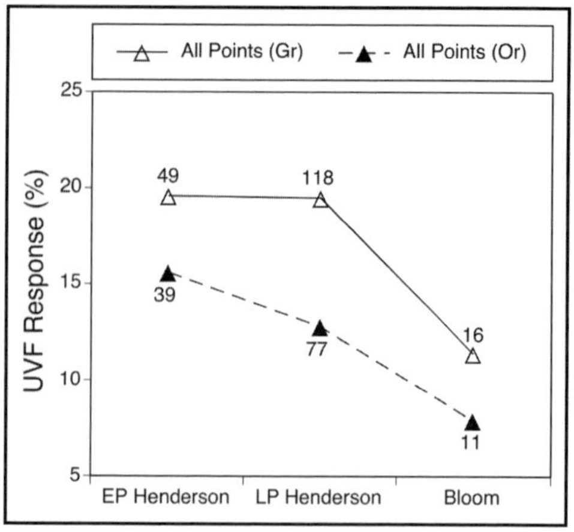

FIGURE 8.3. Proportion of projectile points (all types combined) from Henderson and Bloom Mound that display either light/dark green or yellow-orange UVF response.

between Henderson's late phase and the occupation at Bloom, with access to central Texas beginning to decline sooner.

The patterning seen at Bloom Mound is particularly intriguing. As we discuss below, bison all but disappear in this late fourteenth- to fifteenth-century community, yet trade in exotic ceramics, such as Gila Polychrome and various Chihuahua polychromes, as well as turquoise, obsidian, and marine shell increases to levels well in excess of anything we saw at Henderson. At the same time, projectile points displaying both light/dark green and yellow-orange UVF responses decline in frequency, suggesting that by Bloom times the Roswell villagers had less and less direct access to the Southern Plains. Thus, although bison likely continue to be important in the interregional exchange system, the folks in Roswell no longer seem to be the ones doing the hunting. We return shortly to this intriguing shift in Bloom's economy.

Until now we have been discussing the UVF responses of the projectile points as a group, regardless of type. So here we take a brief look at the Fresnos and Washitas separately. We recovered a total of 73 Fresnos in Henderson's early phase, 145 in the late phase, and 46 at Bloom. Washitas were more numerous at both sites than Fresnos, especially in the late phase: 77 in the early phase, 235 in the late phase, and 67 at Bloom. A perennial question in western North America is whether Fresnos (and their close cousins elsewhere)—small, unnotched triangles—were projectile points in their own right or blanks (preforms) for manufacturing notched forms such as Washitas, Harrells, and others (Adler and Speth 2004; Christenson 1997; Dawe 1987; Jelks 1993). More than likely Fresnos functioned in both ways, some serving as preforms and others being hafted and used without further alteration. However, quantitative comparisons of Henderson's Fresnos and Washitas provide fairly compelling support for the preform idea, at least in the Roswell context. The two point types differ significantly from each other in both size and shape (Adler and Speth 2004). Fresnos are more or less comparable in length to Washitas, but they tend to be thicker, wider, heavier, and

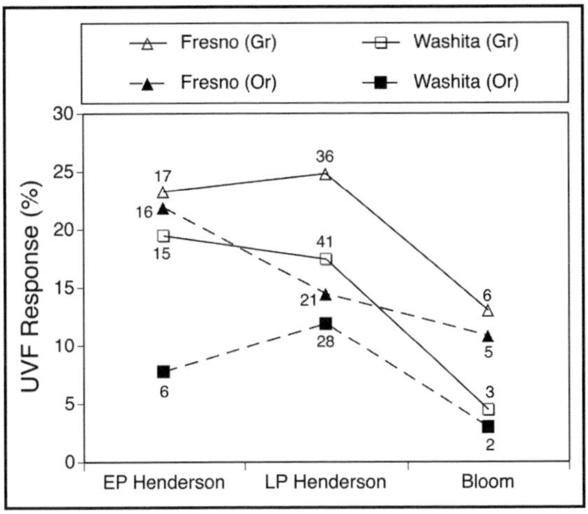

FIGURE 8.4. Proportion of Fresno and Washita points from Henderson and Bloom Mound that display either light/dark green or yellow-orange UVF response.

squatter in overall shape. Fresnos also have a less pronounced basal concavity, and they are less finely flaked.

Archaeologists have often noted that thin, delicately notched projectile points are fragile and, if one is going to transport spare points over considerable distances, it is safer to carry them in unnotched form and add the notches only when the points are actually needed (Cheshier and Kelly 2006; Dawe 1987; Odell and Cowan 1986). Thus, if the villagers were making extended treks out onto the Southern Plains to hunt, we might expect them to carry a supply of preforms, some brought from home, others made at quarries while the hunters were out in the grasslands. Hence, if points were notched only as needed, preforms (i.e., Fresnos) that were made from Southern Plains materials should outnumber finished points that were made from these same materials, and this imbalance might be expected to persist among the points and preforms that were brought back to Roswell at the end of the trip. This expectation again seems to be met, as shown in figure 8.4.

In addition to Fresnos, Henderson yielded relatively crude thick ovate bifaces (91), which we assume (with some hesitation) are roughed-out blanks prepared by the villagers in anticipation of future projectile point needs. If we follow the arguments developed by Parry and Kelly (1987), these bifaces would have been carried by the villagers during periods of high mobility, especially when they were on extended bison hunting treks in the Southern Plains. We therefore expect that many of the bifaces, like the Fresnos, would have been made using Plains raw materials and, as a consequence, would display elevated yellow-orange and green UVF responses reflecting their nonlocal origin.

The data from Henderson again seem to bear this out. Like the Fresnos, comparably high percentages of early phase ovate bifaces produced green or yellow-orange UVF responses (24 percent and 33 percent, respectively). Late phase bifaces also yielded elevated green or yellow-orange UVF values, though more modest ones than in the early phase (17 percent and 16 percent, respectively). De-

TABLE 8.1. Statistical comparison (unpaired t-tests) of metric attributes for Henderson site Washita points made on "local" vs. "nonlocal" materials

Attribute	N	*Mean Difference*	t-*value*	p-*value*
Max. length	131	1.980 x 10-5 cm	2.074 x 10-4	0.9998
Max. thickness	312	2.560 x 10-4 cm	0.04	0.9694
Blade length	186	0.02 cm	0.26	0.7934
Shoulder width	241	0.01 cm	0.54	0.5864
Basal width	154	2.770 x 10-3 cm	0.08	0.9348
Neck width	274	0.01 cm	0.30	0.7633
Left notch ratio	206	0.01	0.10	0.9233
Right notch ratio	112	0.21	1.11	0.2709
Basal concavity	177	0.01 cm	0.29	0.7713

Early phase and late phase combined. The "left" and "right" side designations for notches are arbitrary.

spite two full seasons of excavation at Bloom, we recovered only one ovate biface (with a dark green UVF response). Whether the scarcity of such bifaces is merely a sampling artifact or instead reflects a genuine decline in Bloom's overall mobility remains to be explored more fully as we continue our excavations at the site.

There is a major uncertainty in this discussion of the points. We have argued from the position that the Roswell villagers traveled into the Southern Plains to hunt bison and that, while out in the plains, they were the ones who manufactured most or all of the nonlocal points that found their way back home. It is of course possible that the villagers received these nonlocal points, and point preforms, through exchange with other groups. This in turn might also imply that the bison at Henderson found their way into the village through exchange, not through long-distance village hunting.

There is a way we can explore this issue—by statistically comparing the metric attributes of points made on local materials with the comparable values for the points we consider nonlocal on the basis of their UVF response. If the latter were made by other groups and obtained by the Henderson villagers through exchange, we might expect at least some of the metric attributes to differ. They do not—not even down to the breadth/depth ratios of the notches (table 8.1). The two sets of points are virtually identical in every regard; they almost certainly are the products of skilled flintknappers who belonged to a close-knit craft tradition.

Bloom Mound

We now turn to Bloom Mound, since the occupation of this intriguing little village seems to capture an important "hinge point" in the role that the Roswell communities played within the emerging nexus of interregional exchange and competition. As the work at Henderson progressed and a picture of major economic change began to take shape, we became increasingly curious about how Bloom Mound (LA-2528)—only about 1.5 km downstream and easily visible from Henderson—might fit into the picture. Unfortunately, there seemed to be noth-

FIGURE 8.5. Aerial photo of Bloom Mound taken by Kenneth Cobean sometime in the 1950s, showing rooms excavated by amateurs (north to top of photo). Archived image provided courtesy of Institute of Historical Survey, Las Cruces, New Mexico.

ing left of Bloom. Beginning in the late 1930s, local amateurs had dug there for many years, and by the mid-1950s archaeologists and amateurs alike agreed that little or no in situ deposits remained. What the amateurs had found, recorded in an on-again-off-again dig diary kept by members of the Roswell Archaeological Society, was a small village of only ten rooms—nine contiguous adobe surface structures and an adjacent semisubterranean "ceremonial chamber" (fig. 8.5). The amateurs dug all of them, emptying most, and crisscrossed the site with additional exploratory pits and trenches. They stripped off part of the central "mound" using a blade pulled by a pickup truck to remove the many piles of backdirt and to get at deeper deposits more easily (an unfortunate and destructive event, but one that fortuitously sealed and preserved a series of "bathtub" rooms at the north end of the site).

Despite the site's small size, the amateurs unearthed a remarkable quantity of exotic ceramics, obsidian, marine shell ornaments, turquoise, and perhaps as many as seven copper bells, leading Jane Holden Kelley (1984:455) to characterize Bloom as a "trading center of unusual affluence." According to the amateurs, the entire village may have been torched, perhaps violently destroyed in a single devastating raid, to judge by the many skeletons of victims, several burned, found helter-skelter in room fill and sprawled on house floors (anywhere from fifteen to as many as thirty individuals, according to Wiseman's 1997 and Kelley's 1984 estimates). The wealth of nonlocal items, much more than we found in Henderson's late phase, suggested that Bloom was somewhat later than Henderson and might therefore tell us what happened to the local economy in the decades after Henderson's abandonment.

Everyone, ourselves included, was convinced that Bloom had been completely gutted, and most of the artifacts that had been recovered by the amateurs had disappeared into private collections. Some, particularly those recovered by the Roswell Archaeological Society, had been stored, uncatalogued, in the basement of the Roswell Art Museum, but most were lost in a flood that swept through the museum in the late 1950s or were subsequently discarded because they lacked provenience. The copper bells survived (Vargas 1995), as did a few other noteworthy items because they were on display at the time of the flood. Fortunately, as part of her dissertation research, Kelley (1984) interviewed some of the most active amateurs about their finds and inventoried the collections stashed in the museum basement shortly before the flood. Also, at the invitation of the Roswell Archaeological Society, she excavated one of the original nine surface rooms and finished clearing the floor of the subterranean "ceremonial chamber." These materials, both artifacts and fauna, are now safely curated at Texas Tech University in Lubbock. Kelley (1984) also mapped the site, something the amateurs had never done, even though they had gone through the motions of setting up an elaborate 10- by 10-foot grid system demarcated by large, numbered nails.

We began working at Bloom in 2000 with the hope of at least salvaging economic data from the pothunters' backdirt. We also hoped to get a sample of El Paso Polychrome jar rims large enough to allow us to date Bloom's occupation relative to Henderson's two occupational phases. To our amazement and delight, testing showed that parts of Bloom, particularly at the north end of the site, remained more or less intact, in part sealed by the overburden the amateurs had dragged off the center of the site with a blade. We also discovered that the community was bigger than we had originally thought and had a different layout as well. Instead of being a single room block with just nine surface rooms and an adjacent pit structure, it was a partially, perhaps completely, enclosed rectangular structure surrounding the deep chamber, and with at least twenty to twenty-five rooms, if not more (fig. 8.6).

Like Henderson, Bloom may have had two phases of occupation. These phases, assuming they stand up to future work at the site, may be separated in time by only a few decades, judging by the fact that both have very similar ceramic assemblages. The earlier phase, which we so far have tested only on a limited scale, appears to consist of two parallel tiers of small, semisubterranean "bathtub" rooms situated stratigraphically beneath the surface adobe rooms at the north end of the site. These earlier rooms are also oriented slightly differently than the overlying structure, a difference that may well have been symbolically important to the inhabitants (Fowles 2005).

In 2000 we relocated the original corners of the "ceremonial structure," allowing us to connect Kelley's map to ours. And, as anticipated, seriation of the El Paso Polychrome rims confirmed our suspicion that Bloom dated after Henderson, though perhaps by only a generation or so, indicating that Bloom's heavy involvement in long-distance exchange continued and amplified the process that had begun during Henderson's late phase.

Like the amateurs, we too found human skeletons (six, plus scattered fragmentary remains), but those that we found differed from the unburied and often burned skeletons encountered by the amateurs. Our human remains were all bona fide burials, all interred according to what seems to be the standard pattern for the area—bodies tightly flexed, probably wrapped in some sort of shroud, and

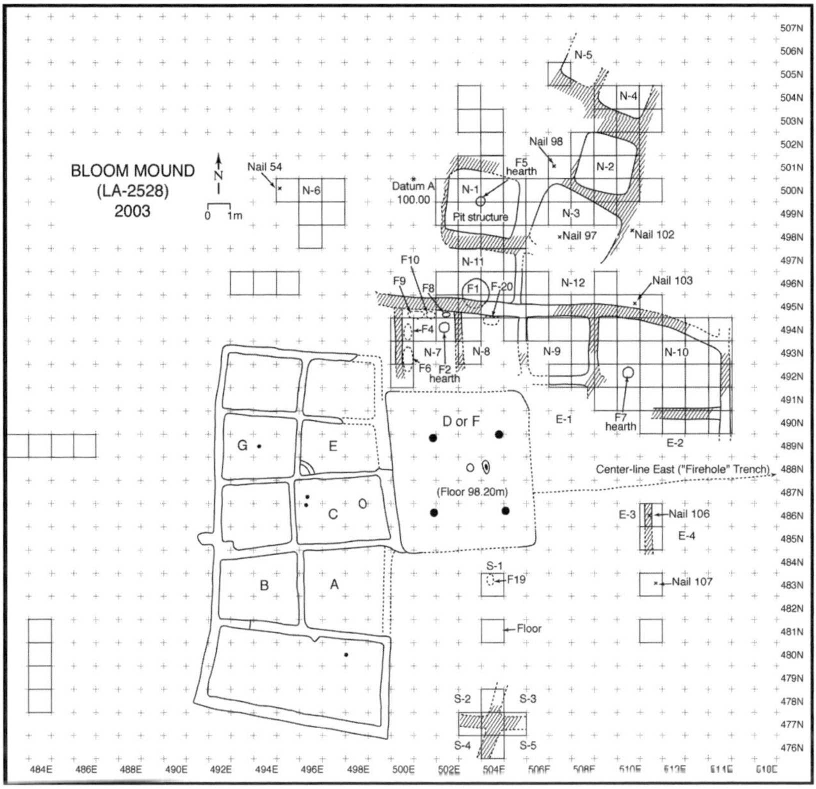

FIGURE 8.6. Map of Bloom Mound (LA-2528) at close of 2003 field season, showing relationship of rooms discovered by University of Michigan excavations in 2000 and 2003 (hachured walls) to Jane Kelley's 1950s map of the nine surface rooms and adjacent pitroom/ceremonial chamber excavated by Roswell amateurs (non-hachured walls). Subfloor burials excavated by the University of Michigan are F4, F6, F8, F9, F10, F19, and F20. Note earlier "bathtub" rooms at north end of site with orientation slightly offset from that of surface room block. Nails are original 10- by 10-foot grid markers used by the Roswell Archaeological Society in the 1930s.

placed in oval pits beneath house floors, close to, and parallel to, the walls of the structures (see fig. 8.6; for details on the Henderson burials, see Rocek and Speth 1986). None were burned. None of the rooms we opened were burned either. Thus, the burials we encountered had been treated as kin, as people who belonged, not as enemies.

In keeping with the evidence for conflict that had been encountered by the amateurs (i.e., numerous burned, unburied bodies), at least one of our burials, an older adult male (Feature 4, age ca. 35–45 years), had clearly met a violent end, with two deep, circular, depressed fractures on his skull, suggesting that he had been bludgeoned to death.[3] He was also missing part of his face. Two young adult women were also missing part of their faces (Feature 6, ca. 20–24 years; Feature 9, ca. 25–30 years). We initially interpreted the facial destruction on the three individuals as evidence of violence, which it may yet prove to be, but after inspecting

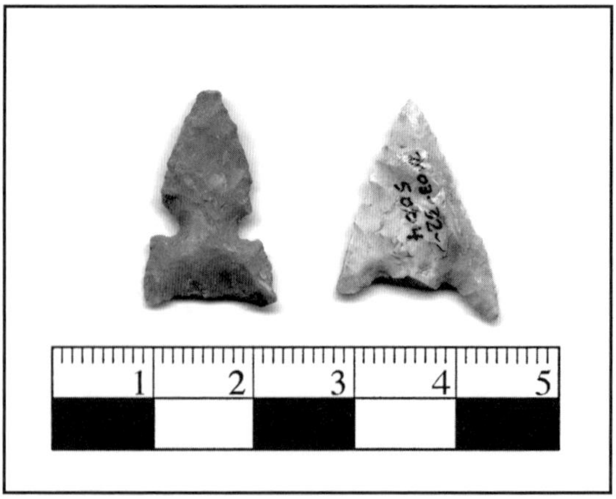

FIGURE 8.7. Projectile points found in association with human burials at Bloom Mound: left, Washita point found with Feature 19 infant; right, Perdiz-like point found with Feature 20 adult male.

the faces David Frayer (personal communication, 2007) recommended that we exercise caution in their interpretation. We can find no clear taphonomic cause for the facial damage (e.g., crushing under the concentrated weight of an overlying rock, rodent or carnivore gnawing, etc.), and the pattern is repeated on three of the four adults we recovered, but we have been equally unsuccessful in finding telltale signs showing that the facial bone had been deliberately cut, smashed, or broken inward. We can discern no fragments of bone still adhering along the margins of the missing face that are depressed inward as though struck by a blunt instrument. The missing bone is simply not evident, although it may yet be preserved deeper within the cranial vault. Because of the very fragile nature of the Bloom crania, we have not removed all of the sediment from within the orbits and vault. Thus, although deliberate destruction of the face, either at the time of death or soon thereafter, remains a distinct possibility, a violent origin for the damage cannot be shown with any degree of certainty.

Nonetheless, we found two projectile points—one Perdiz-like, one Washita—in close proximity to the abdominal area of two of the skeletons, an adult male (Feature 20, ca. 40–45 years, with the Perdiz-like point) and an infant (Feature 19, ca. 3–12 months, with the Washita point; fig. 8.7). Since neither of the points were actually embedded in bone, we cannot be completely certain that they were the cause of death rather than an offering of some sort, although they are suggestive of violence, particularly when added to the facial destruction. Regardless of the uncertainties that persist in determining the cause of death of the burials we encountered at Bloom, the evidence reported by the amateurs and augmented by Kelley's work at the site—unburied skeletons, many burned—clearly testifies to the violence that befell this small community.

The overall picture that is taking shape at Bloom dovetails well with our reconstructions at Henderson (Speth 2004). Like Henderson, Bloom was probably a semisedentary community, with many of the able-bodied adults away from the village each year in the late autumn and winter after the harvest was in, doing at least some bison hunting (albeit considerably less than we observed at Henderson), trading extensively with Pueblos far to the west of Roswell, and perhaps raiding other communities (as at Henderson, the absence of clandestine, below-ground storage pits positioned well away from the rooms argues against Bloom having been totally vacated for some substantial part of each year).

As expected, evidence of long-distance exchange with the Pueblo world was even greater at Bloom than at Henderson, pointing toward increasing involvement in Plains-Pueblo interaction. The most common of these trade items were ceramics, again especially Gila Polychrome, but also "early" Rio Grande glazes, various Chihuahua wares, White Mountain redwares, and others. Using the rims of jars and bowls as a proxy for the entire ceramic assemblage (body sherds from the two sites, numbering well in excess of 100,000 pieces, have not been fully tabulated as yet), the proportion of nonlocal ceramics increases from a mere 1.5 percent of all rims in Henderson's early phase to just over 6.0 percent in Henderson's late phase to 12.5 percent at Bloom. Quantities of marine shell, turquoise, and obsidian follow a similar trend.

However, contrary to what we had expected, the quantity of bison coming into Bloom seems to have declined precipitously. This could turn out to be an artifact of sampling. At Henderson, bison bones were not common in the rooms, particularly during the late phase, and became evident in quantity only when we sampled nonroom contexts. In the plazas we encountered the roasting features copiously filled with bison bones. We therefore proceeded with the view that a similar spatial pattern might hold at Bloom. Yet, when we sampled what we thought would be plaza areas, we encountered remnants of floors and walls. This led to our realization that the Bloom community was bigger than the amateurs had suspected, an important finding in its own right, but it meant that much of our faunal sample came from room contexts. Only with still more testing, farther away from the heart of the village, can we be absolutely certain that the scarcity of bison bone is real and not a sampling artifact. Nevertheless, we have already done enough testing along the peripheries of the site to be reasonably sure that bison were, in fact, much less prominent in Bloom's economy than in Henderson's.

There is another line of evidence—the number of arrowheads—that supports this conclusion. At Henderson we recovered an average of nearly 200 projectile points and point fragments per season. In contrast, at Bloom we found 140 points in two seasons, a recovery rate more than two and a half times smaller than at Henderson. Our screening and recovery procedures were virtually identical at the two sites. Thus, to the extent that points provide an independent proxy for the intensity of big-game hunting, it would appear that hunters from Henderson were far more heavily engaged in the activity than Bloom's hunters. The sharp decline at Bloom in the frequency of points and preforms made on cherts with UVF responses indicating that they had come from the Texas Panhandle and central Texas dovetails well with this conclusion.

Thus, we have a conundrum at Bloom. Trade was clearly up, substantially so judging by the quantities of exotic ceramics and other items found there, yet what we assume to have been the principal commodities the Roswell communities had been contributing to the exchange—products of the bison hunt—were down. Also, unlike Henderson, where we found no evidence of foul play, Bloom was attacked, probably more than once, and probably precisely at those times of year when many able-bodied men and women were away, either hunting or trading, and the community was undermanned.

Competition and Conflict: Ideas and Speculation

The evidence from Bloom provides clues to the nature of the violence and, in the process, what might have been motivating it. In a recent cross-cultural study of warfare in middle-range societies, Solometo (2004) found that deliberate killing of noncombatants (children, prime-adult women, and elderly men) occurred primarily among enemies who were socially distant and often geographically distant as well. Wholesale destruction of structures was also more typical of warfare among socially distant enemies, particularly in contexts where there was little or no prospect of mutual benefit or cooperation in the future. The killing of men, women, and children at Bloom, so apparent from the records kept by the amateurs, as well as the burning of victims and buildings clearly point in this direction (see also Wiseman 1997). These were not just punitive, wife-stealing, or trophy-seeking raids; whoever the enemies were, they were making a serious effort to extirpate the community and its inhabitants.

The deadly seriousness of the conflict is also hinted at by the nearly or completely enclosed layout of the community. Again relying on cross-cultural studies, Solometo (2004) found that communities seldom fortify themselves unless actual conflict, not just the threat of conflict, occurs more or less on an annual basis. If she is right, Bloom may have been locked in a protracted and deadly struggle with other peoples on the margins of the Southwest.

Who were the enemies? Why were they intent on obliterating a small community like Bloom? These of course are the most interesting questions, but the most difficult to answer, especially given the limited data we currently have at hand. At this point we enter into what is admittedly based more on conjecture than on hard evidence. We hope that the ideas we put forward here can be more clearly formulated and tested through additional work at Bloom Mound and elsewhere in the region.

Let us begin with the "who." The two arrow points found among the bones of Bloom victims (Features 19–20) are particularly interesting in this regard, if one is willing to accept that they were the cause of death and not just grave offerings. Both appear to be made on Edwards Plateau chert, and one is a Perdiz or Perdiz-like point, a distinctive and well-known type whose homeland lies to the southeast on the Edwards Plateau (e.g., Black 1989; Hester 1995; Johnson 1994; Ricklis 1992; Suhm and Jelks 1962; Treece et al. 1993) (see fig. 8.7). Perdiz points are not abundant at Bloom (only six so far have been found out of a total of 130 identifiable points, or 4.7 percent), but at Henderson this unmistakable form is absent altogether, even though we recovered more than 570 points complete enough to classify to type (arcsine statistic, $t_s = 4.50$, $p < .0001$; Sokal and Rohlf 1969: 607–10).

Perdiz points are generally thought to appear by about AD 1300 and persist until 1600 or 1650. They are one of the hallmarks of the Toyah phase, the archaeologically defined cultural entity, found throughout central Texas, that is the focus of this volume (Black 1989; Hester 1995; Johnson 1994; Kelley 1986; Prewitt 1981, 1985). Perdiz points, however, are not restricted to the Toyah phase or to central Texas; they are also found in other more or less contemporary Late Prehistoric cultural entities, their distribution extending nearly across the width and breadth of Texas and into northern Mexico. They are very rare in New Mexico, however, even in the southeastern part of the state (Leslie 1978).

Several authors have attempted to link the Classic Toyah with the historically documented Jumanos (Hickerson 1994; Johnson 1994; Kelley 1986; Wade 2003). Although this attribution may be correct, or at least partly so, it seems likely that many other ethnic groups in Texas and northern Mexico also made use of similar points (Wade 2003). For example, Wade (2003:222) and Kenmotsu (2007; Kenmotsu and Wade 2002) show that more than twenty named bands occupied the Edwards Plateau in the early 1600s. Thus, we may never know which specific group or groups may have been fighting with the residents of Bloom, but the Perdiz-like point found in association with one of the skeletons provides a tantalizing hint that the source of at least some of the violence came from the southeast, possibly from the Jumano area of central Texas. The characteristic yellow-orange UVF response of this point is entirely consistent with this idea.

A similar pattern of conflict may be in evidence at the Salt Cedar site, a small Ochoa phase (ca. AD 1300–1500) hamlet or rancheria in Andrews County, Texas, close to the southeastern corner of New Mexico (Collins 1968). The Ochoa phase, defined primarily on the basis of a distinctive brownware pottery type known as Ochoa Indented, is a poorly documented cultural entity found in extreme southeastern New Mexico, east of the Pecos River, and adjacent parts of Texas, extending eastward to about Midland (Corley 1965; Leslie 1970, 1979). Salt Cedar had three or four square to rectangular jacal structures and a dense trash midden, as well as numerous extramural hearths, roasting features, and artifact caches. Animal bones were abundant in the midden, especially bison, as well as smaller numbers of antelope, deer, jackrabbits, and a variety of smaller mammals. Collins (1968) excavated four burials at the site. Two of the individuals, both relatively old adult males (>35 years), had died violently, as evidenced by arrowheads found in various parts of the body cavity that were clearly not there as offerings. In addition, one of the adults had a puncture wound on the right parietal and cutmarks on the frontal that could be the result of scalping. The other two burials, an elderly male and an infant, showed no obvious evidence of violent death. Interestingly, although Perdiz and Perdiz-like points were not common at Salt Cedar (23 of 437 points, or 5.3 percent, a value similar to the 4.7 percent figure we observed at Bloom), four of these points were found within the body of one of the individuals who had met a violent death.

Thus, Bloom Mound and Salt Cedar raise the possibility that groups from central Texas made forays into southeastern New Mexico to attack and kill competitors (including noncombatants) who were engaged in long-distance bison hunting on the Southern Plains. This suggestion, of course, does not rule out the possibility that the inhabitants of Bloom, Salt Cedar, and elsewhere also engaged in hostile exchanges with other groups in other areas. The UVF response data, for instance, suggest that the Roswell communities were hunting bison in the Texas Panhandle as well as in central Texas, and these activities may have brought them into competition and conflict with communities over a wide swath of the Southern Plains.[4]

Although the nature of the conflict seems reasonably clear, and there are hints that some of the conflict involved Toyah peoples from central Texas, its cause is less evident. The answer, however, may be staring us in the face. Henderson's economy underwent a dramatic transformation in the late thirteenth and early fourteenth centuries. Bison hunting, much of it taking place far from the village, increasingly took center stage in Henderson's rapidly evolving economy, and trade with the Pueblos began to flourish at the same time. Westward-focused trade continued to soar a generation or so later at Bloom. Particularly striking about the trade items coming into both villages—at least those items that have been preserved—is that almost all come from the Puebloan world to the west (i.e., ceramics, turquoise, marine shell, obsidian, copper bells, and a macaw found in the backdirt of another pothunted local village known as Rocky Arroyo; see Emslie et al. 1992). We found little—aside from bison and the projectile points presumably used to hunt them—that we can confidently say came from the Plains. What we seem to be witnessing at Henderson and Bloom is the beginnings of intense trade with the Pueblos, and procurement of bison clearly figured prominently in these relationships (Speth 1991, 2004). Dried meat, as a source of protein, may of course have become increasingly important to the eastern Pueblos as they aggregated into large, sometimes huge, communities heavily dependent on farming (Speth and Scott 1989; Spielmann, ed. 1991). Hides may have become even more important than meat in the trade (Creel 1991), in part for robes and other pieces of clothing and footwear, but also as raw material for shields, a need triggered by the destabilizing introduction of a new and far more lethal shock weapon, the backed or recurved "Turkish" bow that rendered traditional Pueblo cane armor obsolete (LeBlanc 1997, 1999). But if the interaction witnessed at Henderson continued and intensified at Bloom, why did bison hunting suddenly decline and socially distant warfare simultaneously become so apparent?

The archaeology of the Toyah phase in central Texas may hold a key part of the answer. A striking feature of Toyah is that many of these peoples, particularly those groups in the more westerly portions of the Toyah area, also began to exploit Southern Plains bison more intensively (but see Dering 2008 for a slightly different perspective), some groups apparently traveling considerable distances to get to the herds (e.g., Johnson 1994; Ricklis 1992; Thompson et al. 2007; see also Mauldin et al., this volume). And judging by the early Spanish chronicles that relate to central and south Texas, fights between groups over access to the herds may have become commonplace:

> After establishing the pueblos of San Ildefonso and Santa Rosa de Santa Maria in the area of the Sabinas River in Coahuila, Captain Elizondo made several suggestions to guarantee the success of the enterprise. One of these recommendations concerned the interdiction of buffalo hunting by the Spaniards in that area. He explained that this was a very sensitive issue among Native groups which, among themselves, led them to defend their rights by the force of arms [*por ser materia mui sensible para ellos, y que afuerza de armas defienden de otras naciones*]. (CA 1674, cited in Wade 2002:174)

On July 3, 1675, Don Antonio de Balcarcel wrote a long letter to the Audiencia de Guadalajara about the problems he was experiencing in Monclova (Wade 1998:404–408). In this detailed letter Balcarcel discussed the issue of the natives' food resources and how the presence or absence of buffalo herds affected the native populations. He related that the buffalo was essential to the livelihood of native groups as a food resource and as the source of their attire. He stated: "This is their permanent attire [buffalo skins], and this is not available everywhere because to get buffalo they have to cross the rio del norte [Rio Grande] where they have great wars and barbarous retaliations over the killing of buffalo" (Wade 2002:179).

Hunters venturing into central Texas from southeastern New Mexico may have faced similarly fierce competition from Southern Plains peoples as bison hunting intensified throughout the region. Toyah folks may also have come into conflict with Roswell and Ochoa peoples over access to trading partners among the eastern Pueblos, although this seems less likely because trade goods emanating from the Pueblos do not appear to be all that common in the Toyah heartland (Johnson 1994). Intense positive interaction and exchange—mutualism in Spielmann's (1991a, 1991b, ed. 1991) view—appear to have been a more common and pervasive development farther to the north in the Texas and Oklahoma Panhandles, where Puebloan trade goods are many orders of magnitude more common than on the Edwards Plateau (Brosowske 2005; Eiselt 2006; Spielmann 1983, 1991b). Whatever the cause—access to herds or trading partners, or some more complex combination of factors—Roswell hunters may have become increasingly embroiled in these conflicts, ultimately forcing them to curtail their bison-hunting activities throughout the Southern Plains.

If the abundance of cherts identified by UVF as Southern Plains materials is any indication, yellow-orange cherts (i.e., central Texas) are always less common in the Roswell sites than the light/dark greens that we believe denote materials from farther north in the Panhandle. This might mean that Roswell hunters always focused more of their bison-hunting activities in the Panhandle than in central Texas. The abundance of yellow-orange cherts begins to decline during Henderson's late phase, whereas the greens do not decline until later, sometime after Henderson's abandonment. This could suggest that Roswell hunters were somehow first squeezed out of central Texas and only during Bloom times were they similarly forced out of the Panhandle. We suspect that by the end of Bloom's occupation the community was no longer actively participating in long-distance bison hunting and had instead taken on the role of "middlemen" in the burgeoning Plains-Pueblo trade. Ultimately, however, lethal conflict may have reduced the small population at Bloom to the point where the survivors were either absorbed by other groups or driven out of the area.

If competition over access to bison lay at the heart of the conflict between peoples on the Edwards Plateau and the inhabitants of the Roswell area, the UVF response of the stone tools and debitage from the Garnsey bison kill becomes particularly interesting. The kill site is located in an intermittent drainage on the east side of the Pecos River, about 20 km southeast of Roswell and 32 km due east of Henderson and Bloom (Speth 1983). Garnsey was the locus of repeated spring kill events dating to about AD 1450, roughly the time that we estimate Bloom was abandoned, give or take a few decades. Garnsey produced only 10 projectile points, but four of them responded with the distinctive yellow-orange light characteristic of central Texas chert. The other six points did not respond to either short- or longwave UV light. Aside from four bifaces, none of which responded to UV light, and 14 retouched tools, three of which responded to light green and four yellow-orange, all of the other lithics from the kill site (N = 598) are small unmodified flakes and tiny retouch and resharpening flakes, many scattered among the butchered bison remains, others concentrated around a hearth in a processing area. Of these, only 7.5 percent fluoresced light or dark green, whereas 30.3 percent responded with the familiar yellow-orange glow of Edwards chert. In light of these completely unanticipated results, it is hard to resist the temptation to attribute the Garnsey kills, not to local Roswell inhabitants as one of us has done ever since he excavated the site in the late 1970s (Speth 1983, 2004), but to uninvited strangers coming into the Pecos Valley to hunt bison from an unknown homeland located somewhere far to the southeast.

Concluding Remarks

The few villages that still remain reasonably intact in the Roswell area are obviously important for understanding local culture history (Emslie et al. 1992; Speth 2004; Wiseman 2002), but their value extends far beyond that. Through these sites we are getting a glimpse of the social and political upheavals that engulfed the Southern Plains during the tumultuous years preceding European contact. If we are right in our reading of the evidence from Bloom, as well as from sites like Salt Cedar, various Antelope Creek sites in the Texas and Oklahoma Panhandles, and many other Late Prehistoric and Protohistoric sites in and adjacent to the Southern Plains (e.g., Bovee and Owsley 1994; Brooks 1994, 2004:342–43), Plains-Pueblo interaction was not just a benevolent bond of economic cooperation and interdependence that sprang up to the mutual benefit of those who participated (see discussion in Vehik 2002; see also Spielmann 1991a); instead, it may at times have been a costly and blood-stained relationship that arose out of the wreckage of more than a century of conflict between scores of competing entities, only a few of which survived to witness the Spanish entrada.

Acknowledgments

First and foremost, we thank Jane Kelley for her wonderful friendship, help, and inspiration over the years. Without Jane's pioneering work in Roswell, we are not sure any of this would have happened. We are also deeply grateful to Regge Wiseman, one of the few archaeologists in New Mexico who has always recognized and valued the great potential of southeastern New Mexico's archaeological record. Over the years that University of Michigan archaeologists have worked in the Roswell area, Regge's unflagging help, knowledge, and insight have been invaluable. We also acknowledge the help of the many other people who, over the years, have participated in one way or another in the excavations and myriad analyses of the Garnsey bison kill, Rocky Arroyo, Henderson, and Bloom Mound. Among these, we owe an especially large debt of gratitude to Dick Ford, Robert H. (Bus) Leslie, Bill Parry, Dave Snow, Dedie Thomas Snow, Kate Spielmann, Henry Wright, and Lisa Young. We also owe a great deal to the ranchers—Skip and Jane Garnsey, Matt and Karen Henderson, Calder and Candy Ezzell, and Jay and Carrie Hollifield—for the many kindnesses and warm hospitality they offered us over the years, and for their invaluable efforts in protecting and preserving these wonderful archaeological treasures. In addition, our thanks go to the Archaeological Conservancy, present owners of both Henderson and Bloom Mound, for their important role in safeguarding southeastern New Mexico's rapidly vanishing archaeological heritage.

Several people helped us specifically with the ultraviolet component of the work. Karen O'Brien first brought our attention to the potential of UVF as a way of identifying Texas lithic materials. Charles Frederick helped us get started, bringing his entire comparative collection of Edwards Plateau chert to the 2007 SAA meetings in Austin so that we could see firsthand just how incredibly variable this material was. We spent an entire evening spread-eagled on the floor of the lobby in the main conference hotel looking at his fabulous collection of Edwards chert. Regge Wiseman shared his insights on the feasibility of UVF analysis with Roswell area materials. Phil Shelley generously loaned us samples from sources in both Texas and New Mexico that greatly expanded our comparative base for the region. Julia Clifton, Anita McNeece, Chris Turnbow, and Dody Fugate of the Museum of New Mexico in Santa Fe helped in the UVF study, providing us with access to collections from lithic workshop sites west of Roswell, as well as additional comparative chert samples from Texas and New Mexico. Kay Clahassey gave us access to her darkroom at the University of Michigan to facilitate the analysis. Kay also took the photograph of the two projectile points illustrated in figure 8.7.

Over the years, financial support for the Roswell work has come from many different sources, including grants from NSF and funds from several different units within the University of Michigan (Museum of Anthropology, Department of Anthropology, College of Literature, Science and the Arts, and Horace H. Rackham School of Graduate Studies). Last but not least, we thank the present volume editors, Nancy Kenmotsu and Doug Boyd, who invited us to participate in the original Toyah symposium in Austin in 2007 and encouraged us to publish this rather lengthy offspring of that stimulating and productive session. We are grateful.

Notes

1. Information provided by Cordelia Thomas Snow, Archaeological Records Management Section, Historic Preservation Division and Museum of New Mexico, Santa Fe.

2. Interestingly, despite many seasons of fieldwork in the Roswell area, we have never encountered any ceramics that came from sources in the Southern Plains, such as Borger Cordmarked.

3. Ages presented here and below determined by Jamie Clark, University of Michigan.

4. For an overview of evidence of violent conflict in the Late Prehistoric Texas Panhandle and adjacent parts of western Oklahoma, see Bovee and Owsley (1994), and Brooks (1994, 2004).

NINE

Toyah

REFLECTIONS ON EVOLVING PERCEPTIONS

Elton R. Prewitt

I appreciate the invitation to comment on this excellent collection focused on the Toyah interval of greater central Texas, a time and cultural phenomenon that encompasses the dynamic transition from prehistory into the written history of that region. Each chapter examines varying aspects of Toyah, and all are thoughtfully researched and presented in logical fashion. Some of the theoretical concepts require effort to understand, and some of the ethnohistorical details are a little tedious, but those concepts and details are critical to advancing our knowledge and understanding of this fascinating regional phenomenon. In reviewing these contributed chapters, I attempt to avoid picking nits; rather, I hope that my comments add to the substance of how we might move forward in constructive research.

Perspectives on the Toyah Phase

KENMOTSU AND BOYD: INTRODUCTION TO THE TOYAH PHASE

Kenmotsu and Boyd provide perhaps the most thorough, succinct, and readable review of Toyah research yet written. The history of research is deftly woven into current theoretical concepts dealing with social interaction at a variety of scales, thus setting the tone and direction for the ensuing specialized discussions. One topic, however, deserves a little amplification.

When Kelley (1947b) initially proposed Toyah as a cultural construct, he saw it as coeval in time and overlapping in regional distribution with the Austin interval (Suhm et al. 1954). What we now see, and accept, as two temporally sequent cultural intervals were not conclusively separated stratigraphically until excavation of Kyle Rockshelter (Jelks 1962). Although there were hints of temporal separation such as at Lehmann Rockshelter (Kelley 1947b), at Belton Reservoir sites (Miller and Jelks 1952), and at Smith Rockshelter (Suhm 1957), it was later that confirmation was made and, importantly, accepted as fact by contemporary researchers. Whether because of the excavation methods used or the palimpsest-style overprinting of open-site occupations, Perdiz points and Scallorn points were found together and were considered contemporaneous until the Kyle Rockshelter excavations provided indisputable evidence for chronological succession.

KENMOTSU AND ARNN: TOYAH AND THE ETHNOHISTORIC RECORD

This chapter written by Kenmotsu and Arnn is a wonderful treat to read. Concisely and logically presented, it contrasts key ethnohistorical documentary data with extant archaeological data in a way that brings them together in a coherent fashion. Some of the group movement and size descriptions can lead to interesting speculation. For example, take Juan Sabeata's report that he and his group of Jumanos traveled to Caddo country in twenty-six days. Presuming a travel rate of 20 to 25 miles per day, which can be achieved by groups traversing established trails, the twenty-six days easily places them among the southern Caddo people in the Crockett to Nacogdoches vicinities.

Variability in the ranges of group mobility, home territories, population densities, and directions of travel suggest several avenues of research. One senses that many groups (nations) infrequently (or never) mentioned in the documents occupied limited territories and lived in small dispersed extended family camps except during seasonal aggregations. This contrasts with the larger (probably) and more gregarious nomadic trader groups (nations) who garnered a lot more "press" from the Spanish simply because they regularly tended to travel widely and "information exchange" (news) was their stock-in-trade. Who is going to attract attention more—the three hundred or so members of a nation that maintains a low profile within a limited area, or the three thousand members of a nation that regularly dispatches trading parties over well-established long-distance routes?

Too, the fact that regular trade routes, long-distance group relationships, and extensive complex social networks were in existence in the sixteenth century suggests that these existed prehistorically as well. I tend to disagree with Kenmotsu and Arnn in their assessment that the archaeological evidence does not support concordance with the ethnographic data about site size. The suggestion that only three sites (Rush, LK201, and possibly Rowe Valley) have evidence that they could support three hundred or so residents is more likely a failure on the part of archaeologists to define sites and site boundaries fully. For example, at Rowe Valley, more than three hundred people set up a haphazard camp for three consecutive years during the Texas Archeological Society field schools there, with the camp covering not much more area than we eventually defined as constituting the archaeological site. The aboriginal camp was much more structured and could easily accommodate three hundred to five hundred persons. However, there are vast expanses of level terrace surface adjacent both upstream and downstream, and those areas never have been tested to see if the site is actually much larger. I can easily envision an aggregation of up to three thousand people camped on this broad segment of river terrace. Because archaeologists typically focus upon "sites," it is likely that larger group aggregate camps are not recognized for what they are.

I suspect sites such as Wheatley (Greer 1976b), Barker (Sorrow 1970), Buckhollow (Johnson 1994), and San Felipe Springs (Mehalchick et al. 1999), among others, also are of sufficient size to host groups larger than we commonly think. Certainly those sites contrast sharply with the smaller Toyah camps at rockshelters and open sites such as Pennywinkle, Loeve, Loeve-Fox, and numerous others. The limited materials at these sites are suggestive of dispersed family camps that differ significantly from the seasonal aggregate camps. An outstanding example of a short-term small family encampment is the as-yet-unpublished La Carneada Site (41WM1012) on the San Gabriel River several miles upstream from Rowe Valley (Rogers and Dixon 2006). This variability in Toyah archaeological site composition certainly seems to support the ethnohistorical record's descriptions.

Views of Toyah Phase Sociocultural Dynamics

ARNN: SOCIOCULTURAL IDENTITY AND THE TOYAH/TEJAS SOCIAL FIELD

In Arnn's first section, a review of major discussions that have focused on either diffusion of a technocomplex or an actual migration of people provides a basis for suggesting that those views be reconsidered in light of anthropological reality. He aptly reminds us that societies, at whatever size level, do not exist in isolation, but that complex interactions among groups occur at varying levels. He goes on to reiterate that these complex relationships documented in the ethnohistorical record surely represent patterns established in prehistory, and that we should use multiple lines of evidence to distinguish varying levels of sociocultural identities within the Toyah.

The second section of Arnn's chapter provides a more detailed review of Toyah regional variation using condensed synopses of a large compilation of individual site reports. This is a marvelous distillation of a huge body of data that provides fascinating views of subsets of Toyah culture. In the subsequent section, Arnn brings to bear the larger body of anthropological literature relevant to examining social identity. Here, he identifies a key problem that archaeologists tend to forget in the minutiae of artifact and feature analysis. In discussing ethnohistorical groups described on the southern High Plains, he cogently notes that most attributes that convey ethnic identity are not likely to survive in the archaeological record.

In the next section, Arnn provides reviews of a subset of ethnohistorical data that is more focused on specific areas within the greater Toyah region. It is complementary to the data presented earlier in the prehistoric section and suggests a number of sociocultural group interrelationships. Perhaps the most striking is the Toyah/Tejas social field as conceptualized in the concluding section. This tantalizing concept is admittedly simple in some respects, but Arnn suggests that three scales of social identity and interaction (community/band, marriage/linguistic group, and long-distance social networks) are present in both the prehistoric and historic record continuum.

I wholeheartedly agree with what Arnn has spent several years researching and has presented so concisely. There are, however, a few additional items to consider. Although disagreeing with some of the details, Shafer's (2006b) proposed concept of "Prairie Caddo" emerging in the northeastern segment of the Classic and Shared Toyah areas during the AD 1000–1200 period, immediately preceding the appearance of the Toyah phenomenon, merits consideration. Such a development provides a basis for sociocultural networks to be in place when bison abundance increases after AD 1200. The archaeologically visible, rapid spread of the bison-related technocomplex could then be explained through a combination of small-group serial migrations and contemporaneous rapid diffusion throughout the already established sociocultural networks. It should also be remembered that not every group receiving the Toyah technocomplex became instant experts in bison processing. For example, Skelton (1977) describes a Toyah-age bison skeleton at 41FY74 that was very sloppily butchered; the hunters knew the basics and had the toolkit, but the execution of the butchering process suggests inexperience with the species.

One item with which I disagree is Arnn's linking the distribution of white-tailed deer with that of Perdiz points. This species' range continues far beyond the eastern boundaries of Toyah, and another species, mule deer (or black-tailed deer), occupies the western segment of Perdiz distribution. I also disagree with the notion of opportunistic deer hunting as opposed to bison hunts by large groups. Small game may have been taken on an opportunistic basis, but I think deer, antelope, and bison most likely were harvested using organized hunts. By that, I do not mean large drive and jump/surround operations as practiced farther north on the Plains; rather, I suspect familiarity with prey habits and habitats allowed strategically planned small-group hunts that took advantage of the observed behavior of each species. Also, I believe—but obviously cannot prove—that this knowledge of species-specific animal behavior formed an integral part of the information exchange that accompanied the tools constituting the visible components of the technocomplex.

In the discussion of the Toyah lithic assemblage, a point is made regarding bifacial versus unifacial projectile point production and the fact that both techniques are seen on the Scallorn and Perdiz types. Considerable research is required before making conclusions, but I will point out that at the as-yet unpublished Rowe Valley site Perdiz points in the lower Toyah component are bifacial whereas those in the upper Toyah component are unifacial. Additionally, a couple of unifacial "Scallorn" points appear in the upper Toyah (as do other point types discussed later).

This also ties in with Arnn's subsequent dilemma relating to whether Austin and Toyah intervals are separable on the south Texas coastal plains; sequentially occupied open camps in low-depositional environments tend to be palimpsests where vertical stratigraphy (hence chronology) cannot be teased from the thin sediments (or soils) using current popular excavation methods.

Similar technological problems are seen in the discussion of Toyah ceramics. Johnson's (1994) analysis of the Buckhollow site has become the touchstone for defining Classic versus Shared Toyah, in large measure on the basis of ceramics. In my view, Buckhollow is an anachronism; many of the ceramics there ostensibly are locally (and sloppily) manufactured in contrast to sites located away from this central isolate. Away from the interior "core" area, in addition to making the variations of Leon Plain wares, Toyah peoples bought pots from the nearest pottery-producing groups, or from traders moving goods along well-established routes. The regional ceramic variations summarized by Arnn should be a wake-up call to reevaluate how ceramics styles are used when inferring sociocultural group identifications and interactions.

KIBLER: THE ROLE OF EXOTIC MATERIALS IN THE TOYAH SOCIAL SYSTEM

The role of exotic materials in the Toyah economic and social system is examined by Kibler largely on the basis of data from the Jayroe site located in the northeastern segment of the Classic Toyah region. Defining "exotics" as Caddo ceramics, obsidian mostly from the Valles Caldera sources, and marine shells from Pacific coast or Gulf of Mexico sources, he argues that they are both rare and not necessities for Toyah folk. Citing the existence of abundant available chert, homemade ceramics, and the prohibitive costs of significant food exchange systems, he questions the role of these nonutilitarian exotic items in the subsistence system in order to support an argument that their presence signifies a strategy for subsistence risk reduction.

To support this proposition, he portrays the environment of the Toyah homeland as subsistence-resource deficient and unpredictable—a contrarian's view to the standard recitation of Eden-like available food resources. After reviewing identified deficiencies Kibler concludes that it is a risky place for Toyah folk to live, then discusses risk management using mobility and exchange strategies. Segueing into an abbreviated comment on Toyah ethnohistory, he aptly observes that the exotic items reflect alliances of social groups and notes the lack of such items in the core of the Toyah homelands, implying that their social networks did not extend into the periphery. After noting several of the regional exotics' distributions around the Classic Toyah margins, Kibler uses the Jayroe site exotics to demonstrate sociocultural interaction with horticultural Caddo groups to the east and Plains Village groups to the north. Pointing out that this is a common pattern for subsistence societies worldwide, he concludes that the unpredictable subsistence base of the Toyah homeland was mitigated through the establishment of external social networks and high mobility, both of which are represented in the exchange of exotic materials.

Although, in large measure, I think Kibler's contribution is positive, there are some problems. In the introductory section he notes his intention to "argue that it is unrealistic to view the Toyah as a *link in an economic interaction sphere* that tied together the adjacent Caddoan people, Plains Villagers, and Puebloan peoples of the Southwest" (emphasis mine). I am not sure that, in a subsistence system wherein risk reduction strategies include exchange through social networking, you can segregate economy as a distinct segment set apart from subsistence. The purpose of the social networks is to reduce economic failure during periods of subsistence stress, a strategy that can take many forms. If he means that Toyah was not a lynchpin between the Caddos and Pueblos, he could be correct; the Plains Villagers fulfilled that role between the northern Caddos and northern Pueblos. However, as other contributors to this volume demonstrate, economic exchange between southern Caddos and southern Pueblos was accomplished through Toyah or Toyah-connected traders.

Turning to Kibler's discussion of the environmental risks in the Toyah homeland, I find it interesting that the presence of numerous springs, both large and small, and extensive river/stream systems are omitted from consideration. If there existed extensive social networks designed to reduce subsistence stress, then within the Toyah homeland these spring oases and riparian bottomlands would have become shared resources within the subsistence economic system of socially networked groups (Taylor 1964). Around the periphery of the homeland, external social networks would have operated in similar fashion and, I suspect, produced the pattern of "exotic" trade items seen in the known archaeological record of the Toyah.

In discussing the ceramics and obsidian from the Jayroe site, Kibler turns to the southern Caddos as a source for the ceramics. For the obsidian, he looks north to the Harrell site on the Brazos River, then beyond to western Oklahoma. Citing well-established east-west exchange by the Plains Villagers of the Edwards Complex, he suggests that the Harrell site represents the southern margin of the Plains Village tradition and thereby implies a north-south exchange system to account for the presence of obsidian at Jayroe. This introduces another avenue of Toyah interaction that merits attention in future studies.

Views of Toyah Phase Subsistence Economy

MAULDIN, THOMPSON, AND KEMP: THE ROLE OF BISON IN THE TOYAH PERIOD

Examination of Toyah subsistence economy opens with a reconsideration of the role of bison, written by Mauldin, Thompson, and Kemp. This chapter takes a contrarian view of how bison figured into subsistence strategies employed by Toyah folk. A brief review of the progression of Toyah research focuses on the identification of this cultural expression as "Plains-like" and on studies subsequent to 1970 that expounded a strong bison presence in the region that followed a hiatus in the terminal Late Archaic to early Late Prehistoric. It is suggested that their data show that there is no bison absence during that time, and that the perceived Toyah abundance is in fact an increase in the importance of logistical hunting strategies during a period of deteriorating bison habitat.

They next review bison availability on the Southern Plains, and they present evidence of bison presence (and abundance) north of the Red River in central and western Oklahoma in addition to the Classic and Shared Toyah regions. They conclude that it is unclear whether Toyah material culture indeed reflects an increase in bison abundance. Next follows a section in which they reconsider the presence of bison in central and south Texas. Data from 114 sites spanning the Late Archaic and Late Prehistoric were examined to determine presence, absence, and NISP when possible. Components were tied to radiocarbon dating where possible, but primary reliance is upon traditional artifact associations.

Their results suggest that bison are not completely absent, but they admit the nearly ubiquitous presence of bison in Toyah components. However, they present data showing that of the thirty-six Toyah components with bison, only seven account for 98 percent of NISP. These data are then used to argue that the Toyah toolkit combined with the few sites with high NISP counts signals a shift in hunting organization and processing. Mauldin and colleagues then review proxy data for bison availability and look at paleovegetation data to show fluctuation in C_4 grasses along with bog pollen data. They conclude that their data suggest a declining bison population throughout the Late Prehistoric, including Toyah.

They then review vegetation using short temporal scales. A primary focus is on the Palmer Drought Severity Index (PDSI) and the projections of variability in soil moisture using a correlation of tree ring data that extends from the present back to AD 1000. Because known periods of multiyear droughts are easily identified, the backward projections are accepted as plausible. High (or positive) PDSI values are associated with increased soil moisture; low (negative) values reflect moisture deficiency. They posit that high values correspond to greater forage availability, yet negative values may show either decrease of forage or expansion of grassland at the expense of forests. Their analysis shows a distinct change in soil moisture availability from less in Late Prehistoric I (Austin interval) to greater in Late Prehistoric II (Toyah interval). Yet they argue that the severity of fluctuations in twenty-five-year data intervals would cause dramatic differences in forage availability, hence a decline in bison numbers.

Finally, they use these data to reconsider the role of bison in Toyah, taking a view that Toyah did not develop in response to the return of bison in large numbers. Several scenarios are presented to account for this apparent disagreement between the environmental and the archaeological data. These are followed by various propositions that key on diversification of resource/diet breadth, and that this reflects intensification in the use of low-return resources. They conclude that traditional interpretations of bison importance in the Toyah are no longer viable.

Overall, this chapter raises good questions regarding past interpretations of Toyah subsistence and its focus on bison procurement. Naturally, I have a few problems with their data review. First, can I trust the compilation of data upon which they base much of their key thesis that bison are archaeologically visible during their initial Late Prehistoric period? Their table 5.2 presenting bison presence for 77 sites omits the very important Toyah component at the Bigon-Kubala site (41WM258) on Willis Creek at Granger Lake (Prikryl 1982). Then, the eight sites with bison present during their initial Late Prehistoric period (LP I, for short) give me pause to wonder. The citation of a single bison bone in LP I at the Loeve-Fox site (41WM230) is in error; levels 1–4, as shown in the first Loeve-Fox report (Prewitt 1974), included both LP I (Austin) and LP II (Toyah) strata. As clearly shown in the second Loeve-Fox report (Prewitt 1982a), bison bones are associated with Toyah, including a partially articulated skeleton with Perdiz, Cliffton, and Young arrow points scattered in and around the carcass. I also question the accuracy of the other sites; some (41HY209T, 41MC296, 41SP120, 41WM130, and 41ZV155) show the difficulties in teasing out stratigraphy in slowly aggrading clay soils with bioturbation, one (41BN33) most likely demonstrates bioturbation in a sinkhole, and another (41BR420) is in a burned rock midden subject to intensive temporal mixing. As a basis for bison presence during the Austin interval, this table provides insufficient data.

This leads to the whole question of Dillehay's (1974) and Huebner's (1991) studies of the presence/absence of bison. As the late David S. Dibble and I discussed at length when we were providing information and encouragement to Dillehay when he began gathering data on the topic about 1972, none of us were thinking in terms of presence versus absolute absence. Rather, we thought in terms of *archaeologically visible* versus *not archaeologically visible*, and *relatively frequent or abundant* versus *infrequent or not abundant*. Herd size, mobility, and habitat vary too widely among bison to consider their presence/absence in absolute terms. Similarly, we did not question that bison were most likely present—and archaeologically visible—*north* of the Red River during the Austin interval.

In looking at both long-term and short-term climate and vegetation change, I am surprised that Hall's Cave was relegated to reflecting local conditions rather than regional patterns, and that only Cooke's (2005) carbon isotope data were used. Toomey's (1993) microfaunal analysis of Hall's Cave correlates very well with the bog pollen data (Collins 1995 and 2004) and is further supported by the Hall's Cave magnetic susceptibility curve (Elwood and Gose 2006). The remarkable congruence of these multiple lines of evidence actually supports the Mauldin et al. thesis that the Toyah interval saw a rapid drying trend. It also is congruent with the onset of the Little Ice Age event, a time when regional climates globally were changing. See Rosen (2007) for an excellent example of climate change in the Near East, including a drying event temporally coincident with our own Toyah interval.

The "Toyah Reconsidered" section relies heavily on decreasing bison abundance due to increasingly patchy grasslands, resulting in resource intensification and diversification, followed by a review of some of Binford's notions about logistical strategies and the resulting types of sites expected to reflect those strategies. I think Mauldin et al. need to stop and rethink some of their perceptions. As I noted at Loeve-Fox (Prewitt 1974 and 1982a), the proliferation of formal and informal tools during the late Late Archaic signaled a shift to what we would now call resource diversification and intensification, and this carried through the Late Prehistoric I (Austin interval). Concomitant with this shift is an ever-increasing incidence of violence that began at the onset of the Late Archaic and continued through LP I. Numerous cemeteries and isolated interments show evidence of violence, suggesting increased competition for all resources.

Contrary to Mauldin et al.'s ending statement, there is precious little evidence of violence during the Toyah compared with the preceding Austin interval. Exceptions include one out of more than twenty individuals in the "mass burial" near Waco (Meroney 1936), two out of seven burials at Asa Warner on the Brazos south of Waco (Watt 1956), and one out of more than thirty interments in Aycock Shelter on Owl Creek near Belton (Watt 1936); in each case, Perdiz points (or "Perdiz-like" points in the case of the Waco "mass burial") are noted in positions suggesting they are the cause of death for the individuals. All three of these sites are on the northeastern periphery of Classic Toyah (Prewitt 1974:Table 4). These four individuals in a population of approximately sixty indicate that only 7 percent met violent deaths; compare this to the Loeve-Fox site Austin interval cemetery where 18 percent (five of twenty-eight) died violently. I also point out that the Coleman Cemetery site (41BX568; Potter et al. 2005) is by interment style and artifact association (however loose)—and the two radiocarbon dates from overlying hearths—suggestive of late LP I rather than LP II (or Toyah). What the bioarchaeological data indicate to me is that the Toyah interval is marked by an abrupt decrease of overt hostility that presumably reflects the emergence of the complex social networks noted in the earlier chapters discussing ethnohistorical data.

Finally, I would note that, yes, bison and the accompanying toolkit have dominated research questions and conclusions in the past. However, that was used as a tool to separate the Toyah interval from earlier cultural expressions. The importance of the full range of resources was not questioned. Interpretations and new avenues of research must build upon past investigations in order to continually refine our understanding of the past.

GILMORE: BONE PROCESSING AND SUBSISTENCE STRESS IN SOUTH TEXAS

Eschewing the broad-brush approach, Gilmore looks at a single site, 41SP220, for clues on bone processing and subsistence stress in southern Texas. After his introduction of the topic, he reviews the environment of the coastal prairies with an eye toward demonstrating the presence of high variability in food and other resources on both short-term and long-term bases. He provides a subregional review of major archaeological sites and pertinent ethnohistorical data along with bioarchaeological findings. These all suggest stress in the subsistence system operating in the south Texas subregion. An excellent discussion shows how fat stored in bones could play various roles in stress avoidance. Protein poisoning and essential fatty acids lead into a discussion on different methods of bone processing and the research methods that can be used to demonstrate the presence or absence of marrow extraction versus bone grease rendering.

This sets the stage for his case study of bones from the Toyah assemblage at 41SP220. Fully expecting to find evidence of bone grease extraction due to the very fragmented nature of his sample, Gilmore found instead that taphonomy had more to do with creating the preserved bone sizes. The results, developed from sophisticated analytical methods developed by Alan Outram and his colleagues, were surprising but clearly suggest that extreme stress processing of the bones could not be demonstrated. The discussion section presents several scenarios to account for the findings, including site occupation during a prosperous time, insufficient quantity of animals/bones to justify bone grease extraction, an increase in diet breadth, and, finally, social activities trumping ecological constraints to alleviate periods of subsistence stress.

Overall, Gilmore has done a great job—establishing a hypothesis and the methods of testing it, describing the results, and providing alternative explanations and avenues of research when his hypothesis proved to be invalid. This is good science, and we need more examples of this kind of study to really get at the heart of the Toyah interval and those who peopled it. I am especially pleased to see the methods currently being refined by Outram and his colleagues being used to examine Toyah faunal assemblages—this is a very positive contribution.

Toyah Phase Viewed from the Outside

BOYD: THE NORTHERN TOYAH PHENOMENON IN THE SOUTHERN PLAINS

Turning to the southern High Plains, Boyd provides a provocative summary of Toyah expressions in a neglected area. Taking a cue, in part, from Shafer's (2006b) "Prairie Caddo" concept, Boyd examines what he terms "northern Toyah." Encompassing the northwestern Classic Toyah area starting at the South Concho River, his northern Toyah area extends onto the High Plains as far north as Palo Duro Creek. Briefly reviewing Toyah background information, he rightly points out that—except for the style of projectile points (Perdiz)—the lithic tools used by these peoples are identical to the suite of stone tools used by their contemporaries, the Plains Villagers. He also suggests that the bone-tempered ceramic types are too generically defined, and that analyses such as INAA might offer better ways to identify source areas. Drawing on Johnson's (1994) review, he suggests an absence of agriculture, then notes an apparent intensive use of deer and antelope as well as plant processing in earth ovens.

An examination of ethnicity and social identity begins with a caution against a priori assumptions that the Jumanos are the historic expression of Toyah. Citing the concepts as too broadly defined, he suggests approaching these topics from a series of arguments developed in Arnn's recent work. The essential argument is that systems of cultural classifications in archaeology that emerged in the mid-twentieth century are inappropriate for seeking small-scale social identities. Drawing upon Schortman's (1989) concepts, Boyd suggests that we work toward defining individual community groups, and that the Jumano model is not what future research should be based upon.

Boyd then turns attention to Johnson's (1994) Shared Toyah area concept for Toyah. Explicitly drawing from Shafer's (2006b) "Prairie Caddo" perceptions and Ricklis's (1992, 1995a, 1995b, 1996) work on Toyah and Rockport interactions along the coastal margins, he explores the archaeological diversity of northern Toyah. A detailed review of the distributions of a variety of contemporaneous projectile point and ceramic styles on the Southern Plains provides a basis for then looking at potential social fields and communities. He points out that the northern Toyah exhibits more stereotypical Plains Village style artifacts, and that there is a greater reliance upon bison procurement in contrast to Toyah sites farther south and southeast. He concludes from this that the northern Toyah represents a boundary zone of social groups situated between at least two other social fields whose backgrounds differed significantly from theirs.

Boyd's concluding section details his thoughts for future research on the northern Toyah. Ecology, social and territorial boundaries, communal hunting, and the need for extensive social alliances are covered in his first subsection. In looking at developing models for the region, he again turns to Schortman (1989) for five research issues that provide a suitable framework for exploring causal relations, increases in social stratification, warfare and competition, trade as a method of communication, and nonelite interactions. The next subsection lays out the always tantalizing topic of Toyah origins. He summarizes several suggestions, mostly drawn from Johnson (1994). Taking Johnson's inferences further, Boyd raises the questions of the Toyah relationship to the Palo Duro and Blowout Mountain complexes. Boyd concludes the section with suggestions about how archaeologists might approach the questions raises in his chapter.

This is an outstanding overview of Toyah materials on the southern High Plains. Boyd raises excellent questions and suggests a variety of ways to explore them. I have few critical comments on this well-conceived analysis. Under the discussion "Ethnicity and Social Identity," I think it would be helpful to bring the work of Wiessner (1983), McBrinn (2005), and others into the consideration and recognition of style and how it might be translated into traits/patterns expected within an archaeological context.

In the subsection "Communities and Social Fields in the Northern Toyah Area," caution should be used with the "Garza complex." Garza and Soto points were defined in print the same year (Runkles 1964; Phelps 1964) by folks working in two distinct geographic areas—the southern High Plains of Texas and the Chihuahuan Desert in central northern Mexico. Although each of these researchers staunchly defends the stylistic distinctions between the two types, I personally do not see a difference. What I do see is a reasonably continuous distribution of Garza/Soto points from the Garza County area south-southwestward across southeastern New Mexico, the western Trans-Pecos of Texas, and into northeastern Chihuahua between Chihuahua City and the area of Presidio and Ojinaga. We do not know the relationships/identities of the Garza/Soto peoples, but I think a look at Beckett's (Beckett and Corbett 1992) work on the Mansos in the El Paso area might be a fruitful place to start. Interactions with the Toyah folk along this long northwestern Shared Toyah boundary might prove an intriguing and productive direction for research.

SPETH AND NEWLANDER: TOYAH AND PLAINS-PUEBLO INTERACTIONS

Speth and Newlander's chapter shifts attention to the western fringe of Boyd's northern Toyah and off the west edge of the southern High Plains. A complex of sites near the confluence of the Hondo and Pecos rivers near Roswell forms a basis for looking at the possibility of social interaction with Toyah (or Toyah-related) groups to the east and southeast, and with Plains Villagers to the northeast. The tongue-in-cheek introductory section gives a humorous review of the place of the eastern extension of Jornada Mogollon in relation to "the Pueblos" and to the Plains. The authors point out, though, that regardless of continuing neglect by most "Southwestern" archaeologists, the eastern Jornada Mogollon peoples participated in the Pueblo exchange system, as evidenced by a variety of exotic artifacts, and they propose that these people may have served as "middlemen" in exchanges between Pueblos and Plains.

After a brief background on the Late Prehistoric near Roswell, they launch into a concise review of excavations and findings at the Henderson site. This pueblo comprises at least seventy adobe pithouse structures that were blocked together, two plazas, and an adjacent series of roasting pits that were filled with not only fire-cracked rocks but a plethora of faunal remains, lithics, and ceramics. A major analytical discovery was the seriation of rim sherds of El Paso Polychrome jars; this not only allowed distinguishing two sequential occupational episodes at this site but provided a basis for temporal sequencing of the other three sites examined in the excavations, placing Bloom Mound as slightly later than Henderson. The economics in the early occupation (ca. AD 1275–1300) appears to be broad spectrum with agriculture supplementing collecting and hunting, and though bison were important they were not a dominant factor. Trade materials, mostly in the form of exotic ceramics, are present but rare.

In contrast, the later occupation at Henderson during the first half (roughly) of the fourteenth century saw significant increases in the quantity and variety of exotic goods. Concomitantly, the quantity of bison bones and projectile points increases dramatically. A bias towards favored utility bones and their concentration in and around public processing locations leads to a conclusion that the inhabitants were procuring the bison elsewhere, transporting the desirable parts home, then processing them into marketable dried meat. Looking to the eastern quadrant for sources of bison, Speth and Newlander segue into a discussion of preferred knapable stone sources and ways to identify the variety of siliceous materials found at Henderson, fixing on ultraviolet florescence as an imperfect—but affordable—method of tentative sourcing. Projectile points from the Texas Panhandle region are much more frequent than those identified as from the Edwards Plateau, suggesting interactions with both regions but more frequently with Panhandle people. The question of whether the points were made by the residents or obtained ready-made through trade could not be answered through analysis of the projectile point metric data.

They then shift their attention down the Hondo River to the nearby Bloom Mound. Professional archaeologists, avocationals, and looters all have dug in this site since the 1930s. Althought the site was thought to be completely destroyed, excavations in 2000 showed remnants of a pueblo of twenty to twenty-five rooms. Sketchy information recorded by avocationals, along with limited fieldwork, allowed Kelley (1984) to postulate that the site was a trading center, as suggested by the unusually abundant quantity and variety of exotic goods recovered. Evidence suggesting the pueblo was sacked and burned was gleaned from the avocationals' notes.

Speth's recent excavations revealed evidence that, like Henderson, Bloom Mound had two sequential occupations. Within some of the houses, flexed burials were found to exhibit inferred fatal trauma in three of six examples of intentional interments. One adult male exhibited bludgeoning of the skull and another adult male and an infant each had a projectile point in the area of the abdomen—one a Perdiz, the other a Washita. These interments are shown to contrast with the violent nature of the frequently burned and uninterred skeletons previously excavated by avocationals. Exotic items surpass the percentages at Henderson, but bison bones are sharply less common. Speth and Newlander rightly point out that this could be a result of sampling error, since excavations have been limited to the room block. Projectile points are significantly less common than at Henderson, and relatively few of these are sourced to the Panhandle of Texas. They note that the kinds of violence seen at Bloom Mound indicate conflict between socially distant groups.

This provides the backdrop for the discussion "Competition and Conflict." They focus on the questions of who the enemies of the Bloom Mound people were, and why these enemies would want to destroy a small trading community. The source of the material of the two points found with individual burials appears to be the Edwards Plateau, and one is typed as Perdiz—one of the hallmarks of the Toyah. Noting that Perdiz is rare at Bloom Mound (six specimens out of 130 typed points) and completely absent at Henderson, the rarity of this type anywhere in southeastern New Mexico leads to a discussion of multiple ethnic/social groups constituting the Toyah. They compare Bloom Mound to the Salt Cedar site in Andrews County, Texas, where Perdiz is rare (23 of 437 specimens) but four were found in the body of a single adult male burial, indicating another example of violence.

Reviewing probable sources and reasons for the pattern of violent conflict involving presumed Toyah groups, Speth and Newlander point to the rapidly changing economy at Henderson, where Pueblo trade increased, then became even more important a short time later at Bloom. They then point out that items from the east seem limited to lithics and bison products—meat and hides. Yet bison hunting as a pursuit declined quickly at Bloom concomitant with an increase in violence. The propensity of Toyah people to exploit bison and to travel long distances in pursuit of these animals, as noted in Spanish documents, leads to a suggestion that Toyah folks ventured into the Southern Plains, generating conflict with eastern Jornada Mogollon communities. They contrast this view with Spielman's perception of positive interaction and exchange (trade) between Plains Villagers and Pueblos farther to the north.

Speth and Newlander suggest that bison procurement during the Henderson occupation derived mostly from the northeast toward the Panhandle because the people were denied access to the southeast, and that during the Bloom occupation they were denied access to the northeast as well. Whether or not the Roswell area pueblos had become middlemen in a trading economy, the result was eventual destruction of the community then living at Bloom Mound. At this point, the authors discuss the Garnsey bison kill some 20 miles to the east in light of the lithics from this series of spring bison-kill events being sourced to Edwards Plateau cherts. Reversing a long-held belief that this site, dating about AD 1450, was the product of local residents, the authors observe instead that it might actually represent a series of incursions by peoples from the southeast (presumably meaning Toyah). They conclude with a suggestion that interactions between Plains and Pueblo peoples were not always sanguine mutual economic cooperation but instead, at times, became violent contests of survival among groups competing for the same resources.

This is an intriguing discussion that presents a very different view of Toyah from the outside. I see a strong correlation between the Roswell area and the northern Toyah presented by Boyd. Between them, a strong case is built in support of conducting carefully planned long-term research into Toyah expressions in the southern Plains adjacent, but well outside, the Toyah "homelands" of central Texas.

Speth and Newlander condense the results of many years of research in the area around the confluence of the Hondo and Pecos rivers into a well-presented tale of a small community and its successes and travails. I have few quibbles with the details, but I do find it a bit odd that, of all the anthropological literature available today regarding social fields, social identity, and reciprocal risk-reduction strategies by economically marginal societies, Spielman's work on Plains-Pueblo exchange is the only example cited (see, e.g., Arnn, this volume). In a similar vein, I encourage Speth to go beyond Binford and use the fascinating work by Outram and his colleagues when dealing with faunal utility indexes, processing, and transportation considerations.

Overall, I find this collection a refreshing overview of the Toyah that provides a variety of topics for further research. Each author or group of authors has pursued their individual topics without being constrained to a particular approach or point of view. Surely it is a coincidence, but the conjunction of the bulk of ethnohistorical data being derived from around the periphery of the Classic Toyah and the varied archaeological data being derived from sites similarly situated strikes me as a little odd. Perhaps "Tio" Lee Johnson (1994) did such a masterful job with the Buckhollow site, followed shortly by Ricklis's (1994) work at the Mustang Branch site that new views within the Toyah heartland were rendered unnecessary. With the exception of Boyd, who made a passing reference, I also find it odd that Creel's (1991) thoughts on the role of bison hides in exchange systems during the Toyah interval are pretty much ignored. Also, there is some degree of ambiguity in several Toyah terms that perhaps reflects a lack of consensus regarding what the Toyah represents and how it should be defined. It probably also reflects an absence of agreement upon chronological terminology in the region, but that is best left for discussion at another time.

A Preview of the Rowe Valley Site

Several contributors to this volume refer to the unpublished Rowe Valley site (41WM437). Although a descriptive report with fully developed conclusions and interpretations is still years away from completion, I provide here a preview of the site's uppermost Toyah component and the direction some of the interpretations *may* take. This synopsis is adapted from a paper I presented to the Texas State Historical Association in 2006.

The Texas Archeological Society's annual field school conducted extensive excavations at the Rowe Valley site in eastern Williamson County, Texas, during three field schools held there in 1982, 1983 and 1984 (fig. 9.1). Infrastructure support was provided by the Travis County Archeological Society based in Austin. I served as archaeologist, directed the fieldwork, and am responsible for the research design, analysis, and reporting. The quantity of data recovered during three years of excavations proved to be so massive that the task of completing the analysis and final report is still in progress.

My approach was taken from that which I previously had used at the Loeve-Fox site (41WM230) a short distance downstream. There, large block excavations (8 m by 16 m) had revealed spatially patterned features and debris suggestive of a series of purposefully structured Late Archaic encampments (Prewitt 1982a). Unconstrained by right-of-way boundaries or project footprints, excavations at Rowe Valley were designed as a series of contiguous 10 m by 10 m blocks. Horizontal controls were by 1 m by 1 m units; initially 10 cm arbitrary levels were

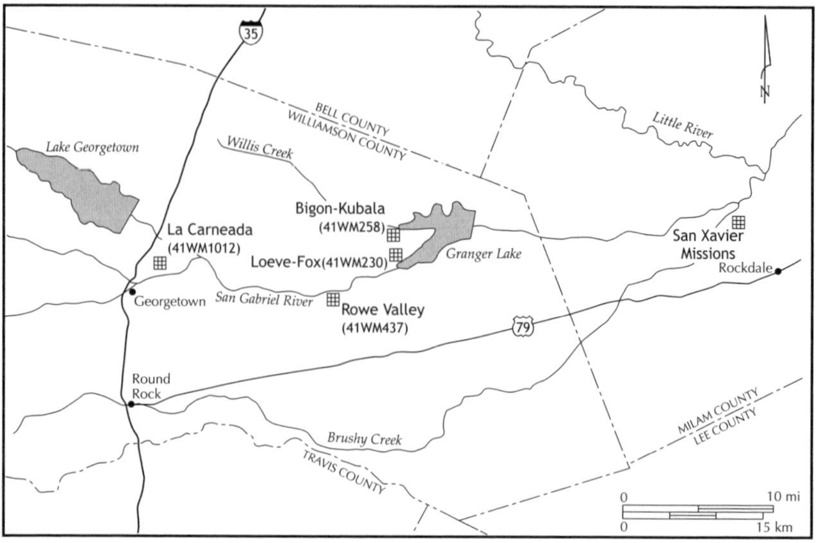

FIGURE 9.1. Location of Rowe Valley site (41WM437) and other sites along the San Gabriel River mentioned in the text.

used as vertical controls, but after realizing that there were two clearly stratified Toyah components we changed to 5 cm levels. Most excavations were in the upper Toyah; sampling of the lower Toyah was limited, and very little sampling of the even lower, and stratigraphically separated, Austin interval was accomplished. I am disappointed that equal sampling of all three components was not possible, but the upper Toyah component yielded the types of spatial data I hoped would be present.

SITE LOCATION AND SETTING

Rowe Valley is located on the south bank of the San Gabriel River in eastern Williamson County about midway between the communities of Jonah and Circleville and about 5 miles north of Taylor. It is contained in a deep alluvial river terrace that supports a grove of native pecan, elm, and hackberry trees. The terrace's fine-grained sediments were deposited during the Holocene epoch. Frequent overbank flooding allows sediments to settle in low-energy stream environments, and over time they can accumulate to great thicknesses, such as the approximately 10 m observed at Rowe Valley.

This site was recorded by Daniel Prikryl in the late 1970s when the Rowe family began mining part of it for fill dirt to be used in construction. A thin layer of sparse burned rocks, flint flakes, and animal bones was noted high in the borrow pit profile. This overlay another thicker zone of burned rocks and flint flakes, but this deeper zone was also darker gray due to charcoal staining. The site is situated on the upstream side of the juncture of a small spring-fed creek with the river. An

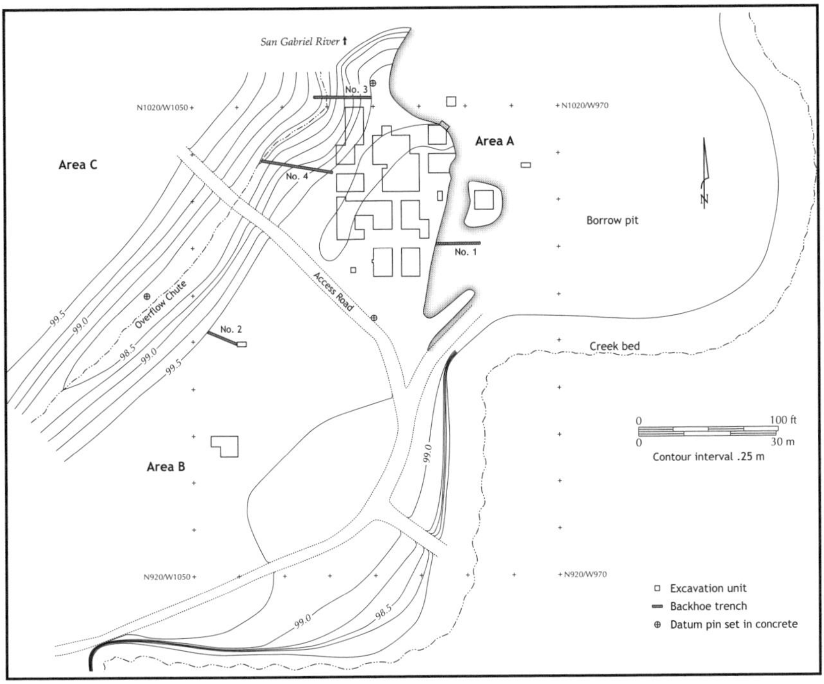

FIGURE 9.2. Plan map of the Rowe Valley site showing locations of excavation units.

overbank flood chute intersects the river upstream from the mouth of the creek and extends through the site (fig. 9.2).

One occupation area is between the chute and the modern river channel (Area C); two occupation areas lie between the chute and the creek, with Area A also fronting the river. The presently known extent of the site was determined through a systematic grid of posthole tests dug to a depth of 60–70 cm. The borrow pit removed at least one-third of the occupation area between the mouths of the chute and the creek (Area A), and it is here that most of our excavations were conducted. Excavations also were limited, for the most part, to the uppermost two isolable occupation layers. These two layers are assigned to the Late Prehistoric age Toyah phase, which dates to about 650–250 years BP, or roughly AD 1300–1700. Here, I focus on the later of the two Toyah occupations, which is thought to date approximately AD 1650–1700.

OCCUPATIONAL FEATURES

Three major types of features were encountered in the upper Toyah at Rowe Valley: resource processing, thermal, and tool manufacturing. The primary resource-processing feature consists of a butchering station on the northwestern side of Area A (fig. 9.3). Here, abundant bones of bison, antelope, and deer were found along with those of other animals such as turtle and various small mammals. Al-

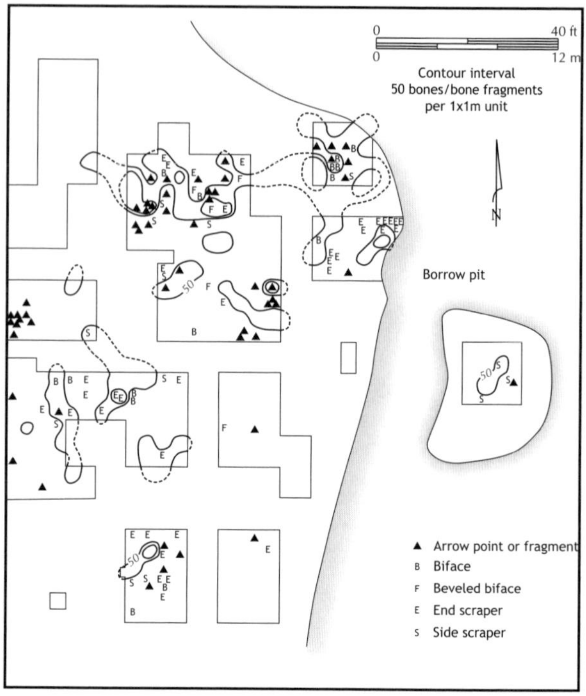

FIGURE 9.3. Raw bone densities (contour) and distribution of bifaces, scrapers, and arrow points in upper Toyah component, Area A, Rowe Valley site.

though the bones of the different animals were generally commingled, there was a concentration of mature deer antlers in the western portion of the butchering station adjacent to a meat-curing station. This suggests the animals were harvested during late fall or early winter. Most of the bones appear to represent adult animals, but a single maxilla fragment of a bison calf indicates an age of six or eight months, again supporting a late fall harvest time. Broken, discarded, and lost tools are scattered among the bones of the butchered animals.

The thermal features include three types of hot-rock cooking facilities, one charcoal- and ash-filled pit, and three small burned clay pits (fig. 9.4). The hot-rock features are present in triplets, with one of each type present in each set. Small basin-shaped pits lined with fire-fractured cobbles are typical hearths containing charcoal and ash associated with this time period. Near, but roughly three meters or so away from each of these hearths, is a smaller hearth that is less structured but contains some charcoal and ash. A similar-size unstructured pile of burned rocks is located a meter or so from these smaller hearths. As noted, these three feature types form triplets, and several sets of them are arranged around the larger charcoal- and ash-filled pit that lacks burned rocks. Two of the three burned clay pits are components of a meat-curing station.

The tool-manufacturing features consist of chipping stations where stone tools were made from locally available chert cobbles (fig. 9.5). These vary from small, well-defined flake concentrations, where only two or three cobbles had been reduced, to larger and more complex concentrations that appear to represent mul-

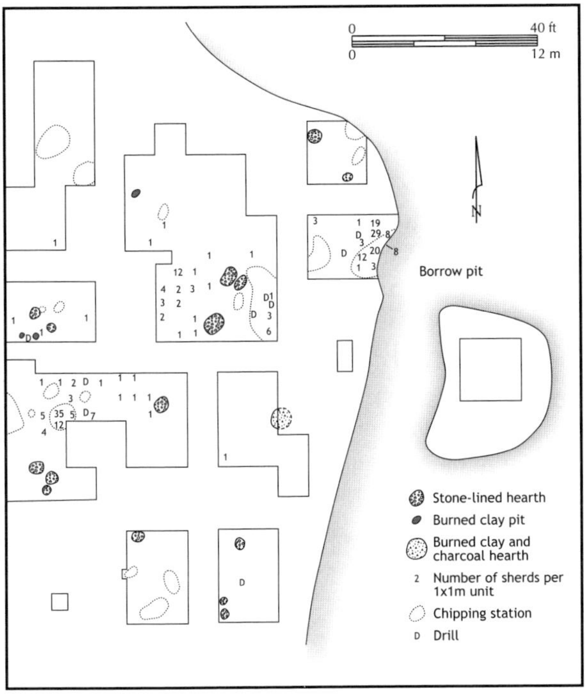

FIGURE 9.4. Distributions of thermal features, chipping stations, drills, and ceramics in upper Toyah component, Area A, Rowe Valley site.

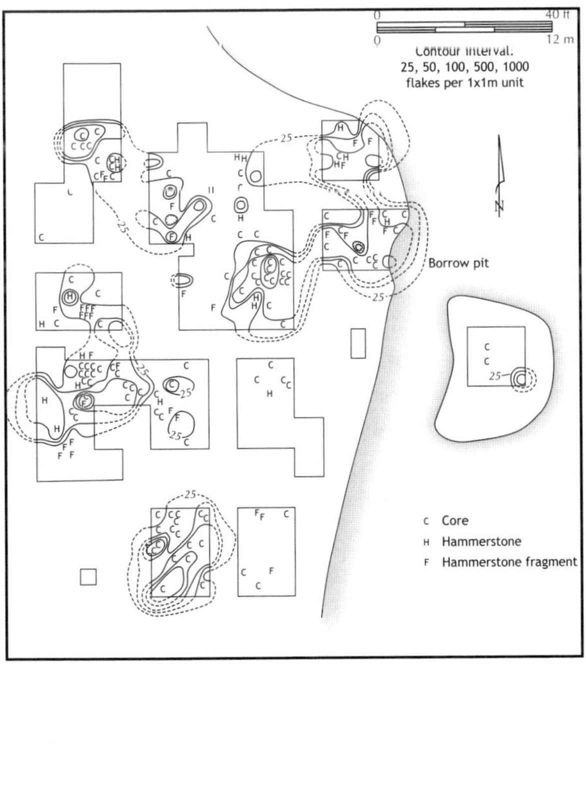

FIGURE 9.5. Raw flake densities (contour) and distribution of chipping stations, cores, and hammerstones in upper Toyah component, Area A, Rowe Valley site.

tiple episodes of knapping. In some, the knapper primarily made arrow points; in others, hide-processing tools such as end scrapers and side scrapers were the dominant items manufactured. Of course, most of the chipping stations exhibit multiple types of tool failures, suggesting that each knapper manufactured a suite of tools. An example of the manufacturing process is shown by a core reassembled from one of the chipping stations; the two major flakes that are missing are in fact blades that were suitable for shaping into end scrapers.

ARTIFACTS

Lithics, ceramics, and modified bones and mussel shells are all present in the materials recovered from Rowe Valley. Weaponry is represented by numerous arrow points. Interestingly, although the Perdiz type of arrow point predominates, there are several other styles present in limited numbers, including Cuney, Guerrero, and Lott. Cuney points tend to be more closely associated with the Caddo region in eastern Texas, Lott points typically are found on the edge of the southern High Plains, and Guerrero points are more commonly found on the Texas coastal plains extending from the Gonzales area southwestward into Nuevo Leon, Mexico. Refurbishing and preparing new arrow shafts are suggested by the presence of small concave unifaces ("spokeshaves").

As one would expect to find in a butchering facility, tools associated with skinning animals, processing hides, and cutting meat are plentiful. These include beveled bifaces, end scrapers, side scrapers, and edge-trimmed flakes (fig. 9.6). All stages of manufacture, resharpening, and breakage are represented in the beveled bifaces. The range of end scrapers varies from large specimens with heavily resharpened and undercut bits to small, relatively delicate flake blades with evenly trimmed bits. The side scrapers also vary from large to small, indicating a range of uses. Edge-damaged flakes are informal tools that were used with little or no modification other than small flake removals that may in fact represent accidental damage occasioned while cutting meat or green hides. Other lithic artifacts such as flake drills used for perforating tasks suggest that after hides were tanned they were made into clothing, bags, shelter coverings, and such.

Ceramic artifacts include bone-tempered sherds from at least eight different pottery vessels. Some of them may represent the Leon Plain type thought to be indigenous to central Texas, but others are from farther afield. The small Patton Engraved jar and the larger Bullard (or Boothe) Brushed jar are both generally associated with southern Caddo groups in the vicinity of Nacogdoches. The burnished orange jar with riveted (or tenoned) handles, however, is more in keeping with Goliad Plain wares commonly associated with the coastal plains region.

Bone and shell artifacts are fairly limited in quantity. A large bone spatulate with a suspension hole was made from a bison rib (Huebner 1987b); it was found in the butchering station, suggesting use to deflesh hides. A few fragments of bone awls were found. Several bone beads were recovered; these were made from

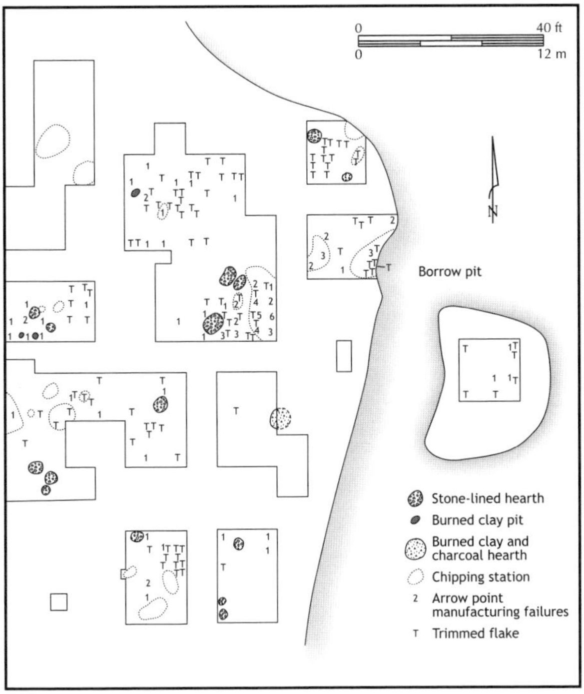

FIGURE 9.6. Distribution of arrow point manufacturing failures and edge-trimmed flakes in relation to thermal features and chipping stations in upper Toyah component, Area A, Rowe Valley site.

as-yet unidentified birds or small mammals. Presumably, most of these beads were sewn onto clothing as decorations. A freshwater mussel shell pendant in the shape of a serrated arrow point was also probably used as clothing ornamentation.

PRELIMINARY INTERPRETATIONS

When the features and artifacts in Area A are plotted on a plan map, a pattern of associations emerges. A single charcoal- and ash-filled pit is surrounded by a 5 m or so wide band that is practically devoid of any debris. Immediately beyond this "clean" circle are several discrete triplets of thermal features. Each of these has one or more chipping stations near them, suggesting a zone of intensive activities that includes multiple heating/cooking facilities and knapping stone tools. On the northwest side of the circular pattern, a butchering station partially intrudes into the other activity areas. Interestingly, the ceramic sherds in Area A are all found within this overlap zone; this strongly suggests that fat or marrow rendering was one of the activities undertaken there.

The overall circular pattern in Area A is typical of various Plains villages recorded during historic times. A central hearth surrounded by a clean community plaza is in turn encircled by a projected twelve sets of cooking facilities reflecting nuclear families that constitute the group (fig. 9.7). Assuming an average nuclear family size of seven persons, Area A could have been populated by about eighty-

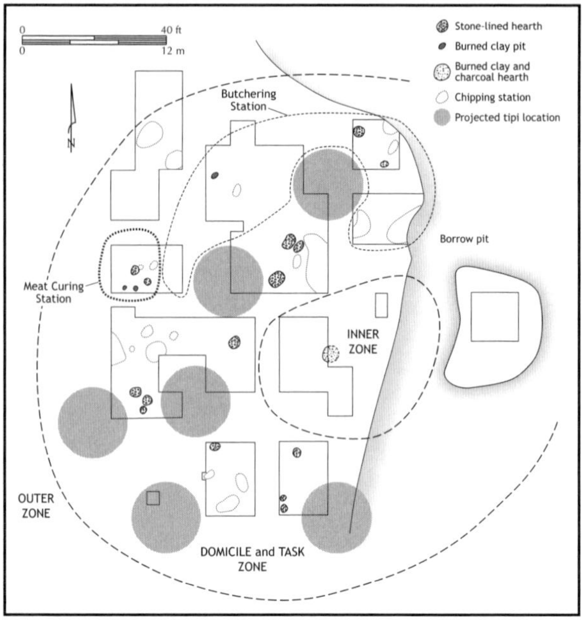

FIGURE 9.7. Preliminary interpretation of camp layout in Upper Toyah component, Area A, Rowe Valley Site.

four people. The immediately adjacent butchering station represents a community activity that involved several, if not all, of the nuclear families, probably amounting to an extended kin group (whether real or fictive).

Although the excavations were concentrated in Area A, limited investigations in Areas B and C indicate that similar patterns may exist there. When the overall pattern of the three site areas is considered, it once again reflects a Plains village, forming a crescent that fronts on a major stream (see fig. 9.2). The size of the known site area suggests a seasonal population aggregation of about 150–300 persons, and the faunal data place the time of occupation as during fall and winter.

No items of European origin, such as horse bones, are associated with the late Toyah phase materials of Area A at Rowe Valley. However, artifacts representing items not manufactured in central Texas suggest ties through trade or other means with at least three other adjacent regions—east Texas Piney Woods, southern coastal plains, and far southern High Plains. This conglomeration of artifacts is at odds with those found in the lower Toyah component at Rowe Valley and at other Toyah phase sites that seem to date earlier within the period. It suggests that Rowe Valley is very late—possibly in the 1650–1700 range—but before significant introduction of European goods such as glass beads, brass tinklers and bells, and metal tools and utensils and the reintroduction of horses. Yet the artifacts suggest that more than one ethnic group was present—indeed that as many as four ethnic groups shared a seasonal aggregate camp.

Historically, ethnic groups were in a state of flux at this time due to the introduction and spread of European diseases and to pressure from expanding European colonization. In 1748 the three San Xavier missions were founded by Spanish missionaries 25–30 miles downstream from Rowe Valley to serve a large multiethnic Native American encampment called Rancheria Grande. This rancheria housed several different "nations," including groups such as Yojuanes, Mayeyes, Ervipiames, Asinais, Nabedaches, Deados, Cocos, and others (Gilmore 1969). Although it is purely speculative at this point, it is entirely possible (as suggested by Kathleen Gilmore in 1983) that the Rowe Valley site represents a late seventeenth-century location of a multiethnic aggregation such as Rancheria Grande, or at least a portion of it, thus explaining the variability in ethnic origins of the artifacts present there. Alternatively, it may represent an encampment of just Toyah folks, with the variety of exotics simply reflecting the extent of their complex sociocultural networks as detailed in this volume.

I think what Rowe Valley eventually may suggest is that there is an evolution in the development of the complex social networks throughout the Toyah interval, and that our inability to look at tightly dated sequential occupations during this period has prevented recognition of this rapid dynamic change. When we can look at very short segments of Toyah, comparable to the intervals Speth and his students have identified in the Roswell area pueblos attacked by Toyah folk, we might be more successful at identifying and understanding the sociocultural interactions. In reality, it is very difficult to find Toyah sites where there is a reasonably clear stratigraphic separation from the preceding Austin materials, and even fewer where there are isolable multiple Toyah components such as at Rowe Valley. This makes the recognition and investigation of extremely short term, single-episode Toyah sites such as La Cameada, just up the river from Rowe Valley, ever more important in the quest for understanding this fascinating culture of collectors, hunters, traders, newsmongers, and survivors.

BIBLIOGRAPHY

The references cited include archival materials preserved in the collections listed below. Individual reports, letters, proceedings, and the like are cited with their original titles. No authors are cited for some of these materials because most citations represent a grouping of letters, reports, queries, and other written material relating to a specific topic and authored by a variety of individuals. Where individual authors are cited, they appear in the references under the author's last name. Some citations of the Archivo del Hidalgo de Parral (AHP) contain the year the document was authored and a capital letter (A, B, C, or D). This archive was microfilmed in the first half of the twentieth century, and copies of the microfilm were distributed to several university libraries in the United States. The documents for a single year could sometimes fit into a single roll. For these rolls, only the year is cited. Some years had too many documents to fit on a single roll. Those years are cited with the year and the capital letter to signify which roll for that year contains the cited document to allow subsequent researchers to search quickly for the document.

Archivo General de Indias, Seville, Spain (cited as AGI)
Archivo General de la Nación, Mexico City, Mexico (cited as AGN)
Archivo del Hidalgo de Parral, Parral, Mexico (cited as AHP)
Biblioteca Nacional de Mexico, Mexico City, Mexico (cited as BN)
Catholic Archives, Austin, Texas (cited as CA)
Edward Ayer manuscripts collection, on file at the Newberry Library, Chicago, Illinois (cited as Ayer)
Saltillo Archives, Saltillo, Mexico (cited as SA)
San Francisco el Grande Archivo, Durango, Mexico (cited as SFG)

ADLER, M. A., AND J. D. SPETH
2004 Projectile Points from the Henderson Site (1980–1981). In *Life on the Periphery: Economic Change in Late Prehistoric Southeastern New Mexico*, edited by J. D. Speth, pp. 350–67. Memoir 37. University of Michigan, Museum of Anthropology, Ann Arbor.

AGI (ARCHIVO GENERAL DE INDIAS)
1591 Carta al Rey Nuestro Señor en su Real Consejo de las Indias. Audiencia de Guadalupe, 66-6-17.
1688 El General Juan Fernandez de Retana Capitán del Presidio de San Francisco de Conchos por su Magistad y Justicia Mayor de esta Jurisdicción. Audiencia de Guadalajara, 66-6-18. Transcript on file, Center for American History, the University of Texas at Austin, box 2Q135.
1693 General Juan Fernandez de Retana Capitán del Presidio de San Francisco de Conchos por su Magestad y Justicia Mayor de esta Jurisdicción por quanto a Llegado a me

Noticia se Halla en la Misión San Pedro de Conchos, dos Relixiosos que an Benido de la Junta del Río del Norte. Audiencia de Guadalajara 76–4–11. Transcript on file, Center for American History, University of Texas at Austin, box 2Q136.

1708 Certificación de Fray Isidro de Espinosa. Audiencia de Mexico, 62–2–29. Transcript on file, Center for American History, University of Texas at Austin, box 2Q146.

1715 Certificacion por Fray Gregorio Ossorio y Fray Juan Antonio Garcia, predicadores y Misioneros en estas Nuevas Miciones de la Junta de el Rio del Norte con el de Conchos. Audencia de Mexico, 61–6–7.

AGN (ARCHIVO GENERAL DE LA NACION)

1682–1683 Correspondencia de Gov. Domingo Gironza Petris de Cruzante. Provincias Internas vol. 35, exp 2. Microfilm on file, Nettie Lee Benson Latin American Library, University of Texas at Austin, roll 31:48–92.

1683 Diario y Derroteo de Juan Dominguez de Mendoza, Cavo y Caudillo de este Pice de Hexército que Ba Caminindo al Descubrimiento del Horiente y Reino de los Texas a Pedimento de Don Juna Sabeata, Indio de Nación Jumana con los Demás Capitanes de Dicha Nación. Provincias Internas 37. Expediente 4. Transcript on file, Center for American History, University of Texas at Austin, box 2Q204.

1684a Autos sobre la Ayuda a el Paso del Norte por Jironsa Petriz de Cruzate, Don Domingo. Provincias Internas 37. Expediente 4. Transcript on file, Center for American History, University of Texas at Austin, box 2Q204.

1684b Autos sobre la Ayuda a el Paso del Norte por Capitán del Presidio, Juan Roque de Madrid. Provincias Internas 37. Expediente 4. Transcript on file, Center for American History, University of Texas at Austin, box 2Q204.

1689–1778 Historia 298. Copias del Padre Talamantes 1689–1778. Autos sobre el Derroteo y Viaje al Río de las Nueces.

1691 Cartas por Juan de la Fuente y Don Diego de Vargas Zapata y Luján. Historia 27. Expediente 2. Transcript on file, Center for American History, University of Texas at Austin, box 2Q178.

AHP (ARCHIVO DEL HIDALGO DE PARRAL)

1640C Averiguación practicada por el Alcalde don Francisco de Escobar Trevión con motivo de las muertes y heridas que hubo al pelear indios Conchos, Sinaloas, y otras naciones. Microfilm on file, Nettie Lee Benson Latin American Library, University of Texas at Austin, frames 1695–1715.

1644A Informes que rinde Fernando Gardea para que vean que su hacienda está muy inmediata a las naciones rebeldes. Microfilm on file, Nettie Lee Benson Latin American Library, University of Texas at Austin, frames 14–29.

1651A Testimonios de los fundamentos que Tubiveron los Indios Para Alzarse y Como el Bovernador dio el Correspondeiente Asinto de Paz. Microfilm on file, Nettie Lee Benson Latin American Library, University of Texas at Austin, frames 204–34.

1652A Sobre la Recitación de la India Felipa de Nación Tobosa. Microfilm on file, Nettie Lee Benson Latin American Library, University of Texas at Austin, frames 217–60.

1653B Autos formados con Motivo de la Venida de Fernando de Obregón y de la Justicia de Guerra contra los Indios. Microfilm on file, Nettie Lee Benson Latin American Library, University of Texas at Austin, frames 804–18.

1654A Autos de Guerra hechos por el Gobernador General don Enrique Dávila y Pacheco, contra los Indios Conchos y Tobosos que roban y matan un carbonero de Santiago de Minas Nuevas el 28 de enero,frames 51–114.

1655Aa Autos de Guerra con Motivos de los Frequentes Abusos que Cometen los Indios Enemigos de la Real Corona. Microfilm on file, Nettie Lee Benson Latin American Library, University of Texas at Austin, frames 231–329.

1655Ab Mandamiento para que se Alisten a la Guerra Algunos Capitanes. Microfilm on file, Nettie Lee Benson Latin American Library, University of Texas at Austin, frames 5–13.

1655B Diligencias sobre el Título de Encomienda de Indios en Favor del Capitán Fernando Gomez. Microfilm on file, Nettie Lee Benson Latin American Library, University of Texas at Austin, frames 640–49.

1670A Autos de Guerra contra los Indios Rebeldes por el Generál Juan Antonio de García. Microfilm on file, Nettie Lee Benson Latin American Library, University of Texas at Austin, frames 4–22.

1673A Relativos a las guerras con los indios enemigos de la Real Corona, para evitar los danos y robos que estos hacen. Microfilm on file, Nettie Lee Benson Latin American Library, University of Texas at Austin, frames 124–36.

1677C Criminal Instruida Don Juan Campos y demás Cumplices sus Compañeros Indios Rebeldes contra la Real Corona. Microfilm on file, Nettie Lee Benson Latin American Library, University of Texas at Austin, frames 2267-EOR.

1716A Documentos Relativos a la Rebelión de los Indios Acoclames y Ococyames y sus Aliados. Microfilm on file, Nettie Lee Benson Latin American Library, University of Texas at Austin, frames 85–265.

AHR, S. W.

1998 Ramifications of Late Holocene Hide-Processing Geographies along the Lower Medina River, Texas. Master's thesis, Department of Anthropology, Texas A&M University, College Station.

ALBERT, BRUCE M.

1999 Early and Protohistoric Agents of Vegetation Change in the Environs of Mission Rosario (41GD2) as Reflected in Palynological Data. *Bulletin of the Texas Archeological Society* 70:189–95.

ALESSIO ROBLES, V.

1978 *Coahuila y Texas en la Época Colonial*. 2nd ed. Editorial Porrua, México, D.F.

ALEXANDER, R. K.

1970 *Archeological Investigations at Parida Cave, Val Verde County, Texas.* Papers of the Texas Archeological Salvage Project 19. University of Texas at Austin.

1974 The Archeology of Conejo Shelter: A Study of Cultural Stability at an Archaic Rockshelter Site in Southwestern Texas. PhD dissertation, Department of Anthropology, University of Texas at Austin.

ALLEY, W. M.

1984 The Palmer Drought Severity Index: Limitations and Applications. *Journal of Climate and Applied Meteorology* 23:1100–1109.

ÁLVAREZ, S.

2000 Agricultores de Paz y Cazadores-Recolectores de Guerra: Los Tobosos de la Cuenca de Río Conchos in la Nueva Vizcaya. In *Nómadas y Sedentarios en el Norte de México, Homenaja a Beatriz Braniff*, edited by M. Hers, J. L. Mirafuentes, M. de los Dolores Soto, and M. Vallebueno, pp. 305–54. Instituto de Investigaciones Anthropolóicas, Instituto de Investigaciones Éstecticas, Instituto de Investigaciones Históricas, Universidad Autónoma Nacional de México, México, D.F.

AMOS, B. B., AND F. R. GEHLBACH

1988 *Edwards Plateau Vegetation: Plant Ecological Studies in Central Texas.* Baylor University Press, Waco, Tex.

ARBINGAST, S.A., L. G. KENNAMER, R. H. RYAN, A. LO, D. L. KARNEY, C. P. ZLATKOVICH, M. E. BONINE, AND R. G. STELLE

1973 *Atlas of Texas.* Rev. ed. Bureau of Business Research, University of Texas at Austin.

ARNN, JOHN W.

2005 Chronology, Technology, and Subsistence: Is That All There Is? *Council of Texas Archeologists Newsletter* (Austin) 29(2): 17–28.

2007 Transformation and Persistence of Indigenous Cultural Identity during the Early Colonial and Late Prehistoric Periods in Texas. PhD dissertation, Department of Anthropology, University of Kentucky, Lexington.

2012 *Land of the Tejas: Native American Identity and Interaction in Texas, A.D. 1300–1700*. University of Texas Press, in press.

ARZAVE, D. P.

1990 *Elementos de Paleografía Novohispana*. Colección Seminarios, Facultad de Filosofía y Letras, Universidad Nacional Autónoma de México, México, D.F.

ATEN, LAWRENCE

1983 *Indians of the Upper Texas Coast*. Academic Press, New York.

AYER, MRS. EDWARD E. (TRANSLATOR)

1965 *The Memorial of Fray Alonso de Benavides, 1630*. Horn and Wallace, Albuquerque.

AYER (EDWARD AYER MANUSCRIPT COLLECTION)

1595 Carta Annua del año 1595. Photocopy of original document in *Nueva Vizcaya Documents*, Ayer Collection, vol. 1.

1691 Diario del viaje a los Tejas por Fray Damien Massanet.

1714 Notícia de las Misiones de la Junta de los Rios por Trasviña Retis.

BAERREIS, D.A., AND R. A. BRYSON

1965 Historical Climatology and the Southern Plains: A Preliminary Statement. *Bulletin, Oklahoma Archeological Society* 13:69–76.

BAHUCHET, S., AND H. GUILLAUME

1982 Aka-Farmer Relations in the Northwest Congo Basin. In *Politics and History in Band Societies*, edited by E. B. Leacock and R. B. Lee, pp. 189–211. Cambridge University Press, Cambridge.

BAMFORTH, DOUGLAS B.

1988 *Ecology and Human Organization on the Great Plains*. Plenum Press, New York.

BANCROFT, H. H.

1886 *History of the North Mexican States and Texas*. Vol. 1, 1531–1800. In vol. 15 of *The Works of Hubert Howe Bancroft*. History Company, San Francisco.

BANDY, PHILLIP A.

1980 *Archaeological Investigations at Sanderson Canyon Watershed Terrell, Pecos, and Brewster Counties, Texas*. Interagency Archeological Services—Denver Office of Archeology and Historic Preservation. Environment Consultants, Dallas.

BARNARD, A.

1992 *Hunters and Herders of Southern Africa: A Comparative Ethnography of the Khoisan Peoples*. Cambridge University Press, New York.

BARNES, THOMAS C., THOMAS H. NAYLOR, AND CHARLES W. POLZER

1981 *Northern New Spain, A Research Guide*. Vol. 1, *The Documentary Relations of the Southwest*. University of Arizona Press, Tucson.

BARSNESS, LARRY

1985 *Herds, Hides, and Horns: The Complete Buffalo Book*. Texas Christian University Press, Fort Worth.

BARTH, F.

1969 Introduction. In *Ethnic Groups and Boundaries: The Social Organization of Culture Difference*, edited by F. Barth, pp. 9–38. Little, Brown and Company, Boston.

BASKETT, J. N.

1907 A Study of the Route of Cabeza de Vaca. *Texas State Historical Association Quarterly* 10(3): 246–79, 10(4): 308–40.

BAUGH, SUSAN

1986 Late Prehistoric Bison Distribution in Oklahoma. In Current Trends in Southern Plains Archaeology, edited by T. Baugh, pp. 83–110. *Plains Anthropologist* 31(114, pt. 2), *Memoir* 21, Lincoln.

BAUGH, TIMOTHY G.

1982 *Edwards I (34BK2): Southern Plains Adaptations in the Protohistoric Period.* Oklahoma Archeological Survey, Studies in Oklahoma's Past 8. Norman.

1986 Culture History and Protohistoric Societies in the Southern Plains. In Current Trends in Southern Plains Archaeology, edited by Timothy G. Baugh, pp. 167–87. *Plains Anthropologist* 31(114, pt. 2), *Memoir* 21, Lincoln.

1991 The Dynamics of Plains-Pueblo Interaction. In *Farmers, Hunters, and Colonists: Interaction between the Southwest and Southern Plains,* edited by K. A. Spielmann, pp. 107–27. University of Arizona Press, Tucson.

BAUGH, TIMOTHY G., AND JONATHAN E. ERICSON

1994 Systematics of the Study of Prehistoric Regional Exchange in North America. In *Prehistoric Exchange Systems in North America,* edited by Timothy G. Baugh and Jonathon E. Ericson, pp. 3–15. Plenum Press, New York.

BAUGH, TIMOTHY G., AND FRED W. NELSON JR.

1987 New Mexico Obsidian Sources and Exchange on the Southern Plains. *Journal of Field Archaeology* 14(3): 313–29.

BECK, LANE ANDERSON

1995 *Regional Approaches to Mortuary Analysis.* Plenum Press, New York.

BECKETT, P. H., AND T. L. CORBETT

1992 *The Manso Indians.* Monograph 9. COAS Publishing and Research. Las Cruces, N.Mex.

BERNARDINI, WESLEY

2005 Reconsidering Spatial and Temporal Aspects of Prehistoric Cultural Identity: A Case Study from the American Southwest. *American Antiquity* 70(1): 31–54.

BETTINGER, ROBERT L.

1991 *Hunter-Gatherers: Archaeological and Evolutionary Theory.* Plenum Press, New York.

BIEDMA, LUÝS HERNÁNDEZ DE

1865 Relación de la Isla de la Florida. In *Colección de Documentos inéditos Relativos al Descubrimiento, Conquista, y Colonización de las Posesiones Españolas en América y Oceania,* 3:437–439. Manuel B. de Quirós, Madrid.

BINFORD, LEWIS R.

1964 A Consideration of Archeological Research Design. *American Antiquity* 29(4): 425–41.

1977 Forty-seven Trips: A Case Study in the Character of Archaeological Formation Process. In *Stone Tools as Cultural Markers,* edited by R. V. S. Wright, pp. 24–36. Australian Institute of Aboriginal Studies, Canberra.

1978 *Nunamiut Ethnoarchaeology.* Academic Press, New York.

1979 Organization and Formation Processes: Looking at Curated Technologies. *Journal of Anthropological Research* 35(3): 255–73.

1980 Willow Smoke and Dog's Tails: Hunter-Gatherer Settlement Systems and Site Formation. *American Antiquity* 45(1): 4–20.

1983 Hunters in a Landscape. In *In Pursuit of the Past: Decoding the Archaeological Record,* by Lewis R. Binford, pp. 109–43. Thames and Hudson, New York.

2001 *Constructing Frames of Reference: An Analytical Method for Archaeological Theory Building Using Hunter-Gatherer and Environmental Data Sets.* University of California Press, Berkeley.

BIRDSELL, J. B.

1953 Some Environmental and Cultural Factors Influencing the Structuring of Australian Aboriginal Populations. *American Naturalist* 87:171–207.

BLACK, STEPHEN L.

1986 *The Clemente and Herminia Hinojosa Site, 41JW8: A Toyah Horizon Campsite in Southern Texas.* Special Report 18. Center for Archaeological Research, University of Texas at San Antonio.

1989 Central Texas Plateau Prairie. In *From the Gulf to the Rio Grande: Human Adaptation in Central, South, and Lower Pecos Texas*, edited by T. R. Hester, S. L. Black, D. G. Steele, B. W. Olive, A. A. Fox, K. J. Reinhard, and L. C. Bement, pp. 17–38. Arkansas Archeological Survey Research Series 33. Arkansas Archeological Survey, Fayetteville.

1997 The Corn Creek Sites, 41MK8 and 41MK9. In *Hot Rock Cooking on the Greater Edwards Plateau: Four Burned Rock Midden Sites in West Central Texas*, Vol. 1, edited by S. L. Black, S., L. W. Ellis, D. G. Creel, and G. T. Goode, pp. 169–206. Studies in Archaeology 22, Texas Archeological Research Laboratory, University of Texas at Austin, and Archeology Studies Program Report 2, Environmental Affairs Division, Texas Department of Transportation. Austin.

BLACK, S. L., AND D. CREEL

1997 The Central Texas Burned Rock Midden Reconsidered. In *Hot Rock Cooking on the Greater Edwards Plateau: Four Burned Rock Midden Sites in West Central Texas*, Vol. 1, edited by S. L. Black, S., L. W. Ellis, D. G. Creel, and G. T. Goode, pp. 269–314. Studies in Archaeology 22, Texas Archeological Research Laboratory, University of Texas at Austin, and Archeology Studies Program Report 2, Environmental Affairs Division, Texas Department of Transportation. Austin.

BLACK, STEPHEN L., LINDA W. ELLIS, DARRELL G. CREEL, AND GLENN T. GOODE

1997 *Hot Rock Cooking on the Greater Edwards Plateau: Four Burned Rock Midden Sites in West Central Texas*. 2 vols. Studies in Archaeology 22, Texas Archeological Research Laboratory, University of Texas at Austin, and Archeology Studies Program Report 2, Environmental Affairs Division, Texas Department of Transportation. Austin.

BLAIR, W. FRANK

1950 The Biotic Provinces of Texas. *Texas Journal of Science* 2(1): 93–117.

BLEED, P.

1986 The Optimal Design of Hunting Weapons: Maintainability or Reliability. *American Antiquity* 51:737–47.

BN (BIBLIOTECA NACIONAL DE MEXICO)

1631 Representación de Comisario Real al Virrey Controversia con el Señor Obispo de Durango por Fr. Francisco Velasco. Leg. 1, núm. 9. On file, University of New Mexico.

1674 *Autos hechos por Francisco Barbarigo, teniente de capitán protector de los indios tlaxcaltecas y guachichiles de la frontera del Saltillo, sobre las provisiones ministradas a los indios en los almachenes de dicha villa. Carta de Fray Juan Larios al Comisario General de la Orden de San Francisco, sobre su entrada a la provincial de Coahuila*. Legado 94, exps. 7 and 8.

BOLTON, HERBERT E.

1911 The Jumano Indians of Texas, 1650–1771. *Quarterly of the Texas State Historical Association* 15(1): 66–84.

1916 *Spanish Exploration in the Southwest, 1542–1706*. Charles Scribner's Sons, New York.

BOMAR, G. W.

1995 *Texas Weather*. 2nd ed. University of Texas Press, Austin.

BOND, C. L.

1978 *Three Archeological Sites at Hoxie Bridge, Williamson County, Texas*. Anthropology Laboratory Report 43. Texas A&M University, College Station.

BOUSMAN, C. BRITT

1998 Paleoenvironmental Change in Central Texas: The Palynological Evidence. *Plains Anthropologist* 43(164): 201–19.

BOVEE, D. L., AND D. W. OWSLEY

1994 Evidence of Warfare at the Heerwald Site. In *Skeletal Biology in the Great Plains: Migration, Warfare, Health, and Subsistence*, edited by D. W. Owsley and R. L. Jantz, pp. 355–62. Smithsonian Institution Press, Washington, D.C.

BOYD, DOUGLAS K.

1995 The Palo Duro Complex: Redefining the Early Ceramic Period in the Caprock Canyonlands. *Bulletin of the Texas Archeological Society* 66:461–518.

1997 *Caprock Canyonlands Archeology: A Synthesis of the Late Prehistory and History of Lake Alan Henry and the Texas Panhandle-Plains.* 2 vols. Reports of Investigations 110. Prewitt and Associates, Austin.

2001 Querechos and Teyas: Protohistoric Hunters and Gatherers in the Texas Panhandle-Plains, A.D. 1580–1700. *Bulletin of the Texas Archeological Society* 72:5–22.

2004 The Palo Duro Complex: Redefining the Early Ceramic Period in the Caprock Canyonlands. In *Prehistoric Archeology in Texas*, edited by Timothy K. Perttula, pp. 296–330. Texas A&M University Press, College Station.

BOYD, DOUGLAS K., JAY PECK, STEVE A. TOMKA, AND KARL W. KIBLER

1993 *Data Recovery at Justiceburg Reservoir (Lake Alan Henry), Garza and Kent Counties, Texas: Phase III, Season 2.* Reports of Investigations 88. Prewitt and Associates, Austin.

BRAUN DAVID P., AND STEPHEN PLOG

1982 Evolution of "Tribal" Social Networks: Theory and Prehistoric North American Evidence. *American Antiquity* 47(3): 504–25.

BRAY, TAMARA L. (EDITOR)

2003 *The Archaeology and Politics of Food and Feasting in Early States and Empires.* Kluwer Academic/Plenum, New York.

BRINK, J. W.

1997 Fat Content in the Bones of *Bison bison* and Applications to Archaeology. *Journal of Archaeological Science* 24:259–74.

BROOKS, CHARLES A.

1978 *Soil Survey of Hill County, Texas.* U.S. Department of Agriculture, Soil Conservation Service, in cooperation with the Texas Agricultural Experiment Station.

BROOKS, JAMES F.

2002 *Captives and Cousins: Slavery, Kinship, and Community in the Southwest Borderlands.* University of North Carolina Press, Chapel Hill.

BROOKS, ROBERT L.

1994 Warfare on the Southern Plains. In *Skeletal Biology in the Great Plains: Migration, Warfare, Health, and Subsistence*, edited by Douglas W. Owsley and Richard L. Jantz, pp. 317–23. Smithsonian Institution Press, Washington, D.C.

2004 From Stone Slab Architecture to Abandonment: A Revisionist View of the Antelope Creek Phase. In *The Prehistory of Texas*, edited by T. K. Perttula, pp. 331–44. Texas A&M University Press, College Station.

BROSOWSKE, S. D.

2005 The Evolution of Exchange in Small-Scale Societies of the Southern High Plains. PhD dissertation, Department of Anthropology, University of Oklahoma, Norman.

BROWN, CLAUDE

1985A Tale of Two Sites: A (41LU34) and B (41LU29). *Transactions of the 20th Regional Archeological Symposium for Southeastern New Mexico and Western Texas*, pp. 143–58. Dawson County Archeological Society, Lamesa, Tex.

BROWN, J. L.

2004 The Lithic Assemblage from the Henderson Site. In *Life on the Periphery: Economic Change in Late Prehistoric Southeastern New Mexico*, edited by J. D. Speth, pp. 368–83. Memoir 37. University of Michigan, Museum of Anthropology, Ann Arbor.

BROWN, KENNETH M., DANIEL R. POTTER, GRANT D. HALL, AND STEPHEN L. BLACK

1982 *Excavations at 41LK67, a Prehistoric Site in the Choke Canyon Reservoir, South Texas.* Choke Canyon Series, Vol. 7. Center for Archaeological Research, University of Texas at San Antonio.

BROWNLOW, RUSSELL K.

2003 *Archeological Investigations at 41WM815, a Blackland Prairie Site, Williamson County, Texas.* Studies in Archeology 36, Texas Archeological Research Laboratory, University of Texas at Austin, and Archeology Studies Program Report 23, Environmental Affairs Division, Texas Department of Transportation, Austin.

BRUMFIEL, ELIZABETH

1992 Distinguished Lecture in Archaeology: Breaking and Entering the Ecosystem-Gender, Class and Faction Steal the Show. *American Anthropologist* 94(3): 551–67.

BRUNE, GUNNAR

1981 *Springs of Texas.* Branch-Smith, Fort Worth, Tex.

BRUSETH, JAMES, AND NANCY A. KENMOTSU

1993 From Naguatex to the River Daycao: The Route of the Hernando de Soto Expedition through Texas. *North American Archeology* 14(2):169–95.

BUFFALOHEAD, E.

2004 Part 1: Dhegihan History: A Personal Journey. *Plains Anthropologist* 49:1–344, Memoir 36.

BURGETT, JESSICA P.

2007 Just Like That, but Different: El Paso Polychrome in the Casas Grandes Region, Chihuahua, Mexico. In *Viva la Jornada: Papers from the 14th Biennial Jornada Mogollon Conference*, edited by J. Jurgena, L. Jackson, and M. Thompson, pp. 53–57. El Paso Museum of Archaeology, El Paso, Tex.

BURMEISTER, STEFAN

2000 Archeology and Migration: Approaches to an Archaeological Proof of Migration. *Current Anthropologist* 41(4): 539–67.

BUTZER, KARL W.

1990 A Human Ecosystem Framework for Archeology. In *The Ecosystem Approach in Anthropology: From Concept to Practice*, edited by E. F. Moran, pp. 91–130. University of Michigan Press, Ann Arbor.

CA (CATHOLIC ARCHIVES)

1674 *Autos en que se da Cuenta de la Entrada.* Box 121, leg. 94, no. 3a.

CABLE, D.

1975 Influence of Precipitation on Perennial Grass Production in the Semidesert Southwest. *Ecology* 56:981–86.

CAHALANE, V. H.

1954 *Mammals of North America.* Macmillan, New York.

CAMPBELL, THOMAS N.

1947 The Johnson Site: Type Site of the Aransas Focus of the Texas Coast. *Bulletin of the Texas Archeological and Paleontological Society* 18:40–75.

1956 Archeological Materials from Five Islands in the Laguna Madre, Texas Coast. *Bulletin of the Texas Archeological Society* 27:7–46.

1988 *The Indians of Southern Texas and Northeastern Mexico: Selected Writings of Thomas Nolan Campbell.* Texas Archeological Research Laboratory, University of Texas at Austin.

1989 *Ethnohistoric Notes on Indian Groups Associated with Three Spanish Missions at Guerrero, Coahuila.* Archeology and History of the San Juan Bautista Mission Area, Coahuila and Texas, Report 3. Center for Archaeological Research, University of Texas at San Antonio.

CAMPBELL, THOMAS N., AND T. J. CAMPBELL

1981 *Historic Indian Groups of the Choke Canyon Reservoir and Surrounding Area, Southern Texas.* Choke Canyon Series Vol. 1. Center for Archaeological Research, University of Texas at San Antonio.

CAMPER, H. A.
1991 Pollen Analysis of Patschke Bog. Master's thesis, Department of Botany, Texas A&M University, College Station.

CARAN, S. CHRISTOPHER, AND VICTOR R. BAKER
1986 Flooding along the Balcones Escarpment, Central Texas. In *The Balcones Escarpment: Geology, Hydrology, Ecology, and Social Development in Central Texas*, edited by Patrick L. Abbott and C. M. Woodruff Jr., pp. 1–14. Geological Society of America, Boulder, Colo.

CARR, J. T.
1967 *The Climate and Physiography of Texas.* Texas Water Development Board Report 53, Austin.

CASHDAN, ELIZABETH A.
1985 Coping with Risk: Reciprocity among the Basarwa of Northern Botswana. *Man* 20:454–74.

CASTEÑEDA, CARLOS E.
1936 *Our Catholic Heritage in Texas, 1519–1936.* Vol. 1, *The Mission Era: The Founding of Texas, 1519–1693.* Von Boeckmann-Jones, Austin.

CHANEY, MARGARET S., AND MARGARET L. ROSS
1971 *Nutrition.* Houghton Mifflin, Boston.

CHESHIER, J., AND R. L. KELLY
2006 Projectile Point Shape and Durability: The Effect of Thickness:Length. *American Antiquity* 71(2): 353–63.

CHIPMAN, DONALD E.
1992 *Spanish Texas, 1519–1821.* University of Texas Press, Austin.

CHRISTENSON, A. L.
1997 Side-Notched and Unnotched Arrowpoints: Assessing Functional Differences. In *Projectile Technology*, edited by H. Knecht, pp. 131–42. Plenum Press, New York.

CLARK, J. J.
2004 Tracking Cultural Affinity. In *Identity, Feasting, and the Archaeology of the Greater Southwest, Proceedings of the 2002 Southwest Symposium*, edited by B. J. Mills, pp. 42–73. University Press of Colorado, Boulder.

CLARK, TIFFANY C.
2006 Production, Exchange, and Social Identity: A Study of Chupadero Black-on-white Pottery. PhD dissertation, School of Human Evolution and Social Change, Arizona State University, Tempe.

CLOUD, WILLIAM A.
2002 Rough Run Burial: A Semi-Subterranean Cairn Burial from Brewster County, Texas. *Journal for Big Bend Studies* (Sul Ross University, Alpine)14:33–84.
2004 *The Arroyo de la Presa Site: A Stratified Late Prehistoric Campsite along the Rio Grande, Presidio County, Trans-Pecos Texas.* Reports in Contract Archeology 9, Center for Big Bend Studies, Sul Ross State University, and Archeological Studies Program Report 56, Environmental Affairs Division, Texas Department of Transportation, Austin.

CLOUD, WILLIAM A, ROBERT J. MALLOUF, PATRICIA MERCADO-ALLINGER, CATHRYN A. HOYT, NANCY A. KENMOTSU, JOSEPH M. SANCHEZ, AND ENRIQUE R. MADRID
1994 *Archeological Testing at the Polvo Site Presidio County, Texas.* Office of the State Archeologist Report 39, Texas Historical Commission, and the U.S. Department of Agriculture, Soil Conservation Service, Austin.

COLLINS, MICHAEL B.
1968 The Andrews Lake Locality: New Archeological Data from the Southern Llano Estacado, Texas. MA thesis, Department of Anthropology, University of Texas, Austin.
1969 *Texas Excavations at Amistad International Reservoir, Fall 1967.* Papers of the Texas Archeological Salvage Project 16. University of Texas at Austin.

1971 A Review of Llano Estacado Archeology and Ethnohistory. *Plains Anthropologist* 16(52): 85–104.

1995 Forty Years of Archeology in Central Texas. *Bulletin of the Texas Archeological Society* 66:361–400.

1999 Named Indian Groups in Texas: A Guide to Entries in the New Handbook of Texas. *Bulletin of the Texas Archeological Society* 70:7–16.

2004 Archeology in Central Texas. In *The Prehistory of Texas*, edited by Timothy K. Perttula, pp. 101–26. Texas A&M University Press, College Station.

COLLINS, MICHAEL B., AND ROBERT A. RICKLIS

1994 Cultural Background. In *Archaic and Late Prehistoric Human Ecology in the Middle Onion Creek Valley, Hays County, Texas*, by R. A. Ricklis and M. B. Collins, 1:11–26. Studies in Archeology 19. Texas Archeological Research Laboratory, University of Texas at Austin.

CONKEY, MARGARET K.

1990 Experimenting with Style in Archaeology: Some Historical and Theoretical Issues. In *The Use of Style in Archaeology*, edited by M.W. Conkey and Christine A. Hastorf. Cambridge University Press, New York.

COOK, E. R., AND P. J. KRUSIC

2004 *The North American Drought Atlas.* Lamont-Doherty Earth Observatory and the National Science Foundation, Colombia University, Palisades, New York. http://iridl.ldeo.columbia.edu/SOURCES/.LDEO/.TRL/.NADA2004/.pdsi-atlas.html.

COOK, E. R., D. M. MEKO, D. W. STAHLE, AND M. K. CLEVELAND

1999 Drought Reconstruction for the Continental United States. *Journal of Climate* 12:1145–62.

COOKE, M. J.

2005 Soil Formation and Erosion in Central Texas: Insights from Relict Soils and Cave Deposits. PhD dissertation, University of Texas at Austin.

COPPEDGE, B. R., D. M. LESLIE JR., AND J. H. SHAW

1998 Botanical Composition of Bison Diets on Tallgrass Prairie in Oklahoma. *Journal of Range Management* 51(4): 379–82.

CORDELL, LINDA S.

1980 *A Cultural Resource Overview of the Middle Rio Grande River Valley, New Mexico.* USDA, Forest Service, Southwestern Region, Albuquerque, N.Mex.

1997 *Archaeology of the Southwest.* 2nd ed. Academic Press, San Diego.

CORLEY, J. A.

1965 Proposed Eastern Extension of the Jornada Branch of the Mogollon Culture. *Transactions of the First Regional Archeological Symposium for Southeastern New Mexico and Western Texas*, 30–36. Lea County Archeological Society, Hobbs, N.Mex.

CORONADO, FRANCISCO VAZQUEZ DE

1870 Carta a su Magestad en que Hace Relación del Descubrimiento de la Provincia de Tigues (20 Octubre 1571). In *Colección de Documentos Inéditos Relativos al Descubrimiento, Conquista y Organización de las Antiguas Posesiones Españoles*, edited by J. F. Pacheco and F. Cardenas, 13:261–68. M. Bernaldo de Quiros, Madrid.

CRAMUSSEL, CHANTEL

2000 De Como los Espanoles Clasificaron los Indios, Naciones y Encomiendas en la Nueva Vizcaya Central. In *Nómadas y Sedentarios en el Norte de México, Homenaja a Beatriz Braniff*, edited by M. Hers, J. L. Mirafuentes, M. de los Dolores Soto, and M. Vallebueno, pp. 275–304. Instituto de Investigaciones Anthropolóicas, Instituto de Investigaciones Éstecticas, Instituto de Investigaciones Históricas, Universidad Autónoma Nacional de México, México, D.F.

CREEL, DARRELL

1990 *Excavations at 41TG91, Tom Green County, Texas, 1978.* Publications in Archeology Report 38. Texas State Department of Highways and Public Transportation, Highway Design Division, Austin.

1991 Bison Hides in Late Prehistoric Exchange in the Southern Plains. *American Antiquity* 56(1): 40–49.

2002 Central Texas Ceramics Project. *Newsletter of the Friends of the Texas Archeological Research Laboratory* (Austin), July 2002.

CREEL, D. G., T. C. CLARK, AND H. NEFF

2002 Production and Long Distance Movement of Chupadero Black-on-white Pottery in New Mexico and Texas. In *Geochemical Evidence for Long Distance Exchange*, edited by M. Glascock, pp. 109–32. Bergin and Garvey, Westport, Conn.

CREEL, DARRELL G., AND GLENN T. GOODE

1997 The Heard Schoolhouse Site, 41UV86. In *Hot Rock Cooking on the Greater Edwards Plateau: Four Burned Rock Midden Sites in West Central Texas*, by Stephen L. Black, Linda W. Ellis, Darrell G. Creel, and Glenn T. Goode, Vol. 1. Studies in Archeology 22. Texas Archeological Research Laboratory, University of Texas at Austin.

DAVENPORT, H., AND J. K. WELLS

1918 The First Europeans in Texas 1528–1536. *Southwestern Historical Quarterly* 22(2): 111–42.

1919 The First Europeans in Texas 1528–1536. *Southwestern Historical Quarterly* 22(3): 205–59.

DAWE, R. J.

1987 The Triangular Projectile Point in Plains Prehistory: A Preform Trade Hypothesis. In *Archaeology in Alberta 1986*, edited by M. Magne, pp. 150–62, 289–302. Occasional Paper 31. Alberta Culture and Multiculturalism, Archaeological Survey of Alberta, Edmonton, Alberta.

D'ALTROY, TERENCE N., AND CHRISTINE A. HASTORF

2001 *Empire and Domestic Economy*. Kluwer Academic/Plenum Publishers, New York.

D'AZEVEDO, W. L. (EDITOR)

1986 *Great Basin*. Vol. 11 of *Handbook of North American Indians*. Smithsonian Institution, Washington, D.C.

DEBOER, W. R.

1988 Subterranean Storage and the Organization of Surplus: The View from Eastern North America. *Southeastern Archaeology* 7(1): 1–20.

DEEDS, SUSAN M.

2003 *Defiance and Deference in Mexico's Colonial North: Indians under Spanish Rule in Nueva Vizcaya*. University of Texas Press, Austin.

DERING, PHIL

2008 Late Prehistoric Subsistence Economy on the Edwards Plateau. *Plains Anthropologist* 53(205): 59–78.

DIAMOND, D. D., D. H. RISKIND, AND S. L. ORZELL

1987 A Framework for Plant Community Classification and Conservation in Texas. *Texas Journal of Science* 39:202–21.

DIBBLE, DAVID S., AND DESSAMAE LORRAINE

1968 *Bonfire Shelter: A Stratified Bison Kill Site, Val Verde County, Texas*. Miscellaneous Papers No. 1. Texas Memorial Museum, University of Texas at Austin.

DICKENS, W. A., AND J. E. WIEDERHOLD

2003 Some Notes on Bison, the Texas Post Oak Savanna, and the Late Prehistoric Period of Texas. *Bulletin of the Texas Archeological Society* 74:31–54.

DIETLER, MICHAEL

1990 Driven by Drink: The Role of Drinking in the Political Economy and the Case of Early Iron Age France. *Journal of Anthropological Archaeology* 9:352–406.

DIETLER, MICHAEL, AND BRIAN HAYDEN (EDITORS)

2001 *Feasts: Archaeological and Ethnographic Perspectives on Food, Politics, and Power.* Smithsonian Institution, Washington, D.C.

DILLEHAY, THOMAS D.

1974 Late Quaternary Bison Population Changes on the Southern Plains. *Plains Anthropologist* 19(65): 180–96.

DI PESO, C. C., J. B. RINALDO, AND G. J. FENNER

1974 *Casas Grandes: A Fallen Trading Center of the Gran Chichimeca.* Vol. 8: *Bone, Perishables, Commerce, Subsistence, and Burials.* Amerind Foundation Series 9. Northland Press, Flagstaff, Ariz.

DRASS, RICHARD R.

1997 *Culture Change on the Eastern Margins of the Southern Plains.* Studies in Oklahoma's Past 19, and Oklahoma Anthropological Society Memoir 7, University of Oklahoma.

DROLET, ROBERT P.

2005 Cultural Impacts on the South Texas Environment: An Archaeological View from the Nueces River Valley. Paper presented at a meeting of the Center of Research Excellence in Science and Technology—Research on Environmental Sustainability of Semi-Arid Coastal Areas, San Antonio, Tex.

2006 Late Prehistoric Occupation of the Lower Nueces River Valley, South Texas. Paper presented at the 77th Annual Meeting of the Texas Archeological Society, San Angelo.

2007 Feature Descriptions: Midden 6, Site 41-SP-220. Manuscript on file, Corpus Christi Museum of Science and History, Corpus Christi, Tex.

DYSON-HUDSON, RADA, AND ERIC A. SMITH

1978 Human Territoriality: An Ecological Reassessment. *American Anthropologist* 80:21–41.

EARLE, TIMOTHY K.

1994 Positioning Exchange in the Evolution of Human Society. In *Prehistoric Exchange Systems in North America,* edited by Timothy G. Baugh and Jonathon E. Ericson, pp. 419–37. Plenum Press, New York.

ECKERT, S. L.

2006 The Production and Distribution of Glaze-Painted Pottery in the Pueblo Southwest: A Synthesis. In *The Social Life of Pots: Glaze Wares and Cultural Transformation in the Late Precontact Southwest,* edited by J. A. Habicht-Mauche, S. L. Eckert, and D. L. Huntley, pp. 34–59. University of Arizona Press, Tucson.

EDDY, F. W.

1973 Salvage Archeology in the Laneport Reservoir District: Central Texas. Report on file, Texas Archeological Survey, University of Texas at Austin.

EISELT, BERNICE SUNDAY

2006 The Emergence of Jicarilla Apache Enclave Economy during the 19th Century in Northern New Mexico. PhD dissertation, Department of Anthropology, University of Michigan.

ELLIS, L. W., G. L. ELLIS, AND C. D. FREDERICK

1995 Implications of Environmental Diversity in the Central Texas Archeological Region. *Bulletin of the Texas Archeological Society* 66:401–26.

ELWOOD, B. B., AND W. A. GOSE

2006 Heinrich H1 and 8200 yr B.P. Climate Events Recorded in Hall's Cave, Texas. *Geology* 34(9): 753–56.

EMERSON, ALICE MARIE

1990 Implications of Variability in the Economic Anatomy of *Bison bison.* Ph.D. dissertation, Department of Anthropology, Washington State University.

1993 The Role of Body Part Utility in Small-Scale Hunting under Two Strategies of Carcass Recovery. In *From Bones to Behavior*, edited by Jean Hudson, pp. 138–55. Center for Archaeological Investigations, Occasional Paper 21. Board of Trustees, Southern Illinois University, Carbondale.

EMSLIE, S. D., J. D. SPETH, AND R. N. WISEMAN

1992 Two Prehistoric Puebloan Avifaunas from the Pecos Valley, Southeastern New Mexico. *Journal of Ethnobiology* 12(1): 83–115.

EPP, H. T.

1988 Way of the Migrant Herds: Dual Dispersion Strategy among Bison. *Plains Anthropologist* 33:309–20.

EPSTEIN, H. E., W. K. LAUENROTH, I. C. BURKE, AND D. P. COFFIN

1997 Productivity Patterns of C_3 and C_4 Functional Types in the U.S. Great Plains. *Ecology* 78(3): 722–31.

EPSTEIN, J. F.

1963 Centipede and Damp Caves: Excavations in Val Verde County, Texas, 1958. *Bulletin of the Texas Archeological Society* 33:1–129.

ESPEJO, ANTONIO

1871a Relación del Viaje, que yo, António Espejo, ciudadano de la ciudad de México, natural de la ciudad de Córdoba, hize con Catorce Soldados y un Relijioso de la Orden de San Francisco. In *Colección de Documentos Inéditos Relativos al Descubrimiento, Conquista y Organización de las Antiguas Posesiones españolas de Améria y Oceanía*, edited by Joaquin F. Pacheco and Francisco Cardenas, 15:101–26. M. Bernaldo de Quirós, Madrid.

1871b Memorial. In *Colección de Documentos Inéditos Relativos al Descubrimiento, Conquista y Organización de las Antiguas Posesiones españolas de Améria y Oceanía*, edited by Joaquin F. Pacheco and Francisco Cardenas, 15:127–46. M. Bernaldo de Quirós, Madrid.

EZZO, J. A., C. M. JOHNSON, AND T. D. PRICE

1997 Analytical Perspectives on Prehistoric Migration: A Case Study from East-Central Arizona. *Journal of Archaeological Science* 24(5): 447–66.

FLINT, RICHARD, AND SHIRLEY C. FLINT

2005 *Documents of the Coronado Expedition, 1539–1542: "They Were Not Familiar with His Majesty, nor Did They Wish to Be His Subjects."* Southern Methodist University Press, Dallas.

FOLMER, H.

1940 De Bellisle on the Texas Coast. *Southwestern Historical Quarterly* 44:204–31.

FORBIS, RICHARD G.

1978 Some Facets of Communal Hunting. In *Bison Procurement and Utilization: A Symposium*, edited by Leslie B. Davis and Michael Wilson, pp. 3–8. *Plains Anthropologist* 23(82), Pt. 2. Memoir 14, Lincoln.

FOSTER, WILLIAM C.

1995 *Spanish Expeditions into Texas 1689–1768*. University of Texas Press, Austin.

1998 *The LaSalle Expedition to Texas: The Journal of Henri Joutel, 1684–1687*. Edited by W. Foster, translated by Johanna S. Warren. Texas State Historical Association, Austin.

FOWLER, C. S., M. DUFORT, M. K. RUSCO, AND P. ESTEVES

1999 In the Field in Death Valley: Julian Steward's Panamint Shoshone Fieldwork. In *Julian Steward and the Great Basin: The Making of an Anthropologist*. University of Utah Press, Salt Lake City.

FOWLES, S. M.

2005 Historical Contingency and the Prehistoric Foundations of Moiety Organization among the Eastern Pueblos. *Journal of Anthropological Research* 61(1): 25–49.

FOX, DANIEL

1979 *Archaeological Investigation of Two Prehistoric Sites on the Coleto Creek Drainage, Goliad County, Texas*. Center for Archaeological Research, Archaeological Survey Report 69. University of Texas, San Antonio.

FOX, GEORGE

1939 Field data and reports on the Harrell Site (NT-5). Manuscripts on file, Texas Archeological Research Laboratory, Archives, University of Texas at Austin.

FRANK, D. A., AND S. J. MCNAUGHTON

1992 The Ecology of Plants, Large Mammalian Herbivores, and Drought in Yellowstone National Park. *Ecology* 73(6): 2043–58.

FREDERICK, C. D., M. D. GLASCOCK, H. NEFF, AND C. M. STEVENSON

1994 *Evaluation of Chert Patination as a Dating Technique: A Case Study from Fort Hood, Texas.* U.S. Army Fort Hood Archeological Resource Management Series, Research Report 32. Mariah Associates, Austin.

FREDERICK, C. D., AND C. RINGSTAFF

1994 Lithic Resources at Fort Hood: Further Investigations. In *Archeological Investigations on 571 Prehistoric Sites at Fort Hood, Bell and Coryell Counties, Texas,* edited by W. N. Trierweiler. U.S. Army Fort Hood Archeological Resource Management Series, Research Report 31. Mariah Associates, Austin.

FRISON, GEORGE C.

1978 Animal Population Studies and Cultural Inference. In *Bison Procurement and Utilization: A Symposium,* edited by Leslie B. Davis and Michael Wilson, pp. 44–52. *Plains Anthropologist* 23(82), Pt. 2. Memoir 14.

GADUS, ELOISE F., ROSS C. FIELDS, AND KARL W. KIBLER

2006 *Data Recovery Excavations at the J. B. White Site (41MM341), Milam County, Texas.* Reports of Investigations 145. Prewitt and Associates, Austin, and Archeology Studies Program Report 87, Environmental Affairs Division, Texas Department of Transportation, Austin.

GALLOWAY, P.

1992 The Unexamined Habitus, Direct Historic Analogy and the Archaeology of the Text. In *Representations in Archaeology,* edited by Jean-Claude Gardin and Christopher S. Peebles, pp. 178–95. Indiana University Press, Bloomington.

GATES, TED, AND ALYCE HART

1977 The Garza Burial. *Transactions of the 12th Regional Archeological Symposium for Southeastern New Mexico and Western Texas,* 145–54. El Paso Archeological Society, El Paso, Tex.

GERHARD, PETER

1982 *The Northern Frontier of New Spain.* Princeton University Press, Princeton, N.J.

GILMORE, K. K.

1969 *The San Xavier Missions: A Study in Historical Site Identification.* Archeological Program Report 16. State Building Commission, Austin.

GILMORE, ZACKARY I.

2007 Bone Processing and Subsistence Security in Late Prehistoric South Texas. MA thesis, Department of Anthropology, Southern Illinois University, Carbondale.

GODDARD, IVES

1979 The Languages of South Texas and the Lower Rio Grande. In *The Languages of North America: Historical and Comparative Assessment,* edited by Lyle Campbell and Marianne Mithun, pp. 355–89. University of Texas Press, Austin.

GOODBY, ROBERT O.

1998 Ceramic Variability in Southern New England. In *The Archaeology of Social Boundaries,* edited by Miriam T. Stark. Smithsonian Institution Press, Washington, D.C.

GOULD, F. W.

1962 *Texas Plants: A Checklist and Ecological Summary.* Texas Agricultural Experiment Station, Texas A&M University, College Station.

GRAVES, MICHAEL W.

1982 Breaking Down Ceramic Variation: Testing Models of White Mountain Redwear Design Style Development. *Journal of Anthropological Archaeology* 1(4): 305–53.

GREEN, L. M., AND T. R. HESTER

1973 The Finnis Frost Site: A Toyah Phase Occupation in San Saba County, Texas. *Bulletin of the Texas Archeological Society* 44:69–88.

GREER, JOHN W.

1968 The Cammack Site: A Neo-American Pit-Oven Ring Midden Site in Val Verde County, Texas. Master's thesis, Department of Anthropology, University of Texas at Austin.

1976a Notes on Bison in Val Verde County, Texas: Additions to Dillehay. *Plains Anthropologist* 21(1): 21–73.

1976b Neo-American Occupation at the Wheatley Site, Pedernales Falls State Park, Blanco County, Texas. *Bulletin of the Texas Archeological Society* 47:89–170.

GREGORY, HIRAM P.

1973 Eighteenth Century Caddoan Archaeology: A Study in Models and Interpretation. PhD dissertation, Department of Anthropology, Southern Methodist University, Dallas.

GRIFFEN, JAMES

1969 *Culture Change and Shifting Populations in Central Northern Mexico*. Anthropological Papers of the University of Arizona 13. University of Arizona Press, Tucson.

1979 *Indian Assimilation in the Franciscan Area of Nueva Vizcaya*. Anthropological Papers of the University of Arizona 33. University of Arizona Press, Tucson.

2000 Observations on the Limitations of Data on the Ethnohistory of Northern Mexico. In *Nómadas y Sedentarios en el Norte de México, Homenaja a Beatriz Braniff*, edited by M. Hers, J. L. Mirafuentes, M. de los Dolores Soto, and M. Vallebueno, pp. 249–73. Instituto de Investigaciones Anthropolóicas, Instituto de Investigaciones Éstecticas, Instituto de Investigaciones Históricas, Universidad Autónoma Nacional de México, México, D.F.

GRIFFIN, JAMES B.

1935 Report on Pottery Sherds from Near Abilene, Texas. *Bulletin of the Texas Archeological and Paleontological Society* 7:57–69.

GRIFFITH, TIMOTHY B., KARL W. KIBLER, AND DOUGLAS K. BOYD

2010 *National Register Testing at 41BQ285, Bosque County, Texas: FM 56 Bridge Replacement at the North Bosque River*. Reports of Investigations 160, Prewitt and Associates, Austin, and Archeological Studies Program, Report 101, Environmental Affairs Division, Texas Department of Transportation, Austin.

GRIFFITHS, JULIETTE

2006 Analyzing the Use of Ceramic Vessels at a Hunter/Gatherer Base Camp (Site MD-1) in the Nueces River Valley, South Texas. Archaeology Field School Report. Manuscript on file, Corpus Christi Museum of Science and History.

GRIFFITHS, J. F., AND R. ORTON

1968 *Agroclimatic Atlas of Texas. Part I: Precipitation Probabilities*. Texas Agricultural Experiment Station Miscellaneous Publication 888. College Station, Tex.

GUCKIAN, WILLIAM J., AND RAMON N. GARCIA

1979 *Soil Survey of San Patricio and Aransas Counties, Texas*. U.S. Department of Agriculture, Soil Conservation Service.

HABICHT-MAUCHE, JUDITH A.

1987 Southwestern-Style Culinary Ceramics on the Southern Plains: A Case Study of Technological Innovation and Cross-Cultural Interaction. *Plains Anthropologist* 32(116): 175–89.

1992 Coronado's Querechos and Teyas in the Archaeological Record of the Texas Panhandle. *Plains Anthropologist* 37:247–59.

HACKETT, CHARLES W.

1926 *Historical Documents relating to New Mexico, Nueva Vizcaya and Approaches Thereto, to 1773, Collected by Adolph F. A. Bandelier and Fanny R. Bandelier*. Papers of the Department of

Historical Research 330, Vols. 1–3. Carnegie Institution of Washington, Washington, D.C.

HADLEY, DIANA, THOMAS H. NAYLOR, AND MARDITH K. SCHUETZ-MILLER (EDITORS)

1997 *The Presidio and Militia on the Northern Frontier of New Spain: A Documentary History*. University of Arizona Press, Tucson.

HAGGARD, J. VILLASANA

1941 *Handbook for Translators of Spanish Historical Documents*. University of Texas, Austin.

HALL, GRANT D.

1998 Prehistoric Human Food Resource Patches on the Texas Coastal Plain. *Bulletin of the Texas Archeological Society* 69:1–10.

2000 Pecan Food Potential in Prehistoric North America. In *Economic Botany* 54(1): 103–12.

HALL, GRANT D., STEPHEN L. BLACK, AND CAROL GRAVES

1982 *Archaeological Investigations at Choke Canyon Reservoir, South Texas: The Phase I Findings*. Choke Canyon Series 5. Center for Archaeological Research, University of Texas at San Antonio.

HALL, GRANT D., THOMAS R. HESTER, AND STEPHEN L. BLACK

1986 *Archaeological Investigations at Choke Canyon Reservoir, Southern Texas: Results of the Phase II Archaeological Investigations*. Choke Canyon Series 10. Center for Archaeological Research, University of Texas at San Antonio.

HALL, GRANT D., AND CHERYL L HIGHLEY

1986 *Archaeological Investigations at 41LK201, Choke Canyon Reservoir, Southern Texas*. Choke Canyon Series 11. Center for Archaeological Research, University of Texas at San Antonio.

HALLENBECK, C.

1940 *Alvar Nuñez Cabeza de Vaca: The Journey and Route of the First European to Cross the Continent of North America, 1534–1536*. Arthur H. Clark, Glendale, Calif.

HALSTEAD, PAUL, AND JOHN O'SHEA (EDITORS)

1989 *Bad Year Economics*. Cambridge University Press, Cambridge.

HAMMOND, GEORGE P., AND AGAPITO REY (TRANSLATORS AND EDITORS)

1929 *Expedition into New Mexico Made by Antonio de Espejo in 1582–1583, as Revealed in the Journal of Diego Pérez de Luxán, a Member of the Party*. Quivira Society Publications 1. Quivira Society, Los Angeles.

1966 *Rediscovery of New Mexico 1580–1594: The Explorations of Chamascado, Espejo, Morlete, and Leyva de Bonilla and Humaña*. University of New Mexico Press, Albuquerque.

HANNAFORD, C. A.

1981 *The Roswell Sites: Archeological Survey and Testing of 24 Sites along U.S. 70 in Chaves and Lincoln Counties, New Mexico*. Note 275. Museum of New Mexico, Laboratory of Anthropology, Santa Fe.

HARD, ROBERT J., AND A. KATZENBERG

2008 Stable Isotope Analysis of Human Bone from the Texas Coastal Plain. Manuscript on file. Department of Anthropology, University of Texas at San Antonio.

HARDESTY, DONALD

1977 *Ecological Anthropology*. John Wiley and Sons, New York.

HART, ALYCE

1976 An Open Report on Probes and Digs of LY42 by Individuals and the Archeological Society of Dawson County. *Transactions of the Eleventh Regional Archeological Symposium for Southeastern New Mexico and Western Texas*, pp. 111–20. Midland Archeological Society, Midland, Tex.

HART, T. B., AND J. A. HART

1986 The Ecological Basis of Hunter-Gatherer Subsistence in African Rainforests: The Mbuti of Eastern Zaire. *Human Ecology* 14:29–56.

HATCHER, MATTIE AUSTIN

1927 Descriptions of the Tejas or Asínai Indians, 1691–1722. *Southwestern Historical Quarterly Online* 30:283–304, www.tsha.utexas.edu/publications/journals/shq/online/vo30/n4/article_6.html.

HEGMON, MICHELLE, AND LYNN E. FISHER

1991 Information Strategies in Hunter-Gatherer Societies. In *Foragers in Context: Long-Term, Regional, and Historical Perspectives in Hunter-Gatherer Studies*, edited by Preston T. Miracle, Lynn E. Fisher, and Jody Brown, pp. 127–45. Michigan Discussions in Anthropology 10. University of Michigan, Ann Arbor.

HELM, MARY S.

1884 *Scraps of Early Texas History*. B. R. Warner and Company, Austin.

HELWING, BARBARA

2003 Feasts as a Social Dynamic in Prehistoric Western Asia: Three Case Studies from Syria and Anatolia. *Paléorient* 29(2): 63–85.

HENDERSON, JERRY

2001 *Excavations at the Rainey Site (41BN33), a Late Prehistoric Sinkhole Site in Bandera County, Texas*. Archeological Studies Program Report 5. Texas Department of Transportation, Austin.

HENIGE, DAVID

1993 Proxy Data, Historical Method, and the De Soto Expedition. In *Expedition of Hernando de Soto West of the Mississippi, 1541–1543*. Proceedings of the De Soto Symposia 1988 and 1990, edited by G. A. Young and M. P. Hoffman, pp. 155–72. University of Arkansas Press, Fayetteville.

HENNING D. R., AND T. D. THIESSEN (EDITORS)

2004 Part II: Central Siouans in the Northeastern Plains: Oneota Archaeology and the Blood Run Site. *Plains Anthropologist* 49:345–625, Memoir 36.

HESTER, THOMAS R.

1975 Late Prehistoric Cultural Patterns along the Lower Rio Grande of Texas. *Bulletin of the Texas Archeological Society* 46:107–26.

1981 Tradition and Diversity among the Prehistoric Hunters and Gathers of Southern Texas. *Plains Anthropologist* 26(92): 119–28.

1995 The Prehistory of South Texas. *Bulletin of the Texas Archeological Society* 66:427–59.

2004 The Prehistory of South Texas. In *The Prehistory of Texas*, edited by T. K. Perttula, pp. 127–51. Texas A&M University Press, College Station.

2005 An Overview of the Late Archaic in Southern Texas. In *The Late Archaic across the Borderlands: From Foraging to Farming*, edited by B. D. Vierra, pp. 259–78. University of Texas Press, Austin.

HESTER, T. R., S. L. BLACK, D. G. STEELE, B. W. OLIVE, A. A. FOX, K. J. REINHARD, AND L. C. BEMENT

1989 *From the Gulf to the Rio Grande: Human Adaptation in Central, South, and Lower Pecos, Texas*. Research Series 33. Arkansas Archeological Survey, Fayetteville.

HESTER, THOMAS R., AND T. C. HILL

1971 An Initial Study of a Prehistoric Ceramic Tradition in Southern Texas. *Plains Anthropologist* 16(52): 195–203.

1975 *Some Aspects of Late Prehistoric and Protohistoric Archaeology in Southern Texas*. Special Report 1. Center for Archaeological Research, University of Texas at San Antonio.

HESTER, THOMAS R., AND R. C. PARKER

1970 The Berclair Site: A Late Prehistoric Component in Goliad County, Southern Texas. *Bulletin of the Texas Archeological Society* 41:1–24.

HESTER, THOMAS R., AND HARRY J. SHAFER

1975 An Initial Study of Blade Technology on the Central Texas Coast. *Plains Anthropologist* 20(69): 175–85.

HICKERSON, NANCY P.

1994 *The Jumanos: Hunters and Traders of the South Plains.* University of Texas Press, Austin.

HIGHLEY, CHERYL LYNN

1986 *Archaeological Investigations at 41LK201, Choke Canyon Reservoir, Southern Texas.* Choke Canyon Series 11. Center for Archaeological Research, University of Texas at San Antonio.

HILLSMAN, M. J.

1992 Evaluation of Visible and Ultraviolet-Excited Attributes of Some Texas and Macroscopically Similar New Mexico Cherts. MA thesis, Department of Anthropology, Eastern New Mexico University, Portales.

HIMMERICH Y VALENCIA, ROBERT

1991 *The Encomenderos of New Spain 1521–1555.* University of Texas Press, Austin.

HITCHCOCK, ROBERT K., AND LAURENCE E. BARTRAM

1998 Social Boundaries in the Kalahari. In *The Archaeology of Social Boundaries*, edited by Miriam T. Stark, pp. 12–49. Smithsonian Institution Press, Washington, D.C.

HODGE, FRANK W.

1910 The Jumano Indians. *Proceedings of the American Antiquarian Society* 20:249–68.

HOFMAN, JACK L.

1984 The Western Protohistoric: A Summary of the Edwards and Wheeler Complexes. In *Prehistory of Oklahoma*, edited by Robert E. Bell, pp. 347–62. Academic Press, New York.

1989 Protohistoric Culture History on the Southern Great Plains. In *From Clovis to Comanchero: Archeological Overview of the Southern Great Plains*, by J. L. Hofman, R. L. Brooks, J. S. Hays, D. W. Owsley, R. L. Jantz, M. K. Marks, and M. H. Manheim, pp. 91–100. Research Series 35. Arkansas Archeological Survey, Fayetteville.

HOFMAN, J. L., R. L. BROOKS, J. S. HAYS, D. W. OWSLEY, R. L. JANTZ, M. K. MARKS, AND M. H. MANHEIM

1989 *From Clovis to Comanchero: Archeological Overview of the Southern Great Plains.* Research Series 35. Arkansas Archeological Survey Fayetteville.

HOFMAN, J. L., L. C. TODD, AND M. B. COLLINS

1991 Identification of Central Texas Edwards Chert at the Folsom and Lindenmeier Sites. *Plains Anthropologist* 36(137): 297–308.

HOLDEN, W. C.

1938 Blue Mountain Rock Shelter. *Bulletin of the Texas Archeological and Paleontological Society* 10:208–21.

HOLLIDAY, V. T., AND C. M. WELTY

1981 Lithic Tool Resources of the Eastern Llano Estacado. *Bulletin of the Texas Archeological Society* 52:201–14.

HUDSON, CHARLES M.

1979 *Black Drink: A Native American Tea.* University of Georgia Press, Athens.

HUEBNER, JEFF

1987a Archaeological Test Excavations at the Burris Site (41VT66) Victoria County, Texas: A Preliminary Summary. *Friends of Archaeology Newsletter* 4:13–16.

1987b A Toyah Horizon Bone Tool from Victoria County. *La Tierra* 14(4): 6–15.

1991 Late Prehistoric Bison Populations in Central and Southern Texas. *Plains Anthropologist* 36:343–58.

HUGHES, JACK T.

1942 An Archeological Report on the Harrell Site of North-Central Texas. MA thesis, University of Texas, Austin.

1969 The Canyon City Club Cave in the Panhandle of Texas. Manuscript on file, Office of the State Archeologist, Texas Historical Commission, Austin.

1989 Prehistoric Cultural Developments on the Texas High Plains. *Bulletin of the Texas Archeological Society* 60:1–55.

HUGHES, RICHARD E.

1989 Notes on Obsidian from the Fort Hood Area of Central Texas. *Bulletin of the Texas Archeological Society* 59:193–99.

HYDE, HAROLD W., ROY H. L. BRUNS, MORRIS F. WILHELM, AND ALAN C. PEER

1992 *Soil Survey of Lavaca County, Texas.* U.S. Department of Agriculture, Soil Conservation, Washington, D.C.

INMAN, BETTY JEAN

1997 The Lithic Artifacts of the Native Americans at the Spanish Colonial Missions, Guerrero, Coahuila, Mexico. Master's thesis, Department of Anthropology, University of Texas at Austin.

INMAN, BETTY, THOMAS R. HESTER, AND T. C. HILL JR.

1998 Archeological Investigations at the Tortuga Flat Site (41ZV155), Zavala County, Southern Texas. *Bulletin of the Texas Archeological Society* 69:11–33.

JACKSON, A. T.

1938 The Fall Creek Sites. In *Annual Report of the WPA and the University of Texas Archaeological Research, Lake Buchanan, 1936–1937*, edited by J. E. Pearce, pp. 111–18. University of Texas Publication 3802. Austin.

JELKS, EDWARD B.

1962 *The Kyle Site: A Stratified Central Texas Aspect Site in Hill County, Texas.* Archaeology Series 5. Department of Anthropology, University of Texas at Austin.

1967 The Gilbert Site: A Norteno Focus Site in Northeastern Texas. *Bulletin of the Texas Archeological Society* 37.

1993 Observations on the Distribution of Certain Arrow-Point Types in Texas and Adjoining Regions. *Lithic Technology* 18(1–2): 9–15.

JENIKE, MARK R.

2001 Nutritional Ecology: Diet, Physical Activity, and Body Size. In *Hunter-Gatherers: An Interdisciplinary Perspective*, edited by Catherine Panter-Brick, Robert H. Layton, and Peter Rowley-Conwy, pp. 205–38. Cambridge University Press, Cambridge.

JOCHIM, MICHAEL A.

1981 *Strategies for Survival: Cultural Behavior in an Ecological Context.* Academic Press, New York.

JOHN, ELIZABETH A.

1975 *Storms Brewed in Other Men's Worlds: The Confrontation of Indians, Spanish, and French, 1540–1795.* Texas A&M University Press, College Station.

JOHN, ELIZABETH A. (EDITOR), AND JOHN WHEAT (TRANSLATOR)

1989 *Views from the Apache Frontier: Report on the Northern Provinces of New Spain by Jose Cortex, Lieutenant in the Royal Corps of Engineers, 1799.* University of Oklahoma Press, Norman.

JOHNSON, GREGORY A.

1982 Organizational Structure and Scalar Stress. In *Social Archaeology: Beyond Subsistence and Dating*, edited by C. Renfrew, M. L. Rowlands, and B. A. Segraves, pp. 389–421. Academic Press, New York.

1989 Dynamics of Southwestern Prehistory: Far Outside Looking In. In *Dynamics of Southwest Prehistory*, edited by Linda S. Cordell and George J. Gumerman, pp. 371–89. Smithsonian Institution Press, Washington, D.C.

JOHNSON, LEROY, JR.

1964 *The Devil's Mouth Site: A Stratified Campsite at Amistad Reservoir, Val Verde County, Texas.* Archaeology Series 6. Department of Anthropology, University of Texas at Austin.

1994 *The Life and Times of Toyah-Culture Folk: The Buckhollow Encampment, Site 41KM16, Kimble County, Texas.* Office of the State Archeologist Report 38. Texas Department of Transportation and Texas Historical Commission, Austin.

1997 *The Lion Creek Site (41BT105): Aboriginal Houses and Other Remains at a Prehistoric Ranchería in the Texas Hill Country (Burnet County).* Texas Historical Commission, OSA, Report 41,

Austin, and Environmental Affairs Division, Archeology Studies Program Report 1, Texas Department of Transportation, Austin.

JOHNSON, LEROY, AND THOMAS N. CAMPBELL

1992 Sanan: Traces of a Previously Unknown Aboriginal Language in Colonial Coahuila and Texas. *Plains Anthropologist* 37:185–212.

JOHNSON, L., JR., D. A. SUHM, AND C. D. TUNNELL

1962 *Salvage Archeology of Canyon Reservoir: The Wunderlich, Footbridge, and Oblate Sites.* Bulletin 5. Texas Memorial Museum, University of Texas at Austin.

JOHNSTON, MARSHALL C.

1963 Past and Present Grasslands of Southern Texas and Northeastern Mexico. *Ecology* 44(3): 456–66.

JONES, OAKAH L., JR.

1988 *Nueva Vizcaya, Heartland of the Spanish Frontier.* University of New Mexico Press, Albuquerque.

JONES, SIÂN

1997 *The Archaeology of Ethnicity.* Routledge, New York.

KALTER, ARDI J., ROBERT M. ROGERS, AND MICHAEL N. SMITH

2005 *Analysis and Reporting for 41FY135, the Sandbur Site, Fayette County, Texas.* Environmental Affairs Division, Archeology Studies Program Report 73, Texas Department of Transportation, Austin.

KARBULA, JAMES

2003 The Toyah Bluff Site (41TV441): Changing Notions of Late Prehistoric Subsistence in the Blackland Prairie along the Eastern Edge of the Edwards Plateau, Travis County, Texas. *Bulletin of the Texas Archeological Society* 74:55–81.

KARBULA, JAMES W., RACHAEL FEIT, AND TIMOTHY B. GRIFFITH

2001 *Changing Perspectives on the Toyah: Data Recovery Investigations of 41TV441, the Toyah Bluff Site, Travis County, Texas.* Hicks and Company, Austin.

KARL, T. R.

1986 The Sensitivity of the Palmer Drought Severity Index and Palmer's Z-Index to Their Calibration Coefficients including Potential Evapotranspiration. *Journal of Climate and Applied Meteorology* 25:77–86.

KATZ, PAUL, AND SUSANA R. KATZ

2002 *Data Recovery at the Bear Branch Site (41CA13), Callahan County, Texas.* PRIAM Project 9906. PRIAM, Panhandle, Tex.

KAVANAGH, THOMAS WHITNEY

1986 Political Power and Political Organization, Comanche Politics 1786–1875. Ph.D. dissertation, Department of Anthropology, University of New Mexico, Albuquerque.

KEELEY, LAWRENCE H.

1996 *War before Civilization: The Myth of the Peaceful Savage.* Oxford University Press, New York.

KELLEY, J. CHARLES

1947a The Cultural Affiliations and Chronological Position of the Clear Fort Focus. *American Antiquity* 13:97–109.

1947b The Lehmann Rock Shelter: A Stratified Site of the Toyah, Uvalde, and Round Rock Foci. *Bulletin of the Texas Archeological and Paleontological Society* 18:115–28.

1955 Juan Sabeata and Diffusion in Aboriginal Texas. *American Anthropologist* 57:981–95.

1986 *Jumano and Patarabueye: Relations at La Junta de los Rios.* Museum of Anthropology, University of Michigan, Ann Arbor.

KELLEY, J. C., T. N. CAMPBELL, AND D. J. LEHMER

1940 The Association of Archaeological Materials with Geological Deposits in the Big Bend Region of Texas. *Sul Ross State Teachers College Bulletin* 21(3): 9–171.

KELLEY, JANE H.

1984 *The Archaeology of the Sierra Blanca Region of Southeastern New Mexico.* Anthropological Paper 74. University of Michigan, Museum of Anthropology, Ann Arbor.

KELLY, ROBERT L.

1980 Hunter-Gatherer Settlement Systems. Master's thesis, Department of Anthropology, University of New Mexico, Albuquerque.

1983 Hunter-Gatherer Mobility Strategies. *Journal of Anthropological Research* 39(3): 277–306.

1995 *The Foraging Spectrum.* Smithsonian Institution Press, Washington, D.C.

KEMP, LEONARD

2008 Buffaloed by Bison. MA thesis, Department of Anthropology, University of Texas at San Antonio.

KENMOTSU, NANCY A.

1994 Helping Each Other Out: A Study of the Mutualistic Relations of Small Scale Foragers and Cultivators in Las Junta de Los Rios Region, Texas and Mexico. Ph.D. dissertation, Department of Anthropology, University of Texas at Austin.

2001 Seeking Friends, Avoiding Enemies: The Jumano Response to Spanish Colonization. *Bulletin of the Texas Archeological Society* 72:23–43.

2007 The Toyah Phase: A Retrospective. Paper Presented at the 72nd Annual Meeting of the Society of American Archaeology, Austin.

2008 Native Peoples of the Trans-Pecos Mountains and Basins during Early Historic Times. Texas beyond History, www.texasbeyondhistory.net/trans-p/peoples/index.html.

KENMOTSU, N. A., J. E. BRUSETH, AND J. E. CORBIN

1993 Moscoso and the Route in Texas: A Reconstruction. In the *Expedition of Hernando de Soto West of the Mississippi, 1541–1543,* Proceedings of the De Soto Symposia 1988 and 1990, edited by G. A. Young and M. P. Hoffman, pp. 106–30. University of Arkansas Press, Fayetteville.

KENMOTSU, NANCY A., AND MARIAH F. WADE

2002 *Amistad National Recreation Area, Del Rio, Texas, American Indian Tribal Affiliation Study Phase I: Ethnohistoric Literature Review.* National Park Service and Archeological Studies Program Report 34, Texas Department of Transportation, Austin.

KESSELL, JOHN L.

1987 *Kiva, Cross, and Crown: The Pecos Indians and New Mexico, 1540–1840.* 2nd ed. University of New Mexico Press, Albuquerque.

KIBLER, KARL W., AND CORY J. BROEHM

2005 Data Recovery at Site 41HM51, Hamilton County, Texas. In *Current Archeology in Texas* 7(1): 18–22. Texas Historical Commission, Austin.

KNAPP, A. K., J. M. BLAIR, J. M. BRIGGS, S. L. COLLINS, D. C. HARTNETT, L. C. JOHNSON, AND E. G. TOWNE

1999 The Keystone Role of Bison in North American Tallgrass Prairie. *Bioscience* 49:39–50.

KNAPP, A. K., J. M. BRIGGS, AND J. K. KOELLIKER

2001 Frequency and Extent of Water Limitation to Primary Production in a Mesic Temperate Grassland. *Ecosystems* 4:19–28.

KRIEGER, ALEX D.

1946 *Culture, Complexes and Chronology in Northern Texas: With Extension of Puebloan Datings to the Mississippi Valley.* University of Texas Publication 4640, Austin.

2002 *We Came Naked and Barefoot: The Journey of Cabeza de Vaca across North America,* edited by Margery Krieger. University of Texas Press, Austin.

KROEBER, ALFRED L.

1939 *Cultural and Natural Areas of Native North America*. University of California Publications in American Archaeology and Ethnology 38. Berkeley.

LAIRD, CAROBETH

1976 *The Chemehuevis*. Malki Museum Press, Banning City, Calif.

LARSEN, CLARK SPENCER

1999 *Bioarchaeology: Interpreting Behavior from the Human Skeleton*. Cambridge Studies in Biological Anthropology 21. Cambridge University Press, Cambridge.

LAUENROTH, W. K., I. C. BURKE, AND M. P. GUTMANN

1999 The Structure and Function of Ecosystems in the Central North American Grassland Region. *Great Plains Research* 9:223–59.

LEBLANC, S. A.

1997 Modeling Warfare in Southwestern Prehistory. *North American Archaeologist* 18(3): 235–76.

1999 *Prehistoric Warfare in the American Southwest*. University of Utah Press, Salt Lake City.

LEE, RICHARD B.

1979 *The !Kung San: Men, Women, and Work in a Foraging Society*. Cambridge University Press, New York.

2003 *The Dobe Ju/'hoansi*. 3rd ed. Cengage Learning, Florence, Ky.

LEHMER, DONALD J.

1948 *The Jornada Branch of the Mogollon*. Social Science Bulletin 17. University of Arizona, Tucson.

LEÓN, ALONSO DE

1909 *História de Nuevo León, con Noticias sobre Coahuila, Tejas, y Nuevo México*. México, D.F.

LEÓN, ALONSO DE

1968 Diario y Derrotero. In *Primeras Exploraciones y Poblamiento de Tejas (1686–1694), Notícias Geográficas e Históricas del Noreste de México*, edited by L. Gomez Candeo, pp. 87–104. Instituto Tecnológico y de estudio superiores de Monterrey, México.

LEONARD, KATHRYN

2006 Directionality and Exclusivity of Plains-Pueblo Exchange during the Protohistoric Period, A.D. 1450–1700. In *The Social Life of Pots: Glaze Wares and Cultural Dynamics in the Southwest, A.D. 1250–1680*, edited by Judith A. Habicht-Mauche, Suzanne L. Eckert, and Deborah L. Huntley, pp. 232–52. University of Arizona Press, Tucson.

LESLIE, ROBERT H.

1970 The Merchant Site, L.C.A.S. E-4. *Transactions of the First Regional Archeological Symposium for Southeastern New Mexico and Western Texas*, 23–29. Lea County Archeological Society, Hobbs, N.Mex.

1978 Projectile Point Types and Sequence of the Eastern Jornada Mogollon, Extreme Southeastern New Mexico. *Transactions of the 13th Regional Archeological Symposium for Southeastern New Mexico and Western Texas*, 81–157. Dawson County Archeological Society, Lamesa, Tex.

1979 The Eastern Jornada Mogollon: Extreme Southeastern New Mexico (A Summary). In *Jornada Mogollon Archaeology: Proceedings of the First Jornada Conference*, edited by P. H. Beckett and R. N. Wiseman, pp. 179–99. New Mexico State University, Cultural Resources Management Division, Las Cruces, and State of New Mexico, Office of Cultural Affairs, Historic Preservation Division, Santa Fe.

LESSER, ALEXANDER

1961 Social Fields and the Evolution of Society. *Southwestern Journal of Anthropology* 17:40–48.

LEWIS, P. J., E. JOHNSON, B. BUCHANAN, AND S. E. CHURCHILL

2007 The Evolution of *Bison bison*: A View from the Southern Plains. *Bulletin of Texas Archeology* 78:197–204.

LIGHTFOOT, KENT G.

1983 Resource Uncertainty and Buffering Strategies in an Arid, Marginal Environment. In *Ecological Models in Economic Prehistory*, edited by Gordon Bronitsky. Arizona State University, Tempe.

LIGHTFOOT, KENT G., A. MARTINEZ, AND A. M. SCHIFF

1998 Daily Practice and Material Culture in Pluralistic Social Settings: An Archaeological Study of Culture Change and Persistence from Fort Ross, California. *American Antiquity* 63:199–222.

LINTZ, CHRISTOPHER, ABBY C. TREECE, F. M. OGLESBY, KARL KIBLER, PATRICK O'NEILL, W. NICHOLAS TRIERWEILER, C. FREDERICK, J. MICHAEL QUIGG, AND A. J. TAYLOR

1993 *Cultural Resource Investigations in the O. H. Ivie Reservoir, Concho, Coleman, and Runnels Counties, Texas*. Vol. 2: *Test Excavations at Prehistoric Sites and Assessment of Rock Cairn Features*. Technical Report 346-II. Mariah Associates, Austin.

LOHSE, JON C.

1999 Lithics from the San Antonio de Valero Mission: Analysis of Materials from 1979 Excavations at the Alamo. *Bulletin of the Texas Archeological Society* 70:265–79.

LORD, K. H.

1977 Faunal Analysis of the Cedar Bridge Sites (41FY74). Appendix V in *Archeological Investigations at the Fayette Power Project, Fayette County, Texas*, by Duford W. Skelton, pp. 237–42. Research Report 60. Texas Archeological Survey, University of Texas at Austin.

LOREN, D. P.

2008 *In Contact: Bodies and Spaces in the Sixteenth- and Seventeenth-Century Eastern Woodlands*. AltaMira Press, New York.

LORRAIN, DESSAMAE

1968 Excavation at Red Bluff Shelter (Sotol Site) X41CX8, Crockett County, Texas. *Transactions of the Fourth Regional Archeological Symposium for Southeastern New Mexico and Western Texas*, pp. 18–39. Iraan Archeological Society, Iraan, Tex.

LOURANDOS, HARRY

1997 *Continent of Hunter-Gatherers: New Perspectives in Australian Prehistory*. Cambridge University Press, New York.

LOW, BOBBI S.

1990 Human Responses to Environmental Extremeness and Uncertainty: A Cross-Cultural Perspective. In *Risk and Uncertainty in Tribal and Peasant Economies*, edited by Elizabeth Cashdan, pp. 229–55. Westview Press, Boulder, Colo.

LYNOTT, MARK J.

1978 *An Archaeological Assessment of the Bear Creek Shelter, Lake Whitney, Texas*. Archaeology Research Program, Research Report 115. Department of Anthropology, Southern Methodist University, Dallas.

1979 Prehistoric Bison Populations of North Central Texas. *Bulletin of the Texas Archeological Society* 50:89–101.

MACDONALD, DOUGLAS H., AND BARRY S. HEWLETT

1999 Reproductive Interests and Forager Mobility. *Current Anthropology* 40(4): 501–24.

MACEARCHERN, S.

1998 Scale, Style, and Cultural Variation: Technological Traditions in the Northern Mandara Mountains. In *The Archaeology of Social Boundaries*, edited by M. T. Stark, pp. 107–31. Smithsonian Institution Press, Washington, D.C.

MADRID, E. R.

1992 *Expedition to La Junta de los Ríos, 1747–1748: Captain Commander Joseph de Ydioaga's Report to the Viceroy of New Spain*. Office of the State Archeologist Special Report 33. Texas Historical Commission, Austin.

MAHONEY, R. B., S. A. TOMKA, R. P. MAULDIN, H. J. SHAFER, L. C. NORDT, R. D. GREAVES, AND R. R. GALDEANO

2003 *Data Recovery Excavations at 41MM340, a Late Archaic Site along Little River in Milam County, Texas*. Archaeological Survey Report 340, Center for Archaeological Research, University of Texas at San Antonio, and Archeological Studies Program Report 54, Environmental Affairs Division, Texas Department of Transportation, Austin.

MALLOUF, ROBERT J.

1987 *Las Haciendas: A Cairn-Burial Assemblage from Northeastern Chihuahua, Mexico*. Office of the State Archeologist Report 35. Texas Historical Commission, Austin.

1989 Quarry Hunting with Jack T. Hughes: Tecovas Jasper in the South Basin of the Canadian River, Oldham County, Texas. In *In the Light of Past Experience: Papers in Honor of Jack T. Hughes*, edited by D. C. Roper, pp. 307–26. Publication 5. Panhandle Archeological Society, Amarillo, Tex.

1990 A Commentary on the Prehistory of Far Northeastern Chihuahua, the La Junta District, and the Cielo Complex. (Translation of "La Prehistória del noreste de Chihuahua: Complejo Cielo y Districto La Junta"). In *História General de Chihuahua 1: Geología y Arqueología*, edited by A. Marquéz-Alameda, pp. 137–62. Universidad Autónoma de Ciudad de Júarez y Gobierno del Estado de Chihuahua, Júarez.

1999 Comments on the Prehistory of Far Northeastern Chihuahua, the La Junta District, and the Cielo Complex. *Journal for Big Bend Studies* 11:49–92.

2004 Unusual Iron Arrow Points from the Marfa Plain. *La Vista de la Frontera: Newsletter of the Center for Big Bend Studies* (Sul Ross State University)16(1): 6–7.

MARSHALL, ANDREW J., AND RICHARD WRANGHAM

2007 Evolutionary Consequences of Fallback Foods. *International Journal of Primatology* 28:1219–35.

MARSHALL, FIONA, AND TOM PILGRAM

1991 Meat versus Within-Bone Nutrients: Another Look at the Meaning of Body Part Representation in Archaeological Sites. *Journal of Archaeological Science* 18:149–63.

MASANET, FRAY DAMIAN (SEE ALSO MAZANET, DAMIEN)

1957 Parecer del Padre Comisario Fray Damian Masanet y demás Religiosos Misioneros, Julio 19 de 1691 años. *Boletín del Archivo General de la Nación* 28:346–81.

MASSON, MARILYN A., AND MARK W. HOLDERBY

1994 Subsistence Patterns at 41HY209 and 41HY202: An Analysis of Vertebrate Faunal Remains. In *Archaic and Late Prehistoric Human Ecology in the Middle Onion Creek Valley, Hays County, Texas*, by Robert A. Ricklis and Michael B. Collins, pp. 403–89. Studies in Archeology 19. Texas Archeological Research Laboratory, University of Texas at Austin.

MAULDIN, R. P.

2003 *Exploring Drought in the San Antonio Area between 1700 and 1979*. Special Report 29. Center for Archaeological Research, University of Texas at San Antonio.

MAULDIN, R. P., R. D. GREAVES, J. L. THOMPSON, C. M. MUNOZ, L. KEMP, B. A. MEISSNER, B. K. MOSES, AND S. A. TOMKA.

2010 *Archeological Testing and Data Recovery at 41ZV202, Zavala County, Texas*. Archaeological Report 409, Center for Archaeological Research, University of Texas at San Antonio, and Archeological Studies Program Report 121, Environmental Affairs Division, Texas Department of Transportation, Austin.

MAULDIN, R. P., C. MUNOZ, AND J. THOMPSON

2008 Assessing Hearth Reuse Frequency through Patterning in Burned Rock Size. Paper presented at the 79th Annual Meeting of the Texas Archeological Society, Lubbock.

MAULDIN, R. P., D. L. NICHOLS, AND C. J. BROEHM

2003 *Archaeological Testing to Determine the National Register Eligibility Status of 18 Prehistoric Sites on Camp Bowie, Brown County, Texas*. 2 vols. Archeological Survey Report 334. Center for Archaeological Research, University of Texas at San Antonio.

MAULDIN, R. P., J. THOMPSON, C. MUNOZ, AND L. KEMP

2009 Hunter-Gatherer Resource Intensification and Changing Patterns of Fire-Cracked Rock Use in Central and South Texas. Poster presented at the 74th Annual Meeting of the Society for American Archaeology, Atlanta, Ga.

MAZANET, DAMIEN (SEE ALSO MASANET, FRAY DAMIAN)

1968 Diario del Padre Mazanet en su Expedición a Texas. In *Primeras Exploraciones y Poblamiento de Tejas (1686–1694), Notícias Geográficas e Históricas del Noreste de México*, edited by L. Gomez Candeo, pp. 225–54. Instituto Tecnológico y de estudios superiores de Monterrey, México.

MCBRINN, MAXINE

2005 *Social Identities among Archaic Mobile Hunters and Gatherers in the American Southwest.* Arizona State Museum Archaeological Series 197. University of Arizona, Tucson.

MCDONALD, J. N.

1981 *North American Bison, Their Classification and Evolution.* University of California Press, Berkeley.

MCELREATH, RICHARD, ROBERT BOYD, AND PETER J. RICHERSON

2003 Shared Norms and the Evolution of Ethnic Markers. *Current Anthropology* 44(1): 122–29.

MEAD, J. F., R. B. ALFIN-SLATER, D. R. HOWTON, AND G. POPJAK

1986 *Lipids: Chemistry, Biochemistry, and Nutrition.* Plenum Press, New York.

MEHALCHICK, GEMMA, KARL W. KIBLER, AMY M. HOLMES, CHRISTOPHER W. RINGSTAFF, AND DOUGLAS K. BOYD

2003 *National Register Testing of 19 Prehistoric Sites on Fort Hood, Texas: The 2000–2001 Season.* U.S. Army, Fort Hood, Archeological Resource Management Series Research Report 47. Prewitt and Associates, Austin.

MEHALCHICK, GEMMA, TERRI MYERS, KARL W. KIBLER, AND DOUGLAS K. BOYD

1999 *Val Verde on the Sunny Rio Grande: Geoarcheological and Historical Investigations at San Felipe Springs, Val Verde County, Texas.* Reports of Investigations 122. Prewitt and Associates, Austin.

MERONEY, W. P.

1936 A Mass Burial near Waco. *Bulletin of the Central Texas Archeological Society* (Waco) 2:58–60.

MERRILL, W.

1988 *Raramuri Souls: Knowledge and Social Process in Northern Mexico.* Smithsonian Institution Press, Washington, D.C.

1994 Cultural Creativity and Raiding Bands in Eighteenth-Century Northern New Spain. In *Violence, Resistance, and Survival in the Americas: Native Americans and the Legacy of Conquest*, edited by W. B. Taylor and F. Pease G.Y., pp. 124–51. Smithsonian Institution Press, Washington, D.C.

MILLER, E. O., AND E. B. JELKS

1952 Archeological Excavations at the Belton Reservoir, Coryell County, Texas. *Bulletin of the Texas Archeological Society* 23:168–217.

MILLER, M. R.

1995 Ceramics of the Jornada Mogollon and Trans-Pecos Regions of West Texas. *Bulletin of the Texas Archeological and Paleontological Society* 66:210–19.

MILLER, M. R., AND N. A. KENMOTSU

2004 Prehistory of the Jornada Mogollon and Eastern Trans-Pecos Regions of West Texas. In *The Prehistory of Texas*, edited by T. K. Perttula, pp. 205–65. Texas A&M University Press, College Station.

MILLS, BARBARA J.

2004 *Identity, Feasting, and the Archaeology of the Greater Southwest.* University Press of Colorado, Boulder.

MINTZ, SIDNEY W. (EDITOR)

1985 *History, Evolution, and the Concept of Culture: Selected Papers by Alexander Lesser.* Cambridge University Press, New York.

MINZENMAYER, FRED E.

1979 *Soil Survey of Jim Wells County, Texas.* U.S. Department of Agriculture, Soil Conservation Service, in cooperation with the Texas Agricultural Experiment Station.

MONTGOMERY, JOHN L.

1978 *The Mariposa Site: A Late Prehistoric Site on the Rio Grande Plain of Texas.* Special Report 6, Vol. 2. Center for Archaeological Research, University of Texas at San Antonio.

MORGAN, R. G.

1980 Bison Movement Patterns on the Canadian Plains: An Ecological Analysis. *Plains Anthropologist* 25:143–60.

MOTOLINÍA, FRAY TORIBIO DE BENAVENTE DE

1971[1555] *Memoriales o Libro de las Cosas de la Nueva Espeña y de los Naturales de Ella.* Edmundo O'Gorman, editor and transcriber. Universidad Nacional Autonomo de México, México.

MUNOZ, C.

2004 Native American Adaptation on the Texas Coastal Plain: A Study of the Dentition from Thirteen Prehistoric and Historic Cemetery Sites. MA thesis, Department of Anthropology, University of Texas at San Antonio.

MURDOCK, GEORGE P.

1949 *Social Structure.* Macmillan, New York.

NATURAL FIBERS INFORMATION CENTER

1987 *The Climates of Texas Counties.* Bureau of Business Research, University of Texas at Austin.

NAYLOR, THOMAS H., AND CHARLES W. POLZER, S. J. (COMPILERS AND EDITORS)

1986 *The Presidio and Militia on the Northern Frontier of New Spain 1570–1700: A Documentary History.* Vol. 1: 1570–1700. University of Arizona Press, Tucson.

NEWELL, F. H.

1891 Hydrography of the Arid Regions. *Twelfth Annual Report of the United States Geological Survey to the Secretary of the Interior, 1890–1891.* Part II. *Irrigation*, by J. W. Powell, pp. 282–90. Government Printing Office, Washington, D.C.

NICKELS, D. L.

2000 The Biesenbach Site (41WN88), Wilson County, Texas: A Study of Toyah Diet-Breadth. Master's thesis, University of Texas at San Antonio.

NICKELS, D. L., AND R. P. MAULDIN

2001 The Project Environment. In *An Archaeological Survey of Twin Buttes Reservoir, Tom Green County, Texas*, Vol. 1, by R. P. Mauldin and D. L. Nickels. Archaeological Survey Report 300. Center for Archaeological Research, University of Texas at San Antonio.

NORDT, L. C., T. W. BOUTTON, J. S. JACOB, AND R. MANDEL

2002 C_4 Plant Productivity and Climate-CO_2 Variations in South-Central Texas during the Late Quaternary. *Quaternary Research* 58(2): 182–88.

NORTHERN, MARTIN JAMES

1979 Archaeological Investigations of the Montgomery Site, Floyd County, Texas. Master's thesis, Department of Anthropology, Texas Tech University, Lubbock.

NUNLEY, J. P., L. F. DUFFIELD, AND E. B. JELKS

1965 *Excavations at Amistad Reservoir, 1962 Season.* Miscellaneous Papers 3. Texas Archeological Salvage Project, University of Texas, Austin.

NUÑEZ, ALVAR CABEZA DE VACA

1992 *Los Náufragios.* Enrique Pupo-Walker, editor. Nueva Biblioteca de Erudicion y Critica, Madrid.

ODELL, G. H.

2008 Interpreting Wichita Lifeways at the Cusp of Contact. *Plains Anthropologist* 53:471–86.

ODELL, G. H., AND F. COWAN

1986 Experiments with Spears and Arrows on Animal Targets. *Journal of Field Archaeology* 13(2): 195–212.

OÑATE, JUAN DE

1871a Discurso de las Jornadas que Hizo el Campo de su Magestad desde la Nueva España a la Provincia de la Nueva México, Año 1596. In *Colección de Documentos Inéditos Relativos al Descubrimiento, Conquista y Organización de las Antiguas Posesiones españolas de Améria y Oceanía*, edited by Joaquin F. Pacheco and Francisco Cardenas, 15:228–76. M. Bernaldo de Quirós, Madrid.

1871b Copia de Carta Escrita al Virrey Conde de Monterrey, Don Juan de Oñate; de la Nueva México, a 2 de Marzo de 1599. In *Colección de Documentos Inéditos Relativos al Descubrimiento, Conquista y Organización de las Antiguas Posesiones españolas de Améria y Oceanía*, edited by Joaquin F. Pacheco and Francisco Cardenas, 16:302–19. M. Bernaldo de Quirós, Madrid.

OUTRAM, ALAN K.

2001 A New Approach to Identifying Bone Marrow and Grease Exploitation: Why the "Indeterminant" Fragments Should Not Be Ignored. *Journal of Archaeological Science* 28:401–10.

2002 Bone Fracture and Within-Bone Nutrients: An Experimentally Based Method for Investigating Levels of Marrow Extraction. In *Consuming Passions and Patterns of Consumption*, edited by Preston Miracle and Nicky Milner, pp. 51–63. McDonald Institute for Archaeological Research, Cambridge, U.K.

2004 Identifying Dietary Stress in Marginal Environments: Bone Fats, Optimal Foraging Theory and the Seasonal Round. In *Colonisation, Migration, and Marginal Areas: A Zooarchaeological Approach*, edited by Mariana Mondini, Sebastian Munoz, and Stephen Wickler, pp. 74–85. Oxbow Books, Oxford, U.K.

PALMER, W. C.

1965 *Meteorological Drought*. Research Paper 45. U.S. Weather Bureau, Washington, D.C.

PARKER, WAYNE

1982 *Archaeology at the Bridwell Site*. Crosby County Pioneer Memorial Museum, Crosbyton, Tex.

1990 The Bridwell Site (41CB27). *Transactions of the 25th Regional Archeological Symposium for Southeastern New Mexico and Western Texas*, pp. 99–114. Midland Archeological Society, Midland, Tex.

PARKMAN, F.

1883 *La Salle and the Discovery of the West*. 12th ed. Little, Brown, New York. [also, Parkman Anthology, Vol. 3. Digital Antiqueria, Morristown, N.J., www.digitalantiquaria.com.]

PARRY, W. J., AND R. L. KELLY

1987 Expedient Core Technology and Sedentism. In *The Organization of Core Technology*, edited by J. K. Johnson and C. A. Morrow, pp. 285–304. Westview Press, Boulder, CO.

PARSONS, MARK L.

1965 *1963 Test Excavations at Fate Bell Shelter, Amistad Reservoir, Val Verde County, Texas*. Miscellaneous Papers 4. Texas Archeological Salvage Project, University of Texas at Austin.

1967 *Archeological Investigations in Crosby and Dickens Counties, Texas, during the Winter, 1966–1967*. Archeological Program Report 7. State Building Commission, Austin.

PARUELO, J. M., AND W. K. LAUENROTH

1996 Relative Abundance of Plant Functional Types in Grasslands and Shrublands of North America. *Ecological Applications* 6(4): 1212–24.

PATTERSON, P. E., AND M. M. FORD

1974 *Oso Creek Flood Control Project Area, Nueces County, Texas: A Report on the Archeological and Historical Resources.* Texas Archeological Survey, Research Report 35. University of Texas at Austin.

PATTON, PETER R., AND VICTOR R. BAKER

1977 Geomorphic Response of Central Texas Stream Channels to Catastrophic Rainfall and Runoff. In *Geomorphology of Arid Regions,* edited by D. O. Doehring, pp. 184–217. State University of New York–Binghamton.

PEDEN, D. G.

1976 Botanical Composition of Bison Diets on Shortgrass Plains. *American Midland Naturalist* 96(1): 225–29.

PEDEN, D. G., G. M. VAN DYNE, R. W. RICE, AND R. M. HANSEN

1974 The Trophic Ecology of *Bison bison* L. on Shortgrass Plains. *Journal of Applied Ecology* 11(2): 489–97.

PERKINS, S. M., S. C. VEHIK, AND R. R. DRASS

2008 The Hide Trade and Wichita Social Organization: An Assessment of Ethnological Hypotheses concerning Polygyny. *Plains Anthropologist* 53:431–43.

PERTTULA, TIMOTHY K.

1992 *The Caddo Nation.* University of Texas Press, Austin.

1995 The Archeology of the Pineywoods and Post Oak Savanna of Northeast Texas. *Bulletin of the Texas Archeological Society* 66:331–59.

1998 Late Caddoan Societies in the Northeast Texas Piney Woods. In *The Native History of the Caddo: Their Place in Southeastern Archeology and Ethnohistory,* edited by Timothy K. Perttula and James E. Bruseth, pp. 69–90. Studies in Archeology 30. Texas Archeological Research Laboratory, University of Texas at Austin.

2001 Hunter-Gatherer Mortuary Practices in the Rio Grande Plains and Central Coastal Plains Archeological Regions of Texas. *La Tierra* 28(3–4): 2–83.

2004 The Prehistoric and Caddoan Archeology of the Northeastern Pineywoods. In *The Prehistory of Texas,* edited by T. K. Perttula, pp. 370–408. Texas A&M University Press, College Station.

PERTTULA, TIMOTHY K., SERGIO A. IRUEGAS, AND HECTOR NEFF

2003 *Caddoan Pottery in Central Texas: Geochemical Analyses of Ceramics from Fort Hood and Vicinity.* U.S. Army, Fort Hood, Archeological Resource Management Series Research Report 51. Prewitt and Associates, Austin.

PERTTULA, TIMOTHY, MYLES MILLER, ROBERT RICKLIS, DANIEL PRIKRYL, AND CHRISTOPHER LINTZ

1995 Prehistoric and Historic Aboriginal Ceramics in Texas. *Bulletin of the Texas Archeological Society* 66:175–235.

PETER, D. E., D. PRIKRYL, O. F. MCCORMICK, AND M. DEMUYNCK

1982 Site Excavation Reports: Primary Contract. In *Archaeological Investigations at the San Gabriel Site Reservoir Districts, Central Texas,* 1:81–297. Institute of Applied Sciences, University of North Texas, Denton.

PHELPS, A. L.

1964 Soto: Proposed Name for a Small Projectile Point, Its Geographical Distribution, and Cultural Associations. In *Cultural Analyzation of Pre-historic Indian Sites of Northern Chihuahua, Mexico,* by Alan L. Phelps, app. A. Special Report 2. El Paso Archaeological Society, El Paso, Tex.

PIEPER, R. D., AND C. H. HERBEL

1982 Herbage Dynamics and Primary Productivity of a Desert Grassland Ecosystem. *Agricultural Experiment Station Bulletin* 695, New Mexico State University, Las Cruces, in cooperation with the U.S. Department of Agriculture.

POLLACK, S.

1983 Style and Information: An Analysis of Susiana Ceramics. *Journal of Anthropological Archaeology* 2:354–90.

POPE, LEON

1991 The Hogue Site (41TY2). *Transactions of the 27th Regional Archeological Symposium for Southeastern New Mexico and Western Texas*, pp. 4–8. South Plains Archeological Society, Lubbock, Tex.

PORTILLO, E. L.

1886 *Apuntes para la Historia Antiqua de Coahuila y Texas*. Miguel Cortina, Saltillo, Coahuila, Mexico.

PORTIS, JOHN, FERN PORTIS, PAT BILLS, AND NELDA BILLS

1968 A Surface Site in Scurry County (41–S.C.). *Transactions of the Fourth Regional Archeological Symposium for Southeastern New Mexico and Western Texas*, pp. 60–64. Iraan Archeological Society, Iraan, Tex.

POSADA, FRAY ALONSO DE

1962 Útiles y Curiosas Noticias del Nuevo Mundo Cíbola y Otras Naciones Confidantes: La Antigua Tradición de Copala, Cuna, no Solo las Naciones Indianas. In *Documentos para Servir a la História del Nuevo México 1538–1778*, pp. 460–82. Coleción Chimalistac, Edición Jose Porrua Turanzas, Madrid.

1982 *Alonso de Posada Report, 1686: A Description of the Area of the Present Southern United States in the last 17th Century*. Alfred Buraby Thomas, editor and translator. Spanish Borderlands Series 4. Perdido Bay Press, Pensacola, Fla.

POTTER, D. R., R. B. PICKERING, AND C. E. MEAR

2005 Salvage Excavation at the Coleman Cemetery Site, 41BX568. *La Tierra* 32(1): 3–64.

POWELL, G. S.

2001 Hunting and Farming between the Plains and the Southwest: Analysis of Archaeobotanical Remains from the Henderson Site, Roswell, New Mexico. PhD dissertation, Department of Anthropology, Washington University, St. Louis, Mo.

POWELL, JOSEPH F.

1987 Stress and Survival: Models of Adaptive Success in the Texas Late Prehistoric. *Bulletin of the Texas Archeological Society* 58:249–66.

PREWITT, ELTON R.

1964 Excavations at the Terri and Lightfoot Sites, Proctor Reservoir, Comanche County, Texas. *Bulletin of the Texas Archeological Society* 31:143–87.

1970 *The Piedra Del Diablo Site, Val Verde County, Texas, and Notes on Some Trans-Pecos, Texas Archeological Material in the Smithsonian Institution, Washington, D.C.* Texas Historical Survey Committee Archeological Report 18. Austin.

1974 *Archeological Investigations at the Loeve-Fox Site, Williams County, Texas*. Research Report 49. Texas Archeological Survey, University of Texas at Austin.

1981 Culture Chronology in Central Texas. *Bulletin of the Texas Archeological Society* 52:65–89.

1982a The 1982 TAS Field School. Rowe Valley, Texas. *Texas Archeology* 26(3): 2–5.

1982b *Archaeological Investigations at the Loeve-Fox Site, Williamson County, Texas*. Reprints in Archeology, Number 1. Prewitt and Associates, Inc., Austin.

1982c *Archeological Investigations at the Loeve-Fox Site, Williamson County, Texas*. Reprints in Archeology 1. Prewitt and Associates, Austin.

1984 1984 TAS Field School, Rowe Valley Site, June 9–17. *Texas Archeology* 28(2): 14–16.

1985 From Circleville to Toyah: Comments on Central Texas Chronology. *Bulletin of the Texas Archeological Society* 54:201–38.

1995 Distributions of Typed Projectile Points in Texas. *Bulletin of the Texas Archeological Society* 66:83–173.

PRICE, T. DOUGLAS, AND JAMES BROWN

1985 Aspects of Hunter Gatherer Complexity. In *Prehistoric Hunter-Gatherers: The Emergence of Cultural Complexity*, edited by T. D. Price and J. A. Brown, pp. 3–20. Academic Press. Orlando, Fla.

PRICE, T. D., M. J. SCHOENINGER, AND G. J. ARMELAGOS

1985 Bone Chemistry and Past Behavior: An Overview. *Journal of Human Evolution* 14(5): 419–47.

PRIKRYL, D. J.

1982 41WM258 (Bigon-Kubala Site). In *Archaeological Investigations at the San Gabriel Reservoir Districts, Central Texas*, Vol. 1, edited and compiled by T. R. Hays. Institute of Applied Sciences, North Texas State University, Denton.

QUIGG, J. M.

1997 Bison Processing at the Rush Site, 41TG346, and Evidence for Pemmican Production in the Southern Plains. In Southern Plains Bison Procurement and Utilization from Paleoindian to Historic, edited by L.C. Bennett and K.J. Buehler, *Plains Anthropologist*, pp. 145–62 *Memoir* 29, Lincoln.

QUIGG, J. M., AND P. DERING

2007 Late Prehistoric Subsistence Economy on the Periphery of the Southern Plains. Paper presented at the 72nd Annual Meeting, Society for American Archaeology, Austin.

QUIGG, J. M., J. D. OWENS, P. M. MATCHEN, G. D. SMITH, R. A. RICKLIS, M. C. CODY, AND C. D. FREDERICK

2008 *The Varga Site: A Multicomponent, Stratified Campsite in the Canyonlands of Edwards County, Texas*. 2 vols. Technical Report 35319, TRC Environmental Corporation, Austin, and Archeological Studies Program Report 110, Texas Department of Transportation, Austin.

QUIGG, J. M., AND J. PECK

1995 *The Rush Site (41TG346): A Stratified Late Prehistoric Locale in Tom Green County, Texas*. Technical Report 816C. Mariah Associates, Austin.

RANDALL, MARK E.

1970 The Archeology of the Lamb County, Texas, Area. *Lower Plains Archeological Society Bulletin* 1:43–53.

RAY, CYRUS W.

1935 The Pottery Complex Artifacts of the Abilene Region. *Bulletin of the Texas Archeological and Paleontological Society* 7:70–88.

REESE-TAYLOR, K.

1995 Appendix F: Petrographic Analyses. In *The Rush Site (41TG346): A Stratified Late Prehistoric Locale in Tom Green County, Texas*, by J. M. Quigg and J. Peck, pp. F-1-F-12. Technical Report 816C. Mariah Associates, Austin.

RICKLIS, ROBERT A.

1987 Archeological Investigations at the McKinzie Site (41NU221), Nueces County, Texas: Descriptions and Contextual Interpretations. *Bulletin of the Texas Archeological Society* 58:1–76.

1990 A Historical Cultural Ecology of the Karankawan Indians of the Central Texas Coast: A Case Study in the Roots of Adaptive Change. PhD dissertation, Department of Geography, University of Texas at Austin.

1992 The Spread of a Late Prehistoric Bison Hunting Complex: Evidence from the South-Central Coastal Prairie of Texas. *Plains Anthropologist* 37(140): 621–74.

1994 Toyah Components: Evidence for Occupations in the Project Area during the Latter Part of the Late Prehistoric Period. In *Archaic and Late Prehistoric Human Ecology in the Middle Onion Creek Valley, Hays County, Texas*, by R. A. Ricklis and M. B. Collins, 1:207–

316. Studies in Archeology 19. Texas Archeological Research Laboratory, University of Texas at Austin, Austin.

1995a The Ceramics of the Toyah Horizon and the Rockport Phase as Indicators of Some Basic Sociocultural Patterns. *Bulletin of the Texas Archeological Society* 66:195–203.

1995b Prehistoric Occupation of the Central and Lower Texas Coast: A Regional Overview. *Bulletin of the Texas Archeological Society* 66:265–300.

1996 *The Karankawa Indians of Texas: An Ecological Study of Cultural Tradition and Change.* University of Texas Press, Austin.

1999 Spanish Colonial Missions of Espíritu Santo and Nuestra Señora del Rosario. *Bulletin of the Texas Archeological Society* 66:133–68.

2004a The Archeology of the Native American Occupation of Southeast Texas. In *The Prehistory of Texas,* edited by T. K. Perttula, pp. 181–203. Texas A&M University Press, College Station.

2004b Prehistoric Occupation of the Central and Lower Texas Coast. In *The Prehistory of Texas,* edited by T. K. Perttula, pp. 155–80. Texas A&M University Press, College Station.

RICKLIS, ROBERT A., AND MICHAEL B. COLLINS

1994 *Archaic and Late Prehistoric Human Ecology in the Middle Onion Creek Valley, Hays County, Texas.* Studies in Archeology 19. Texas Archeological Research Laboratory, University of Texas at Austin.

RIEMENSCHNEIDER, LARRY

1996 The Davis Hackberry Spring Site (41ST87), Sterling County, Texas. *The Cache: Collected Papers on Texas Archeology* 3:13–26. Texas Archeological Stewardship Network, Office of the State Archeologist, Texas Historical Commission, Austin.

RIGGS, AARON D., JR.

1965 LY-4: A Surface Site of the South Plains. *Bulletin of the South Plains Archeological Society* 2:1–35.

ROBINSON, P.

1990 *The Struggler Within: The Indian Debate in Seventeenth-Century Narragansett Country.* [PhD dissertation, Department of Anthropology, State University of New York at Binghamton.] University Microfilms, Ann Arbor, Michigan.

ROCEK, T. R., AND J. D. SPETH

1986 *The Henderson Site Burials: Glimpses of a Late Prehistoric Population in the Pecos Valley.* Technical Report 18. University of Michigan, Museum of Anthropology, Ann Arbor.

ROGERS, DANIEL, AND SAMUEL E. WILSON (EDITORS)

1993 *Ethnohistory and Archaeology: Approaches to Post Contact Change in the Americas.* Plenum Press, New York.

ROGERS, ROBERT

2000 Excavations at Site 41FB255. *Current Archeology in Texas* 2(1): 16–17.

ROGERS, R., AND B. DIXON

2006 *La Carneada (41WM1012): An Early Historic Period Bison Kill Site on the San Gabriel River, Williamson County, Texas.* Texas Antiquities Permit 3266. Report submitted to the Texas Turnpike Authority Division, Texas Department of Transportation, by PBS&J, Austin (Document 060108).

ROGERS, ROSE MARY

1972 Ceramics, Pecos River Drainage Pecos and Crockett Counties, Texas. In *Transactions of the Seventh Regional Archeological Symposium for Southeastern New Mexico and Western Texas.* Dawson County Archeological Society, Lamesa, Tex.

ROSEN, A. M.

2007 *Civilizing Climate: Social Responses to Climate Change in the Ancient Near East.* AltaMira Press, Lanham, Md.

ROSS, R. E.

1965 *The Archeology of Eagle Cave*. Papers of the Texas Archeological Salvage Project 7. University of Texas at Austin.

RUNKLES, FRANK A.

1962 Perdiz Points Found on the South Plains of Texas. *South Plains Archeological Society Newsletter* 4.

1964 The Garza Site: A Neo-American Campsite near Post, Texas. *Bulletin of the Texas Archeological Society* 35:101–25.

RUNKLES, FRANK A., AND E. D. DORCHESTER

1987 The Lott Site (41GR56): A Late Prehistoric Site in Garza County, Texas. *Bulletin of the Texas Archeological Society* 57:83–115.

RUNYAN, JOHN W., AND JOHN A. HEDRICK

1987 Pottery Types of the Southwestern Federation of Archeological Societies (SWFAS) Area. *The Artifact* 25(4): 23–59.

RYDER, PAUL D.

1996 High Plains Aquifer: Hydrogeologic Framework. In Ground Water Atlas of the United States: Oklahoma, Texas, HA 730-E, U.S. Geological Survey. http://pubs.usgs.gov/ha/ha730/ch_e/E-text5.html.

SA (SALTILLO ARCHIVES)

1658 Testimónio de Luis de Morales. Transcript on file, box 2Q259.

SALA, O. E., AND W. K. LAUENROTH

1982 Small Rainfall Events: An Ecological Role in Semiarid Regions. *Oecologia* 53:301–14.

SALINAS, M.

1987 *Indians of the Rio Grande Delta: Their Role in the History of Southern Texas and Northeastern Mexico*. University of Texas Press, Austin.

SALINAS VARONA, GREGARIO DE

1968 Diario del viaje del capitán Gregario de Salinas Varona, en su Expedición del socorro al este de Texas. In *Primeras Exploraciones y Poblamiento de Tejas (1686–1694), Notícias Geográficas e Históricas del Noreste de México*, edited by L. Gomez Candeo, pp. 277–307. Instituto Tecnológico y de estudios superiores de Monterrey, México.

SAYLES, E. B.

1935 *An Archaeological Survey of Texas*. Medallion Papers 17. Gila Pueblo, Globe, Arizona.

SCHOLES, F. V., AND H. P. MERA

1940 *Some Aspects of the Jumano Problem*. Contributions to American Anthropology and History 34. Carnegie Institution Publication 523, Washington, D.C.

SCHORTMAN, EDWARD M.

1989 Interregional Interaction in Prehistory: The Need for a New Perspective. *American Antiquity* 54(1): 52–65.

SCHROEDER, A. H., AND D. S. MATSON

1965 *A Colony on the Move: Gaspar Castano de Sosa's Journal, 1590–1591*. School of American Research, Santa Fe, N.Mex.

SCURLOCK, DAN, WARREN M. LYNN, AND R. THOMAS RAY

1974 *An Assessment of the Archeological Resources of Padre Island National Seashore*. Office of the State Archeologist, Texas Historical Commission Special Reports 11. Austin.

SEACAT, TODD BARRY

1997 The Roots of Prehistoric Warfare in the Southern Plains: A Review of Evidence for Violence and Warfare in Kansas, Oklahoma and Texas. MA thesis, Department of Anthropology, Wichita State University.

SFG (SAN FRANCISCO EL GRANDE ARCHIVE)

1674 Testimónio de haber Salido para la Nueva Conversión de los Indios Bárbaros Chichimecos de la Provincia de Coahuila los Padres Predicadores Fray Juan Larios, Fray

Francisco Peñasco, sacerdotes, y Fray Manual de la Cruz. Transcript on file, Center for American History, University of Texas at Austin, box 2Q248.

SHAEFFER, J. B.

1958 The Alibates Flint Quarry, Texas. *American Antiquity* 24(2): 189–91.

SHAFER, HARRY J.

1969 *Archeological Investigations in Robert Lee Reservoir Basin, West Central Texas.* Survey Report 17. Papers of the Texas Archeological Salvage Project, University of Texas at Austin.

1971a Late Prehistory of Central Texas. Paper presented at the 74th Annual Meeting of the Texas Academy of Science, Nacogdoches, Tex.

1971b *Investigations into South Plains Prehistory, West Central Texas.* Survey Report 20. Papers of the Texas Archeological Salvage Project, University of Texas at Austin.

1977 Late Prehistory of Central Texas. *South Plains Archeological Society* 3:18–27.

2006a Prehistoric Artifacts. In Excavations at Presidio Nuestra Senora de Loreta de la Bahía del Espíritu Santo. *Bulletin of the Texas Archeological Society* 77:95–123.

2006b *People of the Prairie: A Possible Connection to the Davis Site Caddo.* Report prepared for the Archeological Studies Program, Environmental Affairs Division, Texas Department of Transportation, Austin. www.counciloftexasarcheologists.org/publications/PrairieCaddoModule.pdf.

SHAFER, H. J., D. A. SUHM, AND J. D. SCURLOCK

1964 *An Investigation and Appraisal of the Archeological Resources of Belton Reservoir, Bell and Coryell Counties, Texas: 1962.* Miscellaneous Papers 1. Texas Archeological Salvage Project, University of Texas at Austin.

SHAWN, RONNIE

1975 The Bull Hill Site Excavation. *Transactions of the Tenth Regional Archeological Symposium for Southeastern New Mexico and Western Texas*, pp. 1–47. South Plains Archeological Society, Lubbock, Tex.

SHAY, C. THOMAS

1978 Late Prehistoric Bison and Deer in the Eastern Prairie-Forest Border. In *Bison Procurement and Utilization: A Symposium*, edited by Leslie B. Davis and Michael Wilson, pp. 194–212. *Plains Anthropologist* 23(82), Pt. 2. Memoir 14.

SHINKLE, J. D.

1966 *Reminiscences of Roswell Pioneers.* Hall-Poorbaugh Press, Roswell, N.Mex.

SILLIMAN, S.

2005 Culture Contact or Colonialism? Challenges in the Archaeology of Native North America. *American Antiquity* 70:55–74.

SJOBERG, ANDREE

1953 The Culture of the Tonkawa, a Texas Indian Tribe. *Texas Journal of Science* 5(3): 280–304.

SKELTON, D. W.

1977 *Archeological Investigations at the Fayette Power Project, Fayette County, Texas.* Texas Archeological Survey, Research Report 60. University of Texas at Austin.

SKINNER, S. ALAN

1975 Goals for the 1975 TAS Field School. *Texas Archeology* 19(2): 3–5.

SMITH, JAMES E., II

1996 The Rodeo Hill and Third Dam Sites: Two Ceramic-Bearing Sites in Somervell County, Texas. *The Cache: Collected Papers on Texas Archeology* 3:67–75.

SNOW, DAVID H.

1982 The Rio Grande Glaze, Matte-Paint, and Plainware Tradition. In Southwestern Ceramics: A Comparative Review, edited by Albert H. Schroeder, pp. 235–278. *Arizona Archeologist* 15.

1997 "Por Allí No Ay Losa Ni Se Hace": Gilded Men and Glazed Pottery on the Southern

Plains. In *The Coronado Expedition to Tierra Nueva: The 1540–1542 Route across the Southwest*, edited by R. Flint and S. C. Flint, pp. 344–64. University Press of Colorado, Niwot.

2007 Recombining D 'n A: Rio Grande Glaze-Ware Sequence Revisited. Paper Presented at the 2007 Pecos Conference, Pecos National Historical Park, N.Mex.

SOKAL, R. R., AND F. J. ROHLF

1969 *Biometry: The Principles and Practice of Statistics in Biological Research*. W. H. Freeman, San Francisco.

SOLLBERGER, J. B.

1971 A Technological Study of Beveled Knives. *Plains Anthropologist* 16(53): 209–18.

SOLOMETO, J. P.

2004 The Conduct and Consequences of War: Dimensions of Conflict East-Central Arizona. PhD dissertation, Department of Anthropology, University of Michigan, Ann Arbor.

SORROW, WILLIAM M.

1970 *Archeological Investigations at the Barker Site*. Research Report 1. Texas Archeological Salvage Project, University of Texas at Austin.

SORROW, W. M., H. J. SHAFER, AND R. E. ROSS

1967 *Excavations at Stillhouse Hollow Reservoir*. Papers of the Texas Archeological Salvage Project 11. University of Texas at Austin.

SOSA, CASTAÑO DE

1871 Memória del Descubrimiento que Gaspar Castaño de Sosa Hizo en el Nuevo México, Siendo Teniente de Gobernados y Capitán General del Nuevo Reino de León. In *Colección de Documentos Inéditos*, edited by Joaquin F. Pacheco and Francisco Cardenas, pp. 191–261, 283–354. M. Bernaldo de Quirós, Madrid.

SPETH, J. D.

1983 *Bison Kills and Bone Counts: Decision Making by Ancient Hunters*. University of Chicago Press, Chicago.

1987 Early Hominid Subsistence Strategies in Seasonal Habitats. *Journal of Archaeological Science* 14:13–29.

1991 Some Unexplored Aspects of Mutualistic Plains-Pueblo Food Exchange. In *Farmers, Hunters, and Colonists: Interaction between the Southwest and the Southern Plains*, edited by Katherine A. Spielmann, pp. 18–35. University of Arizona Press, Tucson.

SPETH, J. D. (EDITOR)

2004 *Life on the Periphery: Economic Change in Late Prehistoric Southeastern New Mexico*. Memoir 37. University of Michigan, Museum of Anthropology, Ann Arbor.

SPETH, J. D., AND M. LEDUC

2007 El Paso Polychrome Jars: New Insights from Complete Vessels. In *Viva la Jornada: Papers from the 14th Biennial Jornada Mogollon Conference*, edited by J. Jurgena, L. Jackson, and M. Thompson, pp. 33–52. El Paso Museum of Archaeology, El Paso, Tex.

SPETH, J. D., AND A. RAUTMAN

2004 Bison Hunting at the Henderson Site. In *Life on the Periphery: Economic Change in Late Prehistoric Southeastern New Mexico*, edited by J. D. Speth, pp. 98–147. Memoir 37. University of Michigan, Museum of Anthropology, Ann Arbor.

SPETH, J. D., AND S. L. SCOTT

1989 Horticulture and Large-Mammal Hunting: The Role of Resource Depletion and the Constraints of Time and Labor. In *Farmers as Hunters*, edited by Susan Kent, pp. 71–79. Cambridge University Press, New York.

SPETH, JOHN D., AND KATHERINE A. SPIELMANN

1983 Energy Source, Protein Metabolism, and Hunter-Gatherer Subsistence Strategies. *Journal of Anthropological Archaeology* 2(1): 1–31.

SPIELMANN, KATHERINE A.

1982 Inter-Societal Food Acquisition among Egalitarian Societies: An Ecological Study of Plains/Pueblo Interaction in the American Southwest. PhD dissertation, Department of Anthropology, University of Michigan, Ann Arbor.

1983 Late Prehistoric Exchange between the Southwest and Southern Plains. *Plains Anthropologist* 28(102): 257–72.

1989 Colonists, Hunters, and Farmers: Plains-Pueblo Interaction in the Seventeenth Century. In *Columbian Consequences. Vol. 1: Archaeological and Historical Perspectives on the Spanish Borderlands West*, edited by D. H. Thomas, pp. 101–13. Smithsonian Institution Press, Washington, D.C.

1991a Coercion or Cooperation? Plains-Pueblo Interaction in the Protohistoric Period. In *Farmers, Hunters, and Colonists: Interaction between the Southwest and the Southern Plains*, edited by K. A. Spielmann, pp. 36–50. University of Arizona Press, Tucson.

1991b *Interdependence in the Prehistoric Southwest: An Ecological Analysis of Plains-Pueblo Interaction*. Garland, New York.

SPIELMANN, K. A. (EDITOR)

1991 *Farmers, Hunters, and Colonists: Interaction between the Southwest and the Southern Plains*. University of Arizona Press, Tucson.

SPIER, LESLIE

1928 *Havasupai Ethnography*. *Anthropological Papers of the American Museum of Natural History* 29:82–392.

STAHLE, DAVID W., AND MALCOLM K. CLEVELAND

1995 Texas Paleoclimatic Data from Daily to Millennial Time Scales. In *The Changing Climate of Texas: Predictability and Implications for the Future*, edited by Jim Norwine, John R. Giardino, Gerald R. North, and Juan B. Valdés, pp. 49–69. GeoBooks, Texas A&M University, College Station.

STARK, MIRIAM T. (EDITOR)

1998 *The Archaeology of Social Boundaries*. Smithsonian Institution Press, Washington, D.C.

STARK, MIRIAM T., MARK D. ELSON, AND JEFFERY J. CLARK

1998 Social Boundaries and Technical Choices in Tonto Basin Prehistory. In *The Archaeology of Social Boundaries*, edited by Miriam T. Stark, pp. 208–31. Smithsonian Institution Press, Washington, D.C.

STEELE, D. GENTRY

1986a Analysis of Vertebrate Faunal Remains from 41 LK 201, Live Oak County, Texas. In *Archaeological Investigations at 41 LK 201, Choke Canyon Reservoir, Southern Texas*, by Cheryl Lynn Highley, pp. 200–249. Choke Canyon Series Vol. 11. Center for Archaeological Research, University of Texas at San Antonio.

1986b Analysis of Vertebrate Faunal Remains. In *The Clemete and Herminia Hinojosa Site, 41JW8: A Toyah Horizon Campsite in Southern Texas*, by Stephen L. Black, pp. 108–36. Special Report 18. Center for Archaeological Research, University of Texas at San Antonio.

STEPHENSON, ROBERT L.

1950 Archeological Survey of McGee Bend Reservoir, Jasper, Sabine, San Augustine, Angelina and Nacogdoches Counties, Texas: A Preliminary Report. River Basin Surveys, Smithsonian Institution, Washington, D.C.

1970 Archaeological Investigations in the Whitney Reservoir Area, Central Texas. *Bulletin of the Texas Archeological Society* 40:37–257.

STEUTER, A. E., M. STEINAUER, G. L. HILL, P. A. BOWERS, AND L. L. TIESZEN.

1995 Distribution and Diet of Bison and Pocket Gophers in a Sandhill Prairie. *Ecological Applications* 5(3): 756–66.

STORY, DEE ANN, AND DARRELL G. CREEL

1982 The Cultural Setting. In *The Deshazo Site, Nacogdoches County, Texas. Vol. 1: The Site, Its Setting, Investigation, Cultural Features, Artifacts of Non-native Manufacture, and Subsistence Remains*, edited by Dee Ann Story, pp. 20–34. Texas Antiquities Permit Series 7. Texas Antiquities Committee, Austin.

STORY, D. A., AND H. J. SHAFER

1965 *1964 Excavations at Waco Reservoir, McLennan County, Texas: The Baylor and Britton Sites.* Miscellaneous Papers 6. Texas Archeological Salvage Project, University of Texas at Austin.

SUCEC, R.

2008 *Still Ancestral Homeland: An Ethnographic Overview and Assessment of American Indian Histories and Resource Uses Associated with Hill Air Force Base, Utah.* National Park Service, Yellowstone National Park.

SUHM, DEE ANN

1955 Excavations at the Collins Site, Travis County, Texas. *Bulletin of the Texas Archeological Society* 26:7–54.

1957 Excavations at the Smith Rockshelter, Travis County, Texas. *Texas Journal of Science* 9(1): 26–58.

1960 A Review of Central Texas Archeology. *Bulletin of the Texas Archeological Society* 29:63–107 (for 1958).

1962 The White Site: An Historic Indian Burial in Yoakum County, Texas. *Bulletin of the Texas Archeological Society* 32:85–119.

SUHM, DEE ANN, AND EDWARD B. JELKS (EDITORS)

1962 *Handbook of Texas Archeology: Type Descriptions.* Texas Archeological Society Special Publication 1 and Texas Memorial Museum Bulletin 4. Austin.

SUHM, DEE ANN, ALEX D. KRIEGER, AND EDWARD B. JELKS

1954 An Introductory Handbook of Texas Archeology. *Bulletin of the Texas Archeological Society* 25.

SWAGERTY, WILLIAM R.

1991 Protohistoric Trade in Western North America: Archaeological and Ethnohistorical Considerations. In *Columbian Consequences,* Vol. 3: *The Spanish Borderlands in Pan American Perspective,* edited by David Hurst Thomas, pp. 471–98. Smithsonian Institution Press, Washington, D.C.

SWANTON, JOHN

1924 Southern Contacts of the Indians North of the Gulf of Mexico. *Anales, XX Congreso Internacional de Americanistas,* 53–59.

TAFF, JEFFREY A.

2006 Chemical Analysis of Ceramics from the Toyah Archaeological Area. Master's thesis, Department of Anthropology, University of Texas at Austin.

TARR, MATT

2004 Improving Acorn Production, Part I: Factors Affecting Acorn Production of Oaks. *Quality Whitetails* 11(2).

TAYLOR, WALTER W.

1964 Tethered Nomadism and Water Territoriality: An Hypothesis. *Acts of the 35th International Congress of Americanists,* 197–203. Mexico City.

1968 Burial Bundle from Coahuila, Mexico. In *Collected Papers in Honor of Lyndon Lane Hargrave.* Papers of the Archaeological Society of New Mexico, Albuquerque.

TEERI, J. A., AND L. G. STOWE

1976 Climatic Patterns and the Distribution of C4 Grasses in North America. *Oecologia* 23:1–12.

TERÁN, DOMINGO DE LOS RIOS

1968 Diario del generl Domingo Teran de los Rios en su expedición a Texas (1691–1692). In *Primeras Exploraciones y Poblamiento de Tejas (1686–1694), Notícias Geográficas e Históricas del Noreste de México,* edited by L. Gomez Candeo, pp. 2169–224. Instituto Tecnológico y de estudios superiores de Monterrey, México.

THOMAS, GEORGE B.

1978 A Survey and Assessment of the Archeological Resources of Fort Hood, Texas. *Bulletin of the Texas Archeological Society* 49:195–240.

THOMAS, D. H.

1983 *The Archaeology of Monitor Valley I: Epistemology*. Anthropological Papers of the American Museum of Natural History 58(1). American Museum of Natural History, New York.

THOMPSON, J., AND R. MAULDIN

2008 Resource Intensification and Changing Patterns of Thermal Feature Use throughout the Late Archaic and Late Prehistoric Periods in Central and South Texas. Paper presented at the 79th Annual Meeting of the Texas Archeological Society, Lubbock.

THOMPSON, J. L., R. P. MAULDIN, AND S. A. TOMKA

2007 A Research Design for the Analysis of Data Recovered at 41KM69, Kimble County, Texas. Unpublished Report Prepared for the Texas Department of Transportation, Environmental Affairs Division, Austin.

THOMS, ALSTON V.

2005 *Ancient Savannah Roots of the Carbohydrate Revolution in South-Central North America*. Paper presented at the 76th Annual Meeting of the Texas Archeological Society, Austin.

2008 Ancient Savannah Roots of the Carbohydrate Revolution in South-Central North America. *Plains Anthropologist* 53(205): 121–36.

2009 Rocks of Ages: Propagation of Hot-Rock Cookery in Western North America. *Journal of Archaeological Science* 36(3): 573–91.

THOMS, ALSTON V. (EDITOR)

2004 *Yegua Creek Archaeological Project: Survey Results from Lake Somerville State Parks and Trailway, East-Central Texas*. Reports of Investigations 5. Center for Ecological Archaeology, Texas A&M University, College Station.

TOMKA, S. A.

2001 The Effect of Processing Requirements on Reduction Strategies and Tool Form: A New Perspective. In *Lithic Debitage Context, Form and Meaning*, edited by W. Andrefsky Jr., pp. 207–23. University of Utah Press, Salt Lake City.

TOOMEY, R. S., III

1993 Late Pleistocene and Holocene Faunal Changes at Hall's Cave, Kerr County, Texas. PhD dissertation, Department of Geological Sciences, University of Texas at Austin.

TORRENCE, R.

1983 Time Budgeting and Hunter-Gatherering. In *Hunter-Gatherer Economy in Prehistory: A European Perspective*, edited by G. Bailey, pp. 11–22. Cambridge University Press, New York.

1989 Tools as Optimal Solutions. In *Time, Energy, and Stone Tools*, edited by R. Torrence, pp. 1–6. Cambridge University Press, New York.

TPWD (TEXAS PARKS AND WILDLIFE DEPARTMENT)

1984 *The Vegetation Types of Texas*. www.tpwd.state.tx.us/admin/veg/.

TREECE, ABBY C., CHRISTOPHER LINTZ, W. NICHOLAS TRIERWEILER, J. MICHAEL QUIGG, AND KEVIN MILLER

1993 *Cultural Resource Investigations in the O. H. Ivie Reservoir, Concho, Coleman, and Runnels Counties, Texas*. Vol. 4: *Data Recovery from Ceramic Sites*. Technical Report 346-IV. Mariah Associates, Austin.

TRIERWEILER, W. NICHOLAS (EDITOR)

1996 *Archeological Testing of 56 Prehistoric Sites at Fort Hood, 1994–1995*. U.S. Army, Fort Hood, Archeological Resource Management Series, Research Report 35. Mariah Associates, Austin.

TRIGGER, BRUCE G.

1989 History and Contemporary American Archaeology: A Critical Analysis. In *Archaeo-*

logical Thought in America, edited by C. C. Lamberg-Karlovsky, pp. 19–34. Cambridge University Press, New York.

2007 *Artifacts and Ideas: Essays in Archaeology*. Transaction Publishers, New Brunswick, N.J.

TROIKE, RUDOLPH C.

1987 Karankawa Linguistic Data. In *La Salle, the Mississippi, and the Gulf*, edited by R. S. Weddle, pp. 288–301. Texas A&M University Press, College Station.

TURPIN, SOLVEIG

1995 The Lower Pecos River Region of Texas and Northern Mexico. *Bulletin of the Texas Archeological Society* 66:541–60.

VALDES, CARLOS MANUEL

1995 *La Gente del Mezquite, Los Nomadas del Noreste en la Colonia*. Tlalpan, México, D.F.

VAN VUREN, D., AND M. P. BRAY

1986 Population Dynamics of Bison in the Henry Mountains, Utah. *Journal of Mammalogy* 64(3): 503–11.

VARGAS, V. D.

1995 *Copper Bell Trade Patterns in the Prehispanic U.S. Southwest and Northwest Mexico*. Arizona State Museum Archaeological Series 187. Tucson.

VEHIK, SUSAN C.

1977 Bone Fragments and Bone Grease Manufacturing: A Review of Their Archaeological Use and Potential. *Plains Anthropologist* 22:169–82.

1990 Late Prehistoric Plains Trade and Economic Specialization. *Plains Anthropologist* 35(128): 125–45.

2002 Conflict, Trade, and Political Development on the Southern Plains. *American Antiquity* 67(1): 37–64.

VEHIK, SUSAN C., AND TIMOTHY G. BAUGH

1994 Prehistoric Plains Trade. In *Prehistoric Exchange Systems in North America*, edited by Timothy G. Baugh and Jonathon E. Ericson, pp. 249–74. Plenum Press, New York.

WADE, MARIAH

1998 The Native Americans of the Texas Edwards Plateau and Related Areas: 1528–1799. PhD dissertation, Department of Anthropology, University of Texas at Austin.

2001 Cultural Fingerprints: The Native Americans of Texas, 1528–1687. *Bulletin of the Texas Archeological Society* 72:45–54.

2002 Appendix C: Patterns of Buffalo Seasonality during the Protohistoric and Historic Periods in Texas. In *The Smith Creek Bridge Site, 41DW270: A Terrace Site in De Witt County, Texas*, edited by D. Hudler, K. Prilliman, and T. Gustavson, pp. 171–86. Studies in Archeology 35, Texas Archeological Research Laboratory, University of Texas at Austin. Archeology Studies Program Report 17, Environmental Affairs Division, Texas Department of Transportation, Austin.

2003 *Native Americans of the Texas Edwards Plateau, 1582–1799*. University of Texas Press, Austin.

WALKER, D. E., JR.

1999 A Revisionist View of Julian Steward and the Great Basin Paradigm from the North. In *Julian Steward and the Great Basin: The Making of an Anthropologist*, edited by R. O. Clemmer, L. D. Myers, and M. E. Rudden, pp. 60–73. University of Utah Press, Salt Lake City.

WALTERS, EVELYN, AND ROSE MARY ROGERS

1975 Notes on Presence of Indians of Historic Period in Pecos County and Iraan, Texas Area. In *Transactions of the Tenth Regional Archeological Symposium for Southeastern New Mexico and Western Texas*. South Plains Archeological Society, Lubbock, Tex.

WATT, F. H.

1936 A Prehistoric Rock-Shelter Burial in Bell County, Texas. *Bulletin of the Central Texas Archeological Society* (Waco) 2:5–27.

1956 Archeological Materials from the Asa Warner Sites. *Central Texas Archeologist* (Waco) 7:6–29.

1965 Notes on the Clark Site, McLennan County, Texas. *Bulletin of the Texas Archeological Society* 36:99–110.

WATTS, W. C.

1963 Distribution of Pottery in Surface Sites on the South Plains of Texas. *Bulletin of the South Plains Archeological Society* 1:1–25.

WEBER, STEVEN A., AND P. DAVID SEAMAN (EDITORS)

1985 *Havasupai Habitat: A. F. Whiting's Ethnography of a Tradition Culture.* University of Arizona Press, Tucson.

WENIGER, D.

1984 *The Explorers' Texas.* Eakin Press, Austin.

WELSCH, ROBERT L., AND JOHN E. TERRELL

1998 Material Culture, Social Fields, and Social Boundaries on the Sepik Coast of New Guinea. In *The Archaeology of Social Boundaries*, edited by Miriam T. Stark, pp. 3–77. Smithsonian Institution Press, Washington, D.C.

WHALEN, MICHAEL E.

1981 Origin and Evolution of Ceramics in Western Texas. *Bulletin of the Texas Archeological Society* 52:215–229.

WHEAT, C. I.

1954 *Mapping the American West, 1540–1857. A Preliminary Study.* American Antiquarian Society, Worcester, Mass.

WIEDENFELD, C.C.

1986 *Soil Survey of Irion County, Texas.* U.S. Department of Agriculture, Soil Conservation Service, in cooperation with the Texas Agricultural Experiment Station.

WIESSNER, POLLY A.

1977 Hxaro: A Regional System of Reciprocity for Reducing Risk among the !Kung San. PhD dissertation, Museum of Anthropology, University of Michigan.

1982a Risk, Reciprocity, and Social Influences on !Kung San Economies. In *Politics and History in Band Societies*, edited by Eleanor Leacock and Richard Lee, pp. 61–84. Cambridge University Press, Cambridge.

1982b Beyond Willow Smoke and Dogs' Tails: A Comment on Binford's Analysis of Hunter-Gatherer Settlement Systems. *American Antiquity* 47(1): 171–78.

1983 Style and Social Information in Kalahari San Projectile Points. *American Antiquity* 49:253–76.

WILLEY, GORDON R., AND PHILIP PHILLIPS

1958 *Method and Theory in American Archaeology.* University of Chicago Press, Chicago.

WILMSEN, EDWIN N.

1989 *Land Filled with Flies.* University of Chicago Press, Chicago.

WINDBERG, LAMAR A.

1997 Annual Fruit Production of Pricklypear (*Opuntia engelmannii*) and Mesquite (*Prosopis glandulosa*) in Southern Texas. *Texas Journal of Science* 49(1): 65–72.

WINTERHALDER, BRUCE, AND ERIC A. SMITH (EDITORS)

1981 *Hunter-Gatherer Foraging Strategies: Ethnographic and Archeological Analyses.* University of Chicago Press, Chicago.

WISEMAN, REGGE N.

1985 Bison, Fish and Sedentary Occupations: Startling Data from Rocky Arroyo (LA 25277), Chaves County, New Mexico. In *Views of the Jornada Mogollon: Proceedings of the Second Jornada Mogollon Archaeology Conference*, edited by C. M. Beck, pp. 30–32. Contributions in Anthropology 12. Eastern New Mexico University Press, Portales.

1997 A Preliminary Look at Evidence for Late Prehistoric Conflict in Southeastern New Mexico. In *Layers of Time: Essays in Honor of Robert H. Weber*, edited by Meliha S. Duran and David T. Kirkpatrick, pp. 135–46. Archaeological Society of New Mexico 23, Albuquerque.

1999 Cuahuatitlan Burnished: 17th Century Pottery Made in the Valley of Mexico and Found on the Southern Plains of Texas. *Transactions of the 34th Regional Archeological Symposium for Southeastern New Mexico and Western Texas*, pp. 61–65. Midland Archeological Society, Midland, Tex.

2002 *The Fox Place: A Late Prehistoric Hunter-Gatherer Pithouse Village near Roswell, New Mexico.* Archaeology Notes 234. Museum of New Mexico, Office of Archaeological Studies, Santa Fe.

2004 The Pottery of the Henderson Site (LA-1549): The 1980–1981 Seasons. In *Life on the Periphery: Economic Change in Late Prehistoric Southeastern New Mexico*, edited by J. D. Speth, pp. 67–95. Memoir 37. University of Michigan, Museum of Anthropology, Ann Arbor.

WISEMAN, REGGE N., DAVID V. HILL, AND DENNIS MCINTOSH

1999 The Llano Estacado Pottery Project: A Tabulation Report on the Typology Study. *Transactions of the 34th Regional Archeological Symposium for Southeastern New Mexico and Western Texas*, pp. 15–60. Midland Archeological Society, Midland, Tex.

WOBST, H. MARTIN

1974 Boundary Conditions for Paleolithic Social Systems: A Simulation Approach. *American Antiquity* 39:147–78.

WORD, JAMES H.

1963 Floydada Country Club Site (41FL1). *Bulletin of the South Plains Archeological Society* 1:37–63.

1965 The Montgomery Site in Floyd County, Texas. *Bulletin of the South Plains Archeological Society* 11:55–102.

1991 The 1975 Field School of the Texas Archeological Society. *Bulletin of the Texas Archeological Society* 60:57–106.

WORD, J. H., AND C. L. DOUGLAS

1970 *Excavations at Baker Cave, Val Verde County, Texas.* Bulletin of the Texas Memorial Museum 16, Austin.

WRIGHT, J. F.

1997 The Asa Warner Site (41ML46), McLennan County, Texas. *Bulletin of the Texas Archeological Society* 68:215–61.

WYCOFF, D. G., AND J. L. HOFMAN

1982 *Pathways to Plains Prehistory: Anthropological Perspectives of Plains Natives and Their Pasts.* Oklahoma Anthropological Society, Memoir 3, and Cross Timbers' Heritage Association, Contributions 1. Cross Timbers Press, Duncan, Okla.

YELLEN, JOHN E.

1977 *Anthropological Approaches to the Present: Models for Reconstructing the Past.* Academic Press, New York.

YELLEN, JOHN E., A. S. BROOKS, E. CORNELISSEN, M. J. MEHLMAN, AND K. STEWART

1995 A Middle Stone Age Worked Bone Industry from Katanda, Upper Semliki Valley, Zaire. *Science* 268 (5210): 553–56.

ZALDIVER, VICENTE DE

1871 Memorial sobre el Descubrimiento del Nuevo México y sus acontecimientos, Años desde 1595 a 1602. In *Colección de Documentos Inéditos*, edited by Joaquin F. Pacheco and Francisco Cardenas, 16:188–224. M. Bernaldo de Quirós, Madrid.

ZIMMERMAN, L. E.

1996 An Internal Chronology at the Late Prehistoric Henderson Site (LA-1549), New Mexico, as Illustrated by El Paso Polychrome Rim Sherd Indices. Undergraduate honors thesis, Department of Anthropology, University of Michigan, Ann Arbor.

CONTRIBUTORS

JOHN W. ARNN III is an archaeologist with the Environmental Affairs Division of the Texas Department of Transportation in Austin.

DOUGLAS K. BOYD is a Vice President and Principal Investigator for Prewitt and Associates, Inc., in Austin, Texas.

ZACKARY I. GILMORE is a doctoral candidate in the Department of Anthropology at the University of Florida in Gainesville, Florida.

LEONARD KEMP is a Principal Investigator with Geo-Marine. Inc., a subsidiary of Applied Research Associates, Inc., in El Paso, Texas.

NANCY A. KENMOTSU is a Principal Investigator for Geo-Marine, Inc., a subsidiary of Applied Research Associates, Inc., in Yakima, Washington, and a Research Associate with the Texas Archeological Research Laboratory at the University of Texas at Austin.

KARL W. KIBLER is a Principal Investigator for Prewitt and Associates, Inc., in Austin, Texas.

RAYMOND MAULDIN is the Assistant Director of the Center for Archaeological Research at the University of Texas at San Antonio.

KHORI NEWLANDER recently completed his doctorate in anthropological archaeology in the Department of Anthropology at the University of Michigan in Ann Arbor.

ELTON R. PREWITT is a Research Fellow with the Texas Archeological Research Laboratory at the University of Texas at Austin.

JOHN D. SPETH is the Arthur P. Thurnau Professor in the Department of Anthropology and Curator of North American Archaeology in the Museum of Anthropology at the University of Michigan in Ann Arbor.

JENNIFER THOMPSON is an archaeologist with the Center for Archaeological Research at the University of Texas at San Antonio.

INDEX

Page numbers shown in **bold** indicate figures or tables.

TEXAS A&M UNIVERSITY ANTHROPOLOGY SERIES

Making Faces: Using Forensic and Archaeological Evidence, JOHN PRAG AND RICHARD NEAVE

Culture of Stone: Sacred and Profane Uses of Stone among the Dani, O. W. "BUD" HAMPTON

The Archaeology of Death and Burial, MIKE PARKER PEARSON

The Archaeology of Animal Bones, TERRY O'CONNOR

Stories That Float from Afar: Ancestral Folklore of the San of Southern Africa, J. D. LEWIS-WILLIAMS

Archaeological Conservation Using Polymers: Practical Applications for Organic Artifact Stabilization, C. WAYNE SMITH

Rock Art of the Lower Pecos, CAROLYN E. BOYD

The Proto-Neolithic Cemetery in Shanidar Cave, RALPH S. SOLECKI, ROSE L. SOLECKI, and ANAGNOSTIS P. AGELARAKIS

The Prehistory of Texas, TIMOTHY K. PERTTULA

How War Began, KEITH OTTERBEIN

In Search of Maya Sea Traders, HEATHER MCKILLOP

The Osteology of Infants and Children, BRENDA J. BAKER, TOSHA L. DUPRAS, and MATTHEW W. TOCHERI

Human Origins: What Bones and Genomes Tell Us about Ourselves, ROB DESALLE and IAN TATTERSALL

Early Modern Human from Tianyuan Cave, China, HONG SHANG and ERIK TRINKAUS

Race?, ROB DESALLE and IAN TATTERSALL